PERIODS IN
GERMAN LITERATURE

edited by

J. M. RITCHIE

OSWALD WOLFF
LONDON, W.I.

© 1966 OSWALD WOLFF (Publishers) Limited, London W1M 6DR

FIRST PUBLISHED 1966

SECOND IMPRESSION 1968

FIRST SOFT COVER EDITION 1977

ISBN 0 85496 032 5

PRINTED BY LEWIS REPRINTS LTD.,
LONDON AND TONBRIDGE

CONTENTS

Preface

IT must be put on record that my suggestion to Australian colleagues that we might combine to produce a book on the periods and movements of German literature was received at first with considerable caution. All were aware of the dangers inherent in any attempt to carve up literature into sections and particularly in any attempt to force the great work or the great author into the strait-jacket of rigid chronological classifications. Thinking in -isms is not something any teacher would wish to encourage in his students. At the same time we were equally aware that period terms like Classicism, Romanticism and Realism are in constant use, however much we might dislike them and that the need for an analysis of the uses and abuses of such terms, particularly in view of the differing significance of them as applied to various European literatures, is also very great. Hence it was with due reluctance and caution but also with the realization of the need for informed discussion that my Australian colleagues agreed to collaborate with me on this book.

The weaknesses of periodisation are plain for all to see. Not so obvious at first sight are the advantages of this approach. But these too can be considerable. Perhaps they are best revealed in the case of the neglected areas of literary study. Until comparatively recently, for example, few students of German were asked or expected to read any seventeenth century literature. But, for some years now a wide-ranging reappraisal of the once despised "Baroque" has been going on in European literature and art and it would be difficult to plan any survey of German literature which did not include some study of the wealth of the German Baroque lyric, the dramas of Gryphius and Lohenstein and the work of Grimmelshausen whose *Simplicius Simplicissimus* is clearly one of the greatest German novels ever written. As Majut said of the equally suspect *Biedermeier*: "The recognition of an age as a period obedient to its own laws and separated from that which precedes and succeeds it, generally begins with the use of a characterizing name." Hence it was the discussion on the nature and value of "Baroque" as such, as much as the rediscovery and reappraisal of particular works, which has been responsible for the great widening of our literary horizons.

To some extent the same is also true of Rococo literature. For generations this has been condemned as the unnatural, insincere, Frenchified form of art to which, for example, the Young Goethe was exposed in Leipzig, but which he (and through him the *Stürmer und Dränger* and hence German literature in general) fortunately overcame to initiate a truly great, natural, literary German outburst of sincere feeling and experience. Only now are critics beginning to appreciate the wit and irony of German Rococo and in particular the work of Wieland whose *Musarion* is such pure and unadulterated pleasure that it should be essential reading for all students of German literature even if only to prove that all German literature from all periods is not characterized by joyless metaphysics and "depth".

Discussing German literature in terms of periods and movements can too in some cases result in a fairer more balanced view. It has been too easy for some critics for instance to discuss or underestimate Naturalism. Yet as Garten pointed out in his *Modern German Drama* "it put its stamp on European drama for decades" and clearly marks the beginnings of what is now called "die Moderne" in German literature. In the same way Expressionism has for long been dismissed as the violent *Pubertätserscheinung* of a violent age. Only in the last few years has any real attempt been made to arrive at a just evaluation of its undoubted achievements.

But this book is not a rescue operation concerned with the neglected areas of German literature like the *Barock*, *Rokoko* or *Aufklärung*. It reminds us that even the recognized and the known like Realism, Romanticism, Classicism are in constant need of review and reappraisal in the light of newer knowledge and research. Above all, however, it must be stressed that this book is not a history of literature. Many important periods are not discussed or even mentioned. Many well-known figures move freely from one chapter to the next—the divisions are far from rigid and the overlapping is intentionally considerable and not merely a result of the distances separating the various contributors working in different university centres throughout the vast continent of Australia.

J. M. RITCHIE

Problems of Periods and Movements

I

Problems of Periods and Movements

R. B. FARRELL

THIS book is not a history of German literature from the beginning of the Baroque period to the present day, i.e. its main concern is not to present a detailed record of as many writers and works as possible, assigning these to movements and periods and interpreting them in their main lines in their historical context. In so far as such material is used here, it is by way of illustration of the nature of periods and movements, which together with an examination of the names given these is the aim of the book. The problem of temporal divisions and of the course of a movement or period is certainly an aspect of the historical approach to literature, or literary history, which in endeavouring to reveal the relationships between literary phenomena must organize the material by grouping what belongs together by reason of an inner affinity. That we are dealing here with literary and not in the first instance any other kind of history needs to be emphasized since other kinds of history, it is true, may enter into literary study and do throw light on literature. In particular, politico-social history (the sociological approach) and the history of ideas (*Geistesgeschichte*) can make a considerable contribution to the understanding of literature : the writer's reaction to the total situation of his time (intellectual as well as social), the type of sensibility that goes with this, are fruitful sources of inquiry for literary interpretation no less than biography and a knowledge of the genesis of a work. In fact, aesthetic interpretation, if it is to minimize the possibility of error, must be firmly grounded in the knowledge afforded by all these approaches. Literary history will reveal for example to what extent a writer stands in a tradition even if he modifies it, how the practice of one age may still influence that of the following which has a different feeling about life and seeks new forms in which to express it, which aspects of a writer's work are literary convention and the like. This book then is concerned with the meaningfulness (or arbitrariness as the case may be) of the traditional groupings into periods (*Periodisierung*) and movements and, as far as it is necessary, with terminology. The principal division must be a basic unity of character which persists through development and individual variations and diversity. A period, as implied above, must

3

be a literary one, even when the same name, e.g. Romanticism, is applied not only to the other arts, but to other manifestations of the time. Perhaps of all such terms it is *Barock* which has most suffered (because it has in this way been overstretched) by being applied to innumerable areas of the life of the age; none of which means of course that a comparison between the arts of a period and the attempt to grasp the relationship between a literary and a politico-social period may not be instructive.

Histories of literature often divide up their material in such a variety of ways as to suggest the absence of any consistent principle. Not uncommonly the same history will resort to varying principles : now a literary period, however named, now a politico-social period, or a movement, or simply one writer standing for an age if his life and work are extensive and important, or again a group of writers with a rather arbitrary label (e.g. the Lake Poets, the Viennese Drama). English histories of English literature, whether from indifference to the problem or from a deeper insight is not made clear, mostly abandon all attempts at division into periods and content themselves with loose groupings. Periods, where they are used, are given as a century or go by the name of the ruling monarch (e.g. Elizabethan, Victorian) or by what is considered to be the major literary figure in a given span of time (e.g. the Age of Pope), less frequently by the name of some prominent characteristic (e.g. the Age of Reason, the Age of Sentiment). In one case, however, the term used, Romanticism, which designates not just a movement but a period, is based on a large number of characteristics which tend to cohere and is, moreover, international. German historians of German literature, on the other hand, have made a far more serious attempt to come to grips with the problems arising out of periodization, even if with varying success and at times doing violence to facts in order to make them fit into a scheme. In most cases the terms adopted, admittedly sometimes taken from or extended to non-literary phenomena, are meant to refer to a sum of literary characteristics which have some measure of unity about them. Only one of them, the occasional *Vormärz* (i.e. the Metternich period), designates primarily a politico-social, one (*Reformation*), a politico-religious and one (*Aufklärung*) a philosophical division. *Sturm und Drang*, on the other hand, is the only one with an exclusive literary reference.

A question confronting us in the choice of such terms is whether we should be content to regard them as mere labels, as good as any other, and not really affecting our main concern, which is to establish the basic characteristics of this period or that movement, to trace the modifications of these in their rise and decline and to fix their time limits. Most of the terms do suggest vaguely a set of characteristics, rather more clearly in fact in the case of *Sturm und Drang* and *Biedermeier* (the latter, however, with its over-tones of philistinism perhaps making it inappropriate for any but minor writers). It might be argued that with the terms applied to the other arts it is not vital that they should denote exactly the same characteristics; when, however, the same term is used of dif-ferent national literatures, particularly when different epochs are meant, one has to decide whether the common elements become so thinned out and the diverse ones so prominent as to make the term quite vague or whether despite this thinning (or stretching) there is still point in talking about, for example, the various national Romanticisms, Realisms, etc. This, of course, is not to say that a comparison of roughly the same period in various national literatures, no matter what the name given, cannot be illuminat-ing for each. Thus, there is no justification for not comparing the period of German literature, which for a short while was called *Biedermeier* and for which no satisfactory term has been invented, with approximately the same years in English and French (and any other) literature. Of all the terms it is Romanticism which has most firmly established itself in the various national European literatures for approximately the same historical period, different in some important ways though the phenomena it is meant to cover were in the various countries. Classicism or Neo-classicism, on the other hand (complicated by the existence in German of the two terms, *Klassik* and *Klassizismus*) is applied internationally to dif-ferent historical periods (unless we think in terms of very long stretches of time) and has been used, moreover, in very different senses with much resulting confusion.

Any definition of these terms that is meant to account for actual literature must base itself on historical realities and not regard them, as might be suggested by our recourse in some cases to "isms", as absolute essences. If we say that Brentano "wrote Romanticism" (a not very happy form of expression) or even that his poetry is Romantic, we can only mean that it exhibits tendencies in a certain direction, not that it is a complete fulfilment of some possibility we have described as Romantic. This remains true even if we admit that some German poets went farther along the Romantic road than those of any other country. It is, furthermore, essential not to confuse a poet's theory with his practice, however much light the former may throw on the latter. Novalis, for example, hardly found the techniques that would have made pos-sible a far-reaching application of his theory, and when they were found, more than a hundred years later, they were mostly used to

express the negative of what Novalis envisaged. Insistence, however, that the historian's concern is with historical reality and that
it is this that he must interpret in no way precludes him from
attempting to discover the inner intention of a movement or period,
where this is heading, even when its exponents are not fully or
clearly aware of its "whither"; from thinking out the writer's
theory, if necessary to the conclusions the latter himself has
stopped short of. The interpretation of an individual writer or
work or movement in the light of such inner intention can be
illuminating. Thus after 150 years of further development it is no
longer difficult to perceive the historical sense of the inner intention (or impulse) of Romanticism. An interpretation of a tendency
must obviously be in terms of its (often unconscious) goal. From
such considerations it becomes clear that periods and movements,
in so far as they are vital, cannot be regarded as self-contained
units of time unrelated to each other, but rather that it is a
question of tracing tendencies, first as germs embedded and largely
hidden in others which may have a different direction, then
asserting themselves vigorously and dominating a span of years to
which they give their name, finally after the period of their ascendancy, their transformation or submergence in, or even lingering
though less vigorous life alongside, new tendencies. The stages of
their rise and decline in the period of their clear domination are
generally referred to in literary history as *früh*, *hoch* and *spät*,
though the more widespread they are and the greater the number
of writers they embrace, the more complex does the problem of
assigning dates to these stages become. That they do not begin or
end suddenly should, after what has just been said, hardly require
further comment. Dates given are to some extent symbolical. Their
existence before and after the period of their ascendancy, again, is
indicated by literary historians by *vor* and *nach* (thus *Vor . . .*,
Früh . . ., *Hoch . . .*, *Spät . . .*, *Nach-Klassik*). By *nach* of course can
be understood either their continuing influence on other tendencies
or simply belated manifestations of themselves, often in the form
of *Epigonentum* (i.e. when the original impulse is no longer so
vital, though not simply imitative). One must obviously be on one's
guard not to distort historical reality and force it into this pattern
when this does not exist in it; it may, for example, well be that
writers lapse into silence before the late stage of a tendency is
reached.

A further difficulty besetting the terms used as names for historical movements and periods is that some of them are also taken
in the sense of timeless tendencies, i.e. ones that keep recurring in
history. With none is the temptation to employ them in these two

ways perhaps greater than with Realism. To few characterizations are we more prone than to that which declares that a work contains a greater or less degree of realism. Romanticism, in some respects if not in others, got closer to the reality of life than Classicism, though on a total view we would not hesitate to reject the term as an apt description of the former. Since the problem of the realistic portrayal of life is an abiding one in literature, we should expect the future to produce periods for which the most appropriate name might be Realism, important differences though there would probably be between this and the variety that flourished in the second half of the nineteenth century. To surmount the difficulties inherent in the use of a term such as Realism some historians refer to the period of realism in the nineteenth century as *der bürgerliche Realismus*. And similarly, when a reaction set in against Expressionism in the twentieth, realism was avoided in favour of *die neue Sachlichkeit*, a term, however, which has not been given a very precise meaning and so can hardly be said to have established itself. *Barock*, too, has not been limited to the seventeenth century, certain features of Hofmannsthal, for instance, being characterized as such. Not only have classical and romantic been conceived as eternal tendencies of the human mind, but at times the conception has been stated in the extreme form that a man *must* be one or the other. Where the term itself suggests definite characteristics (e.g. realism, impressionism) such dual use seems inevitable. True though it be that the historian's chief concern is to give a correct account of a movement or period and that the name he attaches to this is of secondary importance, the problem of terminology does remain. Without doubt it is in constant need of revision or adjustment in the light of new literary developments.

By this stage of the argument it should be clear not only that movement and period are to be distinguished (though in a few cases they may be practically identical and co-extensive), but that it is far easier to perceive the underlying unity of a movement than of a period. Movements commonly have a programme to which their various exponents stand in a relatively clear relationship. But movements of opposed character may run their course more or less simultaneously, so that the task of finding some deeper unity which would permit the construction of a meaningful period becomes difficult indeed. Most of the traditional terms in fact can be justified better as names of movements than of periods. So it is with *Klassik*, alongside which there are late manifestations of *Sturm und Drang*, even of *Aufklärung*, and the beginnings of *Romantik*. Although for a stretch of years the works of greatest literary value certainly came from the classical camp and formed a considerable body of literary work at that, it is only in this sense that classicism was the dominant tendency; literary history shows that the broad development was basically from *Sturm und Drang* to *Romantik*, important as was the influence of Goethe and Schiller on the adherents of these movements. No less is it true that the literary products of Goethe's old age, which are contemporaneous with *Romantik*, though they are not altogether uninfluenced by the latter, can in no sense be described as Romantic. Historians have tried to see the years from the beginnings of *Sturm und Drang* to Goethe's death as a period consisting of a number of phases which are only opposites within a given framework. To this period they have given various names : the *Goethezeit*; *die deutsche Bewegung* (in as much as certain recurring German characteristics found expression in it, a view which cannot be applied easily to the classical phase); *der deutsche Idealismus* (a term used in the first place of German idealist philosophy, but indicating a mental climate into which Kleist at least does not fit very convincingly). If one regards this as a period, one has to remember that important tendencies of the *Aufklärung* appear purified and synthesized with other elements in the classicism of Goethe and Schiller.

The contemporaneousness of opposed movements can of course be explained in part by the fact that their adherents belong to different generations. This was notably so in the *Goethezeit*. Alongside this we have to set the fact that the tendencies of a writer may be modified, even substantially so, under the influence of the younger generation, or that at some point in his career he may strike out independently along new lines. It may suffice here, to point to the changes that occurred in Goethe's literary lifetime.

Finally, from what has been said, it will be seen that what is frequently called a period may in fact also be seen as a phase of a longer stretch of time, which itself constitutes a period, i.e. a time in which there is a dominant set of basic tendencies. The concept of a period within a period does no violence to historical reality and helps us moreover to distinguish the more enduring and more basic from the less so. In the larger sense there have probably been only two major periods since the Renaissance, the transition coming about gradually but—in the light of subsequent developments —becoming fairly marked in the eighteenth century movements of *Empfindsamkeit* and *Sturm und Drang*. Development is clearly not always in a straight line, and German *Klassik*, while it absorbed something of these two movements into itself, is primarily a culmination of the Renaissance centuries. The basis of these was the belief in the reality of an ordered, intelligible universe, in art as an objective imitation of this in its permanent, typical aspects. Within this framework the differences between *Renaissance, Barock, Aufklärung* and *Klassik* recede as less important.

In the second great period—from the middle of the eighteenth century to the present day—it may at first sight seem that its great diversity, exploding at times into violent opposition, makes even an underlying broad unity unthinkable. During the earlier part we find an outpouring of subjective feeling, a confessional style running its course till it is displaced by objectivity of various kinds and, in more extreme forms, an attempt to exclude the self altogether; later yielding to a different and no less extreme form of subjectivity; a conflict between representational and non-representational literature, one generally dominant at certain times but both existing alongside each other, the latter (known as "modern") becoming more and more the characteristic mode of utterance of the twentieth century, particularly in the lyric but in a modified form at times too in the other genres. We find further the contrast between the literature of affirmation and that of negation, nihilism or the more moderate form we call pessimism; and intimately related to these there is the literature of integration into an order, social, religious and the like, and on the other hand that of alienation from society and forms of religious belief, whether this causes anguish or is gloried in and accompanied by the conviction that the inner world of the artist or indeed the work of art itself is the only true value. Nature, though it lingers on in a few writers, yielded as a theme largely to the portrayal of urban social reality (often, it is true, in the case of Germany, in the form of the small-life idyll), and this in turn to a large extent to the expression of pure inwardness.

Can we in view of this immense variety speak of a period, even if we conceive it in the broadest of terms? First of all, there is in this literature, now more now less distinctly, the atmosphere of crisis, beneath the "Gefühlszauber" of Romanticism no less than in the disillusioned or pessimistic Realism of the nineteenth century, and particularly audible even in George, Rilke, and Hofmannsthal, who in their various ways attempted to assert a meaningful order in which man could live and realize his true self. The problem of our threatened human substance in modern civilization and that of finding or creating a worthy dwelling place for it in the external world appears in countless variations. Though it lingered on in a fragmentary and attenuated form into the nineteenth and twentieth centuries and indeed in many ways formed the basis of school education, belief in a firm order of things, social, natural, intellectual, religious, which had sustained the preceding period, gradually disintegrated in most sensitive minds and left them seeking for a new order in which they could believe.

This intellectual climate established itself of course only gradually, but we can—in historical retrospect—discern its beginnings about the middle of the eighteenth century in the related movements of *Empfindsamkeit* and *Sturm und Drang*. These years may be looked on as the great divide. It was here that individualism in its modern form became a force (prepared, it is true, by the analytical scepticism of the *Aufklärung*). Connected with the decline of the *ancien régime* and the rise of the "Bürgertum" its growth has to be seen in relation to the forms of living created by the latter. Such politico-social phenomena as the striving for political and economic liberalism together with the advance of technological industrialism were in the nineteenth century to produce a civilization with which the imaginative writer had to come to grips by seeing it in its bearing on his idea of man. The problems arising out of individualism and, a little later, the materialistic mass values of an expanding industrial society are two of the most important factors against which the literature of the period must be interpreted. A third is the growth of knowledge about the physical universe (often undermining orthodox religious faith) resulting in a new world picture equal in its impact to the Copernican transformation; but at the same time there is the growing consciousness of the limits of possible knowledge as propounded by the philosopher Kant who also gave birth to the idea of art as an autonomous world, as the creation of the self with laws of its own, i.e. not as an imitation of nature as had been the belief of an earlier period. With the realization of such limits the conviction was shaken that valid statements about the world, about truth are possible. Rationalism continued despite the revolt against it, only in other forms : natural science and its progeny technology, the organization of the State and of social forms. Liberal democracy appears as a blend of rationalism and of the new idea of individuality.

Overwhelmingly, imaginative writers, highly sensitive beings, reacted to the new reality with misgivings if not rejection. The social scene made them uneasy, while even if they shared loss of orthodox religious faith they still felt the need of a metaphysical relationship. Even the Realists of the nineteenth century, who attempted to get close to and portray the social, intellectual and physical reality of life and practised representational art (characteristically, the individuality of details, not the typicality of the Classical artist) tended to be disillusioned. Cultural pessimism was often the response of the spirit to the optimistic belief of the age in progress. Varieties of realism with differing techniques presenting in critical, satirical or pessimistic vein the human condition have persisted to the present day alongside or alternating with more "modern" techniques used by writers (particularly in the lyric) who for the most part have asserted the power of the self to rise above external reality and create its own world. Certainly, at the same time there have been those, mostly sustained by a politico-social or a religious faith, who have shown the world as *heil* and existence as meaningful. Where no sense of crisis threatening this meaning is present it is generally a case of writers of smaller stature.

We have put forward the thesis that it is from the new feeling of individuality confronted with a world of the kind described that the literature of our period springs. That part of it we call "modern" clearly appears in a line of descent from the eighteenth century discovery of individuality, but of course not in a straight line. The phases of development are diverse in character and often in opposition, combined too with other impulses. At the beginning we have Rousseau with his condemnation of an artificial society, his call for a return to nature as a remedy for the ills of civilization, his practice of confessions or self-revelation, and on the German scene Herder with his theories of individuality and development. In the movements of *Empfindsamkeit* and *Sturm und Drang* the sustaining belief is that it is in feeling that individuality most forcefully unfolds itself (reason does not make for individuality). Few words in the literature of the time are more common than "Gefühl" and "Herz". Among other things they signified liberation of the self from conventional restrictions, both social and intellectual. Realization of the self in the external world of reality, in society and nature (in some ways mutually exclusively) was, however, still the main driving force. A world open to the self, an embrace of both was the vision. The motif of a return to nature had a double aspect. In part it was a revolt against an artificial society incapable of further development, but also, and less consciously, against the complexities of life brought about by greater knowledge and expanded horizons with their bewildering contrasts and contradictions, which with the heritage of the *Aufklärung* led to the division of self, to a heightened awareness of the gulf between the self and the world. These movements therefore represent, at least in part, an attempt to restore the oneness of the self with itself and with nature in an age which was losing this oneness and gaining in self-awareness.

Passing over German *Klassik*, which, as the relevant chapter of this book points out, is a culmination of the Renaissance centuries though bearing in itself the marks of its historical lateness, we find that with the early Romantics some of the impulses of the *Sturm und Drang* have become more refined, subtle and at times esoteric. Feeling is no longer glorified one-sidedly, its synthesis with intellectual awareness is demanded. The vision of a primitive oneness has been discarded. In place of a sense of vitality and activity in the real world the self withdraws from this and tries to anticipate through contemplation a transcendent world. Self-awareness has deepened and the subconscious has also been discovered. Above all, the rôle of the self in creating its world is stressed and is in fact a central concern of Romanticism. With this we find the first clear claims of the artist to complete freedom, the tendency to divorce art and social responsibility. Novalis dreamed of a technique which would enable him to suggest the absolute, pure being—by destroying the real. Twentieth century poets (in this preceded by Mallarmé and other French symbolist poets) have devised these techniques, which mostly reveal the absolute of Novalis as nothingness and are thus an expression of nihilism, of alienation from a world that has become meaningless. The experience of estrangement from the bourgeois civilization that was taking shape began early. It was, as we have seen, implicit in the transcendent longing of the early Romantics and was at least one source of the late Romantic glorification of certain traditional values. In Mörike, who belongs to the next generation, we find in some respects an end : not only a deep malaise caused by the atmosphere of the new civilization (which he does not portray), but often a sense of exclusion from nature, with whose power and beauty he can at other times— momentarily and with fluctuation of feeling—achieve an ecstatic sense of oneness and which he can evoke with a sensuousness which not even Goethe can match. After him nature lingers on only in such diluted forms as *Heimatkunst* and the "Dorfgeschichte". After the extravagant dreams of the Romantics the self in Mörike is humble before the power of the object, of things, of social reality, which however he only portrays humorously and in the form of the idyll of small life. The transition to Realism, to the objective depiction of social reality, though for a number of reasons retarded and only partly realized, is now under way. When this impulse, after its more extreme manifestations in Naturalism and Impressionism, ebbs, we have a re-assertion of the supremacy of the self (in the writers sometimes grouped together as Neo-Romantics), above all in Expressionism, which aware of disintegration but also impatient with the world-weariness and beauty-worship of the previous generation, passionately wants to recreate the world. The Expressionists, unlike the earlier generations (e.g. George, Rilke, Hofmannsthal, Thomas Mann) nearly all died young and so, again unlike these, fit fairly neatly into one movement. Partly influenced by Gottfried Benn, whose *Probleme der Lyrik* in 1951 had a profound effect on them, the post–1945 poets have also asserted the power of the self by rejecting the external world—often nihilistically—and creating a pure art world, the world of the poem, which is form and bears little relation to the real world. The self has thus closed in on itself. From the attempt in *Sturm und Drang* days, with a new consciousness of individuality, to build a worthy home for the spirit in the external world, the spirit has withdrawn into itself.

This account of the main lines of literary development from the middle of the eighteenth century, though fragmentary, may suffice to establish the principle that a period and a movement are not self-contained and that any attempt to understand them solely in these terms must fail. Periods, though they have some measure of unity, must be conceived as phases of a longer stretch of time. How, for example, are we to fit Kleist satisfactorily into a short period when basic aspects of his work look forward to a future age? How can we interpret Rilke's "Dinggedichte" or George's Hellenism simply in terms of a period or movement limited in time? An aspect of the diversity with which we are always confronted concerns the genres, which, even if they often have certain period characteristics in common, naturally tend towards forms of expression peculiar to themselves. The specifically modern style of distortion of external reality, abstraction and the like has—in the nature of things—invaded the lyric much more than the other genres (from which, however, it is by no means entirely absent). It follows that a characterization of periods and movements must take into account the history of the genres.

SELECT BIBLIOGRAPHY

G. Baesecke: Zur Periodisierung der deutschen Literatur, *DVjs*, 2 (1924), p. 770.

B. Cavaignac: La succession des générations en histoire, *Bulletin of the International Committee of Historical Sciences*, 10, 1938, p. 574 f.

H. Cysarz: Das Periodenprinzip in der Literaturwissenschaft, in: *Philosophie der Literaturwissenschaft*, ed. E. Ermatinger, 1930.

J. J. Gielen: Breuk of Continuatie?, in: *De Nieuwe Taalgids*, 32 (1938), p. 49 f.

E. Lunding: Stand und Aufgabe der deutschen Barockforschung, *Orbis Litterarum*, 8 (1950), p. 31.

P. Merker: 1926, redigiert von Erna Merker, Neuhochdeutsche Literatur, in: *Reallexikon der deutschen Literaturgeschichte*, Bd. 2, 7 Lfg, 1963, particularly p. 613.

H. P. H. Teesing: *Das Problem der Perioden in der Literaturwissenschaft* (Groningen, 1948).

M. Wehrli: *Allgemeine Literaturwissenschaft* (Bern, 1951), p. 139 ff.

Austin Warren and René Wellek: *Theory of Literature* (London/New York, 1949), chapter: Literary History, p. 263 ff.

René Wellek: Periods and Movements in Literary History, in: *English Institute Annual*, 1940, pp. 73–93.

René Wellek: Period, in: *Shipley's Dictionary* (New York, 1943), p. 428.

Baroque

II

Baroque

J. H. TISCH-WACKERNAGEL

THE notoriously bewildering complexity of this still half-submerged literary continent is mirrored only too accurately in the amazing Babel of terminology. By considering critically the appropriateness of a number of terms currently used, this essay will try to bring some method into the terminological madness, offer a more clearly circumscribed idea of the meaning of "Baroque" and, where necessary, reshape the content of the term in order to define more adequately the inner unity in the "spannungsreiche Miteinander des Gegensätzlichen"[1] of German seventeenth century literature.

I

The etymology of baroque is still relatively obscure and uncertain, but it seems at least likely that as an adjective—meaning "odd, striking, extravagant"[2] it stems from a fusion of at least two major sources, viz. (*a*) from the irregular, oddly shaped rough pearl (Portuguese : *pérola barroca*, cf. Spanish : *barrueco*, French : *perle baroque*, German : *Brockenperle*) and (*b*) from the logical term *baroco* denoting the fourth mode of the second figure in the scholastic nomenclature of syllogisms.[3] Unlike other period terms, baroque does not characterize an essential quality of the age and was not coeval with the phenomena it is now supposed to bear on. The German *barock* (ck because of short o; the derivative adj. and adv. *barockisch* are defunct) derived from the French adj. *baroc*, *baroque* (1531) which Campe translated as "schief, wunderlich, seltsam". The first recorded example of its use to denote style seems to go back to Zachariä in 1754—"im barokschen Geschmack" (cf. "en goût baroque"), but it is not before the later eighteenth century that the word is applied to the art and taste of the preceding unclassical era, and till about 1900 its meaning was predominantly negative ("excessive, chaotic, irregular"). The German noun which is both neuter and masculine dates from about 1850. The writings of Nicolai, Lessing (who significantly employs "Barockgeschmack" for Klopstock), Winckelmann (whose baroque affinities should not be forgotten), Goethe (whose use is somewhat am-

17

biguous), Schiller, Nietzsche and others, yield a wealth of instructive examples, among the best of which is the couplet from
Wieland's delightful *Der Neue Amadis* :[4]

Barockischer konnte man nichts als Blaffardinen sehn
Von Kopf zu Gürtel so schrecklich, als bis zum Knöchel schön

(it continues) :

Von unten der besten Nymphe von Vanloo zu vergleichen,
Von oben ein Ideal um Vögel zu verscheuchen.

A serious handicap from which the term baroque has not yet
fully recovered is its genesis in the realm of art history! It appears
to have been Jacob Burckhardt who, under the influence of
Kugler, limited this descriptive, "previously free floating adjective"
to the style of a historical period, namely the counter-reformation
"decadence" of Renaissance architecture.[5] While the great Basle
scholar still shows something of an antibaroque bias,[6] his eminent
pupil Heinrich Wölfflin was the first to appreciate baroque art in
its own right. To maintain that he also inaugurated the literary
use of the term is erroneous, but nevertheless his seminal categories
—"linear-painterly", "closed-open form", etc.—with which in
his *Kunstgeschichtliche Grundbegriffe*, 1915, he suggestively con-
fronts Renaissance and Baroque art in structural, primarily visual
terms, did make an almost hypnotic impact on later generations
of critics who often all too schematically transferred them to the
alien medium of literature.

The introduction of Baroque as a literary concept radiated
mainly from propagators in the German-speaking countries, and its
rise to popularity, and the vogue of the literature described by it,
rode on the wave of the Expressionist generation's enthusiastic feeling of contemporaneity and elective affinity. Much of the feverish
revival and revaluation inaugurated by the Expressionists rested
on a subjective misunderstanding of seventeenth century works and
produced, besides some perceptive pioneering studies, a flood of
abstruseness that proved extremely harmful to the reputation of
Baroque scholarship. While fully conscious of what L. Forster has
called the "modernity of the baroque"[7] and of interesting parallels
with the poetry of our troubled time, one must have strong reser-
vations against anachronistically linking Baroque with Expressionism, Romanticism or with the spirit of Gothic art, as too against
the indiscriminating application of the term to the Old Saxon
Heliand ("Stabreimbarock" (Genzmer)) and Wolfram as well as
Gottfried Keller, Rilke and Dürrenmatt. This fashionable practice
is suspiciously similar to the distorting typological or phenomeno-

logical use of baroque as a non-historical category, as a universal principle or recurrent constant (e.g. in polar contrast to an ideal Classicism).

II

The Baroque poses vexed problems of periodization, and there is still startling diversity of opinion as to its chronological extension which, like the heated discussions about its content, has substantially detracted from the value of the term. Generally, dates given vary from 1600 and 1610 at one end to anything between 1680 and 1710 at the other, but time limits have been extended by some to 1575 (or even 1550) and 1750 respectively. Let us first examine the situation at the end of the sixteenth century before turning to the situation at the end of the seventeenth and the beginning of the eighteenth centuries.

(a) *Sixteenth century:* Even if one does not favour an all too flexible Baroque, stretched to comprise Waldis, Sachs, Manuel, Wickram and Fischart with his often "mannerist" style, one cannot help discerning indications of a change in taste and spirit around 1575.[8] Hence the turn of the century cannot be taken as the simple dividing line between the old and the new. No such strict periodization can take account of non-conformist figures such as the gifted anonymous translator of Jan van der Noot whose *Olympia* epic anticipated *Frühbarock* in metrics and diction almost fifty years before Weckherlin and Opitz.[9] Few would nowadays conceive of the time-span 1470–1600 or of the tumultuous Reformation period as a uniform German "Renaissance", despite the vital stimuli from Renaissance countries absorbed by Germany in this time, for there was clearly no German vernacular Renaissance poetry worth mentioning. (Similarly the application of the concept of Renaissance to the whole of the German seventeenth century must also be rejected as deficient in historical justification and utterly confusing.) In fact the traditional pattern of a fierce antagonism between Renaissance and Baroque is based on a fallacy and there is solid evidence of an artistically fruitful continuity in the poetic theory, textures and motifs of the Humanists into the seventeenth century. The vast cosmopolitan body of form-conscious Neo-Latin poetry (which exerted an influence even on the *Kirchenlied* as well as on the belated development of a German poetic language) has long been known to have adumbrated and moulded characteristic tendencies of the German Baroque—not to speak of the remarkable Neo-Latin *oeuvre* of Gryphius, Fleming and other highly educated polyglot poets. We should not overlook how firmly some of the "baroque" elements of German seventeenth century poetry are rooted in the Latin tradition of the sixteenth century and earlier.[10]

(b) *Eighteenth century* : Literary historians studying the development from Baroque to *Aufklärung* have become increasingly aware that formulae such as "Irrationalism-Rationalism" suggesting a tidy sequence of epochs are unequal to the task of separating them. But although the transformations dividing the two have been recognized as long-drawn out processes—there is still a wide unexplored transitional zone—the fundamental problem of the baroque stratifications in early eighteenth century literature has remained unsolved.[11] Figures of transition include authors as widely different in stature and sensibility as Weise, Reuter, Leibniz, Günther, Wernicke, Abschatz, Pyra, Schnabel, Brockes, Bodmer, Gottsched and Haller; Rococo has been called a "step by step transformation of the baroque inheritance"[12] and the old controversy whether Klopstock, whose obtrusive subjectivism is as unbaroque as could be imagined, can be rated a *Barockdichter* still flares up occasionally, perhaps because the historical position of his *"Neubarock"*[13] is so strangely ambiguous.

The temptation to expand the confines of the Baroque period right up into the time of the young Goethe is no doubt a real one, since everyday life, culture and literary activities were then still appreciably determined by seventeenth-century traditions, and indeed, a strong baroque affinity on the part of Goethe has repeatedly been posited, to say nothing of the colourful baroque elements in the work of Schiller who in language of metallic musicality resuscitated religious baroque drama in terms of moral heroism and whose poetry often recalls the most sonorous utterances of the seventeenth century. But the (irrefutable) argument that many baroque ideas, institutions and works were still living forces at least during the first half of the eighteenth century does not permit us to declare the whole era as actually baroque, as Kettler does in his *Baroque Tradition in the Literature of the German Enlightenment 1700–1750*.[14] Hazard's well-known analysis of European thought and other studies have firmly established that what, for Germany, we commonly refer to as *Aufklärung* in philosophy as well as in letters, came into being well within the seventeenth century already. And the reader who fresh from the religious didacticism of Gryphius and Grimmelshausen moves into the secular, political and irreverently pragmatic world of Lohenstein, Weise or Reuter already witnesses a chilling change in spiritual climate and a drastic shift in the handling and significance of form that will dispel any illusions about the unity of the Baroque.

III

If we choose to think of Baroque as a period, then we must accept it as one that comprises numerous movements and trends of differing ideological content and stylistic expression in various geographical areas as well as in different social strata. We must resist the inclination (particularly noticeable in German scholars) to invest the seventeenth century with artificial coherence; we must respond without presuppositions to its crowded richness, its paradoxical contrasts and dualities (such as the seeming dichotomy between a poet's secular and religious poetry), comprehending them as integral facets of this Protean epoch in which individual works and genres run a bewildering gamut of styles and moods; the lyric, for instance may speak in resounding public strains, or with hymnal ardour and mystical abandon, or with folksong-like simplicity, or with bold eroticism couched in a glittering display of Petrarchist conceits. We would look in vain for linear chronological consistency, as we are dealing with a web of tautly intertwined strands. We should not underestimate the magnitude of the changes taking place during the century itself (even within one and the same clearly defined field such as the *Jesuitendrama*!) nor the wide spectrum of mental attitudes. Different literary genres reach their culmination in different decades. The seventeenth century novel for example encompasses an amazing multiformity, ranging from the political-ethical type to the intimately-psychological and the bawdily realistic and amply demonstrates that genres should not be treated as static absolutes and that dates "are rather signposts than divides".[15]

Historians of German baroque literature often attempt to marshal the recalcitrant material in this great time span with the aid of certain subdivisions, namely four modifications of the basic period term : (1) *Vor-* (Pre-), (2) *Früh-* (Early), (3) *Hoch-* (High) and (4) *Spät-* (Late) *barock*.

(1) *Pre-Baroque* : Dates vary from 1570–90 to 1620–30 respectively. Figures who should be considered as immediate precursors of the Baroque include Henry Julius Duke of Brunswick (1564–1613) whose *Vincentius Ladislaus* (1594) is more akin to the woodcut-like angularity of Reformation drama than the sophistication of Gryph's *Horribilicribrifax* (another braggart comedy); Paul Schede-Melissus (1539–1602), writing under Ronsard's influence and known for his Neo-Latin poetry and his translations of the psalms which, however, were eclipsed by the conservative plainness of A. Lobwasser's version; Th. Höck (1573–1658), an individualist whose work has a Renaissance flavour, Christoph von

Schallenberg (1561–97), Jacob Regnart whose *Lieder* bearing the stamp of Italian style appeared in the year of Hans Sach's death, 1576; J. W. Zincgref (1591–1635) who strove to combine the popular tradition with the humanistic type of poetry, and other members of the *Heidelberger Dichterkreis* (around Opitz). Where does the versatile Martin Opitz (1597–1639) himself belong? The evidence overwhelmingly indicates that he is not so much an inaugurator of a completely new era as a belated courtly Renaissance figure. In view of his acute fame-consciousness, his worldly stoical creed, his religious eclecticism and the narrowly rationalistic aridity of his doctrines and style one is hardly justified in according the epithet "baroque" to this seventeenth century man of letters who, blessed with an unfailing flair for the need of the hour and rare single-mindedness followed his mighty national (but not entirely unselfish) aim to create a stylish vernacular poetry founded upon the noble heritage of the European Renaissance and capable of vying with the advanced artistic achievements of other Western nations. By industriously making available suitable literary models and by pontificating with scanty apparatus but ample self-confidence on poetic and metrical rules, this untiring mediator and adroit organizer accidentally prefigured and stimulated many baroque features, but himself remained immersed in a humanistic outlook and wedded to the Latin tradition. His peculiar position instructively reflects the genesis of baroque literature in Germany where a single century had to accommodate what occupied two or more centuries elsewhere. In providing some momentous literary antecedents of the Baroque, but standing apart from it stylistically and ideologically, Opitz strikingly embodies the important Renaissance component of the seventeenth century.

The best term to apply to Opitz is perhaps *Vorbarocker Klassizismus* (VBK) coined by Richard Alewyn as a characterization of the poets of the so-called First Silesian School.[16] Its counterpart is the congenial post-baroque *Klassizismus* around Gottsched who, for once in agreement with his militant Swiss antagonist Bodmer (and also with Leibniz) hailed Opitz as Germany's greatest poet and the "Father of German Poetry". The classicist continuity governing Opitz' reform in theory and practice is, it is true, one of the main ingredients of the Baroque proper. In the case of Opitz, however, this Renaissance vein would appear too unmitigated, the artistic and spiritual connection with High Baroque too slender. Opitz lacks, for instance, the expansive abundant baroque imagery to warrant even the designation Early Baroque. Apart from a welcome gain in precision for our period concept, one decided advantage of Pre-Baroque Classicism lies in its implied recognition that Baroque itself is bestridden by manifestations of an unmetaphysical and uninspired classicism. Unfortunately, to use VBK (or the label *Opitz-Zeit*) for the whole era 1600–40 may encourage the notion that Opitz' classicism in its entirety *precedes* the actual Baroque. Such an image of the period would exclude essential baroque works like Böhme's *Morgenröte im Aufgang* (1612) as well as Gryph's *Sonn- und Feiertagssonette* (published 1639). Pre-Baroque, and Pre-Baroque Classicism, therefore, will be more profitably confined to a group or movement with the dynamic figure of Opitz as its focal point.

(2) *Early Baroque* : This term, in textbooks the name attached to the decades from 1610–30 to about 1640–50, is usable if one wants to bring out that an author or a work form part of the Baroque, albeit yet in a stage of gestation, less determinate than its full advent. The Silesian mystic and philosopher Jakob Böhme (1575–1624) for example is potentially thoroughly baroque in his religious search for the cosmic harmony but he did not live beyond the year in which Opitz' slight but influential *Buch von der Deutschen Poeterey* appeared. Johann Hermann Schein (1586–1643) is another. His songs (as distinct from Höck's) have undergone the crucial transition from Renaissance to Baroque. Georg Rudolf Weckherlin (1584–1653), despite vigorous links with the popular sixteenth century, also embraces Renaissance values, and yet his poetry while controlled by courtly discipline is affected by the evolving baroque style. He has a contrast-figure representing the ascetic, missionary aspect of Early Baroque in a fellow-Swabian, the Jesuit Jakob Bidermann (1578–1639) whose powerful Latin drama *Cenodoxus* (1602) unmasks the ungodly pride of stoic Humanism with almost late-medieval vehemence. The courageous Friedrich von Spee (1591–1635), another Jesuit, with his tender mystical verse the outstanding Catholic poet of the century, eschews the literary conventions of the fully fledged Baroque. Paul Fleming (1609–40) the unsurpassed master of the Early Baroque lyric in form, if not in spirit, presents a more complicated picture, since his work, the pinnacle of German Petrarchism, is also indebted to more homely models. Fleming outgrows his Opitzian phase, but no development towards a (hypothetical) "hochbarocker Individualstil" (Viëtor) should be read into his more mature poems; as Pyritz has convincingly shown, Fleming rather becomes a prefiguration of Günther, as an outsider anticipating eighteenth century lyrical attitudes.

(3) *High Baroque* : Dates for this bulky main compartment commonly oscillate between 1640–50 and 1670–90, but most literary historians have acknowledged that any meaningful concept

of High Baroque has to be centred in the monumental work of Andreas Gryphius (1616–64). High Baroque is taken as the natural flowering of the prevailing literary and imaginative forces of the period, implying the fullest realization of Baroque and thereby (but not primarily) a certain value judgement. One might say that High Baroque is characterized by more marked contrasts, growing rhetorical (and also mannerist) tendencies as well as greater artistic balance and deeper thematic integration of formal patterns apparent for instance in the way Gryphius endows the dialectics of the sonnet with religious urgency. Despite its heightened moral and Christian preoccupation, High Baroque (as against Late Baroque) retains and if anything enhances the un-subjective, impersonal qualities of the era. Nevertheless, neither Gryph's work nor High Baroque as a whole should be viewed as assessable in static or schematic terms. And the briefest of surveys of other authors falling under that heading confirms that High Baroque is so varied as to defy rigid codification. Catharina von Greiffenberg (1633–94) is comparable to Gryphius in her concern with the praise of God; Laurentius von Schnüffis (1633–1702) with his homilectic pastoral poetry strikes a more popular note; Kaspar Stieler's (1632–1707) lyrics combine songlike charm with unsuspected vigour; the *Cherubinische Wandersmann* of Angelus Silesius (Johannes Scheffler, 1624–77) betrays the characteristic tension between artistry and devotion, casting ideas of German mysticism in the pointed High Baroque form of antithetic epigrams, whereas Scheffler's forerunner Daniel Czepko (1605–60) could be seen as partially Early Baroque. Another "transitional" writer whose contrivedly elegant output eventually leads beyond High Baroque and whose connections with the *Sprachgesellschaften* of his time may remind us of their rôle in the implementation of baroque poetic and linguistic legislation is Philipp von Zesen (1619–89). He has much in common with Joh. Klaj (1616–56), G. Ph. von Harsdörffer (1607–58) and S. v. Birken (1626–81), who on the soil of the staid but inventive town culture of Nuremberg indulge in an allegorizing pastoral escapism and create a questioning experimental *Wortbarock* capable of musical and onomatopœic bravura effects behind which lies a whole philosophy of language. The singable, pious and pronouncedly bourgeois lyrics by the *Sterblichkeitsbeflissene* of the *Königsberger Dichterkreis* (H. Albert 1604–51, S. Dach 1605–59, and the more mundane R. Roberthin 1600–48), who write without a theoretical programme, form a significant contrast to the stupendous mannerists on the Pegnitz.

The "logocentric" (Stöcklein) poetry of Christian Hofmann von Hofmannswaldau (1617–79) has long been denigrated as florid

Marinism and decadent Late Baroque, but in view of the underlying seriousness of his "metaphysical frivolity" (G. Müller), the
emblematic complexity of his much arraigned imagery, and his
long neglected religious verse, these outmoded judgements should
be rectified by regarding him as essentially a High Baroque
author, not diametrically opposed but rather complementary to
Gryphius (with whom he was on friendly terms). Much in the
unorthodox work of the "ecstatic visionary" Quirinus Kuhlmann
(1651–89) already points to Late Baroque, but there may be a
good case for leaving him "the man without a label".[17]

(4) *Late Baroque* : Dates normally associated with this term
which has been severely invalidated by loose use and derogatory
undertones, range from 1670–75 to about 1690–1700 or beyond.
Nothing could more strikingly illustrate the literally epoch-making
transmutation from High to Late Baroque than the dissimilarity
between the cosmic-transcendental idealism of Gryphius' dramas
and the Machiavellian realism permeating the secularized courtly
tragedies of his "pupil" Daniel Casper von Lohenstein (1635–83)
who portrays life no longer paradigmatically as *Schein* (appearance), but as full-blooded *Sein* (essence)! Since the days of the
Enlightenment, critics have not tired of stigmatizing Lohenstein as
an exponent of unsavoury and immoral *Schwulst*, and only comparatively recently have these well-worn strictures been replaced
by less jaundiced and better informed critical estimates and his
Trauerspiele recognized as highly dramatic and intricately struc-
tured works governed by the basic polarity of erotic and political
energies.[18] What, then, is meant by the "Lateness" of certain
baroque works and authors? If we also take into account the production of lesser authors, and epigones, such as the sensational
melodramatic pieces by Hallman (c. 1640–1706) and Haugwitz
(1647–1706) or much of the verse in the early volumes of the
unabashedly ribald *Neukirchsche Sammlung* what can be seen? A
breaking-up of the closely interweaving textures of High Baroque;
an overpowering extrovert intensification of movement, sensuousness
and antithesis; an unambiguous shifting of emphasis from ethical
and religious values to resourceful pragmatism adumbrating the
Enlightenment, but also to an orientalistic Exoticism hardly surprising in an age of colonial and missionary activities as well as
Turkish wars; a tendency to engineer effects that surprise and
dazzle, to manipulate devices and to pile on exterior ornaments
for their own sake, to wrest images from their network of baroque
correspondences, to let formalism dominate over a content whose
forces may be almost spent, to exaggerate structure to the point
of distortion and unbalance; or—this possibility is often lost sight

of besides the vast hypertrophies of form—a whittling down to austere economy. Of course, not all of these factors will occur all at once in one Late Baroque work, and those that do may not all bulk equally large. Changes in the mental climate may chronologically outrun metamorphoses in form and vice-versa, and a "historical" verdict must weigh one aspect against the other. A glance at yet another genre may exemplify this need. While Ziegler's intensely theatrical Lohensteinian *Banise* of 1689 may be appropriately styled Late Baroque, the capacious courtly political novels of Anton Ulrich Duke of Brunswick (1635-1714) have plausibly been claimed to mirror in their masterly tectonic composition the world view of High Baroque. But the all-seeing author's absolute sovereignty over the multiple threads of the plot, so unforgettably evoked by Catharina von Greiffenberg in her dedicatory poem to the third volume of the Duke's *Aramena*,[19] rather reveals an optimistic or wistful secularization of the idea of Divine Providence and therefore, a final stage, a "Late" Baroque outlook.[20]

No period term is exhaustive, and from conceding that individual authors, e.g. Wolf Helmhardt von Hohberg (1612-88) may only be marginally baroque, it would seem only a step farther to staking out baroque-free zones in the literary landscape of the seventeenth century. But it alarmingly undermines the validity of our term if, as has been suggested by some, the Protestant *Kirchenlied* and its unrivalled master Paul Gerhardt (1607-76) who movingly merged the popular (e.g. sub-courtly diction) with the artistic (e.g. the antithetical structure of the baroque stanza) are ruled out as totally at variance with the Baroque. With a deplorably retrograde use of "baroque" as no more than a synonym for overembellished style, even one of the two greatest figures of High Baroque and indeed of the age, Grimmelshausen (*c.* 1622-76), has been declared as standing outside the bounds of the term which becomes plainly useless if it precludes central writers or relegates them to the fringe. Admittedly, Grimmelshausen, an engaged satirical "popular" writer, rooted in the sixteenth century, and at the same time the author of gallant novels aiming at more courtly tastes, is somewhat enigmatic and difficult to place; his perennially human *Simplicissimus*, for years misunderstood as an *Entwicklungsroman*, has ironically enough been singled out as both a typical example of baroque style and as an un-baroque precursor of eighteenth century attitudes. If profound distrust of the times and the insight that the soul finds peace only in God are tantamount to a rejection of the Baroque, then Grimmelshausen, who utilizes baroque devices to unmask courtly wordliness, answers the description. But isn't his inexhaustible "metaphysical picaresque novel" (Forster) rather the truest, most universal realization of what a less wilfully limited notion of High Baroque should imply: Christian outlook clothed in a didactically effective and artistically accomplished form? A comparison with the delightful, boisterously realistic novels of the Austrian Johannes Beer (1655–1700) who outwardly employs similar motifs but without Grimmelshausen's moral and theological connotations would make this abundantly clear.

Other subsidiary terms have been suggested instead of Baroque— *First and Second Silesian Schools, Schwulst, Alamode, Galante Dichtung*, etc. but owing to their restricted nature and frustrating duplication, their usefulness is tantalizingly small. The terms *First and Second Silesian School*, in the past at least often taken as the equivalent, the first of *Frühbarock* (but including Opitz) and the second of *Spätbarock*, left Gryphius marooned in the no-man's land between and are now generally discarded as obsolete misnomers fostering illusions about regional homogeneity. Similarly *Schwulst* with its virulent deprecatory flavour, and *Alamode* which refers to excessive outlandishness and affectation as well as to the patriotic reaction against such derivative cosmopolitanism do not provide suitable substitutes either for Baroque in general or for the florid but far from universally decadent Late Baroque. And to treat *Galante Dichtung*, actually the frivolous, dallying, French-orientated poetry of Neukirch, Hunold-Menantes and Abschatz simply as a synonym for Second Silesian School or Late Baroque as a whole, fails to do justice to the ramifications of literary fashions and critical fronts during the crucial decades between the 1680s and 1720s or early 30s, the so-called "galante-curieuse Epoche", in which devitalized, moribund and disintegrating Baroque over-lapped and compromised extensively with Early Enlightenment Classicism (to which *Galante Dichtung* yielded without much of a struggle) and also with Rococo. And finally, the recent introduction of the term *Frührokoko* (Singer) for the transitional literature around 1700 (if not for the *Galante Dichtung* itself) does not seem fortunate as it unduly stretches Rococo and glosses over the persistence of baroque elements into the eighteenth century.

IV

The term Baroque originated as a stylistic one, but despite the poets' concern with form and their awareness of genre, the real aims of baroque literature do not reside in formal excellence, and the concept of Baroque should not be narrowed down to style alone. There is no baroque uniformity of literary expression even within High Baroque. To gear it to isolated verbal devices deprives Baroque of its historical precision besides ignoring the relative weight of such aspects in each individual work, since supposedly baroque traits, e.g. the much cited asyndeton (*Worthäufung*) may belong to a much older tradition; and to insist on the specifically baroque nature of say, the rich Petrarchan imagery of Fleming would, on these exclusively stylistic grounds, render Scaliger and Bembo baroque figures, too.

On various occasions, Baroque has (with suspect arguments) been interpreted as the revival of a certain racial (Nordic) or national (German, Hispanic) spirit, and a steady flow of psychological-philosophical speculations has engendered the ubiquitous verbal phantom of the "Baroque Man" with his tormented "Baroque Soul" forever alternating between conflicting existential rôles. Other card-board models of the age, and the patently anachronistic ghosts of emotional subjectivism and individualism have not yet been completely exorcised from seventeenth century studies. The copious, often mutually exclusive definitions in terms of *Zeitgeist* and ideology, of foggy -isms (Voluntarism, Illusionism) or pretentious bipolar formulae of the "spirit and flesh" variety show up the merits but even more the pitfalls of rhapsodic *Geistesgeschichte* and its practice of distilling ideas from literature. Few would deny the centrality of festive ostentation, hierarchical order or the obsession with "vanitas", decay, and devouring time in baroque mentality and art. But while the polarity of worldly glory and eternal salvation, for one, is very real and typical, our grasp of the period has, on the whole, not been appreciably furthered by oracular theories reiterating its antithetic and dualistic character. The well-entrenched views that the seventeenth century is predominantly an age of crisis, anguish, tension, pessimism and passive suffering blatantly disregard the positive values of hope and trust, the spiritual conquest over momentanism and anxiety, the mystically serene as well as the dramatic-heroic element in the Baroque. And if one seeks the identity of the period in the realm of ideas alone, it is again advisable to remind oneself that what "appears baroque to many observers may also be medieval or simply universally Christian . . .,"[21] or classical, or Neo-Latin, and the artistic intention and emphasis of each idea, topos or motif—be it "Adieu Welt", "carpe diem", "constantia", "fortuna", the feeling of transience or "the world's a stage"—has to be elucidated in each instance.

As regards the value of historical, political and denominational factors as constituents of a definition, one may well ask whether they do not tend to obscure the fact that literature and society, while related, are not co-incidental. To identify Baroque, e.g. with dynastic Absolutism runs counter to the disillusioning reality of an atomized Germany under the superstructure of a powerless and distant Empire. This is not to deny that Absolutism was a major facet of the age, transposing religious concepts (e.g. divine hierarchy) to the political sphere but also modifying man's interpretation of his relationship with God.

To equate Baroque with *Counter-Reformation* has long enjoyed pseudo-historical respectability, irrespective of the factual and chronological fallacies underlying this assumption which in no way takes cognizance of the Protestant Baroque. Without belittling the fascination and power of the *Ordensdrama* and other branches of Catholic literature, one has to refute any denominational and regional schematizing as untenable. Even the hackneyed North–South division in terms of *Wort- und Bürgerbarock* as against *Bild- und Kaiserbarock* can only serve as a preliminary orientation. Neither Catholicism nor Protestantism can stake an exclusive claim to the German Baroque, in whose literature syncretism is widespread; in Gryphius, for example, who has been described as having created a kind of Jesuit drama in a Protestant mould.

Nor was Baroque confined to any particular geographical area. Nevertheless, literary life did largely shift from its sixteenth century centres in the South-west to the North-east, and Silesia, occupying a peculiar position within the Empire, attained prominence through poetic works that at least for a while flourished under favourable material and political conditions. Generally speaking, the devastation and misery of the Thirty Years' War as formative background to baroque literature have been exaggerated.

Sociological definitions of the Baroque tend to keep too rigidly to the courtly sphere and to pass over sermons and devotional literature, satirical writings, the unsophisticated folk-song, the popular novel, etc. Only a minority of the practising poets lived at court and connections between authors and courtly society were on the whole tenuous. *Aulica Vita*, the courtly life, may even be reduced to the very image of "vanitas" and diabolical worldliness by baroque literature, which is mainly borne by the rising middle class in cities such as Hamburg, Königsberg and Nuremberg. There is no doubt that the so-called *anticourtly* current did provide an articulate counterpoint in seventeenth century culture—Heidelberg and Straßburg with its valiant *Aufrichtige Tannengesellschaft*, in opposition to the exotic emblem of the *Palmenorden*, were amongst its bastions and the barbs of satire, striking at *Alamode* pomposity and the insincerity of courtiers, amongst its favourite weapons. But the intricacies and fluctuations of this anticourtly strain have been persistently oversimplified. J. Lauremberg (1590–1658), e.g., despite his polemical use of homely Low German against the courtly *Alamode* craze, maintains intimate links with the courtly sphere much more so than H. M. Moscherosch (1601–69) for example with his hard-hitting satire *Wunderliche und Wahrhaftige Gesichte Philanders von Sittewald.* Similarly displays of patriotic purism against the interlarding of German with foreign words can be found in popular as well as courtly *Sprachgesellschaften.* The first great master of the epigram, Fr. von Logau (1604–55), was a penetrating critic of the courtly age, but he neither writes for the masses, nor is he free from baroque artistry. The spectacular stagecraft of Jesuit drama in Habsburg Vienna caters for *all* social classes. The mingling of elements in Johann Khuen's (1606–75) poetry about the Virgin Mary suggests a courtly impact on South German popular Catholic verse. The assertion : "the antinomy of courtly and anticourtly is the central axis of the baroque"[22] is therefore disputable and ignores, *inter alia*, possible tensions between Court and Nobility. And Gryph's comedies alone would suffice to illustrate that we are not dealing with irreconcilable polarities but rather with an interplay of complementary opposites.

Pushed to its extreme consequence, the sociological approach has caused Marxist critics to dismiss the whole concept of Baroque as obscuring class distinctions, to reject Late Baroque as the literary medium of feudalism and to build up the comedy of the period as an antifeudal genre with a bourgeois hero. Here one must admit that the great social shift was indubitably gathering strength in the seventeenth century. But many bourgeois elements in baroque literature had made their appearance much earlier and can be traced back through the age of Luther to the popular traditions of the Middle Ages. Such continuity is discernible in the pulpit oratory of Catholic preachers such as Abraham a Sancta Clara (J. U. Megerle, 1644–1709) whose ebullient style blends this heritage with Humanist learning—or in the moral satire of the *Alamode* battle, and most impressively perhaps in the work of Gryphius which has affiliations with the religious poetry and drama of the Middle Ages as well as with the didacticism of the Reformation.

v

The existence of a "European Baroque" is being assumed rather too optimistically in recent years though the term is still by no

means generally accepted and has been exposed to dramatic vicissi-
tudes in some countries.[23] Clearly it is almost impossible to decoct
a common denominator of a synchronistic unity of tone and spirit
even for literature alone and still less for all the arts, when one
considers the complications caused by the timelag, e.g. between
baroque poetry and baroque music or architecture! Hence it is not
surprising that many modern critics view the whole concept of
Baroque with suspicion and have considered what might be from
the viewpoint of German studies, the value of other names used
for the Western literatures of the seventeenth century? *Manier-
ismus* (Mannerism), in which Curtius and others have seen an
anticlassical constant, has become an overworked blanket term.
To advocate its usefulness as an uncommitted replacement for
Baroque is to disregard its commitments in art history and its
derogatory connotations (excess, degeneration, lack of balance,
subjectivism). To equate Mannerism (or "Baroquism", meaning
mannerist Baroque) sweepingly with *Barock* as a whole can only
produce a onesided and idiosyncratic notion of that period—the
category of Mannerism plays no part of any consequence in many
of its works, including its greatest. To apply "mannerist" loosely
to High or Late Baroque writers has, e.g. in the case of Hofmannswaldau and Lohenstein, obscured the true nature of their
art.

Metaphysical, which has been extended to continental literatures
as, for example, in F. J. Warnke's *European Metaphysical Poetry*
is inevitably fraught with the association of "a loosely knit group—
if that—of poets around John Donne", and for that reason alone
has to be declared unsuitable, although interesting typological
parallels between German baroque and English metaphysical poetry
can be found. And similar but still more cogent arguments rule out
Préciosité as *précieux* may even purport a reaction against
Baroque. Other nationally restricted designations such as *Culter-
anismo, Conceptismo, Gongorismo*, etc. prove in no way inter-
changeable with Baroque, indeed their relationship with the latter
is not yet satisfactorily explored. To label German or the whole
of European literature with these or other terms implying exotic
exaggeration throws the picture out of focus. *Marinismus* too,
which in German has become a collective epithet for obscure and
frivolous seventeenth century extravagance, should if used at all
be confined to the colourful mannerist products of Silesian Late
Baroque—the results of Spanish-Italian influences running wild,
unchecked by a courtly centre. It should not be viewed as the
apogee of Baroque. Significantly enough, the Second Silesian
School (for which *some* textbooks substitute *Marinismus*) was

violently attacked by Enlightenment critics who at the same time respected and even commended Gryphius and Fleming.

VI

As a literary term "Baroque" should be rescued from the prejudices, stigmas and hereditary taints of its pejorative beginnings. It should not be a mere synonym for "in bad taste", "twisted", "turgid", for "lacking in harmony" or "attracted to the ornate". There is a good deal more to it than an outburst of lavish decoration and uncontrolled movement between the earthier matter-of-factness of the sixteenth, and the neoclassicist stiffness of the early eighteenth centuries; but to see Baroque as the heyday of facile toying with soulless topoi and self-sufficient stylistic devices is equally incorrect.

Are we to take baroque purely as a nominalistic tag with a heuristic value, or as a historiographic means to describe a period style? Various dangers besetting the application of the term have already been touched upon. One that cannot be overemphasized is the intrusion of Goethean concepts (*Symbol, Erlebnisdichtung*, organic form, etc.) and the denunciation of Baroque as lacking in them. Equally misleading, is the pan-aesthetic approach. There is still a tenacious proneness to compare Baroque apologetically with a normative *Klassik*, instead of a readiness to look upon baroque authors as exponents of a period, devoted to the objective implementation of genres and supra-personal ideologies. Another distorting factor lurks in excessive selectiveness that scales Baroque down to a single group (e.g. the Nuremberg poets) or phenomenon (e.g. Viennese court opera).

I would like to suggest a concept of Baroque that is centred in, but not restricted to a core of works of literary quality, spiritual depth and structural discipline, a re-appraisal that would place mannerist and predominantly secular poets on the periphery. I would also recommend that *Early, High* and *Late* Baroque should not function primarily as chronological markers—after all, Gryph's *Kirchhofsgedanken* and Lohenstein's *Cleopatra* both belong to the same year 1656, for example—but as abbreviated references to the totality, and not merely to the stylistic fabric of a work; to such reciprocity or correlation as may exist between its components, as e.g. in the characteristically baroque interaction of theme and form in Gryph's splendidly complex *Horribilicribrifax*.[24] This would aid us to differentiate adequately between coeval but disparate works such as *Simplicissimus* and Hallmann's *Marianne*, both 1669.

What, then, is typically baroque? Rather than conclude with a theoretical pronouncement, I quote one of Gryph's most perfect sonnets which through its lucid architectural concentration may convey that Baroque need not be identical with chaotic irrationalism; on the contrary, this poem *Abend* stands for Baroque as intricately wrought, strongly rational *Mass- und Formkunst*.

Der schnelle Tag ist hin/die Nacht schwingt jhre fahn/
Vnd führt die Sternen auff. Der Menschen müde scharen
Verlassen feld vnd werck/Wo Thier vnd Vögel waren
Trawrt jtzt die Einsamkeit. Wie ist die zeit verthan!
Der port naht mehr vnd mehr sich/zu der glieder Kahn.
Gleich wie diß licht verfiel/so wird in wenig Jahren
Ich/du/vnd was man hat/vnd was man siht/hinfahren.
Diß Leben kömmt mir vor alß eine renne bahn.
Laß höchster Gott mich doch nicht auff dem Laufplatz gleiten/
Laß mich nicht ach/nicht pracht/nicht lust/nicht angst ver-
    leiten.
Dein ewig heller glantz sey vor vnd neben mir/
Laß/wenn der müde Leib entschläfft/die Seele wachen
Vnd wenn der letzte Tag wird mit mir abend machen/
So reiß mich auß dem thal der Finsternuß zu Dir.[25]

Abend, part of a cycle on the times of day, participates in the intensive polarity of *Time* and *Eternity* around which so much of Gryph's work revolves, and its religious humility offers an illuminating contrast to the more humanistic side of the age whose stoic manifesto, Fleming's sonnet *An Sich*, proudly celebrates Man's mastery over fate and cultivates form, the refuge of so many seventeenth century poets, not as an intimation of divine reason ordering a disjointed world but as a near-pagan pledge of worldly immortality.

Here, crystallized in fourteen alexandrine lines, we recognize some of the pivotal elements in the mainstream of German Baroque :

1. Christian faith, not untroubled but unwavering, and a paradigmatic didacticism that does not allow subject matter (e.g. history in *Catharina von Georgien*), motif (nature in stanza I of *Abend*!) or literary medium (Renaissance sonnet) to acquire a relevance of their own. Even the very rhetoric of Gryphius is subordinated to his "mission" of celebrating Christian virtues, vindicating human self-denial and submissiveness, and of depicting eschatology and eternity in visionary images. There was much truth in J. E. Schlegel's remark that Heaven created Gryph's dramatic characters.

Abend, meditative and ending in prayer, is rich in biblical allusions (cf. I Cor. ix. 24, and Phil. iii. 13) that call to mind the close kinship between Gryph's poetry and devotional literature.

If we associate, as I think we must, High Baroque with the edifying "theological stylus" (Grimmelshausen) in literary garb, the modifier *Late* becomes indispensable once these Christian impulses have been ousted by wordlier motivations.

2. With its abstract, un-subjective metaphors of earthly transitoriness, *Abend* epitomizes the inherently religious imagery that constitutes another integral part of the era which already Herder was inclined to style "emblematic". Gryph's whole work draws upon a body of images (whose ancestry is traceable back to Renaissance and Middle Ages at least), subservient to the poetic expounding of a Christian world picture, a system of universal references, deictic, exemplary, and ultimately metaphysical in character. (Small wonder that the Enlightenment critics like Breitinger frowned upon this kind of "dark hieroglyph.") Recent research has substantially borne out the assumption of the fundamentally emblematic nature of baroque poetry and greatly enriched our understanding of baroque drama by demonstrating its consistently emblematic structure.[26]

3. In seventeenth century scholarship, a trend towards a synthesis of methods has been gaining ground, after decades of myopic dissection of isolated motifs and stylistic traits. Only by integrating the stylistic with the ideological—and sociological—aspect, will an approach equal to the task of analysing the fusion of rhetorical classicism and allegorical medievalism in the many-sided *oeuvre* of Gryphius be developed.

In most genuinely baroque works a particular type of structure will be found which, though radically different from the inseparable oneness of Goethean poetry, provides baroque works with a constitutive unity. Baroque drama, closely interlinking the physical and the otherworldly, perhaps most clearly lays bare the interaction between *Struktur-* and *Epochenkräfte* (Just); e.g. the curtain screening off the rear of the stage is a vehicle for theatrical effects but also for abrupt transformations of ideological import.

The pattern of organization, or rather demonstration, of a baroque work interlocks with its "message" (a word justified for so didactic a period)—overtly for instance in the religious symbolism of numbers (*Zahlenkomposition*) or in more oblique disguises. Baroque authors tend to operate with several levels, to make ingenious use of shifting perspectives, of minutely planned antithetical and symmetrical mirror-designs, of fugal and polyphonic techniques, of paradoxical polarities and a peculiarly seventeenth century brand of irony; they exploit dialectically the multiple and mutable implications of emblematic images and scenes, the "Umschlägigkeit der Bilder" (Schöne). But they will nevertheless observe the primacy of content over form, or, in Grimmelshausen's famous metaphors, of the kernel over the husks, of the moral pill over the sugar-coating. We cannot understand Baroque unless we realize that underneath massed conceits and stylistic disintegration there glows a desire to announce truths transcending human utterance and therefore straining the language to breaking-point. And where Baroque, giving the lie to its modern reputation, achieves balance, it is less of an immanent than of an excentric nature as befits an age that looked beyond the physical world for its ultimate orientation.

Baroque, in the last analysis incommensurable, embraces dichotomy and tensions as well as reconciliation of polar opposites, but it does not strive for a harmonious spiritual-worldly synthesis. When, as in Late Baroque, the religious energies are completely counterbalanced by a secular pull, we are no longer encountering genuine representatives of this last universally Christian epoch. In High Baroque whose central position we have stressed, the predominance of the metaphysical over the anthropocentric, of the Christian over the classical values and doctrines is hardly ever in doubt. Our concepts of Early and Late Baroque should be revised accordingly.

It has been maintained that all national versions of baroque art show a classical undercurrent, and Baroque has even been demoted to a mere sub-division of a Renaissance Classicism spanning several centuries. But to raise *Klassizismus* to the dominant of German Baroque levels the profound differences within the period, and to juxtapose, as is often done, Gryphius and Corneille begets fictitious analogies and obliterates the rift separating the Frenchman's "haughty culte du moi" (de Mourgues) from the Silesian High Baroque drama that upheld a critical reserve towards the "tragédie classique"; the almost total absence of influences is revealing.

Gryph's achievement, "the fusion of biblical language, personal religious emotion and humanistic-rhetorical linguistic form"[27] his endeavours to forge a synthesis, remarkable for its creative boldness, of medieval and modern, of the sixteenth and seventeenth centuries, of the popular and the courtly, of antiquity and Christianity, furnishes the landmark from which any conspectus of German Baroque has to obtain its bearings.

No definition, however flexible, will capture the essence of the age and still allow for developments pointing to the future, for the "Verpersönlichung" in Fleming's mature lyrics, the psychological sentimentalism of Zesen's *Rosemund* or the secularity of Lohenstein's tragedies.

If the notion of Baroque emerging from this essay is at least adequate for the more central phenomena, its inability to be comprehensive need not cause concern if it has driven home the elusiveness and richness of one of the most captivating chapters in the history of German literature.

NOTES

1. Albrecht Schöne, *Das Zeitalter des Barock. Texte und Zeugnisse. Die deutsche Literatur*, III (Munich, 1963), p. IX.
2. Cf. *OED*, Vol. I, 1933, reprinted 1961, p. 678 "irregularly shaped, whimsical, grotesque, odd".
3. Cf. Lowry Nelson, Jr., *Baroque Lyric Poetry* (New Haven and London, 1961), pp. 3 ff: René Wellek, "The Concept of Baroque in Literary Scholarship" (first published in *JAAC*, 5 (1946)), pp. 77–109, reprinted in: R.W., *Concepts of Criticism*, edited and with an introduction by Stephen G. Nichols, Jr. (New Haven and London, 1963), pp. 69–114 (hereafter cited as Wellek I), see especially pp. 69–76, passim, and R.W., "Postscript 1962", op. cit. pp. 115 ff. (hereafter cited as Wellek II). See also C. T. Carr, "Origin and Diffusion of the word 'Baroque'", *Forum for Modern Language Studies, I* (1965), pp. 175–190.
4. VII, st. 30, *Sämtliche Werke* (Leipzig, 1839) XV, p. 101 f.
   Than Blaffardine naught more baroque could possibly be found—
   She was as horrible from head to waist as she was gorgeous from
       waist to ankles.
   Viewed from below: a match for Vanloo's finest nymphs—
   Viewed from above: a sight to scare away the crows.
5. Cf. A. Buker, "The Baroque S-T-O-R-M: A Study in the limits of the Culture-Epoch", *JAAC*, XXII/3 (1964), p. 304.
6. He objects, however, to a sweeping disparagement of the Baroque, especially in his mature *Cicerone*, see Werner Kaegi, *Jacob Burckhardt* (Basel, 1956), III, p. 508.
7. *German Poetry 1944–1948* (Cambridge, 1949), pp. 31 f., cf. p. 53.
8. Cf. P. Merker, "Die Anfänge der deutschen Barockliteratur", *GR* VI (1931), 113.
9. Cf. L. Forster, "Fremdsprache und Muttersprache. Zur Frage der polyglotten Dichtung", *Neophilologus* 45 (1961), p. 183.
10. See Karl Otto Conrady, *Lateinische Dichtungstradition und deutsche Lyrik des 17. Jahrhunderts* (Bonn, 1962).
11. Cf. J. H. Tisch, "Gottsched's Dramas between Baroque and Enlightenment". Proceedings of the IXth Congress AULLA, ed. by Marion Adams, Melbourne, 1964, 120 ff.
12. Helmut Singer, *Der deutsche Roman zwischen Barock und Rokoko* (Cologne-Graz, 1963), p. 88.
13. Cf. H. O. Burger, "Deutsche Aufklärung im Widerspiel zu Barock und 'Neubarock'", in: *Formkräfte der deutschen Dichtung* (Göttingen, 1963), especially p. 73.

14. H. K. Kettler: *Baroque Tradition in the Literature of the German Enlightenment 1700–1750* (Cambridge, n.d.). See also K. Berger, *Barock und Aufklärung im geistlichen Lied* (Marburg, 1951).
15. R. Wellek, "Period in Literature", *Dictionary of World Literature*, ed. Joseph T. Shipley (New York, 1943), p. 909.
16. *Vorbarocker Klassizismus und griechische Tragödie. Analyse der "Antigone"-Ubersetzung der Martin Opitz* (Darmstadt, 1962), Wiss. Buchgesellschaft, Reihe "Libelli", LXXIX (first published *Neue Heidelberger Jahrbücher* 1926), pp. 3–63.
17. Cf. E. Rotermund, *Christian Hofmann von Hofmannswaldau* (Stuttgart, 1963); Kuhlmann: A. Menhennet, *YWMLSt*, XXV (1963), p. 327 (there in regard to K's religious thought).
18. See *Die Trauerspiele Lohensteins* (Berlin, 1961), by Klaus Günther Just, the editor of the critical edition of the *Trauerspiele*.
19. *Deutsche Barocklyrik* ed. Max Wehrli, 3rd ed. (Basel, 1962), p. 26.
20. Cf. H. O. Burger, "Deutsche Aufklärung . . .", *Formkräfte*, p. 62 ff.
21. Wellek I, p. 107.
22. E. Lunding, "German Baroque Literature", *GLL* NS III (1949) p. 3 (but see also II). The original anticourtly thesis put forward by Erika Vogt (*Die gegenhöfische Strömung in der deutschen Barockliteratur*, 1932) is considerably invalidated by incorrect presuppositions and a precarious vacillation between the realms of moral outlook and sociology. See also O. Brunner, *Adeliges Landleben und europäischer Geist* (Salzburg, 1959).
23. For details see e.g. Wellek I, pp. 81 ff. and Wellek II, pp. 117 ff.
24. See my article "Braggarts, Wooers, Foreign Tongues and Vanitas . . .", *AUMLA*, XXI (1964), 65 ff., especially 72 ff.
25. Andreas Gryphius, *Gesamtausgabe der deutschsprachigen Werke*, Vol. I, *Sonette*, ed. Marian Szyrocki (Tübingen, 1963), p. 66.

Evening

The rapid day is gone; her banner swings the night,
And leads the stars aloft. Men's wearied hosts have wended
Away from field and work; where beast and bird attended,
Now solitude laments. How vain has been time's flight!
The vessel of our limbs draws nearer to the bight.
In but a little while, just as this light descended,
Will I, you, what we have, and what we see be ended.
E'en as a runner's track seems life within my sight.
Great God, grant me that I in coursing do not blunder!
Nor joy trick me nor fear nor woe nor earthly wonder!
Let Your unfailing light my comrade be and guide!
When my tired body sleeps, grant that my soul be waking,
And when the final day my eventide is making,
Then take me from this vale of darkness to Your side!

G. C. Schoolfield, *The German Lyric of the Baroque in English Translation* (Chapel Hill, Uni. of North Carolina Press, 1961).

26. See the recent publications by Albrecht Schöne, particularly his illustrated *Emblematik und Drama im Zeitalter des Barock* (Munich, 1964).

27. Paul Böckmann, *Formgeschichte der deutschen Dichtung*, I (Hamburg, 1949), p. 424.

SELECT BIBLIOGRAPHY

In addition to the works by Schöne (notes 1 and 26), Wellek (note 3), Conrady (note 10), the first four essays in *Formkräfte* (see note 13) and the anthologies of Wehrli (note 19) and Schoolfield (note 25), the following publications are regarded as particularly important (the emphasis in this selection being on the discussion of problems similar to those touched upon in our chapter, rather than on literary history as such):

R. Alewyn (and others), *Aus der Welt des Barock* (Stuttgart, 1957).

R. Alewyn (ed.), *Deutsche Barockforschung. Dokumentation einer Epoche* (Cologne, 1965—only seen *after* my chapter had been completed). An anthology, and bibliography, of representative and pioneer work by Cysarz, Peuckert, Nadler, Hirsch, Strich, v. Wiese, Fricke, Kayser, Lugowski, Benjamin, Milch—to mention some not referred to in our notes and bibliography—and others, from the 'twenties to the mid-'thirties.

W. Fleming, (Introductions to) *Barockdrama*, 6 vols. (Leipzig, 1930–33) (DLE, Reihe Barock, Barockdrama).

L. Forster, *The Temper of Seventeenth Century German Literature* (London, 1952).

E. Lunding, "Stand und Aufgaben der deutschen Barockforschung", *Orbis Litterarum* VIII (1950), p. 27 f.

H. Pyritz, *Paul Flemings Liebeslyrik. Zur Geschichte des Petrarkismus* (Göttingen, 1963—enlarged reprint of the author's *PFs deutsche Liebeslyrik*, Leipzig, 1932).

J. Mark, "The Uses of the Term 'Baroque'", *MLR* XXXIII (1938), p. 547 f.

J. H. Scholte, article. "Barockliteratur", *RL* I2 (marred by retrograde attitude; cf. article "Alamode").

R. Stamm (ed.), *Kunstformen des Barockzeitalters* (Berne, 1956), (especially the essays by Stamm and by H. Tintelnot).

E. Trunz, "Die Erforschung der deutschen Barockdichtung..." *DVjs* XVIII (1940), Referatenheft If.

K. Viëtor, *Probleme der deutschen Barockliteratur* (Leipzig, 1929).

The main handbooks on the period are:

C. von Faber du Faur, *German Baroque Literature* (New Haven, 1958).

P. Hankamer, *Deutsche Gegenreformation und deutsches Barock in der Dichtung* (Stuttgart, 1935; 1947; the 1964 reprint omits the extensive bibliography compiled by H. Pyritz which is being revised for separate publication).

G. Müller, *Deutsche Dichtung von der Renaissance bis zum Ausgang des Barock* (Potsdam 1926–28) (reprint, Darmstadt, 1957).

R. Newald, *Die deutsche Literatur vom Späthumanismus zur Empfindsamkeit* . . . (Munich, 1963–4).

(For different reasons, none of these books represents the approach and insights of modern scholarship.)

Special issues of periodicals include: *Revue des Sciences Humaines* (1949), *MLN*, German issue (1962), and *EG* (1964).

Rococo

III

Rococo

R. H. SAMUEL

"ROCOCO" in German literature is not a "movement" but an attitude and mood which expressed itself in certain works, themes and genres and reflects certain social tendencies of the age. As a general term it is borrowed from the style in architecture and the visual arts of the *ancien régime* before the French Revolution. The origin of the term Rococo is obscure. After the outbreak of the Revolution artists trying to express their ideas in new forms consciously distanced themselves from the style of the *ancien régime*. They found the essential emblem of the preceding age in the diminution of a rock (French : *roc*) into small fragments (French : *rocaille*), or heaps of pebbles clustered around a sea-shell. Playing with words such as *roc, rocaille, rocailleux* led to the coining of the word *rococo* at the end of the eighteenth century in the atelier of the French painter Jacques Louis David whose disciples pointed to the—seeming—meaninglessness of ornamental diffusion so characteristic of post-baroque style. The term, therefore, had a strongly pejorative, even abusive, meaning which it retained in general in the nineteenth century. Not until early in the twentieth century was an objective appreciation of the stylistic characteristics of the period attained and the term was also applied to literary phenomena.

The "Rococo" style grew out of the Baroque style and yet introduced a diametrically opposed art form and view of life. It developed under the Regency (1715–23) and spread to Germany where it found its consummation in the multifarious courts of the Holy Roman Empire. Its essential characteristics are the dissolution of established forms. The monumental lines of Baroque art were pierced and corrupted, as it were, by detailed superimposed ornamentation. The arbitrary and irregular curves of a sea-shell with its infinite variations became the basic model. Everything was reduced in size and prettified. Playfulness, elegance, charm, ease, refinement, gracefulness was the intended effect. Instead of massive organization of material there was constant and shifting movement, the eye was never allowed to rest, but had to absorb an abundance of seemingly unorganized, fancifully twisted and interlaced ornamental detail. This love of detail is, in particular, dis-

43

played in interior decoration, in furniture, in applied art and the small appliances of life. It is the time when pretty, apparently useless, articles abound. The massive invasion of Chinese Art, which began in the last quarter of the seventeenth century, gave a powerful impetus to Rococo art, and the successful imitation of the process of china manufacture by Johann Böttger in Meissen in 1709 "provided the Rococo period with the raw material that enabled it to transform its ultimate intentions into artistic action".[1]

Rococo culture was basically aristocratic and emanated from the great courts of Europe. It reflects, in particular, the style of life developed at the court of Louis XV and of the French aristocracy in its salons where the rigid ceremonial of the previous age was exchanged for informality and easy-going social behaviour. Its underlying nature was aimlessness and, stemming from this, frivolity, *esprit* (wit), make-believe, and a worldly epicureanism which advocated serene enjoyment of life and *galante* form. The epicurean and *galante* literature of the later seventeenth and the early eighteenth century is exemplified in French *chansons* and the new playful form of *Vaudevilles*, precursors of the comic opera.[2] The latter with their rural setting and popular contents signify the longing of high society to return to the joys of a simple life, which in turn is expressed in the settings of shepherds and shepherdesses in courtly and aristocratic festivities as mirrored in the paintings and tapestries of the time and repeated a hundredfold on chinaware and china figures. This mode of writing also spread to England where Shaftesbury, Prior, Pope, John Gay and later Fielding and Sterne adapted its mood to English conditions.[3]

In the wake of Rococo culture which invaded the German courts in the second quarter of the eighteenth century its literary equivalent followed quite naturally. Although Rococo culture flowered mainly in Roman Catholic western and southern Germany and in Austria, the literary scene of the German-speaking regions was dominated by Protestant writers from northern and central Germany and from Switzerland. However, one of the most important centres of Rococo culture was the court of Dresden under the Elector Augustus the Strong (1649–1733) and his son Augustus III (1733–63). In Berlin Frederick the Great (1740–86) developed a somewhat tempered "Prussian" Rococo. The upper middle classes in cities such as Hamburg and Leipzig adopted the Rococo style to a certain extent. It must be borne in mind that almost every one of the middle-class writers in the eighteenth century—writers of aristocratic origin were the exception throughout—either depended on or were at one time or other in the service of princes or aristocrats.

German Rococo literature flourished from the third to the sixth decade of the eighteenth century. The number of writers and poets who adopted its style—with many it was only a passing phase—is legion and only a few names and characteristic works will be mentioned in this essay.

The first German writer influenced by the wave of Rococo culture was Friedrich von Hagedorn (1708–54). His background is of interest. He was one of the few writers of aristocratic origin, but was born in Hamburg where his father was Danish Ambassador. His years in England as Secretary to the Danish Ambassador in London from 1729 to 1731—here he met Pope, Thomson and Händel and married an English woman—were of formative importance. He returned to Hamburg as Secretary to the "English Court" and became the centre of a dining-club, a circle that developed a gracious form of high conviviality. Hagedorn devoted his "muse" entirely to the entertainment of his friends and frequent visitors from abroad in accordance with the sociable nature of Rococo literature. Writing is to him not a profession, but a "playmate of his leisure hours". The preface to his first collection of occasional poems under the significant title *Versuch einiger Gedichte oder Erlesene Proben poetischer Nebenstunden* (1729) stressed the convivial aspect of poetry and the initial poem *An die Dichtkunst* epitomizes the essence of the new style. His lodestars are not the Iliad or Aeneid whose authors sang of the strength and virtues of heroes. To write of "higher things" and for eternity is not for him. His aim is to learn from Horace how one can please through genuine "wit". He canvasses that poetry which soothes life, diminishes sorrow and promotes happiness. He knows that later ages will find petty what he considers to be important and in this kind of poem—he also wrote different ones—he does not wish to compete with his contemporaries in creating heroic or philosophical literature. He commends his trifles (*Kleinigkeiten*) to an understanding public and does not claim immortality for them.

This unpretentiousness is characteristic of the Rococo style. Hagedorn preached, in his own interpretation of the classical tradition, prudent moderation, a smiling insight into the weaknesses of men, serene wisdom, and he spoke not as a courtier but as a man of the world who found in the social conviviality of a patrician Republic some equivalent for courtly and aristocratic society. He showed the German middle class how social life can be built on the basis of friendship between like-minded persons of high education and breeding. The contents of his Rococo poetry are presented in the costume of classicistic Baroque, but prettified and reduced in scale. His "Odes" are singable and were published with music composed by Valentin Görner, the music director of Hamburg's Protestant cathedral. These two created the Rococo *Lied* which was to influence German lyrics for decades to come.

A new element, the Anacreontic one, was brought into German literature through the younger group of the "Halle Poets", J. W. Gleim, J. P. Uz and J. N. Götz who studied together in 1738–39 and ushered in the literary Rococo style on a large scale. They worshipped Anacreon as their guiding star and went back to the Greek sources, not, however, to the works of the sixth century B.C. poet themselves, but to the imitations of the more popular parts of Anacreon's five last books of poetry, songs of love, wine and youth, written by anonymous poets in the Hellenistic age between the second century B.C. and the fourth century A.D. This "Anacreontic" poetry is preserved in a Heidelberg manuscript of the early tenth century A.D. which contains a collection of sixty songs under the title : *Convivial Half-Iambics of Anacreon of Teos and Anacreontia*. Since the editio princeps by Henri Estienne (Henricus Stephanus) of 1554[4] the songs had exerted a strong influence first in France and then in England, just as in Germany sporadic traces of Anacreontic poetry can be found in the sixteenth and seventeenth centuries. But the elevation of "Anacreon" as a teacher of a particular philosophy of life as well as an artistic mode did not occur until the early forties of the eighteenth century.

The treatment of Anacreontic themes by writers of the Baroque age as compared with those of the Rococo period highlights the difference between the two modes in a significant way. The Baroque writers' lust for life, even their longing for Arcadian simplicity, is always placed against the religious background of the transitory nature of life, against the constant presence of decay and death.

The sombre note that envelops all Baroque writing is eliminated by the Rococo writers. Through the medium of the Anacreontia —which the Halle poets translated from the Greek into rhymeless German verse[5]—they imagine they have discovered in Anacreon a man who has mastered life from youth to old age by being cheerful, eliminating life's stings, disregarding life's burdens (wealth, war, politics, the dread of death, etc.) and allowing oneself to be guided by χάρις (grace) and refinement and by those mythical incarnations of χάρις, the χάριτες or Graces. Through these qualities Anacreon and those who adopt his way of life attain true wisdom.

> Anakreon, mein Lehrer
> Singt nur von Wein und Liebe;
> Er salbt den Bart mit Salben,

Und singt von Wein und Liebe;
Er krönt sein Haupt mit Rosen ...
Und singt von Wein und Liebe ...

so begins the first collection of Gleim's poems entitled "Experiment
in frolicsome songs".[6] These fifty-one poems made their author
famous overnight and released a veritable torrent of like-minded
poetry over the next twenty-five years to such an extent that hardly
any writer of repute—Lessing, Gellert, Klopstock, Goethe among
them—could fail to be drawn into this whirlpool if only as a
passing phase.

The mood from which Anacreontic poetry sprang was one of
protest against certain prevailing tendencies of the time. First of all
it turned against the heroic tendencies of both Baroque and early
Enlightenment writing, the glorification of war and the idealization of the great in the social hierarchy. Christian Felix Weiße
expressed more strongly than Hagedorn this anti-heroic trend in
Rococo literature, for instance in an adaptation of Horace's Ode
to Maecenas (II, 12) which itself had drawn its theme from the
Anacreontia :

> Ich singe nicht der deutschen Adler Kriege,
> Den Stolz der Könige, der Weltbezwinger Siege,
> Nicht jenes Meer von Blut und Tod ...[7]

just as Gleim declared that his songs were not "blutig" and as Karl
Christian Reckert begins a short idyll :

> Nicht dem Ruhm des Eroberers, nicht der blutigen
> Feldschlacht, nicht den sterbenden Helden, weihe
> die Muse ihr zärtliches Lied ![8]

Here social criticism begins to creep into Anacreontic writing as
witnessed again by Weiße, who does not wish to deal with :

> .... jen Gebürg von Schlößern und Palästen,
> Wo unter Reigen sich unnütze Schmeichler mästen,
> Indeß des Bürgers Thräne fließt
> Und sein erkargtes Brod begießt.[9]

Other targets of these writers were the sublimity and severity of
metaphysical poets such as Haller, the cosmic enthusiasm of Klopstock, the patriarchic and seraphic epics of Bodmer and the early
Wieland, and finally the tearful and ascetic otherworldliness of the
Pietist movement, which had its stronghold in Halle, the birth-
place of Gleim's and his friends' early "experiments".

Against these trends the Rococo writers display a purely secular view of the world and stand for cheerful affirmation of life, for full enjoyment of the happy and the beautiful things that are offered on this earth, for harmony of body and soul, for simplicity and naturalness, for good taste and discernment. The latter, in particular, led to a gentle irony which mocked at all things that are considered great and accepted as immovable convention. This determines also the form of the new poetry. The sublime is rejected. The eagle, says Gleim, is sublime, to be sure, and he reveres him; but if he sees Jove's lightning issue from his claws, dread and horror befall him; he adds, significantly : his thunder disturbs my peace, why all the noise?

> Sein Donner störet meine Ruh :
> So großer Lärm, wozu? Wozu?

He prefers the little dove which Anacreon sent from his tiny township. Just as the pretty dove is preferable to the fearful eagle so small poems, gently fluttering, are preferable to the rolling form of the ode cultivated by Klopstock and his disciples. Gleim is prepared to grant this form its rightful place on the Parnassus, but he doubts whether they will be read.

> Die kleinen Verse, die bescheiden
> Gern neben sich die großen leiden,
> Gelesen werden sie mit Freuden,
> Gelobt wird ihre Harmonie . . .[10]

So he sums up with the unpretentiousness which all Rococo writers display as a matter of aesthetic faith. Nor do they pretend that their writing is a reflection of experience in their lives, that their Dorises, Daphnes and Chloes, their Amynts and Seladons, their bucolic and arcadian scenes populated with Nymphs, Dryads, Amors and hosts of other sylvan deities are anything but stage settings or that the carefree philanderings and suggestive situations that take place in this environment are based on actual adventures, in short that their poetry is *Erlebnisdichtung*. On the contrary, poetry is consciously divorced from life. Gleim pronounced this as an aesthetic principle in the preface to the second issue of the *Versuche* . . . —the preface is disguised as an address by Doris to her reader :

> Never draw from the writing of poets conclusions as to their morals. You will be deceived; for they write merely to display their wit, even if thereby they expose their virtue to suspicion. They don't characterize themselves as they are, but as the nature of their poetry demands it, and they give preference to that

system which offers them the best opportunity of being witty. The mathematical evidence of the Wolffians does not embellish a single poem, and the universal wisdom of Plato is an unsuitable subject for frolicsome songs.[11]

Witz then is the foremost instrument of the Rococo poet and to be "witty" is his foremost function. To develop *Witz*—the word became in German an equivalent to *esprit* in the eighteenth century—the Rococo writers forged a new terminology and eventually a new language. The Rococo *Witz* is, however, different from that of the Enlightenment. Christian Wolff had defined it as a combination of ingenuity and imagination (*Scharfsinnigkeit und Einbildungskraft*).[12] The intellectual process of *Scharfsinnigkeit* was lightened and loosened by the Rococo writers through playfulness. Again Gleim set the tune :

Ich will singen, ich will spielen . . .[13]

This playfulness added to wit produces *Scherz* which could be defined as wistful gaiety. According to the early Rococo theoretician G. F. Meyer, it contains an element of ingenuity (*Scharfsinnigkeit*) and has the effect of "cheering up our inner disposition in such a way that all anxiety is expelled from our soul".[14] *Scherz* thus became the fundamental principle of a new artistic style. Eventually it was personified and *Scherz* joined the retinue of Amor with graces and amorettoes.[15] The overriding significance of *Scherz* explains why this term appears as the title of so many Rococo publications.[16]

The element of playfulness with its inherent gentle irony necessitated a vocabulary new to the diction customary in literary expression. The Rococo tendency to diminution[17] and prettification in the name of elegance and gracefulness, of simplicity and naturalness and lightness of touch, naturally shied away from grandiloquence, emphatic forcefulness, from *Machtwörter* (as Breitinger called them)[18] as a means of metaphorical usage. Instead Rococo writers emphasized gentleness and refinement. "Agreeable" epithets abound such as *artig* (gentle mannered), *angenehm, reizend; hold, zart, zärtlich; still, leise, heimlich, milde, gelind, fein*; expressions of a happy mood such as *froh, fröhlich, heiter, munter, vergnügt* and *schalkhaft*; compounds with colour concepts such as *silber* and *gold* (*glänzend* for instance). Among nouns *Lust* and *Wollust* (in the sense of delight), *Verlangen* and *Entzücken* predominate and diminutives abound (or the adjective *klein* qualifies nouns). But superlatives too have a diminutizing effect as in compounds with *aller* (e.g. *allerliebst, allerhöchst*). Certain verbs reflect the tendency to express constant movement, e.g. *tanzen, tänzeln, trippeln, herum-flattern*; water metaphors belong to this category, e.g. *rieseln, schmelzen, ergiessen,* whereas *säuseln* denotes the gentle breeze of the ubiquitous Zephyr. Superimposed on this vocabulary is the whole edifice of the Arcadian world which determines the Rococo view of nature and landscape.[19] The treatment of love—which is frequently frivolous, but rarely lascivious—is exemplified by the verbs *schäkern* (dally) and *tändeln,* though both go beyond the amorous field in their use. *Tändeln* became a significant key-word derived from the noun *Tand* (m. originally Latin *tantum*), a worthless ware. The noun from *tändeln = Tändeley* is listed for the first time in 1691 and once more denotes in Rococo idiom playful trifling, with the meaning of flirting on amorous occasions. The effect intended by all these word preferences was *Anmut,* that happy medium of well-balanced harmony, that final artistic target of all Rococo culture : grace and charm.[20]

The language of Rococo is occasionally interspersed with the language of sentimentality (*Empfindsamkeit*). Pastoral poetry and the form of the idyll are often responsible for this, the latter being a genre which does not lend itself easily to irony and which by its very nature has a sentimental undercurrent. The blending of Rococo and sentimentality is most striking in the work of Salomon Gessner (1733–88)[21] whose *Idyllen* (they soon spread over the whole civilized world) mark one of the summits of German literary Rococo. For Gessner the idyll has a cleansing effect; it heals the wounds of civilization which city life has inflicted on mankind. Gessner, the first to turn his countryman Rousseau's ideas into creative poetry, takes Theokritos as his model; however, he believes that the latter's *Gemählde* are not products of the imagination but realistic reproductions of actual conditions and are not applicable to his own time :

> when the husbandman has submissively to hand over to the Princes and the cities the fruit of his hard labour, and where oppression and poverty have made him morally depraved, cunning and base.

He, therefore, wants to lead his reader to the "beauty of nature" in which he, Gessner, is always as "happy as a shepherd in the golden age and richer than a king". He appreciates in Theokritos the lack of "epigrammatic wit" and turns against the artificial and affected nature of the bucolic craze in high society.[22]

Thus Gessner's work is bound to be sentimental because it constitutes a conscious flight back into a supposed "golden age" of unspoiled simplicity, naturalness, and goodness. At first glance his idylls appear to stand outside the scope of literature. Yet by stating that he wishes to present his subject matter with "agreeable nonchalance" a first contact with the Rococo style is established. Added to this we have the all-pervading atmosphere of bucolic life in a classical environment which he unfolds with a charming lightness of touch. The well-known description by a Faun of his broken pitcher may serve as an example :

Auch war der schöne Bacchus eingegraben. Er saß in einer Laube von Reben, und eine Nymphe lag ihm zur Seite. Ihr linker Arm unschlang seine Hüften; den rechten hielt sie empor, und zog den Becher zurück, nach dem seine lächelnden Augen sich sehnten. Schmachtend sah sie ihn an, und schien ihn um Küße zu flehen, und vor ihm spielten rein gefleckte Tiger; schmeichelnd aßen sie Trauben aus der Leibesgötter kleinen Händen.[23]

In contrast to this Rococo scene diluted with sentimentality an example of undiluted Rococo can be found in Johann Christoph Rost's "Die Schäferstunde".[24] In this rhymed tale of 185 lines of different rhythmical quality, divided into seventeen small chapters of different length, the narrator, taking his reader constantly into his confidence tells of the seduction of the shepherdess Doris by the shepherd Amynt with a freedom that would be lascivious were it not tempered by subtle irony. The initial chapter in which the author refuses to write a sublime "Heldenlied" ends with the lines :

Die Schäferstunde hat die Helden selbst bezwungen,
Wer sie besingt, der hat den größten Held besungen.

The reader's suspense—only "pretty female readers" are assumed—is heightened by passages which interrupt the flow of events and intimate coming delights. For instance, when the "hour" (l'heure du berger) approaches, the narrator observes :

Was euer Blick hierbei zu fürchten hat,
Wird im Gebüsche nur geschehen.
Doch sollte hier und da ein Blatt
Vom Zefir weggewehet werden,
So messet mir die Schuld nicht bei;
Seht weg, seht hinn, es steht euch alles frei.
Ich kann den Winden nicht gebieten ...

The difference between Gessner and Rost can be observed in one and the same motif appearing in both examples and signifying their authors' different attitudes. In "The Broken Pitcher" a nymph in the arms of Pan is transfigured into a whispering reed in order to evade seduction. Doris, in "Die Schäferstunde", also prays to the gods for the boon of transfiguration, but she implores them expressly "to spare the human figure" and accordingly a thick rose bush envelops the lovers. The story, built according to the rules of a fable, ends with a salacious moral.

Rost and Gessner constitute two contrasting poles in Rococo literature, the frivolous and the moralistic, between which an infinite variety of modes of expression became possible. Christoph Martin Wieland created a synthesis of the two extremes and gave German Rococo its final philosphy of art and life.

Wieland's conversion from the mystic dedication of the Pietists' otherworldliness (which he had mingled with a platonic spirituality and Klopstock's seraphic enthusiasm) to *Weltfreudigkeit*, an uninhibited affirmation of life, took place in Switzerland late in the seventeen-fifties, when he turned away from the severe puritanism of his host Johann Jakob Bodmer. His friendship with and admiration for Gessner and his work was an important step in the new direction. The break-through followed when soon after his return to his native Biberach he was admitted at the age of twenty-nine into the circle of Friedrich Count Stadion, who in 1761 relinquished his position as the virtual regent of the Electorate of Mainz and retired to his resplendent castle of Warthausen near Biberach. Here Wieland experienced and, for a time, enjoyed all the facets of aristocratic and courtly Rococo civilization "en miniature", the parks and gardens, the richly endowed library, the gallery of exquisite paintings. Through the old Count, the well-bred man of the world, *causeur*, *amant*, enlightened, politically astute, he learned to see the world realistically, without illusions and with a fair dose of scepticism, even with regard to the life of high society.[25] This led him to attempt to influence the world through an unobtrusive, veiled didacticism clothed in gay, ironic form. The foundation of all of Wieland's enormous "rococo" opus was laid in Warthausen. His incredibly fertile imagination was bridled and tempered by a keen perception that was open to the arguments of enlightened philosophy. He widened his horizon in Warthausen by the study of all the great works of world literature and philosophy, and his receptive mind adapted these with sovereign skill to his artistic purposes. Far more widely read than any contemporary writer he broadened the subject matter of contemporary literature well beyond the anacreontic field. In ancient life and civilization he was a real scholar with an intimate knowledge in particular of the Hellenistic and Roman world. Medieval romance, oriental fairy tales (Arabic, Persian, Chinese), Cervantes, Ariosto, Tasso, and the whole orbit of French civilization filtered into his writing, its structure as well as its style. The artistic transition from the seraphic to Rococo style was his sustained translation into German of twenty-one plays by Shakespeare. Significantly he began with plays of pure imagination, with *The Tempest* and *A Midsummer-Night's Dream* (1762) playing down the Baroque features and emphasizing the humane side of Shakespeare's genius.

Whereas Shakespeare was instrumental in shaping Wieland's new artistic style, another Englishman, Lord Shaftesbury, had even before his return from Switzerland provided him with the basis for a new philosophical outlook that—in the Warthausen environment—bound together the trends he had studied. The Hellenic spirit expressed according to Shaftesbury the order and harmony of the world in its clearest form. The beautiful was to him the harmonious and in accord with the ideal of Kalokagatheia was identical with the virtuous and the good. Therefore man should endeavour to balance out his intellectual energies : the egotistic and the altruistic, the physical and the mental, and thereby attain "moral grace". Goethe, not without reason, called Wieland the twin brother of Shaftesbury.[26] But he failed to see the aspect of sceptical irony with which Wieland spiced the ideal of moral grace, the "Schein von angenehmer Nachlässigkeit", which he perceived in Shaftesbury's concept of order.[27]

Ma morale n'a rien de ce que j'appelle la Morale des Capucins. Je vise au Caractère de *Virtuoso*, que Shaftesbury peint si admirablement dans tous ses écrits

he had written from Switzerland,[28] and the Virtuoso as the man of the world revealed himself in the four *Comische Erzählungen* which burst upon the German public in 1765 like a bombshell. These "Scherzhafte Erzählungen" were a sally into pure Rococo, sensuous, witty and urbane, elegant in the flow of rhythms and rhymes, daring in their highly modern adaptation of ancient mythical stories such as "The Judgement of Paris" or "Diana and Endymion", ironical in their direct approach to the reader, original in their taking the Gods down a few pegs and putting mortals a few up. Yet, these small pieces of filigree were but the first steps in a new field; they were the transition to social poetry written not in the isolation of a contemplative individual, but for a sophisticated public. Wieland told Gessner with pride of Count Stadion's amazement that "all this could be said in the German language". One year earlier, Moritz August von Thümmel had, in the wake of Pope's *Rape of the Lock*, published an epyllion *Wilhelmine oder der vermählte Pedant. Ein prosaisch-comishes Gedicht* which was inspired by a fellow courtier's challenge to show that the

German language was capable of reaching the grace and elegance of French prose. This was, indeed the aim of what may be called the "high" phase of German Rococo, and Wieland was, simultaneously with Thümmel, engaged in just this remoulding of German prose. He now reached out into the more massive field of the novel—a genre so far not cultivated by any German Rococo writer—first on a smaller scale in *Die Abenteuer des Don Sylvio von Rosalva* (1764), then on a larger scale in *Geschichte des Agathon* (1766–67). As with Thümmel, French and English models converged. Thümmel, as others before him, found in Pope's mock-heroic miniature epic a congenial form to serve his particular end. Wieland took his lead from the "comic novel" which had in the eighteenth century turned from the gross, crude and gargantuan to the sophisticated, urbane and sociable. Fielding's *Tom Jones* (1749) was in this respect a new beginning and provided Wieland with many stimuli in matters of style, narrative-technique and even content. *Don Sylvio* takes the place of *Tom Jones* in German literature and is even more significant in this respect than *Agathon*. Superficially an imitation of *Don Quixote* with the difference that the hero lives in a dream world of enchanted palaces, fairies, magicians, dragons, dwarfs and hobgoblins, it has a didactic purpose. The original edition bore the title : *Der Sieg der Natur über die Schwärmerey, oder die Abentheuer des Don Sylvio de Rosalva, Eine Geschichte worinn alles Wunderbare natürlich zugeht.*[29] It is the playful and witty way in which Wieland submerged and veiled his didacticism which marks the new departure. At the beginning of Book V he explains his intentions. With an attack on the literary output of the Pietists, which includes his own former voluminous writing, he once and for all disposes of the past.[30] He is serious in spite of the mockery he displays, because by playful insinuation, by "speaking the truth laughingly" he attains the two purposes he now considers to be the essence of art : entertainment and education. He has found a vantage point from which he is able to probe into every facet of human life, whether concerning the individual or the community. By seeing the world as a colourful masquerade he is able to uncover the follies of men without moralizing and without being aggressive. At the same time he allows his imagination full rein, as for instance in the fairy tale of Prince Biribinker, which forms the climax of *Don Sylvio*, a gem of pure Rococo phantasy reflecting its gracefulness on the one hand and making fun of it on the other. Because this tale is so fantastic it serves the ultimate educational purpose of the novel, "Entzauberung". Disenchantment from now on is the main theme of Wieland's work, but the term has a positive meaning, as a liberat-

ing force [31] of a kind indicated in the subtitle of his first novel :
Sieg der Natur über die Schwärmerey. *Schwärmerei* is usually rendered into English as "fancy", but it is more; it is an exaltation of
concepts and sentiments, which—because they become muddled
and hazy—determine judgments and actions at the expense of
clarity and reason.

Wieland aims at liberating man from many kinds of *Schwärmerei*—to him the greatest of human follies—metaphysical, idealistic, mystical, supernatural, superstitions, as well as from
mannerisms in everyday life including love-making. A dialogue
between the milk-maid and Prince Biribinker in which the fanciful
language of sentimentality is contrasted with the "natural"
language of the girl may serve as the best example :

> Nachdem seine zärtliche Elegie zu Ende war, antwortete ihm die
> schöne Schäferin, mit einem Blick, welcher kaltsinniger anfing als
> aufhörte : Ich weiß nicht, ob ich Sie recht verstanden habe,
> wollten Sie mir alle diese Weile her nicht sagen, daß Sie mich
> lieb hätten?—Himmel ! daß ich Sie liebe ! rief der entzückte
> Biribinker, sagen Sie, daß ich Sie anbete, daß ich meine
> schmatchtende Seele zu Ihren Füßen aushauche.—Sehen Sie,
> antwortete die Schäferin, ich bin nur ein ganz einfältiges
> Mädchen, ich verlange nicht, daß Sie mich *anbeten* sollen, und
> Sie sollen auch *Ihre Seele nicht aushauchen*, denn ich denke
> nicht, daß Sie deren zu viel haben; ich würde wohl zufrieden
> seyn, wenn Sie mich nur *liebten* ... (italics are Wieland's).[32]

In *Musarion oder die Philosophie der Grazien. Ein Gedicht in
drey Büchern* (1768) the synthesis of the two trends in Rococo finds
its consummation. Whereas the burlesque predominates in *Don
Sylvio*, all is mellow and serene in this perfectly constructed little
verse epic. Again the victory of "nature" over "fancy" is the main
theme, but both are now clearly defined and moulded into a
"philosophy". The setting in *Don Sylvio* is Spain, the land of Cervantes, with a superimposed world of fairies and enchanted
castles in the mind of the hero as contemporary Rococo creations
manipulating nature artistically.[33] *Musarion* is placed like *Agathon*
in a classical environment which enabled Wieland to develop his
"philosophy of the Graces", as taught by Musarion to her fickle
lover Phanias who inclines to extremes of every kind. This "philosophy" of the joyful life, attained at the end of the story, has as its
basic element moderation : accepting what nature and fate offer,
preferring to look at the bright aspects of life, it refuses to probe
into the mysteries of the unknown which the Gods benevolently
hide from man; it is not angry with the fools on this earth but

smiles at them; it pities those who err and keeps away from the hypocrites. It looks at the world dispassionately knowing it to be neither Elysium nor hell, not so depraved as censorious moralists depict it nor as glowing as young poets see it when intoxicated by wine and love. This "philosophy" does not preach or exalt virtue, it exercises it from a sense of good taste without expecting reward.[34]

In this way Wieland attained a position between rationalism and sensualism, between pure Rococo and sentimentality, between the frivolity of the *Comische Erzählungen* and the heavy philosophical speculation of *Agathon*, between the burlesque of *Don Sylvio* and the solemnity of a Gessner idyll. This golden mean, this combination of the culture of wit and the culture of feeling[35] is also reflected in the form which is a blending of comedy, satire, didactic tale and serene idyll, a blending of irony and serious argument in which didacticism and argument are always lightened by playful urbanity and unconventionality of expression. In particular, didacticism is tempered by the mere fact that the dispenser of the philosophy of the graces, the representative of Shaftesbury's moral grace and inward beauty, is an Athenian hetaera.

Goethe stated that among the works of Wieland which he read during his student years in Leipzig, *Musarion* had the strongest effect upon him because "it was here that I believed I saw antiquity alive and revived".[36]

The question arises : which kind of "antiquity"? Rococo classicism is as far removed from the rigid moralistic classicism of Enlightenment, which stressed Roman virtue and republicanism as the ideal, as it is from Winckelmann's aesthetic Neo-Hellenism. Rococo classicism has its setting not in the Periclean, but in the Hellenistic age which had spread Greek culture over the whole civilized world and in this process absorbed elements of other, in particular oriental, cultures. It was an age in which the older religious faith had lost its cosmic substance and dissolved into a welter of tales about gods and minor deities, demigods, "heroes" and mortals intertwined in adventures mostly of an amorous nature.[37] The stress had shifted from the heroic and sublime to the refined and sophisticated, the frivolous and the satirical. The philosophy of Epicurus (341-270 B.C.) was conceived at the very beginning of the Hellenistic age and constituted a counterweight against the systems of Plato and Aristotle. The poetry of Catullus, Horace and Ovid, the Anacreontia and the bucolic works of Theokritos, and of Virgil were the models for the Rococo age as were the prose Romances of the second and third centuries A.D. (Apuleius, Longinus and Heliodorus) which provided a broad canvas of late Hellenistic life and civilization. They opened up a new image of the "classical" world : the late stage of a civilization and society akin to the Rococo phase of the eighteenth century so that the former became a symbolical image of the latter. Wieland felt this kinship most strongly when he studied and finally translated the works of Lucian of Samosata, a contemporary of Apuleius. In an essay introducing the translation,[38] Wieland painted a lively picture of declining Hellenistic culture in the "silver" age of the Roman Empire. Lucian is seen by Wieland as the healer who combated the evils of his time "with the sarcasm of cold-blooded reason" and made it his business to "unmask all kinds of lies and deception . . . false idols of superstition, false prophets, false philosophers". He succeeded because his intellectual forebears were Democritos and Epicurus, not Pythagoras and Plato. Lucian, the flower of a late culture, achieved for his age what Wieland attempted for his own time, i.e. to show how man can stand on his own feet in an age without genuine religious foundation by finding his "humanitas". In this he was a conscious antagonist of Winckelmann's idealization of only one aspect of Hellenic life. He intentionally deflated the "classical" elevation of Periclean Greece and demonstrated the all-too-human and the seamier sides of its society, in *Agathon* on a serious level, in *Musarion* in a lighter, in *Die Abderiten* in a satirical vein.[39]

Wieland represents German literary Rococo at its highest level, which, attracted by the epicurean and eudaemonistic trends of this late phase of Greek culture, that had percolated through the centuries, formed its own image of antiquity, a blending of joyous Anacreontism with Socratic irony, Horacean wisdom with Lucianic lucidity. Wieland's *Musarion*, reflecting this image in its simplest form, is also the artistic climax of what Rococo could achieve. At the same time this literary mode stood at the cross-roads. During the 'fifties it had successfully withstood the onslaught of the Swiss school of writers which culminated in 1757 in Wieland's own vicious attack on the Anacreontics, and on Uz in particular, in the letter of the Prussian Court Chaplain Sack, with which he prefaced the "Empfindungen eines Christen".[40] Wieland's intellectual and literary conversion had strengthened the Rococo camp enormously and given it depth and breadth. But the appearance side by side with *Musarion* of the correspondence between J. G. Jacobi and Gleim[41] incited the old champion Johann Jacob Bodmer to enter the lists once more. His pamphlet : *Von den Grazien des Kleinen. (Im Namen und zum Besten der Anakreontchen)*[42] is a bad tempered yet not unjustified attack on the Rococo mode of writing. He analyses its style, the "Kleine Manier", the diminution of all concepts of life, of linguistic usage, of metres and genres, the endless repetitions of the same motifs, the cult of the bosom. The gross sentimentality interwoven with Rococo imagery which characterizes the cult of friendship as revealed in the Jacobi correspondence signifies indeed a low ebb of Rococo literature and readily lent itself to ridicule. Though Jacobi's "Briefchen und Liederchen" are Bodmer's main target, he ranges over the whole field of Rococo literature and concludes with a blow at Wieland the apostate by comparing *Musarion* with his earlier works written under his, Bodmer's guidance.

We can therefore expect to see the poet who has written the philosophy of the graces receive the plaudits of those reviewers on whom the hexameters of his *Abraham in Afflication* and his grave-yard singing somnambulistic *Letters from the Departed* produced no effect.[43]

Although Bodmer clung stubbornly to the patriarchic, seraphic and sublime line in literature and writes with the righteous indignation of a puritanical defender of Christian morality who sees the virtue of the daughters of Germany endangered by the "German Gressets", his new sortie coincided precisely with a change in Germany's intellectual climate.

H. W. Gerstenberg who ten years earlier had published *Tändeleyen*, one of the highlights of Rococo literature, now sounded the clarion call of a new departure which, reinforced by Herder's theories of history, literature and art, by the public condemnation of Wieland through the Göttinger Hain in 1773—they singled out his incomplete verse epic *Idris* (1767) for burning— and by the ever increasing output of the *Sturm und Drang* movement seemed to seal the fate of Rococo as a literary force.

Yet Rococo literature was not dead. First of all it had made an important contribution to German language and literature which could not be suddenly obliterated. It had brought about what almost amounted to a revolution in the evolution of the German language. It had given it a touch of subtlety and urbanity, wistfulness and agreeableness which it had never had before. What humour there had been was either rough and coarse or stiff and stilted. The entirely new feature of German Rococo style was its ironical flavour : subtle hints, suggestive innuendoes, equivocal ambiguity, allusive double-meaning—all combining to sharpen the wit of the reader. Prose became more natural—in the simple genres such as the short tale and idyll—and more complicated in the novel. Verse became more supple and melodious. A far larger scale of sensations and emotions than before was given expression. The images of the mirror and the veil opened up new perspectives and gave the world of reality a new meaning. Diversification in metres as well as in genres burst the strait-jacket into which the writer had been laced hitherto. The "Kleine Manier" led to mannerism, indeed, but also had a liberating effect. The *Lied*, the epyllion, the comic tale, the short verse epic, the idyll, the pastoral play, the *Singspiel*, even the comic *Romanze* as invented by Gleim not only changed the whole temper of artistic creativeness but also attracted a responsive reading public and had more ties with *Volkspoesie* than meet the eye at first sight. The skill and artistry acquired in the exercise in "kleine Formen" eventually led to the rebirth of the German novel. The sober scepticism so characteristic of the Rococo mood engendered an awareness of social problems and with it a deeper psychological insight and a readiness to self-criticism which not only laid bare the follies of humanity but also resulted in an understanding of human nature and in the vision of a well balanced humanism. This humanism, precarious as it was, is the particular German contribution to Rococo culture. German literary Rococo was never a mere imitation of French models; it could not be, for the social conditions were lacking. German literary Rococo was essentially a middle-class phenomenon; it picked up many crumbs from the aristocratic tables but was unable to digest the rarer dishes, nor did it wish to. It rather amalgamated certain external features of French Rococo stylistic forms with the witty and relaxed style of Fielding and Stern and Shaftesbury's gentlemanly ideal of perfect equilibrium. Its supreme achievement, however, was that it infused the moral system of Enlightenment with a sense of lightness, cheerfulness and grace. It reduced its severity to the humanly possible, and its solemnity to the humanly acceptable. It made good taste the yardstick of philosophical contemplation as well as of artistic creation, and good taste meant avoidance of excess and exaggeration, the natural flow of imagination and sentiment tempered by the demands of reason. The work of art had to serve first of all the human desire for entertainment, but this urge was guided, imperceptibly, towards a higher and freer form of life.

German Rococo did not produce any outstanding genius in the field of literature as it did in the fields of music and architecture, or as France did in the fine arts and England in the field of the novel. But it did influence the German literary scene profoundly and was not simply swept away by subsequent literary styles. It was never a "movement", but, as has been said in the beginning, an attitude. As such it had its impact on every German writer of the eighteenth century, major and minor (e.g. Klopstock, Lessing,

Bürger, Heinse, Matthias Claudius, Goethe, Schiller, Jean Paul, Novalis, Heinrich von Kleist), frequently in the early stages of their careers. However, the Rococo attitude also filtered into the later work of these writers and many threads lead from it to Weimar classicism and neo-humanism and to the early Romantic movement. At the same time Rococo authors continued to write, to be re-edited and widely read well into the early nineteenth century. Wieland, for instance, wrote his *Geschichte der Abderiten* and *Oberon* (1780) during the decade when the *Sturm und Drang* movement was sweeping the literary scene; both were enthusiastically received. However strongly the Rococo attitude was deprecated throughout the nineteenth century, it was never entirely submerged and a definite revival of interest occurred in the first decade of the twentieth century.[44]

A study of the effect and aftermath of German literary Rococo after its apparent demise is lacking, but would be of absorbing interest and produce surprising results.[45]

NOTES

1. Cf. Max von Boehn, *Deutschland im 18. Jahrhundert* (Berlin, 1922) p. 362.
2. A typical collection of this manner of poetry can be found in *Nouveau Recueil de Chansons choisies*, 8 vols. (Paris 1731–35).
3. As to the importance of English "Rococo" literature for Germany see A. Anger, *Literarisches Rokoko*, p. 21 ff. and passim.
4. Ἀνακρέοντυος Τυίου σμποσιακά ἡμιάμβια καὶ Ἀνακρεόντια Cf. ed. J. M. Edmonds, The Loeb Classical Library, Elegy and Iambus, vol. II (London, 1931).
5. The translation was begun in Halle and eventually published in 1746 as *Die Oden des Anakreon in reimlosen Versen* by Götz and Uz.
6. *Versuch in Scherzhaften Liedern* (1744)—the first critical edition of which was published by Alfred Anger, Niemeyer (Tübingen, 1965).

   > Anacreon, my teacher
   > Sings only of wine and love;
   > He scents his beard with scent,
   > And sings of wine and love;
   > He crowns his head with roses,
   > And sings of wine and love. . . .

7. "Der Inhalt meiner Lieder" in *Scherzhafte Lieder* of 1758, see Alfred Anger (ed.), *Die Dichtung des Rokoko. Nach Motiven geordnet* (Tübingen, 1958), p. 5, hereafter referred to as Anger's anthology.

   > I sing not the wars of the German eagles,
   > The pride of kings, the victories of world-conquerors,
   > I sing not of that sea of blood and death. . . .

8. "An Phyllis" in *Scherze* (1766), s.v. Anger's anthology, p. 8.

Not to the glory of the victor's name,
Not to the bloody field of battle,
Not to the dying heroes,
Let the Muse devote her tender song.

9. See note 7.

Yon citadel of mansions and palaces,
Where amid dancing and pleasure,
The flatterer lives off the fat of the land,
While the tears of the honest citizen
Fall on his hard-won bread.

10. "An Johann Georg Jacobi, damals Professor in Halle" (i.e. 1766–68), cf. Anger's anthology, p. 7.

The small poems, the humble ones
Are read with pleasure,
Praised for their harmony.
So they don't mind the big ones....

11. Anger, edition Niemeyer, p. 71. Examples of this anti-metaphysical attitude can be found in Uz ("Magister Duns") and Johann Matthaeus Dreyer ("Der Weise"), Anger's anthology pp. 69 and 63.

12. cf. Eric Blackall, *The Emergence of German as a Literary Language* (CUP, 1959), p. 387 ff. and the whole chapter on "The Culture of Wit and Feeling", pp. 387–429.

13. "Die Anfrage", ed. Anger, p. 75, "I want to sing, I want to play...."

14. Meyer *Gedanken von Scherzen* (1744), p. 105. See Blackall, op. cit., pp. 388 and 392. Adelung defined *Scherz* as "eine witzige Rede... welche andern zur anständigen Belustigung dienen soll" (Wörterbuch, ed. 1807, p. 1427).

15. Cf. i.a. Wieland's *Musarion*, ed. Anger, Reclam 1964, lines 19 and 67.

16. Cf. i.a. Anger's anthology, list of sources, p. 160 ff.

17. I.a. indicated by the many collections of poetry entitled *Kleinigkeiten*, starting with Lessing 1751.

18. *Critische Dichtkunst*, vol. 2 (1740). Cf. Blackall, op. cit., p. 280 ff.

19. Cf. A. Anger, "Landschaftstil des Rokoko" in *Euphorion*, vol. 51 (1957), pp. 151–191.

20. In Rococo idiom *Anmut* corresponds to French *grâce*, frequently rendered as *Grazie* (f.) and personified in the plural *Grazien*.

21. *Daphnis. In dreyen Büchern*, 1754 (in the preface Gessner calls it "einen kleinen Roman", it is a pastoral novel). *Idyllen von dem Verfasser des Daphnis*, 1756 (enlarged in later editions).

22. The quotations are taken from Gessner's preface to the idylls, *Salomon Gessners Schriften. Zweyter Band*, Zürich, 1782, p. 5 ff.

23. "Der Zerbrochene Krug", op. cit., p. 29.

Beautiful Bacchus too was entrenched. He sat in a wine grove and a nymph lay by his side. Her left arm encircled his waist; the right hand she held aloft and drew back the beaker for which his laughing eyes longed. She gave him a languishing look, and seemed to be

62   PERIODS IN GERMAN LITERATURE

pleading for his kisses, while at his feet played finely speckled tigers;
fawning they ate grapes from the dainty hands of the Gods of Love.
24. In *Schäfererzählungen* (1742), cf. Anger's anthology, pp. 131–137.
L'heure du berger has vanquished even the heroes
Whoever sings of it, has sung of the greatest of all heroes.

What your timid eyes might fear to behold
Will happen only in the bushes.
But should Zephyr now and then
Blow away a leaf or two
Then don't blame me;
Look or look away, the choice is up to you.
I have no control over the winds.
25. For descriptions of Stadion, Warthausen and Wieland's life there
see F. Sengle, *Wieland* (Stuttgart, 1949), pp. 141–150 (a picture of
Warthausen on p. 145) and R. Benz, *Die Zeit der deutschen Klassik*
(Stuttgart, 1953), p. 42 ff.
26. In the funeral oration on 18 February 1813.
27. In letter to Zimmermann, 6 October 1758, *Briefwechsel*, ed. Seiffert,
Berlin, 1963, p. 363.
28. To Zimmermann, 12th March, 1758, ibid., p. 326.
29. Cf. *C. M. Wielands Werke* ed. by F. Martini (and others) Carl
Hanser, München, 1964, vol. I, p. 18–30. The first English translation
entitled "Reason Triumphant over Fancy; Exemplified in the singular
Adventures of Don Sylvio de Rosalva. A History in which every
marvellous event occurs Naturally" appeared 1773 in 3 vols. Reprint
Routledge, London, 1904, with introduction by Ernest A. Baker.
30. Cf. ed. Martini, p. 193; ed. Baker, p. 221 f.
31. In book VII, ch. 1 (ed. Martini, p. 349) Wieland explains the
difference between *Don Quixote* and his own novel. The former's
purpose is to make fun of outmoded customs and attitudes, the latter
is "unsern Helden von der Bezauberung seines Gehirns je bälder je
lieber zu *befreien*" (Wieland's italics).
32. Book VI, ch. 2, ed. Martini, p. 294.
When his tender elegy was finished the lovely shepherdess answered
him with a look that did not stop with the cold indifference it started
with: I don't know if I have understood you properly, weren't you
trying to tell me all this time that you love me?——Merciful
Heavens! Love You! exclaimed Biribinker in transports. Say rather
that I adore you, that my languishing soul expires at your feet.——
Look here, the shepherdess replied, I'm only a simple maiden, I
don't expect you to *adore* me, and there is no need for *your soul to
expire* for I don't suppose you have all that much; I should be quite
content, if you just *loved* me. . . .
33. Cf. Book VII, ch. 1, op. cit., p. 353, where Sylvio, in the process
of disenchantment, walks in a Rococo "labyrinth" of summer-
pavilions, groves, cascades, Greek temples, pagodas, statues, etc. and
realizes: "that all this, however much it might look like an enchant-

ing region, was in fact a work of art, which guided by a poetic imagination had contrived to create such a pleasing whole out of the ingenious fusion of various elements of natural beauty with the imitative arts."

34. Cf. edition A. Anger, Reclam, Stuttgart, 1964, lines 1410–1428, also Wieland's foreword to the second edition, addressed to Felix Weiße, ibid., p. 6.

35. See Blackall, op. cit., p. 414.

36. "Hier war es, wo ich das Antike lebendig und neu wieder zu sehen glaubte." *Dichtung und Wahrheit*, book VII (ed. Trunz, Hamburg 1955, vol. IX, p. 271).

37. B. J. Hederich's *Gründliches mythologisches Lexikon* (1st ed., 1724) was an inexhaustible source in the eighteenth century.

38. Lucian's works appeared in 6 vols., 1788–89. Quotations from the essay are in the edition of the translation that appeared in 1911 (Georg Müller, München, 5 vols.; vol. 1, pp. 1–32).

39. Cf. W. E. Yuill's introduction to his edition, *Die Geschichte der Abderiten, IV. Buch* (O.U.P., 1964), p. 24 f.

40. The letter, which Wieland omitted in later editions, is reprinted in D.L.E., Reihe Aufklärung, vol. 7 (1935), pp. 268–80. August Sauer deals with all phases of the dispute up to 1760 in *J. P. Uz. Sämtliche poetische Werke*, 1890, reprint: Wissenschaftliche Buchgesellschaft Darmstadt 1964, pp. XX-LXII.

41. "Briefe des Herrn Jacobi", Berlin 1768.

42. "In der Schweiz 1769" (22 pp.). Reprint in F. Ausfeld *Die deutsche Anakreontik des 18. Jahrhunderts* (Strassburg, 1907), pp. 153–162.

43. "Von den Grazien des Kleinen", p. 21: cf. Aufhaus, op. cit., p. 162. Bodmer refers here to Wieland's epic *Der Geprüfte Abraham* and *Briefe von Verstorbenen an hinterlassene Freunde*, both 1753.

44. In 1903 Arno Holz issued an anthology entitled *Aus Aurgroßmutters Garten. Ein Frühlingsstrauß aus dem Rokoko* (Carl Reissner, Dresden, 238 pp.), illuminated by several hundred Rococo vignettes.

45. A. Anger in *Literarisches Rokoko*, op. cit., pp. 31–33, gives valuable suggestions in this direction.

BIBLIOGRAPHICAL NOTE

For full biographical information on all facets of Rococo literature the following two publications by Alfred Anger should be consulted:
(1) *Literarisches Rokoko*, Metzler, 1962 (Sammlung Metzler No. M25).
(2) Deutsche Rokoko-Dichtung. Ein Forschungsbericht. Metzler. Stuttgart 1963 (=offprint from *Deutsche Vierteljahrsschrift für Literatur- und Geistesgeschichte*, vol. 36 (1962) pp. 430–479; 614–618).
Since 1963 the following major publications have appeared:
(3) Carr, C. T.: Two Words in Art History II. Rococo. *Forum for Modern Language Studies*. Vol. I (1965), p. 266–281.
(4) Lauffer, Roger: *Style Rococo, Style des "Lumières"*. Paris 1963.

(5) Mähl, Hans Joachim: *Die Idee des goldenen Zeitalters im Werk des Novalis. Studien zur Wesensbestimmung der frühromantischen Utopie und zu ihren ideengeschichtlichen Voraussetzungen.* (Heidelberg 1965) (cf. esp. ch. II and III: Vergils Arkadien-Vorstellung, pp. 58–84; Die Arkadien-Vorstellung als Uberlieferungslinie vom Mittelalter zur Neuzeit, pp. 103–186).

(6) Singer, Herbert: *Der deutsche Roman zwischen Barock und Rokoko* (Literatur und Leben, Neue Folge, Bd. 6) (Köln-Graz 1963).

Enlightenment and Storm and Stress

IV

Enlightenment and Storm and Stress

J. D. STOWELL

NO term of literary history should be more amenable to definition than the term *Aufklärung*, Enlightenment. An age dedicated to the eradication of error and the rational exploration of nature and all spheres of human endeavour must surely bear a name commensurate with these aims, a name which can be defined in one brief, clear, illuminating sentence. Pope's famous epitaph for Newton springs instantly to mind :

> Nature and Nature's Laws lay hid in Night;
> God said, Let Newton be!—and all was Light.

This wittily blasphemous epigram succinctly expresses a belief in the orderly structure of a universe created by a benevolent deity for the instruction and delight of man. It reveals too a sense of a breach with the ignorant past and a proud advance into a future bright with the radiance of reason. It is hard for us to avoid the vision of Newton throwing a great electric switch; but with such a formulation the shadow of doubt immediately rises over the landscape of our metaphorical terminology. The term *Enlightenment* and the age to which it is customarily applied can be no more satisfactorily isolated and summarily dealt with than any of the other labels we use as orientation guides to map the human spirit. To quote Horace's *Art of Poetry*, "If I labour to be brief, I am bound to be obscure". It is a particularly happy paradox that the first men of the Enlightenment did not know they were enlightened (as we now understand the term); it is also amusing that the word as now used may well have its origins in mysticism. The English word *Enlightenment* is a nineteenth century translation of the German *Aufklärung*,[1] and German dictionaries document the first use of the word in its sense of referring to the intellectual and cultural progress of the human community—"probably" under the influence of Leibniz's theory of Monadology—in the work of Wieland, writing in 1770.[2] The metaphor of clarity and light as a source of knowledge and truth is of course of great antiquity, but this does not automatically make it part of the province of rationalism. Part of the survival of baroque elements in the eighteenth century is the considerable strain of mystical language found in current speech and especially in the writing of Leibniz himself who is frequently named as the founder of the philosophy of the German Enlightenment.[3] At its widest reach, the term may be used to refer to any process of intellectual development, and this vagueness is reflected in the usage of histories of literature. Gero von Wilpert suggests that any movement of sceptical rationalism may be given the name of *Aufklärung* and cites the ancient sophists as an example.[4] In the modern world, the rise of science and the decline of theology are seen as marking the progress of enlightenment; the names of Copernicus, Kepler, Galileo and Newton, of Bacon, Hobbes, Locke and Hume, of Descartes, Spinoza and Leibniz remind us that our own age, which believes in the value of the quantitative spread of knowledge, education and prosperity, and the overcoming of superstition and inequality among men, reaches well back into the past for the presuppositions by which it lives. It is also characteristic of our age that we have less trust in the power of reason as an efficient instrument for solving the problems of the world than some earlier rationalists had; but even in the eighteenth century doubts were expressed about the efficacy of reason; it is therefore pertinent to ask if the recognition of the limitations of reason are part of true enlightenment. This sort of question troubled the best minds of the later eighteenth century and they therefore rejected the thoroughgoing rationalism of their fathers without abandoning themselves to despair or embracing mysticism.

The critical temper is of course the mainspring of Kant's philosophy, and this is the tone we find in his essay on Enlightenment which is frequently quoted as a definition of the age. Published in the *Berlinische Monatsschrift* in 1784, the essay was seen as a reply to a correspondent who had complained some months earlier that the term *Aufklärung* had become current coin without ever having been properly defined. The essay begins with a stimulating exhortation :

> Enlightenment is the emergence of man from a state of self-inflicted immaturity. Immaturity is the inability to use one's understanding without guidance from another; it is self-inflicted when its cause is not to be found in defective understanding, but in the lack of courage to use this understanding without another's guidance. *Sapere aude!* Have the courage to use your *own* understanding—this is the watchword of the Enlightenment.[5]

Kant continues by attacking apathy and cowardice which inhibit the search for truth; he draws a careful distinction between the free exercise of critical thought on a theoretical level and the necessity for compromise with convention in practical living, for he believes in gradual improvement and shuns revolution; he sees the best chance for increasing enlightenment in attacks on religious intolerance, and he sees his own age in terms of a tempered optimism :

> If it is asked : Do we live in an enlightened age? then the answer is : No; but we do live in an age of Enlightenment.[6]

These sentiments are clearly as valid today as when they were first written, but it was during the eighteenth century in Germany that the process of the liberation of the individual, begun by the Renaissance, cut short by the Thirty Years' War and held in check by the other-worldly concerns of the Baroque, underwent an accelerated development. Recipes of all kinds were tried in the search for the perfecting of the individual and society. Whether rational or irrational, hard-headed or sentimental, utopian or arcadian, revolutionary or conservative, these experiments in forms of existence or expression were all critical of the existing order and were directed towards the discovery of the best path by which man could realize the greatest degree of freedom and happiness on this earth. For the past 150 years we have been feeding on the insights established during the eighteenth century; the number of "neo" terms which sprinkle the pages of literary studies bear witness to this fact. The limits of the possible were reached by the Early Romantics; terms like Rationalism, Pietism, Rococo, Sensibility, Storm and Stress and Classicism are just so many specialized aspects of the process which issues into the complete eclectic freedom of the artist as expressed in Friedrich Schlegel's famous fragment on *Universalpoesie*. Seen from this point of view, it seems an error to limit the term *Aufklärung* to a name for the period of time and the thought and literature it embraces between the years 1720 and 1770. Yet, by and large, this is what is done in most histories of literature which speak of the *Sturm und Drang* as "replacing" the *Aufklärung*[7] or "fighting against the limitations of the *Aufklärung*",[8]—what the *Sturm und Drang* fights against is a cold and commonsense rationalism which is dogmatic and authoritarian and therefore scarcely deserves the name of enlightenment at all.[9]

Kant's essay describes a critical habit of thought; to discover the image of the ideal man of the age we must go to the poet Schiller who draws the following sketch in deliberately flattering contour at the beginning of his long allegorical poem, *Die Künstler* :[10]

Wie schön, o Mensch, mit deinem Palmenzweige
stehst du an des Jahrhunderts Neige,
in edler, stolzer Männlichkeit,
mit aufgeschloßnem Sinn, mit Geistesfülle,
voll milden Ernsts, in tatenreicher Stille,
der reifste Sohn der Zeit,
frei durch Vernunft, stark durch Gesetze,
durch Sanftmut groß und reich durch Schätze,
die lange Zeit dein Busen dir verschwieg,
Herr der Natur, die deine Fesseln liebet,
die deine Kraft in tausend Kämpfen übet
und prangend unter dir aus der Verwildrung stieg!

Schiller's paragon is noble, proud and virile, alert in mind and body, filled with busy creativity and dignified assurance. Entirely orientated towards this life and the increase of its blessings, he is conscious of the historical processes modelling his acceptance of law and the rule of reason, and he appreciates that his control over himself and external nature is a finely-balanced achievement, the result of sympathetic understanding rather than tyranny. For a more realistic description of the current state of enlightenment, we may turn to Wieland, writing in 1788, the year which also saw the composition of *Die Künstler*. After delivering a tirade against continuing religious intolerance, he is comforted by his "good genius" in the following words:

What's the use of trying to deceive yourself ... Never, as long as men are what they are, will light entirely swallow up darkness. The reason of the few will never gain the upper hand over the ignorance, apathy, reeling fantasy, poverty of spirit and faint-heartedness of the many.[11]

But having accepted this correction, Wieland determines to concentrate on the limited hope which must always spring anew in the world.

The sophisticated acceptance of the limits of reason and enlightened progress in the world which speaks in the work of Kant, Schiller and Wieland is the attitude characteristic of German Classicism. It only became possible after more than a century of familiarization with the central thoughts of the great philosophers of the previous century. At this point it is useful to recall some of these central thoughts.[12] The subjectivity of Protestantism, which rejected the authority of the Church as a mediator between the individual soul and God, received its modern philosophical formulation in the philosophy of the mathematicians Descartes, Spinoza and Leibniz. Descartes (*Discourse on Method*, 1637), resolved to doubt all that was not self-evident, that is, perfectly clear and distinct; and so set the fashion in scepticism and rational clarity which later had such a destructive effect on orthodox religious dogma. His assertion that the only thing of which we can have immediate knowledge is the individual mind and its ideas encouraged introspection and elevated the value of the human mind to heights unknown before. His positing of the existence of the world of extension, parallel to but independent of the mind, insisted on a dualism of mind and matter which gave rise to the poles of Idealism and Materialism between which European thought has oscillated ever since. The problem of the relationship between mind and body, subject and object, is a critical one for the eighteenth century. Spinoza, whose *Ethics* appeared posthumously in 1677, reduced this dualism to a monism. There is only one single infinite substance (deus sive natura); finite souls and the extension of matter are merely aspects of the great logical whole, emanations of divine thought. This pantheism (violently attacked by the Churches as atheism) is completely deterministic, since everything which happens is a determination of God, but it is also optimistic, for Spinoza believes we should try to adopt as far as possible the standpoint of God and see all things *sub specie aeternitatis*, to take always the long view and see things whole.

Leibniz, whose published work appeared between 1695 and 1714, broke this one substance again into an infinite plurality of substances, because he believed all predicates are contained in the notion of a subject and no two subjects are identical. These substances he called Monads (Greek μονάς = one; unit), borrowing the term and the similarity of the notion perhaps from Giordano Bruno. The whole universe consists of these unextended foci of force, "souls" or intelligences. Each monad is locked in its own individuality and neither acts on others nor can be acted upon by others (in his quaint expression, it is "windowless"). Each contains within itself its whole pre-determined history which it gradually unfolds to full realization. Each represents and reflects the whole universe from its own point of view. The difference between individual monads is seen as a difference in the intensity and clarity with which each reflects the whole and Leibniz posits a hierarchy of being, a graded series from the most obscure monad (smallest particles of matter) to the most perfect and clear—God—who has chosen to control the independent activity of all the other monads in creation according to a pre-established harmony which results in the best actual world from all those logically possible.

This system, though deterministic like Spinoza's and therefore abhorrent to the theologians, was seen by Leibniz as affording excellent proof of the existence of God who is necessary as the architect of the pre-established harmony.

All these systems derive logically from simple premises according to rigorous thought : Spinoza's *Ethics* is arranged like the theorems of geometry; Leibniz's thought is intimately connected with his work on the infinitesimal calculus. The theologians' objections to their conclusions, the abstract nature of their reasoning and their own hesitancy in proposing revolutionary views (either from respect for authority or fear of reprisals) meant that the advanced thought of these men only gradually overcame the force of inertia exerted by established opinion. Spinoza and Leibniz had far more impact on the writers of Storm and Stress, Classicism and Romanticism than on earlier writers.

In the meantime the empirical philosophy of England as formulated by John Locke (*An Essay concerning Human Understanding*, 1690), deriving from Descartes and influenced by the mechanical cosmology of Newton (*Principia Mathematica*, 1687) was more quickly absorbed as being more readily understood by the wider middle-class audience for whom he wrote. His influence was transmitted to Germany through Voltaire and *les philosophes* and through the "moralizing weeklies" which were closely modelled on the English journals of the early years of the eighteenth century. Suspicious of abstract metaphysical speculation, Locke rejects innate ideas and founds all knowledge on experience :

> Let us then suppose the mind to be, as we say, white paper, void of all characters, without any ideas; how comes it to be furnished?... To this I answer in one word, from experience : in that all our knowledge is founded, and from that it ultimately derives itself.[13]

He is not very much concerned with how the sensations of experience come to imprint themselves on the mind nor whether they have some underlying substance as external cause, he is more interested in the way complex ideas are built up from the simple elements of experience. The mind is to be observed as the scientist observes nature, and the laws of association of ideas are to be plotted like the motion of the planets in space :

> ... three-dimensional Newtonian space has its counterpart in the inner "space" of the mind over which the inner eye—the faculty of reflection—presides.[14]

This empiricism leads eventually, particularly in France, to a thoroughgoing materialism. The most famous example is found in the formulation of La Mettrie of *L'homme machine* (1748). In his view, mind is reduced to being merely a function of the body and therefore entirely capable of regulation. It is this cold machine-like functionalism which Goethe's Werther detests, but it is the orderliness of the machine which the rationalists praise.

To live an orderly life in the pursuit of perfection results necessarily in that happiness which is the reward of virtue, according to Leibniz. Locke preached the virtue of prudence and Christian Wolff, the popularizer of Leibniz, points out that it is prudent to pursue enlightenment. Virtue is therefore no longer to be found in obedience to the commandments of God, but in the dictates of enlightened self-interest and utilitarianism.

The logic of reason also permeates all thought on art in the first half of the century. Boileau's *Art Poétique* (1674) remains valid until questioned by the expressive theories of the *Sturm und Drang*. According to Boileau, "Nature is truth" and "only the true is beautiful" which means that the logical orderliness of reason is the beautiful.[15] The artist is a man in whom the faculty of *Wit*, defined by Wolff as "a faculty of the mind by which similarity is noted", is developed to a (slightly) higher degree than in his fellows.[16] Poetry is therefore merely an elaborate form of discourse; the writer conceals his meaning in a metaphor or story and the reader unwraps the meaning, gets at the "moral". According to Gottsched, the literary theorist of early Enlightenment in Germany, the poet must know as much as possible in order to exercise his talent for intellectual penetration as far as possible.[17] H. K. Kettler, in his book, *Baroque Tradition in the Literature of the German Enlightenment*,[18] demonstrates convincingly that the poetics of rationalism stretch from the seventeenth to the eighteenth century; the only difference in practice is a greater sense of propriety in later writers. The reason for this shift in taste is accounted for by the spread of culture into broader levels of the populace. In the fifty years between 1670 and 1720 practically nothing of literary value was published in Germany. The cultural scene was dominated by the French-speaking courts; the Universities were dominated by Latin, the language of scholasticism. In 1682 and 1697, Leibniz, whose own works were written mainly in French and Latin, pleaded in the name of patriotism and enlightenment for the restoration of German as a language of learned discourse. In 1687, Christian Thomasius, lecturer at the University of Leipzig and one of the earliest fighters for enlightened principles in the field of law, sullied the notice-board with the announcement, written in German, of a course of lectures to be given in German on the basic rules of sensible, prudent and polite behaviour.[19]

E. A. Blackall states the implications of this action in dramatic terms :

His fixing of the notice in the vernacular to the university screens was a symbolic gesture reminiscent of Luther's nailing his theses to the door of the church at Wittenberg. It was a gesture to flout authority, a typical gesture from Thomasius whose whole activity was concerned with the overthrow of prejudice and rigid super- stition.[20]

His own German was clumsy and laced with Latinisms, but it was spirited. He anticipated the advent of the moral weeklies with his journal, *Die Monatsgespräche*,[21] a monthly review of new books couched in semi-learned, semi-popular language, intended both to amuse and instruct the general reader. But the spread of popular journalism did not really begin until an example had been set by the English. Steele and Addison, in *The Tatler* (1709–11) and *The Spectator* (1711–12) became the spokesmen of upper middle-class morality, opposing licentiousness and refining taste. The first German imitation was *Der Vernünftler* (1713–14), published in Hamburg and offering skilful translations of *The Spectator*. The enthusiasm for this kind of improving literature is indicated by the statistics : 500 such journals appeared in Germany during the course of the century, as compared to 200 in England and twenty- eight in France.[22] Besides spreading refinement in manners, these journals were the forcing-houses in which German prose-style was rapidly brought to polished and graceful maturity.

The example of Addison's urbanity was complemented in 1720 by the robust terseness of Defoe's style in an excellent translation of *The Life and Strange Surprising Adventures of Robinson Crusoe*. The combination of the adventures of an individual in a state of nature and the expression of a deep sense of piety could not fail to impress the contemporary German public. The trans- lation itself was a tremendous success and produced imitations in all corners of Germany. The best of these, J. G. Schnabel's *Wun- derliche Fata einiger Seefahrer* (1731–43) describes a utopian idyll far from the artificialities of European society, an ideal of peaceful felicity under the patriarchal rule of the natural leader of the community. Rationalism, sensibility and conservatism are all here combined to a kind of harmless domesticity—the perfection of eudaemonistic moral theory. *Robinson Crusoe* had turned the novel-reading public towards English novelists. Swift's *Gulliver's Travels* appeared in German translation in 1728, Richardson's *Pamela* in 1742 and *Clarissa* 1748–53, Fielding's *Joseph Andrews* in 1745 and *Tom Jones* in 1749–51. The only offering from Germany in the first fifty years of the century was Gellert's *Das Leben der schwedischen Gräfin von G.* (1748). Like Pamela, Gellert's Countess is smugly virtuous; the blows of fate she must suffer (loss of beloved husband, his sudden return after she has married another, the unwitting incest of her children etc.) are accepted with a rather devastating stoicism; Gellert's chaste style seems as frigid as his heroine when he tells of exciting adventures and emotional crises; he is much more at home with the shorter form of the verse fable.

The aims and achievements of the early *Aufklärung* are most easily seen in the two didactic poets, Brockes and Haller. Barthold Heinrich Brockes was a well-to-do Hamburg merchant who determined to devote himself to the praise of the Creator through the exploration of Creation in verse. Between 1721 and 1748 his *Irdisches Vergnügen in Gott* grew to nine volumes. In meticulous detail he enumerates the delights of nature, often with striking images, but the general level of his work seldom rises above the following rather clumsy attempt to explain away the problem of evil in teleological terms :

> Auch der Luchs ist schön und schädlich; er ist voller Raubbegier;
> Aber dennoch ist es uns ebenfalls ein nützlichs Tier,
> Zwischen Katzen und dem Tiger scheint's ein Mitteltier zu sein;
> Seine Haut ist gelblich fleckig, auch wohl etwas grau zuweilen.
> Sie sind aus der Maßen fertig, ihre Speise zu ereilen,
> Sehn so scharf als sonst kein Tier. Zwischen Bergen, Fels und Stein
> Leben meist die Katzenlüchse, wenn die Kälberlüchs' hingegen
> In den dickverwachsnen Wäldern insgemein zu wohnen pflegen.
> Für die Schwerenot und Krampf wird die Luchsklau uns verschrieben
> Und mit ihren Bälgen werden große Handlungen getrieben.[23]

Occasionally a conceit succeeds, as in the frequently anthologized "Kirschblüthe bei Nacht", where he tells how he saw some blossoms in an orchard at night which seemed to be of the purest white, until suddenly he noted with surprise the greater whiteness of a star shining through the branches. A later poet would have left us with the image, but Brockes cannot resist explicitly drawing the moral :

> Wie sehr ich mich am Irdischen ergötze,
> Dacht' ich, hat Gott dennoch weit größre Schätze.
> Die größte Schönheit dieser Erden
> Kann mit der himmlischen doch nicht verglichen werden.[24]

Albrecht von Haller, a Swiss scholar of encyclopaedic learning, provides us with an example of the penetration of the mechanistic view of the universe into poetry in his unfinished ode "Über die Ewigkeit".

> Unendlichkeit! wer misset dich?
> Bei dir sind Welten Tag', und Menschen Augenblicke,
> Vielleicht die Tausendste der Sonnen wälzt itzt sich,
> Und tausend bleiben noch zurücke.
> Wie eine Uhr, beseelt durch ein Gewicht,
> Eilt eine Sonn', aus Gottes Kraft bewegt;
> Ihr Trieb läuft ab, und eine zweite schlägt,
> Du aber bleibst, und zählst sie nicht.[25]

This vision of the majestic clock-work of interstellar space is a perfect example of what Kant later described as the mathematically sublime. Haller heaps one galaxy on another, only to conclude that he cannot in this way approach to a knowledge of God. The heavens declare the incommensurable nature of divinity. We find verses very like this in Schiller's early poetry, for example in his "Die Größe der Welt", written almost fifty years later. In Die Alpen, Haller assembles his learning to praise the simple life of the Swiss herdsmen of the Bernese Oberland. In thirty-nine ten-line stanzas he elaborates every aspect of the life of the mountain-dwellers and the splendid setting in which they live and contrasts it with the evils of civilized life. The images are often laboured with conventional circumlocutions :

> Belebt die Blumen-Flur mit steigendem Gewässer,
> Theilt nach Korinths Gesetz gehaune Felsen ab;[26]

it takes modern wit some time to realize that Haller is speaking here of fountains and architectural columns, but perhaps he may be excused for the florid "Silesian" manner since he is contrasting complex forms of luxury with the simple life. The didactic sententiousness of the whole poem is reflected in the form of his stanzas; each ends with a couplet expressing some moral reflection on the matter of the stanza.

The desire for express moralizing also explains the popularity of the fable. Gellert gives an informative and amusing account of his being summoned to the presence of Frederick the Great who had chanced to hear of the poet's work from the English ambassador (!) and is almost shocked to learn that Gellert is even esteemed for his fables in Paris. The poet—according to his own account—replies to the king's domineering manner with respectful wit, and in answer to Frederick's request tells his fable "Der Maler in Athen". Here is how he reports the event :

I told him the fable of the Painter of Athens. When I came to the moral, he said : "And now, the moral?" I told him the moral.

The King : That's good, that's very good! I really must compliment you. I didn't think of that; no, that's really very pretty, both good and short. Where did you learn to write like that?[27]

The account is not only remarkable for its revelation of the king's ignorance of German literature; even more surprising is that he needed to hear the moral before giving the royal approval. The Fable was imported from France both for its Rococo form and its moral instruction. The critic, Gottsched, gives a great deal of space to the discussion of fables in his *Versuch einer critischen Dichtkunst vor die Deutschen*. His definition of "Die Fabel", however, does not bother to distinguish between the different meanings of plot, story and moral tale. It is "a fictional occurrence, invented to harbour a particular moral precept, or rather to render it more readily perceptible".[28] Provided the moral is clear and the invention does not tax his credulity too much, Gottsched is prepared to accept any fable as the best of literature. Gellert's fables are mostly couched in terms of gentle mockery; Lessing later reduced the form to laconic brevity, deliberately omitting the "moral" for the sake of the immediacy of impact and because he had come to mistrust the mechanical nature of traditional poetics, while Wieland, in *Die Abderiten*, inflated the fable of Demosthenes about the Ass's Shadow to the mock-heroic proportions of a political allegory. Gottsched's *Critische Dichtkunst* is the shrine of early *Aufklärung* poetics. It was first published in 1730 and consists of two parts; the first discusses the nature of poetry and the poet, the second enumerates the genres according to a loose classification on the pattern of lyric, epic, dramatic, operatic. In Gottsched's view the poet is *born* with some talent but must also be *made* by close study of the rules; his education must lead him to control his imagination. The essence of poetry is the imitation of nature, but nature for Gottsched is largely human nature obedient to the rule of reason, therefore he stresses the importance of a coherent "invention" with a moral precept at its base. Anything fanciful (*das Wunderbare*) can only be permitted if it is also credible; so all divine figures should be capable of explanation as consistent allegories, representation of passion should never become ridiculous through exaggeration, the wonders of nature are permissible if real. Reasonable probability (*Wahrscheinlichkeit, vraisemblance*) also dominates his view of the theatre, so he rejects the opera and monologues, insists on the preservation of the unities with ludicrous pedantry, insists on the historical accuracy of costume-design and on the preservation of the decencies of station : for example, the characters of comedy should be normal citizens, at the most Barons, Marquises or Counts, not because the great do not commit follies but because it would be an offence against public decency to show this on the stage. Although in the theory of rationalism the mind is free to pursue critical enquiry in an uninhibited way, it is nevertheless presumed that one eternally valid result will be arrived at. Originality is therefore to be feared rather than praised, and Gottsched is proud of the fact that he has consulted the best of authorities from Aristotle to Voltaire and incorporated their findings in his work.[29] These remarks were made in the second edition of the *Critische Dichtkunst* which appeared in 1737 and also carried unfavourable judgements on the improbable nature of Milton's imagery in *Paradise Lost*. Among other objections, he does not like the idea that the architecture of Pandaemonium is an ornamented doric! *Paradise Lost* had been translated by Johann Jakob Bodmer of Zürich in 1732. He and his friend, Johann Jakob Breitinger, had published a weekly, *Discourse der Mahlern* (1721–22) in which the influence of Addison can be seen. Influenced by the empirical English attitude, they looked first at works of literature and used them to test the rules in opposition to Gottsched's method. Translating from Addison's *Essay on Imagination* and the French critic Dubos, they appealed to the power of creative imagination, operating through striking imagery, to give expression to inward states of mind and emotion. In 1740 Bodmer published a defence of Milton, his *Kritische Abhandlung von dem Wunderbaren in der Poesie und dessen Verbindung mit dem Wahrscheinlichen*. Here imagination is allowed to explore the province of the possible as well as the plausible and Bodmer pleads the advantages of a rich emotional life over one of cool rationalism. Breitinger's *Kritische Dichtkunst*, published in the same year, is a theory of poetry which stresses the importance of making poetry vital by creating sensuous, concrete imagery. Somehow it ought to have the immediacy which was supposed to reside in the visual arts (ut pictura poesis), while words from which literature is made are merely abstract counters. Gottsched saw his position threatened by these works and an acrimonious feud ensued which, however, petered out through inertia. It was all too bloodless and abstract, since neither party really had an immediate understanding of artistic creativity. Both parties to the quarrel did useful groundwork on language; Gottsched in his *Deutsche Sprachkunst* (1748) gave rules for the correct usage of German while Breitinger's stressing of powerful expressions (*Machtwörter*) and Bodmer's discovery of the forthright simplicity of medieval German helped to prepare the ground for the later rich harvest. It must also be remembered in Gottsched's favour that by working with Caroline Neuber's troupe of actors and by translating and publishing plays, even bad ones, he helped in the general revival of the theatre in the eighteenth century as a mirror of middle-class morals. Gottsched's influence waned as the desire for some expression in literature of a more familiar emotional life became more insistent. The phenomenon of *Empfindsamkeit* (Lessing translated the English "sentimental" by the word "empfindsam" in 1768) is frequently seen as an anti-rationalist movement, springing, like Pietism, from the native springs of genuine feeling.[30] But these things are also direct products of the general secularization of culture carried through by the early Enlightenment. The intellectual religion of the scholars could not appeal to the wider populace; effusions of fine feeling and indulgence in melancholy and effete tenderness are harmless surrogates for real passion in a world governed by standards of common-sense decency and propriety. The modern equivalents of these sentiments are found in the women's journals which trace their descent from the moral weeklies via the family journals of the nineteenth century :

> The sentimentalism which was so prominent in literature was an extension of this originally religious attitude to other objects. Instead of anxiously observing and, one may almost say, whipping up their feelings towards God, ... many transferred their attention in a similar way to their friends and lovers, to nature and literature ... At the other extreme are the family dramas and novels, with their faithful reflection of feeling in everyday life, mainly feeling enjoying social approval, a man's affection for his wife, his children, his dog, his old arm-chair.[31]

For a time the high seriousness of literary pursuits was eclipsed by the relative insignificance of escapist literature in the form of Anacreontic Rococo, sentimental idylls in verse and prose and the absorption of the English domestic tragedy and French *comédie larmoyante* into the theatrical repertoire. The literature of sentiment underwent its first apotheosis in the publication in 1748 of the first three cantos of Klopstock's *Der Messias*. To his contemporaries Klopstock's poem seemed to fulfil the demand for a great poet to arise and create an exemplary work in the German language—a demand which had been repeated in vain for fifty years. The poet himself had conceived his task with missionary zeal. While still at school he had determined to embark on the greatest subject, the redemption of mankind, in a form to vie with Homer, Virgil and Milton, whose *Paradise Lost* he had come to know in Bodmer's translation. The poem is written in imitation of classical hexameters, freely adapted to the natural stress rhythms of German, but to modern ears it sounds faltering and clumsy. In the windy spaces of an abstract cosmology Klopstock created a vessel in which the vague desire for intensity of feeling could be contained. There is something arid about the whole conception of the epic and this is borne out by the fact that Klopstock's inspiration flagged. The poem was not finished until 1773 and was subjected to three subsequent revisions; by then Klopstock's "seraphic" tone had been replaced by the more palpable directness of Goethe's "Storm and Stress" lyrics. Although the visions of *Der Messias* tend towards over-refined abstraction and sublimity, there is great power in the dynamic use of verbs to express surging restless movement. It is almost as though Klopstock anticipates Lessing's distinction between poetry and the plastic arts as the difference between nervous energy and repose.[32]

In the religious hymn, "Die Frühlingsfeier", written in 1759, both macrocosm and microcosm are created with a breathless urgency. The Creator is no longer a distant, benevolent deity but a shattering presence, the old testament Jehovah who comes on the wings of the Storm to annihilate and exalt his creatures at will :

Seht ihr den Zeugen des Nahen, den zückenden Strahl?
Hört ihr Jehovas Donner?
Hört ihr ihn? Hört ihr ihn,
Den erschütternden Donner des Herrn?

Herr! Herr! Gott!
Barmherzig, und gnädig!
Angebetet, gepriesen
Sei dein herrlicher Name!

Und die Gewitterwinde? Sie tragen den Donner!
Wie sie rauschen! wie sie mit lauter Woge den Wald durch-
    strömen!
Und nun schweigen sie. Langsam wandelt
Die schwarze Wolke.

Seht ihr den neuen Zeugen des Nahen, den fliegenden Strahl?
Höret ihr hoch in der Wolke den Donner des Herrn?
Er ruft : Jehova! Jehova!
Und der geschmetterte Wald dampft![32A]

The free rhythms of this powerful language burst the bonds of conventional prosody in giving utterance to the exalted emotional state of the poet. Such language had an immediate magical effect on the new generation, shown definitively in the famous passage of Goethe's *Die Leiden des jungen Werthers*, where the mere name "Klopstock", spoken by Lotte after a thunder-storm, is sufficient to release in Werther a cascade of blissful sentiment. But Klopstock did not always write in such exalted tones. Schooled on the Classics, he was accustomed to search for a patterning in his verse which could allow it to range far from normal prose patterns to achieve concentration of expression. The freedom attained in such poems has been compared with Picasso's portraits of the 1940s.[33] Such a comparison shows how far the lyric had been liberated from the constraints of Gottsched's classifying poetics.

A similar liberation of the creative powers was almost carried out by Lessing for the German theatre. Lessing is accorded the honour of being both the best writer of rational Enlightenment and also the toughest critic of that movement. Though he annihilated Gottsched for his pedantic observance of the rules, his own plays are obedient to the Aristotelian canon; though he praised Shakespeare and the English theatre and claimed that the native German genius should follow the direction taken in England, his own plays are more nearly derived from the French model of Diderot. In *Miß Sara Sampson* (1755) and *Emilia Galotti* (1772) he provided the German stage with its first successful domestic tragedies, the latter almost becoming real tragedy. His comedy, *Minna von Barnhelm* (1763) is one of the few traditional comedies to be found in German. *Nathan der Weise* (1779) treats the theme of religious tolerance in intellectualized blank verse, preaching the relative value of revealed religions before the great truth of reason that all men are brothers in their search for perfection and virtue, and that the validity of their beliefs will be proved by their actions in this world, not through adherence to a system of dogma. Lessing's conviction is expressed in two ways in the play; allegorically, in the story of the three rings, by which Nathan earns the respect and friendsl ip of the noble Saladin, and symbolically, when it is revealed that the representatives of the three major religions, Christianity, Judaism and Mohammedanism are in fact members of one family. This lesson in tolerance and practical religion, hammered home with great forcefulness, was the result of five years of controversy with Church authorities on the right to the free discussion and publication of unorthodox views. This championship of the cause of freedom of speech alone makes Lessing a great "Enlightener", but his own views on religion as expounded in *Nathan der Weise* and in the pamphlet of 1780, *The Education of the Human Race*, show him also to be a keen scholar of Leibniz and Spinoza, as he declares his belief in an ultimate millenium when revealed religions will be seen only as so many discarded husks, historical episodes in man's struggle to arrive at a state of totally autonomous morality.

His fundamental optimism also accounts in part for the particular interpretation he gave of Aristotle's theory of tragedy and his own inability to write tragedy. The new formulation of Aristotle grew gradually from a dissatisfaction with the ruling French taste and the theories of Corneille, theories which Gottsched had adopted for Germany. In the *Hamburg Dramaturgy* (1767–69) Lessing treated the problem of the aim of tragedy and the nature of tragic catharsis in great detail, expanding the basic view he had established ten years earlier in correspondence with his friends Nicolai and Mendelssohn.[34]

The essence of his theory is that he sees in tragedy an instrument for arousing the emotions of fear and sympathy in the audience. The "fear" he speaks of is not the "terror" of earlier theorists, but a self-directed sympathy :

> He [Aristotle] speaks of sympathy and fear, not pity and terror; and his fear is by no means the fear excited in us by misfortune threatening another person . . . it is the fear that the impending calamities . . . might also befall ourselves . . . In a word, this fear is sympathy referred back to ourselves.[35]

The sentiment of sympathy is enlarged to a general principle of philanthropy, a loving idenfication with all our fellows :

> And it is this love, say I, which we can never entirely lose towards our fellow-creatures, which smoulders inextinguishably beneath the ashes by which our stronger emotions are covered, and which only awaits a favourable wind . . . to be blown into the flame of compassion.[36]

The "purgation" of older theories becomes a strengthening purification; sympathy is enlarged in reflection to an aesthetic category :

> This fear [for ourselves] we carry away with us, and as it helps as an ingredient of sympathy to purify our sympathy, it now helps to purify itself as a passion *capable of independent continuous existence* (my italics)[37]
> . . . (to put it briefly) this purification rests in nothing else than in the transformation of passions into virtuous habits.[38]

Tragedy therefore is allotted a highly moral aim, not narrowly moralizing, but extending the range of emotional life, of generosity of heart. The theory arises in an age of sentiment and had enormous repercussions on subsequent drama.

The release of a fine flood of emotion forms a great part of the intention of Lessing's first play, *Miß Sara Sampson*. Sara herself weeps for her lost virtue, her father weeps at her predicament and her seducer weeps at his own cruelty.

And so the play goes on, as if the secret of stage success for every character were : weep, and the world weeps with you. The strange thing is that it did. At the first performance, so Ramler wrote to Gleim, the audience sat as still as statues for three and a half hours, and wept.[39]

They did not weep nearly as much at his *Emilia Galotti*, which is a far better play and one which has provoked constant debate since its first appearance. The action and psychological subtlety of motivation are so compressed that the play has called forth admiration and rejection in turn. It was a challenge to contemporary imitators and remains a challenge to interpretation.

As a prototype of the Storm and Stress plays of Goethe and Schiller and as an extension into practice of Lessing's theory, it deserves closer attention; here, only the barest outlines of plot and theme can be given.

Hettore Gonzaga, the reckless and emotionally irresponsible Prince of Guastalla, is shortly to enter on a political marriage but has fallen in love with Emilia Galotti, child of an upright and high-minded colonel, Odoardo, who loves his daughter to distraction and is zealously concerned for her honour. She is about to marry Count Appiani, a decent but otherwise unremarkable bridegroom. When the Prince learns of this marriage, he is so distracted that he permits his favourite, the cynical and unscrupulous Marinelli, to set about a plan for the seduction of Emilia which results in Appiani's death and the compromising of Emilia's virtue —actually, in the eyes of the world, as declared by Orsina, the Prince's former mistress, and potentially, in Emilia's own feelings. She protests she would not be safe against temptation when told she must be detained in custody while an inquiry into Appiani's murder is carried out. In these circumstances she and her father both conclude (with astonishing haste) that only death can avoid this dishonour and so Galotti stabs his daughter and delivers himself up to justice.

The tragic impasse lies in the fact that *all* the major characters worship Emilia as the ideal of all that is lovely. Such perfection is simply not possible in flesh and blood and so to preserve the image, the reality must die. Our sympathy is involved for the human condition which can know, but not possess, perfection. It is possible to accept this fate with sorrowful or stoic resignation or to protest violently against it. The writers of *Storm and Stress* protested; to do so they were obliged to see the tragedy as caused by outward social conditions, to regard the play as a polemic against tyranny, or they rejected it as being too cold and mechanical since they wished to live on in the illusion that some place could be found to build an Eden far from the madding crowd. This was the solution to the problem of society in Lessing's comedy, *Minna von Barnhelm*, but even there the balance is only precariously maintained; it takes a very wise king and an unusually tenacious heroine to bring about the happy end.

In all of Lessing's work we see criticism of the past and suggestions for lines of development in the future. In his *Laokoön oder über die Grenzen der Malerei und Poesie* (1766) he had used an analysis of Homer's technique of consecutive description to crack open one of the century's hoary old chestnuts; whether poetry should imitate the visual arts or vice-versa. In proving to his own satisfaction that they were essentially different in kind, that the plastic arts are static while poetry is dynamic,

> he had opened the floodgates into the stagnant stream of German verse; and into Goethe's channel there flowed, gurgling and bubbling, foaming and frothing, the mobile, flexible, vitally energetic and gallantly dynamic finite verb.[40]

Lessing championed Shakespeare against the French dramatists, but it was Wieland who first made Shakespeare's texts available to the German reading public, in his prose translations (1762–66). Rendered more prosaic and "reasonable" than the originals, these translations were soon bettered by the new generation of Shakespeare-enthusiasts, but they had first to learn from him. As a novelist Wieland wrote in the cultivated Rococo manner, but his intentions remained didactic; behind the brilliant surface is a hard core of sound common-sense. The philosopher Democritos in *Die Abderiten* is not so much there to comment on the elaborate follies of his fellow townsmen as to provide a foil against which these follies may be judged. Of his first novel he wrote that "wit and irony, along with the regular employment of the five senses, have always been considered the best specific for excesses of enthusiasm and super-stitition"[41] and his long-lived journal, *Der Teutsche Merkur* (1773–1810) has rightly been assessed as the monument of a "vast and exciting adult-education task".[42]

The process of enlightenment as a liberation from the chains of traditional patterns of thought proceeded only slowly during the first fifty years of the century, in the sixties it became agitated, in the seventies tradition was overthrown and the "creative life" of the emotions was prized more highly than the reflective powers of the mind.

The expression of this irrationalism in German literature during the seventies goes by the name of *Sturm und Drang*, Storm and Stress. The source of the term is clearly known. It was a title invented in 1776 by the self-styled "apostle of genius", Christoph Kaufmann, for F. M. Klinger's drama, called originally *Wirrwarr* (confusion, chaos) and the name was quickly adopted, at first mainly by detractors, to characterize the style and attitudes of the group of writers who were associated with Goethe in Straßburg, Frankfurt and Weimar during the seventies. The name *Storm and Stress* expresses well the turbulent excitement of these young men who saw any form of energy, even if destructive, as a desirable stimulant to emotional power. The young hero of Klinger's play is so filled with a sense of his own passionate lust for experience that he wishes he could be stretched over a drum to get a new sense of extension or be loaded into a pistol barrel waiting for the explosion of release, and Goethe's Faust imagines himself as a destructive elemental power, something beyond the limits of ordinary human society :

> Ha ! bin ich nicht der Flüchtling, Unbehauste,
> Der Unmensch ohne Zweck und Ruh,
> Der wie ein Wassersturz von Fels zu Felsen brauste,
> Begierig wütend nach dem Abgrund zu?[43]

Emotional turbulence, however, was only one aspect of the movement, and some writers prefer the term *Geniezeit*,[44] which stresses the importance of the idea of the creative originality of the individual and the artist. An early term, *Göthisieren*, reminds us that the movement would probably never have crystallized without the informing force of his genius, but naturally it had to be dropped when Goethe's genius developed in other directions.

It is a mistake to try to isolate *Storm and Stress* from the general flow of ideas in the eighteenth century. To call it pre-Romanticism or pre-Classicism, as is sometimes done, has not much more value than saying that these writers grew up and influenced others, and it denies the debt they owe to the struggle for freedom of expression in life and art which had gathered momentum throughout the century. H. B. Garland stresses the central importance of the personality and creative drive of Goethe for the whole movement, pointing out how many different writers entered his orbit, blazed for a short while and then vanished into the outer darkness, either of madness (Lenz), practical affairs (Klinger, Wagner) or aesthetic dilettantism (Maler Müller).[45] But one writer, no matter how great, can scarcely be said to make a movement, an idea which suggests a conscious programme and a journal such as the Romantics of Jena developed in the *Athenäum*. The contribution of Goethe, Herder and Merck to the *Frankfurter Gelehrte Anzeigen* does not seem large enough to warrant its being called a real forum, and the conscious dissemination of a programme stems more from Goethe and Herder than any of the others. Superficial badges of solidarity, like the affectation of dressing in the clothes of Werther or solemnly dancing round a druidical oak, as was done by the original founders of the Göttinger Hainbund, may be attributed either to youthful fancy or the fashion in sensibility. What appears superficially as a movement is rather a reflection of Goethe's power on the one hand and the general demand of the spirit of the age for artistic expression. The rationalism of earlier *Aufklärung* had done little to encourage imaginative writing, the emphasis was on criticism, the creation of a reading public, the creation of a theatre which required new plays and the creation of a need for the experience of literature. These desires had been largely encouraged and satisfied by foreign imports before the seventies. It was now time to test the home-grown product.

Goethe's life, before his meeting with Herder in Straßburg in 1770, had been spent largely in acquiring the education expected of his upper middle-class station. The poems written in Leipzig are mostly in the conventional Rococo manner; even a poem like "Die schöne Nacht", breaks the convention only in a very civilized and sentimental way, hindsight makes us sensitive to every possible clue to Goethe's later development. The intensity of the religious exercises and the fascination with alchemy which occupied him during his convalescence in Frankfurt give a first clue to his search for new paths of knowledge. But with his stay in Straßburg, the impact of Gothic architecture, of Herder's new insights into history and literature and of his love-affair with Friederike Brion all combined to produce that creative response to the world which goes by the name of genius. The direct singing joy of the poem "Mailied" and the dramatic, pulsing urgency of "Willkommen und Abschied" may be read as models of what Hamann and Herder required from the poetic power of language.

The release of creative genius was prepared by the philosophy of Rousseau who re-asserted the primacy of the "feelings" as the peculiar essence of the individual. This thought can be traced back to the spiritualized universe of Leibniz's Monadology. In his *Discourse on the origin and causes of inequality among men* (1754) and his *Social Contract* (1762), Rousseau taught that civilization had wandered into degenerate paths from an original state of nature, a lost paradise. Mankind must retrace its steps in order to reconstruct a society which will allow for the full development of the individual. How this is to be done is not very clear, nor very practical, but Rousseau has a vision of a free association of equals. His ideas were popularized through his novels, *The New Héloise* (1762) and *Émile* (1762) which is a recipe for an education which proceeds naturally and without constraint to develop individual potential.

At the same time Hamann, in Königsberg, was publishing his thoughts on the nature of language as a direct expression of the total being of man. Goethe summed up Hamann's views in the following words :

Everything man undertakes to perform, whether it be brought forth in word, deed or what you will, must spring from all powers acting in consort; all discreteness is to be rejected.[46]

In his *Aesthetics in a Nutshell* (1762), Hamann insists on the primacy of imagery as the source of all creation. Just as God created the world with an image : Let there be light! so all language which is used creatively, i.e. figuratively, is a similar creation. He even seems to suggest that poetry is older than creation :

Poetry is the mother-tongue of the human race; like gardening, older than the soil; [like] painting, [older] than words; song— than rhetoric; parables—than syllogisms; barter—than trade . . . The whole treasure of human knowledge and happiness consists in images;—the first appearance and the first pleasure in nature are joined in the command : Let there be light![47]

This is the most extreme statement of the idea of man, the poet, as a second maker. Herder knew Hamann in Königsberg and had learned from him the proud claim of creative language. In a number of early essays he develops these thoughts until they are given final expression in a prize essay written for the Berlin Academy in 1770 on the subject of the origins of language, "Über den Ursprung der Sprache". Like Lessing in the *Laokoön* he favours the definition of language as moving sound and claims that all sensuous impressions come to us originally as sound and gesture and thus receive articulation. Language picks up the world around us and forms it into an intelligible creation. A corollary of this theory comes out in the essay, "Über Ossian und die Lieder alter Völker",[48] where Herder points out that the more primitive languages are richer in expressiveness, closer to the source of the creative act; the songs and lays of simple cultures are *wild*, *lebendig*, *freiwürkend*, *sinnlich*, *lyrisch*, *handelnd*. They show *der freie Wurf* and *Tiefe des Eindrucks*. All this power is lacking in our modern over-civilized culture and we must somehow attempt to recapture the immediacy and directness of earlier ages by recreating our language. This is the task of the poet who has a greater sensitivity to words than most men whose senses are dulled by convention. The theory is entirely modern and still commands our assent. Herder writes very persuasively, drawing examples of folk-poetry from all corners of the globe which he interprets with considerable critical skill, showing the extreme sophistication of technique in the most artless songs, a sophistication to be contrasted with the technical refinements of cultured poetry.

The theory was later expanded to show the organic nature of the whole of human history, and this entailed the praise of the past as a more genuine and vital age than the present. Herder collected folk-songs and begged his friends to do the same. This whetted their appetite for the simple rhythms and direct expression they found there and set them imitating. Goethe's "Heidenröslein" is often taken for a folk-song and yet in comparison with the genuine article it is seen to reflect the complex sensibility of the modern poet for whom life is problematic.

The ideal of genius was now launched; "it became the slogan of the day", Goethe reports in *Dichtung und Wahrheit*. The concept is fed by support from England, where R. Woods had written an *Essay on the Original Genius of Homer* (1769), translated into German in 1771, basing his thoughts on E. Young's *Conjectures on original composition* (1759) which speaks of a man's genius "rising as the sun from chaos" and stresses the importance of introspection :

> Therefore dive deep into thy bosom; learn the depth, extent, bias and full fort of thy mind; contract full intimacy with the stranger within thee . . .[49]

Young's language is not as tricksy as Hamann's, but it is still highly emotive, as must be expected from one who elevates the expressiveness of the passional life of the individual soul. This is both the strength and weakness of the idea of genius. Literature becomes strongly confessional in tone, as one soul calls to another and expresses its experience of the world. With the overthrow of the rules of composition it seemed as though all critical standards had been abandoned. The *ABC for big children* (Vienna 1782) gives the following satirical entry for *Originalgenie* :

> *Original genius.* Only to be understood by normal geniuses. Not to be grasped by the profane, who don't possess the organ for it, don't know what Storm and Stress is. The profane man not struck in the vitals by it, but in later years saves his blushes for having been an original genius.

One form of critical standard is, however, given in the elevation of folk-poetry to a natural basic form. Any imitation of the natural-ness of folk-poetry may claim approval. So Gerstenberg wrote his *Gedicht eines Skalden* (1766) and started with Klopstock, a fashion in bardic song. The danger of this sort of standard is reflected, however, in the success of Macpherson's *Lays of Ossian*, a con-fidence-trick of genius, since it gave to the age of sentiment an ideal projection of their vision of the primitive life.

The genius may also attempt to lend his work conviction by the strength of his utterance and the sheer forcefulness of his person-ality. This explains the cultivation of *Titanism*, the cult of the great hero, great man or great criminal. Prometheus is the presid-ing deity, Caesar and Mahomet are also venerated. Goethe, in his speech written for a Shakespeare festival, "Zum Schäkespeare Tag" (1771) combines the views of Shakespeare as a natural, elemental folk-poet and a rival to Prometheus :

> Most of these gentlemen [French and frenchified critics]
> take particular exception to his characters.
> And I cry Nature! Nature! nothing so much Nature
> as Shakespeare's men.
> And then they're at my throat.
> Give me air, that I may speak!
> He contended with Prometheus, trait by trait
> he formed his men in the same way, but
> in colossal size; that is why we fail to
> recognize our brothers; then he inspired them
> with the breath of his spirit, he speaks through
> all of them and we see their relationship.[50]

The style suits the subject and the declamatory pathos. Gersten-berg's *Ugolino* (1768), the first drama of Storm and Stress, is one long surge of pathetic utterance, which is supposed to reflect Shakespeare's style. It is written in prose and is divided into the conventional five acts, but there is no real justification for this division, since the play merely follows a line of rising crescendo as it traces the gradual starvation of Count Ugolino and his two sons. They pass through various stages of nobility, self-sacrifice, misery, hallucination and bestiality as death approaches. An exquisite touch of horror is provided when the thirteen year old Anselmo determines to satisfy his hunger by gnawing at his mother's corpse, after realizing that his young brother who has just died might contain too much poison!

> In meinem Herzen empört sich's und ruft: Iß nicht Anselmo, iß nicht von diesem Fleische. Ein guter Rat! Dies Fleisch könnte mir schaden; es ist vergiftet. Hieher winkt der Versorger. Ein offner Sarg, der einen weiblichen Körper voll himmlischer Schönheit für mich aufbewahrt! Soll ich? Glück! Soll ich? Ich folge dir, Glück! Meine Zähne knirschen! Der Wolf ist in mir! Ha! verwünscht will ich sein, wenn ich dieser Weibsbrust schone! (Indem er sich über den Sarg erhebt, fällt der Deckel.)[51]

Goethe's *Götz von Berlichingen* is likewise an "imitation" of Shakespeare, and in the figure of Götz we see the ideal of the historical hero projected, a rough but upright individual, a fighter for independence and the old German virtues against the sophistry of modern power politics. The multiple plots are extremely complicated and analytic development is abandoned for an "epic" technique, telling the story in a great number of short, chronological scenes.

The drama was the most favoured form because it was most immediate and alive, combining gesture and speech into a microcosm of the world. Not many of these enthusiastic geniuses handled dialogue well, they were too inspired to listen to normal speechrhythms, and most of the plots are stereotyped, being concerned with social injustices (the brutality of army life, the corruption of courts and princes, the inequality of the estates), or with conflicts within nature (the hate between two individuals who struggle to outdo each other as titans but who ought to love each other as brothers, fathers and sons, etc.). Lessing's *Emilia Galotti* is a model for most of these plays but none of them approached Lessing in subtlety of motivation or economy of means, until Schiller published his *Kabale und Liebe* twelve years later.

One play which would have surpassed it remained largely unknown. This was Goethe's original conception of his Faust-drama, now known as *Urfaust*. In it are combined most of the familiar themes; the titanic striving of "Faustian" man, the criticism and rejection of dead learning, the worship of nature as the living substance of God, the brutality of the age as shown in the example of Auerbach's Cellar, and the tenderness of youth and young love in the figure of Gretchen. It also contains, like Goethe's epistolary novel, *Die Leiden des jungen Werthers*, the criticism of the age; for it shows us that the ideal of unchecked passion is ultimately self-destructive. Werther and Faust both have a sentimentalized view of human nature, they are poseurs when contrasted with the simplicity of Gretchen and the urbane evil of Mephistopheles; they long to be drawn into the richness of life, but they are dreamers in love with an ideal, the perfection sought for by the Enlightenment, the true substance behind shifting appearances.

NOTES

1. *OED* gives first use in 1865, claiming only pejorative use, though the 1846 usage also seems suitable.
2. *s.v.* "Aufklärung" in H. Paul, *Deutsches Wörterbuch*, 5. *Auflage* (Tübingen, n.d.) and *Trübners Deutsches Wörterbuch* (Berlin, 1939). "Aufklärung", "aufklären" and "aufgeklärt" had of course existed before (1691), but in the meaning of "clear", "distinct" and "rational", i.e. without the sense of development so important to Leibniz's monads.
3. *v.* E. A. Blackall, *The Emergence of German as a literary language, 1700–1775* (Cambridge, 1959), p. 34. Cf. R. W. Meyer, *Leibniz and the Seventeenth-century Revolution*, trans. J. P. Stern (Cambridge, 1952), for an account of Leibniz as representative of the Baroque Age.
4. G. von Wilpert, *Sachwörterbuch der Literatur* (Stuttgart, 1955, rev. 1959); *v.* also W. Windelband, *A History of Philosophy*, trans. J. H. Tufts (New York, 1893, rev. 1901), p. 437.
5. Immanuel Kant, *Beantwortung der Frage: Was ist Aufklärung?* Werke in 6 Bdn., ed. W. Weischedel (Darmstadt, 1964), p. 53.
6. Kant, p. 59.
7. F. J. Schneider, *Die Deutsche Dichtung der Geniezeit* (Stuttgart, 1952), in *Epochen der Deutschen Literatur*, III/2, p. 1.
8. H. Hettner, *Geschichte der deutschen Literatur im achzehnten Jahrhundert*, rev. G. Erler (Berlin, 1961), Bd. II, p. 7.
9. Cf. Roy Pascal, *The German Sturm und Drang* (Manchester, 1953), p. xiv.
10. Text according to the *Nationalausgabe*. Schiller wrote to Körner (9 February 1789): "Ich eröffne das Gedicht mit einer 12 Verse langen Vorstellung des Menschen in seiner jetzigen Vollkommenheit; dies gab mir Gelegenheit zu einer guten Schilderung dieses Jahrhunderts von seiner besseren Seite."

How glorious, o Man, with palm in hand,
Here at the century's gate you stand,
In manly pride sublime.
Alert of sense, with spirit overflowing,
Serenely grave, in quiet power glowing,

Maturest son of time.
Strong in the law, free through reason's measures,
Through mildness great, and rich in treasures
Which you yourself kept long concealed from view:
Great Nature's Lord! Though bent beneath your yoke,
In loving contest still she can your power provoke,
And thus from savage state to present glory grew.

11. In *Zeichen der Zeit, ein deutsches Lesebuch*, Bd. I, ed. W. Killy (Frankfurt, 1962), p. 26.

12. For a more detailed introduction see Windelband, *A History of Philosophy*, Parts IV and V, and Bertrand Russell, *A History of Western Philosophy*, pp. 522–701.
Leibniz, *Discourse on Metaphysics*, trans. P. G. Lucas (Manchester, 1953), paras. VIII–XVI, gives an excellent introduction to his thought.

13. Essay (Book II, Ch. I, Sec. 2).

14. Isaiah Berlin, *The Age of Enlightenment* (New York, 1956), p. 19.

15. See F. J. Schneider, *Aufklärung* (Stuttgart, 1948), in *Epochen der Deutschen Literatur* III/1, p. 29.

16. Cf. J. C. Gottsched, *Versuch einer critischen Dichtkunst* (Leipzig, 1751), p. 102.

17. See Gottsched, p. 105.

18. Kettler, *Baroque Tradition in the Literature of the German Enlightenment*, 1700–50 (Cambridge, n.d.).

19. The full title ran: "... ein Collegium über des Gratians Grund-Reguln, Vernünfftig, klug und artig zu leben."—The lectures were introduced by a pamphlet bearing the significant title: "Welcher Gestalt man denen Frantzosen in gemeinem Leben und Wandel nachahmen solle?"

20. *The Emergence of German*, p. 12.

21. Full title of first issue: "Schertz- und Ernsthaffter, Vernünfftiger und Einfältiger Gedancken, über allerhand Lustige und nützliche Bücher und Fragen, Erster Monat oder JANUARIUS."

22. *s.v.* "Moralische Wochenschriften", G. von Wilpert, *op. cit.*

23. Translation:
Lynxes are famed for their beauty and danger, truly fearsome carnivores;
Nevertheless, we must confess it, there are uses for their paws.
'Twixt the lesser cats and tiger they adopt a middle state;
Spotted yellow is their tegument, though some are grey, I hear relate.
Impelled by appetite voracious, upon small beasts they haste to dine,
Spying their prey with keenest eyesight; small lynxes live in desert climes
Among the mountains, rocks and cliff-scapes. The great lynx on the other hand
Is found among the thickest thickets, generally in forest lands.
Lynx-claw is famed as a specific for cramps and epileptic fits,
While merchants prize their spotted hides, and sell them widely as carpets.

For a more generous appraisal of Brockes, see W. F. Mainland, "Brockes and the Limitations of Imitation", in *Reality and Creative Vision in German Lyrical Poetry*, ed. A. Closs (London, 1963).

24. Translation:
> However much in earthy things I take my pleasure,
> Thought I, God still can boast of many a greater treasure.
> The greatest beauty of this earth falls far,
> Far short of any heavenly star.

25. Translation:
> Eternity! who can measure you?
> For you whole worlds are but a day, and men mere moments,
> Perhaps the thousandth star is rolling now
> With a thousand more remaining yet to come.
> Just as a clock receives its soul through weights,
> So does the sun run on by heaven impelled;
> Its mechanism tires and now a second starts
> But you remain and count them not.

26. Translation:
> Enliven the flowery mead with rising waters,
> Divide the hewn out cliffs by Corinth's law;

27. *Oxford Book of German Prose*, letter from Gellert to Fräulein Schönfeld (19 December 1760).

28. Gottsched, *Critische Dichtkunst*, p. 436.

29. Ibid., Vorrede zur zweiten Auflage p. XXVII.

30. See Hettner, Vol. I, p. 286.

31. W. H. Bruford, *Theatre, Drama and Audience in Goethe's Germany* (London, 1950), p. 118.

32. See below for discussion on *Laokoön*.

32A. Translation:
> Do you see the Near One's witness, the flashing bolt?
> Do you hear Jehovah's thunder?
> Do you hear it? Do you hear,
> The terrible thunder of the Lord.
>
> Lord! Lord! God!
> Merciful and gracious!
> Adored and praised
> Be your glorious name!
>
> And the winds of the storm? They carry the thunder!
> How they roar! how their surging waves rage through the woods!
> And now they are quiet. And slowly recedes
> The black cloud.
>
> Do you see the new witness of the Near One, the flying bolt?
> Do you hear, high in the clouds, the thunder of the Lord?
> It calls: Jehovah! Jehovah!
> And the shattered wood smokes!

33. Blackall, *Emergence of German*, p. 349.
34. *Die Hamburgische Dramaturgie* consists of 104 bi-weekly issues of a series of review articles which Lessing was required to write as part of his duties as "Dramaturg", production adviser to the newly formed "National Theatre" in Hamburg. The reviews were expected to be criticisms of the theatre programme, but Lessing typically used them as a vehicle for the dissemination of ideas and made no apology for doing so.
35. Lessing, *Hamb. Dram.*, No. 75.
36. Ibid., No. 76.
37. Ibid., No. 77.
38. Ibid., No. 78.
39. Bruford, *Theatre, Drama and Audience*, p. 148.
40. E. M. Butler, *The Tyranny of Greece over Germany* (Cambridge, 1935), p. 70.
41. In a letter to Gleim, quoted by Hettner, Vol. I, p. 672.
42. D. van Abbé, *Christoph Martin Wieland* (London, 1961), p. 153.
43. Translation:

> Ah! am I not the fugitive, the homeless,
> The monster without goal or peace,
> Who roared like cataracts across the rock-face,
> Raged thirsty down towards the deep abyss?

44. As F. J. Schneider.
45. H. B. Garland, *Storm and Stress* (London, 1952).
46. *Dichtung und Wahrheit*, Bk. XII.
47. *Sturm und Drang, Kritische Schriften* (Heidelberg, 1959), p. 121. See Blackall, p. 441, for extensive commentary.
48. Ibid., p. 507.
49. E. Young, *Conjectures on Original Composition*, in *Eighteenth-Century Prose* (Penguin, London).
50. In *Sturm und Drang*, p. 697.
51. Act V, *Sturm und Drang, Dramatische Schriften*, p. 54–55. Translation:

There's rebellion in my heart which cries: Don't eat Anselmo, don't eat of this flesh. Good counsel! This flesh could harm me; it is poisoned. This way the Provider beckons. An open coffin, and in it lies a female form of passing beauty, kept safe for me! Shall I? Fortune, shall I? I follow, Fortune! My teeth grind! The wolf is in me! Ha! I will be cursed if I should spare this woman's breast! (As he stretches up over the coffin, the lid falls.)

BIBLIOGRAPHY

Anthologies

F. Brüggemann, *Deutsche Literatur in Entwicklungsreihen* (Weimar and Leipzig, 1928 ff.), *Reihe Aufklärung*.
Sturm und Drang, Kritische Schriften, ed. E. Löwenthal (Heidelberg, 1959).

Sturm und Drang, Dramatische Schriften, 2 vols., ed. Löwenthal and Schneider (Heidelberg, 1959).

Surveys and Studies

H. Hettner, *Geschichte der deutschen Literatur im achtzehnten Jahrhundert*, rev. G. Erler (Berlin, 1961), 2 vols.

F. J. Schneider, *Die deutsche Dichtung der Aufklärungszeit* (Stuttgart, 1948), Vol. III/1 of *Epochen der deutschen Literatur*.

F. J. Schneider, *Die deutsche Dichtung der Geniezeit* (Stuttgart, 1952), Vol. III/2 of *Epochen der deutschen Literatur*.

H. A. Korff, *Geist der Goethezeit*, 4 vols. (Leipzig, 1923; rev. 4th. ed. 1958), Vol. I, *Sturm und Drang*.

J. G. Robertson, *A History of German Literature* (London, 1931; rev. E. Purdie, 1959).

A. Köster, *Die deutsche Literatur der Aufklärungszeit* (Heidelberg, 1925).

H. M. Wolff, *Die Weltanschauung der deutschen Aufklärung* (Bern, 1949).

W. Windelband, *A History of Philosophy*, trans. J. H. Tufts (New York 1901).

Bertrand Russell, *A History of Western Philosophy* (London, 1946).

W. H. Bruford, *Germany in the Eighteenth Century* (Cambridge, 1935).

W. H. Bruford, *Theatre, Drama and Audience in Goethe's Germany* (London, 1950).

E. A. Blackall, *The Emergence of German as a Literary Language, 1700–1775* (Cambridge, 1959).

P. Hazard, *The European Mind (1680–1715)*, trans. J. L. May (London, 1953); original title, *La crise de la Conscience Européenne* (Paris, 1935).

H. K. Kettler, *Baroque Tradition in the Literature of the German Enlightenment 1700–1750* (Cambridge, n.d.).

J. G. Robertson, *Lessing's Dramatic Theory*, ed. E. Purdie (Cambridge, 1939).

H. B. Garland, *Lessing* (Cambridge, 1937).

H. B. Garland, *Storm and Stress* (London, 1952).

R. Pascal, *The German Sturm und Drang* (Manchester, 1953).

R. Unger, *Hamann und die Aufklärung* (Berlin, 1911).

A. Gillies, *Herder* (Oxford, 1945).

B. Fairley, *A Study of Goethe* (Oxford, 1945).

W. Witte, *Schiller* (Oxford, 1949).

Classicism

V

Classicism

R. B. FARRELL

IN discussing the term "classicism" in relation to German literature it is necessary to distinguish between two German terms :
Klassik and *Klassizismus*, which apart from a few doubtful
examples are not applied by German literary historians to the same
writers and works. *Deutsche Klassik* is the name given to a span
of years in German literary history, which, while views differ as
to their end and particularly to their beginning, are for the rest
fixed : the years between Goethe's trip to Italy in 1786 (sometimes
his return in 1788) and Schiller's death in 1805, i.e. Goethe's middle
years and those of Schiller's maturity. Historians intent on exclud-
ing everything that cannot be made to conform to rigidly unified
principles contract still further and speak of "*Klassik* in the narrower sense", meaning the years of friendship between Goethe and
Schiller, 1794–1805; a limitation, however, which, granting that
in these years classical principles were clearly formulated, does not
exhibit a much more unified character in the imaginative literature
produced than would appear if the preceding years were included.
Other views would extend the period forward by a few years to
include a work like *Pandora* (1808), occasionally still further to
Die Wahlverwandtschaften (*The Elective Affinities*) (1809), while
others again take it backwards to Goethe's early Weimar years
after 1775 when, outgrowing his *Sturm und Drang* turbulence and
subjectivity, he began to seek objective laws in the moral and
natural spheres. More often these years are referred to as "Early
Classicism", a time of preparation. If we go back still further, to
Winckelmann, Lessing and Wieland we undoubtedly find something of what we are accustomed to regard as classical (a kind of
"Pre-Classicism"), but fused with other elements. Similarly, Goethe's
classicism did not end abruptly even with *The Elective Affinities*,
it persisted till the end, but became much less uncompromising,
modified as it was by his efforts to come to grips with the nineteenth century and by his acceptance of cultures other than Greek.
We may regard it as a kind of "Post-Classicism".

It is of course with the period known as *Klassik* that this
chapter is concerned, and, as far as its history is traced, first of all
and very briefly, with its preparation in the stages where classical

tendencies begin to emerge (in the widest sense the bulk of the eighteenth century is preparation) and then with its heyday. To clarify certain of its central features, however, a brief description of *Klassizismus* and a comparison of the two will be helpful.[1] In brief, *Klassizismus* is applied to works, writers and periods that derive their principles (and often their materials) from a genuine classicism, ultimately from ancient Greece or Rome, but remain largely imitative and one-sided. Thus, some of the literature of the German *Aufklärung*, and particularly Gottsched, is characterized as *Klassizismus* (with Opitz as an early form of it), and too with some justification writers who came after Goethe such as Platen and the *Münchener Dichterschule* (a label, however, which does not exhaust Platen). Quite obviously, on the other hand, there is a Goethe heritage which appears merged with, at times conflicting with, other tendencies in the nineteenth and even twentieth centuries. With this "classical-romantic" heritage in such writers as Mörike, Stifter, Grillparzer, Stefan George, there is, however, no question of imitation or any justification for the label *klassizistisch*.

Both terms, furthermore, have been applied by German critics to non-German literature, *Klassik* above all to the French writers of the seventeenth century from about 1660 to 1685, a period— significantly brief—of original creativeness rooted in French society, however much its writers may have believed they were fulfilling the principles of the ancients. Sometimes, too, though with resulting confusions, *Klassik* has been applied to the Elizabethan age of English literature in that this represents a culmination and flowering of the national genius.[2] It may be said immediately that if this view—that *Klassik* is simply a flowering of the national spirit—is accepted, the term loses many characteristics that we traditionally associate with classicism and in particular its close association with the literatures of Greece and Rome. The exuberance and individualism of the Elizabethans and the absence of the sense of an aesthetic norm in their work remove it far from the world of Racine or the classical Goethe. In so far as there is in a Shakespearean tragedy a pervading sanity despite the terrible events it unfolds it might indeed be taken as akin, at least in this respect, to the classical outlook, but on the other hand it is at least open to question whether the re-assertion of the moral order at the end of the play is always convincing in its attempt to present a basically sound world order. The "rottenness" of the world from which Hamlet suffers is suggestive rather of the romantic than the classical spirit. This same view of *Klassik* is also responsible for its application to the great flowering of medieval German literature around 1200. The case for such a view, a *Staufische Klassik*, has been argued by K. H. Halbach,[3] who, moreover on the basis of this interpretation sees a *Klassik* appearing about every three hundred years, the years 900 and 1500 being other culminating points. (Scherer had thought in terms of 600 years). Certainly, medieval literature of this period had polish and something of a norm about it, particularly linguistically; on the other hand medieval literature in general has been seen as an expression of revolt, of romanticism overthrowing the classical authority, i.e. the Church—a seductive interpretation perhaps but one which ignores all sorts of problems.[4]

As for *Klassizismus*, it is often used by German historians, e.g. for the Augustan Age of eighteenth century English literature, sometimes for the whole period up to pre-romanticism. If this learned much from French models of the *grand siècle* and from ancient Rome, it is nevertheless wide of the mark to imply that it is imitative or derivative, growing as it did out of English life. On the other hand, its temper is eminently critical, it lacks the wholeness, which includes the emotional profundity characteristic of *Klassik*, whether this be a question of fifth century Athens, the age of Racine or that of Goethe. The same is true of the first half of the French eighteenth century, the age of *les philosophes*, critical, sceptical, disintegrating, and as such, therefore, inimical to the sense of integration of man with his world and of man within himself found in a literature described as *Klassik*. In its external imitation of such qualities as balance and symmetry *Klassizismus* is often described as "glatt" (smooth).

The two terms, again, are used of the other arts. *Klassizismus* is applied to the visual arts, particularly architecture, and denotes a style that consistently took antiquity as its model, and is in the history of German art the only term to be used of Goethe's contemporaries, though Claude Lorrain and Poussin in seventeenth century France are accorded the epithet *klassisch*. On the other hand *Klassik* is the term applied to the great age of German music, to Gluck, Haydn, Mozart and, with qualifications, to Beethoven, composers whose music possesses not only excellence but excellence of a particular kind, perhaps a kind of Rococo classicism. (If it were merely a question of outstanding excellence Bach would have to figure on the list.)

So far, the argument has suggested that there is far from complete agreement in the use of the terms: *Klassizismus* includes the English "pseudo-classicism" as well as "classicism" (sometimes, however, reserved for the original Greek variety) and "neo-classicism"; *Klassik* excludes "pseudo-classicism", but, unlike any of the English terms, is also used of periods which do not stand in a close relationship to Greece and Rome. Our discussion, furthermore, has referred to certain characteristics constantly associated with these terms. Before adding to these and showing how they have a tendency to cohere, it will serve the aim of this preliminary clarification to refer to the origin and later development of the term "classicus" in Latin. Originally used to denote the first and wealthiest class of Roman citizen, that subject to the highest taxes, it easily acquired the sense of "best" or "excellent", and in the second century A.D. was applied by Aulus Gellius in his *Noctes Atticae* (Book XIX) to writers in the sense of excellent, "scriptor classicus" as opposed to "scriptor proletarius"; the sixth and last class of citizens was designated by the latter term. From the Renaissance on its equivalents in modern western European languages (E. "classical", F. "classique", G. "klassisch") have been in common use, first in reference to the literatures of Greek and Roman antiquity, whose excellence was felt to have created a norm, a model for all time, later to works of modern European literature which possess the same sort of excellence and above all have an affinity to Greek and Roman. Its application to periods which lack this affinity is recent. The noun "classic" (G. "Klassiker"), however, has for long been used of a work or writer of great excellence who has consequently withstood the test of time, no matter what the type of literature be. Thus Grimmelshausen's *Simplicissimus* and Thomas Mann's *Buddenbrooks* are held to be classics no less than Goethe's *Römische Elegien*. Another use of the English term "the classics", without qualifications, refers exclusively to Greek and Roman literature, a meaning not shared by the G. "Klassiker". In English, again, there are two adjectives, "classic" and "classical". The latter refers—and in good use exclusively— to the arts and the type of culture associated with them (a "classical" education is one in which the study of Greek and Latin plays a prominent part). On the other hand "classic" (G. for this sense has only "klassisch") refers to other things and means well-established, often with the sense of well-tried and therefore with the suggestion of worthy of imitation. Thus : classic diplomacy; a classic answer (to meet a well-defined situation); a classic example (e.g. of ineptness as well as of skill); the disease ran its classic course. The last two examples serve to show that the idea of excellence is not always present and that in fact that of the well established, the clearly typical, the essential, predominate, connotations, it will be seen later, also inherent in the term "classical" as applied to literature and art.

To judge whether the period of German literature under review can justifiably be called classical we need to see it in relation to the whole history of classical literature from the Greeks through the Renaissance up to the end of the eighteenth century, for the terms is European and should in consequence not be allowed to differ in essentials from one national literature to another.[5] In classical theory Aristotle remained the main source on which later exponents drew. What he attempted to do was to base his theory on observation of Greek practice, not to work out strict principles *a priori*. It was left to later theorists to codify his ideas rigidly. Of the famous unities, for example, Aristotle insists only on that of action; those of place and time received the force of dogma only at the time of the Italian Renaissance. Aristotelianism in literary theory then dominated the so-called Renaissance centuries, i.e. till about the middle of the eighteenth, rigid at first (e.g. Sir Philip Sidney), still more so with Gottsched, but towards the end finding in Dr. Johnson in England a more liberal interpreter and in the German Lessing, from inside Rationalism, a critic who held that Shakespeare better fulfilled the spirit of the rules than did Racine. In a general way, however, literary practice illustrated theory, particularly the conception of literature as mimesis. While it would be a mistake to see all the literary manifestations of these centuries as classical simply because they stand more or less in the Aristotelian tradition, this long period nevertheless has a broad, if loose, unity, which changes in literary style cannot obscure. The phases we have called classical (those of Racine, the English Augustans, the middle Goethe), have something of a culmination about them, suggesting a balance and harmony that can only come from an order that has reached its zenith. Goethe's and Schiller's historical position is at the very end of this order, in fact after its end as a vital force in life and when a new social and intellectual order was already clearly in the making. In literature the latter is reflected, as an early stage of modernity, in the second half of the eighteenth century as Rousseauism, in Germany as *Empfindsamkeit* and *Sturm und Drang*. Our problem then is largely to determine whether classical German literature is fully classical in the traditional sense or whether because of its historical position it has elements of modernity. After all, before they turned towards classicism Goethe and Schiller had passed through an acute period of *Sturm und Drang*. And in the years of their "High Classicism", moreover, romanticism, of which they were aware, was fast getting under way.

If German classicism has to be studied against the background of European classicism as a purified synthesis of preceding movements of the eighteenth century, particularly of the *Aufklärung* and of *Sturm und Drang*, which avoids the excesses and the one-sidedness of both, it must equally be viewed as a phase in the development of literature from about 1770 to 1830 (Goethe's productive lifetime). It forms a part of what has sometimes been called the *deutsche Bewegung* though not very illuminatingly, because the classical phase which is its highest achievement is cosmopolitan and not rooted in German life. This "German Movement" which also covers romanticism and its aftermath is clearly given this name because of the great upsurge of genius in these years. It will then be seen that the broad development is from *Sturm und Drang* to romanticism, even though the impact of Goethe's and Schiller's classicism was to be felt for a long time to come, retarding perhaps the full advent of modernity longer than would otherwise have been the case.

At this point it is appropriate to inquire into the characteristics that appear in literature to which the epithet "classical" is accorded, but without limiting ourselves to the German scene. One basic quality, from which many others are inseparable, is the reflection in literature of wholeness in life, a quality that distinguishes Greek man, at least of the great age. It implies all-sidedness, a harmonious development of all sides of the self, none over-developed at the expense of others. Thus it implies further a harmony within the self and furthermore a harmony of the self with its world, with its society, however much it may find itself beset by problems and even though tragedy be recognized as an inevitable part of the human condition. Thought and action hold each other in a state of balance and fructify each other. Unlike the situation in the Age of Rationalism reason will not stifle depth of feeling, nor will the reverse be the case as with *Sturm und Drang*. The essential oneness of the trinity (the good, the beautiful and the true) is an abiding experience and belief, in contrast with that of our modern age which, for example, feels the beautiful to be neither true nor good, and in general the moral to be at variance with the aesthetic, life with art.

Such an attitude has certain pre-suppositions : above all trust in the world, which basically responds, sustains the individual and enables him to feel that he belongs to it, binding him to it in love and joy. Where there is no feeling of belongingness (a state of being contrasting utterly with the alienation of the modern artist) the classical spirit does not reside. Implied further is that the phenomena of the world and the social order have a stable meaning and a value in human terms, are worthy dwelling places of the artist's spirit, again in contrast to the modern situation, where the things of the world have lost their meaning or at best retain a fugitive and uncertain one. Such oneness with the world tends, almost by definition, to be naive, to be taken for granted. In such a world, such a society the individual will possess, as T. S. Eliot points out in his essay *What is a Classic?*, a high degree of maturity, a maturity which is the culmination of the development of society, accompanied, to be sure, by struggle and ferment but which in its final stage confers the sense of having "arrived", of having achieved universal and permanent values and of embodying in itself valid laws, of having mastered life. A feeling of sovereignty over one's world, which does not exclude reverence and a sense of one's due place in it, is a concomitant; a restraint, which is not coldness but rather a sense of measure, a serenity that is nevertheless compatible with depth of feeling, dignity, nobility and elevation of tone. These human qualities are reflected in the work of art, not necessarily as subject-matter though they may often constitute it or be adumbrated in it, but as style, an outstanding characteristic of which is balance, the constant creation of a sense of wholeness through complementary opposites, of completeness, of the circle closing itself. Urbanity, ease and gracefulness will often be associated with this balance. A style that feels it has achieved the essential, the permanent, will also regard itself as normative, will be conscious of its own rightness. This is true not only of its view of life, but of its use of language, where it will confine itself to established forms and vocabulary.

Hand in hand with such an attitude of optimism, that the world is a meaningful cosmos, has value and is adequate to man, goes a second important characteristic of the classical spirit : objectivity. The classical self looks outward to the world, unlike the romantic, which seeks to transcend it and turns inwards. The intelligibility of the world is taken for granted as is also the adequacy of the mind to perceive truth, and knowledge of such truth is regarded as the proper concern of the artist. Whereas in his inwardness the romantic tends to make his work more an expression and exploration of his feelings, his inner world, including its sub-conscious layers, than of the external world, the classical artist remains objective, description of feeling being incidental, feeling indeed being in no way absent but permeating the work as a tone rather than as something given a name and talked about. Experience in the social and natural world (particularly the former) is therefore the material of literature. It is in this sense that Aristotle's theory of mimesis (imitation of nature) holds good for the classical poet. Not photographic, naturalistic reproduction of externals, however, is meant, but a revelation of what is essential in nature conceived as a rationally ordered whole and behaving in accordance with laws.

The essential, the permanent, the universal in nature and in human nature, not the accidental and transitory nor the uniquely individual is the province of art as seen by the classical spirit. Thus in the social sphere types, not unique individuals with their local colour, are the concern of the artist. In so far, however, as this objectivity is thought of as realism it has little to do with nineteenth century realism with its portrayal of a multiplicity of accidental details characteristic of a milieu. The presentation of the essential conceived as the manifestation of an eternal law of nature and, because it is the essential, in a clear and simple form is the hall-mark of classical art. The classical artist is normally one who is in possession of this feeling for life, not one who seeks it.

Another central tenet of the classical outlook from Aristotle on (though doubted by Plato) is that art educates, that it has a moral effect or at least offers the possibility of moral improvement. As far as literature is concerned, this does not imply that it must be overtly didactic or that it must only hold up models of good conduct for us to admire and to follow. Rather does its moral effect lie in our being brought into vital contact with essentials, with truth, (literature being a replica of reality thus conceived) and in the heightened awareness of these made possible by literary presentation. Since the world is a meaningful cosmos, its truth must be moral, and the work of art, whatever deviations from the norm it presents, adumbrates this moral order. It is basically a wholesome world, which can therefore be affirmed. It is a view which has had a tenacious life, celebrating revivals after the classical age proper had closed and after opposed views had gained wide acceptance. In none perhaps was the revival more forceful than in Mathew Arnold, who substantially re-affirmed the classical position. Modern art on the other hand pre-supposes the self-sufficiency of the aesthetic experience. In ancient Greece, where art was intimately associated with religion and with the life of the Greek as a citizen, it understandably was thought to have such a moral effect. And till the advent of modernism, art has tended to celebrate and glorify what it held to be good, likewise by implication even when it portrays the destruction of the good.

Klassik is a phrase of German Neo-Hellenism, but is not co-extensive or identical with it.[6] For this reason the latter would be an inappropriate label for our period, although it is a powerful current in the eighteenth century and is not altogether a spent force in the nineteenth and twentieth. Certainly, German classicism is grounded in the experience of Greece (much less in that of Rome) and without this would have been inconceivable. From J. J. Winckelmann (1717–68) came the most vital impulse through his discovery and interpretation of Greek sculpture, but its history has also to be traced through Lessing, Wieland, Herder, Heinse, Humboldt, to say nothing of Goethe, Schiller and Hölderlin and, in his beginnings, Friedrich Schlegel. In his *Thoughts on the Imitation of Greek Works in Painting and Sculpture* (1775) Winckelmann saw in Greek statues an expression of "eine edle Einfalt und eine stille Größe". The relevant passage, which was to have such a decisive influence, runs :

> The general pre-eminent characteristics of Greek masterpieces is a noble simplicity and a calm grandeur both in position and in expression. Just as the depths of the ocean ever remain calm, however much the surface may rage, so does the expression in the figures of the Greeks with all their passions show a great and self-possessed soul.

Here began the Apollonian view of Greece as measure, serenity, light, nobility in statuesque form, a view which dominated German classicism till a Dionysian side of Greece (glimpsed by Hölderlin and drawn on by Kleist in his *Penthesilea*, 1808) displaced it. With Goethe and Schiller the Greek way of life, turning art with its educational function into a religion, superseded Christianity (in whose dogmas anyhow they did not believe) as an ideal for living. If, however, the attitude to Christianity was on the whole hostile during the specifically classical years, it is equally true that at least in certain respects the classical ideal of "Humanität" was not altogether inconsistent with Christian ethics. In Goethe's later years, too, his aversion to Christianity—despite many fluctuations and inconsistencies—mellowed. A desperate attempt to unite the two was made by Hölderlin. That Christianity and classicism were not mutually exclusive and could in fact interpenetrate each other is amply demonstrated by the French seventeenth century example. In the case of Goethe and Schiller the opposition of the two is to be explained not only by the influence of the *Aufklärung* and its scepticism, but also by the radical nature of their attempt to embrace Greek values.

We turn now to a number of general features of German classicism. What above all has made critics doubt whether there is such a thing as German classicism in the full sense of a movement dominating a period and growing out of the national life is the fewness of the writers who can be assigned to it. Hölderlin, Kleist and Jean Paul are placed by literary historians in an indeterminate region between classicism and romanticism (Hölderlin closer to the former, it is true, for which reason he is treated, although briefly, in this chapter). Wieland is thought of as belonging predominantly to Rococo though as moving at times towards classic-ism, and Lessing to the *Aufklärung* though transcending it. Wilhelm von Humboldt (1767–1835), an exponent of certain aspects of the classical idea of man in its embodiment in institu-tions, belongs in the history of ideas and education not literature. A similar reservation applies to Winckelmann, who, although his influence on Goethe was profound, was more of an art historian and critic than a literary artist; while J. H. Voss (1751–1826), if he is associated with classicism, can hardly lay claim to this in any other way than through his translation of Homer. There remain only Goethe and Schiller, who themselves can be described as classical only for a part of their creative life, and then not in a complete sense, Schiller in fact at times being thought of as more baroque or (by the French) as more romantic than classical.

This restriction (and many other features besides) are due, at least in part, to the lateness of German classicism, which meant that, unlike other manifestations, the conditions out of which such a literature normally grows (a particular type of society, view of the world and the like) were not present, at any rate not as vital forces. In the eighteenth century the European world was rapidly changing, with the beginnings of modernity discernible to percep-tive minds. By the time Goethe and Schiller entered their classical phase the far-reaching revolution of individualism and subjectiv-ism had already manifested itself in the literature of *Sturm und Drang*; romanticism, which, if in some respects it looked back-wards, also looked forwards, was taking shape; and in the later years of our period the classical position was being undermined by Kleist, whose work Goethe instinctively disliked not on purely aesthetic grounds (his literary judgements were often broadly moral in character) but as symptomatic of a deep disturbance in man's relationship to the world, of shattered trust in a world that had become incomprehensible. In an age of change a critical aware-ness of the foundations and values of a social order, of a way of life may be expected, and in their work, imaginative and critical alike, Goethe and Schiller reveal their awareness. It is a peculiar characteristic of German classical literature that it endeavours to make these foundations of the classical world explicit in poetical terms, and that its exponents are imbued with the pedagogical desire to educate a public to absorb these particular values. Where-as French classicism was primarily an "esthétique", the content being general human problems, the content of German classical literature revolves largely round the idea of "Bildung" (self-shaping), the classical conception of man (known in literary history as the "Humanitätsidee").[7] It was furthermore an affirmation of these values and an answer to the questions : when is man fully man, how can he best realize his nature? If the answer is a vision of a better life with something of a utopia about it, the difficulties of achieving it under modern conditions are far from being glossed over. German classical literature is therefore highly conscious, the expression of a desire or a need rather than of a possession, a desire to create (or to revive) a certain type of man and society rather than simply a picture of man and his doings in a secure, well-established order of things. In no sense did this literature grow naturally out of and reflect a society comparable with that which revolved round the closely knit and relatively small court of Louis XIV in France, that was not only sustained by its feeling of ascendancy but unquestioningly fulfilled its principles and laws; or with that broader English society of the first half of the eighteenth century, to which its members had a strong sense of belonging and in which each had and knew his due place.

Undoubtedly, there was a Rococo court society in many German centres—Goethe's style catches something of its atmosphere—but it had neither the brilliance, the creativeness nor the compelling power of the French court. Although at this time Germany witnessed an unparalleled flowering of genius, this was not closely associated with power in the larger centres, at any rate as far as literary and intellectual life were concerned. Vienna and—for all Friedrich's enlightenment—Berlin had failed to rise to the occasion, and very few of the innumerable petty rulers were genuinely interested in the things of the mind, even if they found use for architects and musicians. Goethe paid his ruler full tribute for all he tried to do, but in the last analysis he found Karl August's Weimar inadequate and after ten years felt a desperate need, not solely attributable to the self-denial he had to practice in his relationship with Frau von Stein, for a freer, more spacious and more developed society. Moreover, he was fully aware that neither here nor anywhere else in Germany did the social foundations of a classical literature exist. That he so often found it necessary to insist that art must be sociable and closely linked to life is a measure of the extent to which he missed these pre-suppositions in German lands and, furthermore, was unhappy about the kind of art which implied their absence. In his essay *Der Literarische Sansculottismus* (written 1795), though he defends the achievements of German writers against attack, he states quite unambiguously the necessary conditions for the emergence of a classical literature and admits their absence in Germany. The result was that the man of letters and the intellectual, isolated as they were from society and a meaningful rôle in the conduct of affairs, tended to turn inwards, in literary terms from the representation of man in society (mimesis of the objective world) to the expression of the inner self and to the construction of ideal worlds. Goethe consciously struggled against this state of affairs. His Werther takes his own life not merely because of an unhappy love affair but because his exclusion from a rôle in practical affairs commensurate with his abilities drives him into an excess of inwardness from which the only escape is a violent one. Goethe was made of sterner stuff than the character he created, but he needed the experience of Italy, of the oneness with life that he found there, before the classical poet in him could fully mature.

A son of the eighteenth century and deeply rooted in it, Goethe nevertheless described the shape of future events and, particularly in his post-classical years, made a determined effort to come to terms with the new age. The picture we gain of him is that of a man seeking his way between the great antinomies of his age and, precisely because his finger was on the pulse of events, expressing on occasions opinions which, to say the least, were not consistent. Any view of him as living above the struggle in a state of Apollonian calm ignores much of the evidence. His statement that he had never known more than three weeks of unclouded well-being must be set against others about the goodness of life, just as his injunction to think well of man must be thought of together with his recurrent moods of despair about him. If he lamented the absence of a society, he was none the less clear that the days of the *ancien régime* were drawing to a close and that change was necessary, But the course and implications of the French Revolution remained an abiding problem for him as also for Schiller, so much so that their literary work, above all their classical phase, cannot be fully understood without constant reference to it. It enters directly into several of Goethe's works (e.g. *Hermann und Dorothea, Die Natürliche Tochter*) and indirectly into others. Schiller, ardent apostle of freedom as he was, was shaken by its excesses and its general course and was led in consequence to a deeper consideration of the nature of man and of freedom, while Goethe became a believer in evolution and an opponent of revolution. In no sense did they feel attuned to a real existing society, at best to an ideal one consisting of great men from all ages and countries. Hölderlin for his part, completely alienated from the life of his times, looked longingly to ancient Greece, asking with regard to the office of poet in his own day : "... und wozu Dichter in dürftiger Zeit?" (and to what end a poet in a barren age?).

Goethe's trust in the senses, his antagonism to abstract, mathematical science (witness his dislike of Newton) go some way to explaining his fear of a civilization based on the latter as well as his preference for the classical world and suggest furthermore, that at any rate in one part of his being he was pre-disposed towards this. Yet he and Schiller lived in an intellectual realm which was destroying its own foundations just as surely as the French Revolution was destroying an order of society. The relationship of German classicism to Kant was a complex one, but it seems safe to say that Kant with his view of the rôle of mind in constructing our world, e.g. in the categories of place, time and causality, undermined classicism with its belief in an objectively knowable cosmos. The conception of art too, set out in the *Critique of Judgement* as an autonomous world, free, in a word not subservient to morality, religion or anything else, was not in accord with classical theory. While Kant at the time may have been as much a symptom as an influence he indubitably provided a theoretical justification for the absolute art of the moderns. Not that Kant was basing his theory on anything but traditional art; the extreme implications that could be drawn from it for modern art were no part of his intention.

Although Goethe's purely theoretical pronouncements are anything but systematic, there are scattered throughout his writings ample statements to show unmistakably the direction of his thought. The "Antikes" of his essay *Winckelmann und sein Jahrhundert* (1805) contains a passage that is of such central importance for his classical outlook that it must be quoted :

Man is capable of much through appropriate use of individual powers, he is capable of the extraordinary through the combination of several faculties; but the unique, the quite unexpected he accomplishes only when all qualities unite in him in equal measure. The latter was the happy lot of the ancients, especially of the Greeks in their best time; to the first we moderns have been reduced by fate.

When the healthy nature of man works as a whole, when he is aware of himself in a world that has greatness, beauty, dignity and worth, when a harmonious feeling of well-being confers pure, untrammeled delight, then the universe, if it could be conscious of itself, would exult as having reached its goal and marvel at the culmination of its own evolution and essence. For what purpose is served by the profusion of suns and planets, and moons, of stars and milky ways, of comets and nebula, of worlds that have evolved and are evolving if finally a happy man cannot unconsciously rejoice in his own existence?

In one and the same way the poet lived in his imagination,

the writer of history in the political, the scientist in the material world. All held fast to the nearest, the true, the real, and even their fantasies had bone and marrow. Man and the human are esteemed as the highest value, and all his inner, his outer relationships with the world are portrayed just as they are seen with a sense of greatness. As yet feeling and reflection were not atomized, as yet that hardly curable division in the powers of man had not taken place.

Such an antique nature, in so far as it can be claimed of any one of our contemporaries, had appeared again in Winckelmann . . .

Here we have—ascribed to antique man—the conception of wholeness, his sense of belonging to a world he can affirm as having value, the joy such a relationship gives him, his strong attachment to the real, in short a state of being Goethe calls "healthy", which recalls his later famous statement to Eckermann : "The classical I call healthy, and the romantic diseased." (2 April 1829.)[8] The dichotomy of modern man is the condition with which this vision is always contrasted, and it is around the problem of wholeness and dichotomy that Schiller's philosophical writings revolve. A fundamental treatment of the problem of moral action in the light of classical wholeness forms the substance of Schiller's essay "On Grace and Dignity" (1793). Departing from and modifying Kant's rigorism, according to which an action ceases to be moral once it is in harmony with our inclinations, Schiller maintained that we are only moral when our actions proceed from a character that is good, in other words when our inclinations impel us in this direction. A character in which such a balance of duty and inclination appears Schiller calls a "schöne Seele " (beautiful soul). In a condition in which the ethical has become nature, body and soul are in harmony and interpenetrate each other, man achieves "grace". Schiller recognized, however, that there are many situations in life when such oneness of inclination and duty are not possible, when the moral law demands a supreme effort of the will, a sacrifice of self, of life. Man, in rising to this demand, achieves "dignity". The capacity for "grace" and "dignity" reveals the human being at his highest reach. In this way Schiller resolved the clash between Goethe's "nature" and Kant's rigorism. His mature tragedies portray man called upon to show "dignity", which in aesthetic terms we experience as the sublime ("On the Sublime", appeared 1801). The *Letters on the Aesthetic Education of Man* (1794–95) develop this view of man in relation to the aesthetic. Disappointed with the realities of the French Revolution Schiller came to believe that man needs not only political freedom but inner (moral) freedom and—in conformity with the classical outlook—that the way to moral action lies through the purification of the self afforded by aesthetic experience, the nature of which he examines. Yet it is characteristic of Schiller that in the same essay he paves the way for the doctrine of the autonomy of art, for the view of art as a religion and ultimately that of art for art's sake not life's sake. Again, his belief that the nature of art is such that form annihilates matter brings him close to Kant and modern theory. Quite clearly Schiller's view of man proceeds from a vision of him as he ought to be, not from his actual realization. In history, he thought, the Greeks had gone farthest towards making the vision a reality. He himself on the other hand was ever conscious of the clash of opposites, of a hardly eradicable dualism, which of course predisposed him towards the drama as his natural mode of expression.

The *Sturm und Drang* writers (and the youthful Goethe among them) had been concerned with such motifs as nature, freedom, immediacy of feeling, individuality, genius and the power of the self to create the world. When Goethe moved to Weimar, he began to outgrow these; rather, however, in their one-sidedness than as a total abandonment. The early Weimar years (i.e. preceding the flight to Italy in 1886) usher in a period of search for objective law, in the moral and the natural spheres alike, an attitude of patient submission of the self to the object in an effort to know it and to allow this knowledge to shape one's conduct towards and feelings about the world. ("Bildung", far removed from Rousseauistic primitivism, implied conscious cultivation.) In the light of what we have said earlier about the objectivity of classicism this was clearly a period of preparation, of struggle for mastery of self and life. The same years witness the beginnings of his scientific studies, which, morphological in character and, in their unmodern method, relying on observation by the eye followed by conjecture, culminated during his Italian sojourn in the idea of the *Urpflanze*, the typical plant, its essential structure or being. This amounted to a divination of the inner intention of nature, and in the same way he thought that Greek statues were a completion of this inner intention, which is of course rarely realized in actuality. His little essay *Simple Imitation of Nature, Mannerism, Style* (1789) represents style as the making manifest of this intention in sensuous material. His scientific thinking and his theorizing about art are therefore closely linked. In himself Goethe, however, was still far from the happy harmony of morality and impulse which he (and Schiller and Hölderlin with him) was to think characteristic of Greek life. Recognition of the existence of an objective moral law, the overcoming of self, an attitude of submissiveness and humility—such are the themes and the atmosphere of much of Goethe's literary work of these years, both of the hymns and of *Iphigenie auf Tauris* (not recast into final iambic verse form till the Roman period).

Iphigenie's struggle with herself to subdue selfish promptings, her healing power over others, a moral effort quite in keeping with Christianity, such is the substance of this play. However, though Iphigenie is prepared to pay the price of "dignity", the world (Thoas) responds to her example so that payment is spared her. And that she has no wish for martyrdom or even to continue her civilizing work amongst the Taurians is made abundantly clear : she longs above all to return to Greece and for a happy life in a congenial world. Her moral purity causes her to be truthful, grateful and just towards Thoas, but it does not fill her with missionary zeal or the will to self-sacrifice in such a cause. Her sense of measure and her freedom from fanaticism are unmistakable. The atmosphere of her wished-for world (Greece) is conjured up by the harmony and balance of the style, and it is through this that we witness the moral struggle, but like Goethe, she has not yet set foot in it.

In Italy Goethe sought and achieved not only insight into the nature of (classical) art but found, in all strata of the population, a way of life (a heritage of classical antiquity), which seemed to him eminently desirable : naturalness, freedom from all dichotomy, from the scruples and ravages of conscience, joy which expressed itself as a capacity to live intensely (and at the same time gracefully) in the present moment, whether in love or in the every-day practical affairs of life. A re-reading of Homer in Sicily presented him with the image of a way of life which unquestioningly accepted the real and was based on immediacy of experience. On return to Weimar, Goethe, strongly under the impression of the pagan unity of body and soul, nature and spirit he had found still alive in Italy, took into his house a vivacious young flower-girl, Christiane Vulpius, who lived with him as his *de facto* wife till he married her much later. The literary expression of this temper of mind, the *Römische Elegien* (1788–90), show in their subject matter the fruitful and basic oneness of sensual experience, appreciation of and creativity in art and intellectual awareness, while their classical metres help to reinforce the suggestion of contented and joyful union with life and mastery of the world in which the self moves. In this they do express something of the classical spirit; yet, it is hardly possible to resist the impression, particularly in the fifth

elegy, the best known of them all, that Goethe was being too conscious about his beliefs, indeed that these poems, whatever their
merits, were written to embody a thesis. To the writer of this article
at any rate it does not seem possible to detect irony in their statements and images. In labouring the foundations of a way of life
Schiller clearly goes much farther than Goethe, who, if he is no less
sententious, better succeeds in allowing such thoughts, characters
and incidents to grow naturally out of the concrete substance of
the work. Nevertheless, in *Hermann und Dorothea* (1796–97)
Goethe makes it patent that he is extolling solid, permanent human
qualities embodied in the German "Bürger" as against if not all
that the French Revolution stood for, at least many of its actual
manifestations.

The most detailed statement of the classical "Humanitätsidee"
under the conditions of contemporary life is to be found in Goethe's
Bildungsroman, Wilhelm Meisters Lehrjahre (1795–96) with its
gospel of knowing one's possibilities and limitations, of "Bildung"
through life, of balancing thought with activity in society. Wilhelm
is guided, without his knowledge, by the society of the tower, by
which we are to understand : life. In other words, the world
responds; it is basically so constituted that man can generally make
something of himself, even if there is an element in it beyond his
control, exemplified here in the fates of Mignon and the harper,
that may destroy him. This underlying optimism was shaken by the
time Goethe came to write *The Elective Affinities* (1809), a work in
which many factors conspire to wreck a harmonious and happy
relationship with the world and to leave the central character,
Ottilie, originally naive and possessing "grace", no other choice,
if she is to preserve her integrity, than to achieve "dignity". Yet,
however much his view of the possible relationship between man
and life has changed, the work is in substance no less classical than
Schiller's tragedies, and it is a good deal more satisfyingly classical
in its style and its construction.

That in the years following the Italian journey Goethe viewed
the relationship between the poet and society as problematical, as
not permitting under modern conditions the realization of the total
human being, i.e. the union of the poet and the man of action, is
fully documented in his *Torquato Tasso* (completed 1789). Here
the court society is not presented with unqualified approval since,
in as far as it accepts the poet, it sees in him largely an instrument
wherewith to outshine other courts. As in *Iphigenie auf Tauris* the
style with its balance and harmony, adapted it is true to the needs
of the situation, suggests the achievement of balance, of the unity
of the two, and it is against this impression that the events of the

play are seen. The work furnishes ample evidence of how Goethe foresaw what was to become in increasing measure the artist's situation in life, driven back from society into his inwardness, into alienation, the basic condition of the modern artist.

In his classical years Goethe undoubtedly succeeded best when he treated a modern theme in a classical style, as in the play just discussed. But he did not always do this. Impelled by the malaise with which his surroundings and contemporary events in general filled him and by the results of his and Schiller's theorizing he was seized more and more by the desire to live like a Greek, to treat only Greek materials exclusively in the Greek manner. This was the phase of his undeviating classicism, his Graeco-mania (a mania to which Schiller succumbed much less). In the visual arts he instituted prizes for the best paintings in the classical manner and was not deterred by attempts that were totally uninspired. However, after his failure to make headway with *Achilleis* (1799), an antique subject in antique form, he began to realize that such an extreme position about the Greeks was untenable. Classical metres yielded gradually to German, while for subjects he turned not merely to contemporary European life but also to non-European cultures. Nevertheless, his conviction that the Greeks, even if they had not produced the only culture, were unsurpassed in their realization of true humanity persisted till the end as did also his belief that they could be a fruitful influence in modern life.

His final word—in symbolical form—on this fruitfulness was spoken in the Helena Act of *Faust II*, parts of the beginning of which were composed about 1800, but which was completed as a whole only by 1826 (date of publication), when not only his years of doctrinaire classicism lay far behind him but he had also seen what romanticism, by now on the decline, was. Though at Schiller's insistent urging during the years 1797–1805 he had added to Part I as well as thought about Part II, the mental climate of these years was, if we except the symbol of Helena, not favourable for work on *Faust*. The bringing back of Helena from the shades, her marriage with Faust, their son Euphorion, and his death by recklessly attempting to fly, Helena's disappearance, leaving only her veil which in turn dissolves into clouds that transport Faust back to his own country—all this is a symbol not only of the reception of the Greek spirit into the modern western world, but also of the heyday of its influence and its decline, and finally of what remains from it all as a fruitful possession. But despite the beauty of its style, in which antique metres (as well as, in other parts, modern rhyme) are an important element, this episode (as also the "Klassiche Walpurgisnacht" preceding it) can only be read as Goethe's comment on and summing up of classicism. It lacks the reality of the genuine thing and, in being a comment on itself looks forward to more modern methods.

In writing his essay *Über Naive und Sentimentalische Dichtung* (1795), in which he sees the antique as naive and the sentimentive (reflective) as modern, an important motive with Schiller was to justify his own more modern manner against Goethe's, in whom he saw a synthesis of both. In other words, Schiller was aware that he was fundamentally a modern, and though he too saw the Greeks as unexcelled be became in his later years somewhat sceptical about the myth that had been created round them. His Hellenism was already evident in 1788 with his *Die Götter Griechenlands*. In this poem the gods of Greece are played off against Christianity, which for both Goethe and Schiller, was incompatible with antique wholeness, engagement with life, self-fulfilment in the here and now. Yet despite this Hellenism the question arises as to the extent, if at all, to which Schiller can be regarded as classical. The tragedies on the whole give a dark picture of life, wholeness lives in them as an idea rather than as a reality. Though his style often arranges the material in complementary polarities and though he stands foursquare as he weathers the storm, he nowhere creates the sense of resting in the real things of the world, of sensuous reality enfolding him (as Goethe does). His gaze is fixed on the ideal, he is filled with moral fervour, he lacks "grace". Even his classical metres have an inner restlessness about them.

If Goethe and Schiller portrayed man in the midst of social reality and believed that he must fulfill himself in this sphere, Hölderlin's concern was with the gods; his infatuation with the Greeks led him to seek wholeness not in society, from which he felt that the gods had withdrawn, but in union with nature, which he experienced as divine. His own age, he thought, was living in the night of history. Hyperion, a young Greek of this time, in the novel of the same name, is disillusioned with his own countrymen and with Germans, but responds deeply to the beauty of the spring. Not only the ideal vision of Greece (admittedly Hölderlin came in the course of time to see a non-Winckelmannian, Dionysian element in it), but still more his transcendence of the social, and the exalted feeling accompanying this put a distance between Hölderlin and the fully classical poet.

If the conditions of classical literature were largely lacking in Germany, we still have to ask, since the proof of the pudding is in the eating, what the result was. The sense of a need rather than of a possession and the desire to educate a community in a way of life have certainly left their mark on German classical literature, but in varying degrees. Whatever Goethe's themes were, his embeddedness in nature, his ability to evoke the atmosphere of the lasting reality of the present, the full moment, the sense of wholeness informing his style, all this, despite at times an enigmatic irony, disposes us to accept him as classical to an extent we cannot do with other German writers. With the qualifications indicated we may then accept a German classicism less as the designation of a period than as the dominant tendency of a short span of years, dominant less in reference to a broad national movement than to the number and excellence of the work produced by its few exponents. It represents the culmination of the Greek-Roman strand in European literature and at the same time a transition to something else. The latter characteristic does not so much dilute the meaning of the term classicism as reveal the tradition in its last stages, still with power to give birth to a considerable body of great works reflecting in their range a way of life, and before it declined into anaemic imitation or at best spasmodic manifestations in isolated works. Disregarding the ambiguity of the term in the meaning of general excellence on the one hand and on the other excellence of a particular kind, usages that are firmly established, we may still ask whether the interests of clarity have been served by taking *Klassik* in the sense of any excellence that is the culminating point of a development instead of reserving it for excellence that has a close affinity with Greek and Roman antiquity. It is conceivable that, although a further flowering of the antique spirit is hardly a possibility, there will be culminations of other kinds. If *Klassik* were applied to these the term would lose its significance as the designation of a specific character. There is on the other hand some justification for the existence of the two terms. *Klassik* (in the restricted sense) as well as *Klassizismus* in as much as they are not used of the same works of literature and have, moreover, the advantage of distinguishing the imitative, the borrowing of externals, the ill-digested from what is classical in spirit.

NOTES

1. Herbert Cysarz: *Reallexikon der deutschen Literaturgeschichte* (Berlin, 1954). See also Alexander Heussler, *Klassik und Klassizismus in der deutschen Literatur* (Bern, 1952).
2. For brief statements see the article on "Klassik" in *Das Kleine Lexikon der Weltliteratur* by Herman Pongs and *Sachwörterbuch der Literatur* by Gero von Wilpert (Stuttgart, 1959). For articles on "Klassik" and "Klassizismus" see this and the last mentioned work as well as Wolfgang Kayser, *Kleines Literarisches Lexikon* (Bern, 1961).

3. K. H. Halbach, "Zu Begriff und Wesen der Klassik" in *Festschrift für Paul Kluckhohn und Hermann Schneider* (Tübingen, 1948).
4. Herbert Grierson, "Classical and Romantic" in *The Background of English Literature* (London, 1925).
5. See: Henri Peyre: *Qu'est ce que le Classicisme* (Paris, 1942).
6. On German Hellenism see W. Rehm: *Griechentum und Goethezeit* (München, 1952); and in English H. Trevelyan: *The Popular Background to Goethe's Hellenism* (London, 1934); and his *Goethe and the Greeks* (Cambridge, 1942); also Henry Hatfield: *Aesthetic Paganism in German Literature* (Cambridge, Mass., 1964).
7. See Paul Kluckhohn: *Die Idee des Menschen in der Goethezeit* (Stuttgart, 1946). For an elaborate analysis, mostly over-patterned, of the underlying ideas of the Age of Goethe see H. A. Korff's *Geist der Goethezeit* (5 vols., the second volume being devoted to the classical phase), (Leipzig, 1923–57).
8. See Erich Jenisch: "Das Klassische nenne ich das Gesunde und das Romantische das Kranke" in *Goethe, Neue Folge der Jahrbuchs der Goethe-Gesellschaft*, vol. 19, 1957. For a comparison of classicism and romanticism, worked out neatly as opposites, Fr. Strich: *Deutsche Klassik und Romantik* (Bern, 1949).

SELECT BIBLIOGRAPHY

Comprehensive bibliographies are given by (a) H. Cysarz at the end of his article on "Klassik" in *Reallexikon der deutschen Literaturgeschichte*, Band I, Lieferung 19 (2nd edition), Berlin, 1958 (date of this Lieferung); (b) H. W. Eppelsheimer in *Handbuch der Weltliteratur* (3rd edition), (Frankfurt/Main, 1960), under the heading "Deutsche Klassik"; (c) Wilhelm Kosch in *Deutsches Literatur-Lexikon*, volume 2, (Bern, 1952) in article "Klassisch".

Benz, Richard: *Die Zeit der deutschen Klassik* (Stuttgart, 1953).
Benz, Richard: *Wandel des Bildes der Antike in Deutschland* (München, 1948).
Cysarz, Herbert: *Reallexikon der deutschen Literaturgeschichte* (articles on "Klassik", "Klassiker", "Klassizismus") (Berlin, 1954f.).
Eliot, T. S.: *What is a Classic?* (London, 1945).
Grierson, Herbert: "Classical and Romantic" in *The Background of English Literature* (London, 1925).
Halbach, K. H.: "Zu Begriff und Wesen der Klassik" in *Festschrift für Paul Kluckhohn und Hermann Schneider* (Tübingen, 1948).
Hatfield, Henry: *Aesthetic Paganism in German Literature* (Cambridge, Massachusetts, 1964).
Heussler, Alexander: *Klassik und Klassizismus in der deutschen Literatur* (Bern, 1952).
Jenisch, Erich: "Das Klassische nenne ich das Gesunde und das Romantische das Kranke" in *Goethe, Neue Folge des Jahrbuchs der Goethe-Gesellschaft*, vol. 19 (1957).

Kayser, Wolfgang: *Kleines Literarisches Lexikon* (articles on "Klassik", "Klassizismus"), vol. 1, 3rd ed. (Bern, 1961).

Kluckhohn, Paul: *Die Idee des Menschen in der Goethezeit* (Stuttgart, 1946).

Korff, H. A.: *Geist der Goethezeit* (5 vols.) (Leipzig, 1923–57).

Newald Richard: *Deutsche Philologie im Aufriss* (article "Klassisches Altertum und deutsche Literatur", vol. 2) (Berlin, 1960).

Peyre, Henri: *Qu'est ce que le Classicisme* (Paris, 1942).

Pongs, Hermann: *Das Kleine Lexikon der Weltliteratur*, 2nd ed. (articles on "Klassik" and "Klassizismus") (Stuttgart, 1956).

Rehm, Walter: *Griechentum und Goethezeit*, 3rd ed. (München, 1952).

Schultz, Franz: *Klassik und Romantik der Deutschen*, vol. 1 Die Grundlagen der klassisch-romantischen Literatur 1780–1830; vol. 2 Wesen und Form der klassich-romantischen Literatur 1780–1830, 2nd ed. (Stuttgart, 1952).

Strich, F.: *Deutsche Klassik und Romantik*, 4th ed. (Bern, 1949).

Trevelyan, H.: *The Popular Background to Goethe's Hellenism* (London, 1934).

Trevelyan, H.: *Goethe and the Greeks* (Cambridge, 1942).

Wilpert, Gero von: *Sachwörterbuch der Literatur*, 2nd ed. (articles on "Klassik" and "Klassizismus") (Stuttgart, 1959).

Romanticism

VI

Romanticism

LAWRENCE RYAN

IN Novalis' novel *Heinrich von Ofterdingen* the poet Klingsohr, when discussing the nature of poetry in terms that obviously represent an important aspect of the author's own views on the subject, places marked emphasis upon the necessity of reflection and self-awareness, of sobriety and clarity :

> Nothing is more indispensable to the poet than insight into the nature of every poetic operation, acquaintance with the means of attaining every objective, and presence of mind to select the most fitting means according to time and circumstances...The young poet cannot be too cool or reflective... Poetry must be conducted above all as a strictly regulated art.[1]

The kind of consciousness and awareness demanded here seems not quite reconcilable with certain views of Romanticism fashionable at least in England, which regard it as having sacrificed form and sobriety, closeness of perception and treatment of real things to a somewhat unclear evocation of an irrational world dominated by the forces of nature and the unconscious. But to reduce Romanticism to such an attitude would be as incomplete and misleading as, for example—to illustrate by reference to a now largely superseded view of German Classicism, to define the latter in terms of a so-called ideal of "humanity" or "Bildung". And it would be equally inadequate to regard the so-called "satanic" Romanticism as the only kind, to seize upon those aspects of the movement that, viewed unhistorically, might seem to be peculiarly "modern", or, while placing undue and tendentious emphasis on the fact that German Romanticism arose in a country that more than a hundred years later produced National Socialism, to perpetuate the fallacy of confusing "post hoc" and "propter hoc". By the same token, those whose main access to German Romanticism is through the musical rendition of some of its more trifling works (those of Eichendorff, Brentano or Mörike, or even the worse poems of Heine), are liable to misjudgement. In a sense, German Romanticism provides a more decisive refutation of many of the grounds on which it is fashionable for Romanticism to be decried than does the comparable literature of most other countries. The

emphasis placed by Novalis—and others—on the central importance of reflection in poetic production may therefore provide a
useful starting point.

To proceed in this way may seem at first sight to involve an
undue limitation of the subject. A brief methodological consideration seems therefore indicated, in order that we may justify our
neglect of the concept "Romanticism" itself. Unfortunately, much
contemporary criticism has not succeeded in freeing itself from the
all too inviting temptation to deduce the characteristics of a supposed period of literary history from the word chosen to designate
it, thus assuming—implicitly or explicitly—that the word itself is
to be regarded as an entity with certain intrinsic properties of its
own. To attempt to establish a relationship between the more
"popular" and the allegedly more "scientific" ("wissenschaftlich")
meanings of the word Romanticism would be no less futile than, for
example, to situate the term "classical", regarded as a category of
literary periodicization, within the whole range of meanings that
the word "classical" seems to connote, ranging from the "classical"
as the outstanding instance of anything whatsoever to the
"classical" as that pertaining to ancient times; we shall consequently refrain from taking into account the more common connotations of the word "romantic", in order to avoid as far as possible
—precisely within the framework of an enterprise that is by its
whole conception peculiarly liable to this fault—the danger of
substituting a juggling with words for the recognition of historical
peculiarity. Similarly, it is not our intention to take as a starting
point for the characterization of a literary trend such unhistorically
framed questions as : What is Classicism? What is Romanticism?
or : What is Realism?, and to give as an answer some equally unhistorical formula, such that Classicism is determined by a "sense
of wholeness", Romanticism by a "longing for the infinite", or
Realism by the "observation of the actual". For this would also
involve the substitution of arbitrarily manufactured entities for the
complex variables of historical development. This is of course not
to deny that one might trace the actual history of the term
"Romanticism" (this has been adequately done),[2] or compare what
one might for convenience agree to call German Romanticism with
literary manifestations in Germany and elsewhere—even if the
conclusions often reached by devotees of so-called comparative
literature (for example, that within the framework of European
literature the whole movement of German literature "between the
date of Klopstock's *Messiah* (1748) and the death of Goethe
(1832)"[3] must be called "romantic") do not add very much to our
insight into the complexities of German literature. In particular,

we wish to avoid that facile polarization of the classical and the
Romantic that has often been attempted in literary studies, but
whose inapplicability is readily demonstrable; thus our brief reference to Hölderlin in the course of these remarks is by no means
intended to deny that in a meaningful sense he embodies "classical"
tendencies in German literature to as great a degree as any other
writer. If one is to embark at all on the somewhat foolhardy
enterprise of organizing German literature in terms of a string of
period concepts, it would seem comparatively fruitful to attempt
here to isolate and describe only some of the various tendencies
that are frequently designated "Romantic", in order thus to show
at least a partial consistency within a limited sphere, rather than
making any claim to giving a comprehensive account. The restric-
tiveness of the following remarks should be understood in this sense.

As already suggested, the concept of poetic reflection may provide a starting-point. This implies the view that modern poetry is
essentially compounded both of creative production and philosophical reflection, indeed that it attains its poetic character only
by the incorporation of reflection. The diagnosis given by various
Romantic writers of their own historical situation accords with
this view that the present age is to be characterized in terms of a
dichotomy—or, according to emphasis—of a synthesis of the creative and the reflective, of nature and spirit. Such a belief found
one of its more famous formulations in the writings of Schiller,
who in his treatise *Über naive und sentimentalische Dichtung* distinguished the modern relationship to nature from that of the ancients :
the modern writer no longer *is* nature, but "seeks" that union with
nature that has been precluded by the development of self-
consciousness. Thus his goal is no longer the achievement of a
perfectly realized coalescence, but an infinite approximation to
an essentially unrealizable ideal. The "sentimentality" (not to be
confused with the common meaning of the word) of modern poetry
is precisely its awareness of the discrepancy between nature and
spirit and its consistent determination by that awareness. In a
similar vein, Friedrich Schlegel, whose essay *Vom Studium der
griechischen Poesie* is one of the more important Romantic writings, regards "reflection on the relationship of the real and the
ideal" as a constituent characteristic of modern literature. His
brother August Wilhelm Schlegel, whose lectures contributed much
to the popularization of Romanticism, makes a similar point :
ancient literature was one of "possession", that of modern times
one of "longing", which no longer "stands firmly upon the ground
of the present", but goes back and forth between memory of the
past and presentiment of the future. On the whole, "feelings are

more inward, the imagination less corporeal, thought more contemplative"; whereas the Greek ideal of humanity was "perfect unison and equilibrium of all forces", the moderns "have come to an awareness of inner duality which makes such an ideal impossible; therefore the striving of its poetry is to reconcile these two worlds, the spiritual and the sensual, between which we are divided", even though this reconciliation can of course no longer take the form of the "original consciousless unity of form and matter", but is a "more inward interpenetration of both as two contraries".[4] Similar views are put forward by Hölderlin in his contrasting of the Greek and the "Hesperian", of the Greek "sons of nature", who in art gave expression to a "beauty" that was still undifferentiatedly divine and human, and the modern writer, who is at first excluded by his reflectiveness from immediate access to "all transforming enthusiasm". And Hegel defines Romantic art in related terms, as determined by an "inwardness" that is constituted by the spirit's finding itself through self-negation :

> The simple, undifferentiated totality of the ideal is dissolved and falls into the double totality of external appearance and a subjectivity turned in upon itself, so that the spirit may through this separation attain a more profound reconciliation in its own element of the inward ... Thereby the spirit gains consciousness of having its otherness, its *existence*, as spirit in itself and thus for the first time of enjoying its own infinity and freedom ... This raising of the spirit *to itself*, through which it gains in itself that objectivity that otherwise it had to seek in the external and the sensual, and feels and knows itself in this unity with itself, constitutes the basic principle of Romantic art.[5]

This formulation of Hegel admittedly places the emphasis somewhat differently from the Romantic writers themselves (from whom Hegel expressly distances himself in various of his writings), but a certain correspondence is nevertheless evident. The Romantics were concerned, however, less with the inwardness of the self-mediation of the subject than with its belongingness to a whole gradated system of worldly existence; or, to put it differently, subjective categories were at the same time regarded as functions of objective existence. That is to say, Romanticism was closely allied with philosophical Idealism and must be viewed against the background of the Idealist attempt to reconcile the dichotomy of the self and the world by postulating a dialectical process of the self-finding of the subject through its external realization. A brief characterization of some of the main impulses of Idealism is therefore in place.

Historically speaking, Idealistic philosophy goes back in a sense to Kant, who attempted to provide a new basis of metaphysics by mediating between the opposite extremes of rationalism, with its naive construction of the suprasensual and the divine, and the empiricism and scepticism of Hume and others. But although the intention of his "Copernican revolution", by which perception is no longer to be conditioned by objects, but rather appearances by perception, was to establish the limitations of human perception, bound as it is on the one hand by the material object of apprehension, on the other by the transcendentally effective categories of its own operation, the effect of Kant's philosophy was rather to stimulate reflection on the self-subsistent and creative elements of subjectivity. This can be seen in the philosophy of Fichte, who indeed describes his own *Wissenschaftslehre* as but a developed and enlightened form of Kant's philosophy, namely as an attempt to reconcile the two main aspects of Kantian dualism, the "active" (willing) and "passive" (perceiving) functions of the mind. In fact, a very great deal of Idealistic philosophy—and of Romanticism—can be regarded as an attempt to mediate between the two poles of this opposition and to present all human thought, indeed the totality of existence, as the emanation of a single universal principle of being.

Fichte found the unifying principle in the process of the self-constitution of consciousness as such : he called his main work the *Wissenschaftslehre* because it presents a reflection upon reflection itself, and reveals the transcendental presuppositions of consciousness such as are contemplated by the philosopher in the act of "intellektuelle Anschauung"—which Fichte defines as reflection upon the act of consciousness itself, as awareness on the part of the philosopher of the "absolute" consciousness that is a condition of subjectivity as such. In his explanation of those experiences that are "accompanied by a feeling of necessity", that seem to be conditioned by an external world, he establishes that their apparent "object" is—from the point of view of the philosophical insight just characterized—in reality but a "Nicht-Ich" posited by the "Ich" as a necessary concomitant of its positing of itself (for the nature of the "Ich", of subjectivity, is *self*-consciousness, constituted by an "activity returning into itself", which therefore implies the existence of an apparent external barrier and stimulus—which Fichte calls the "Anstoß"). In other words : subjectivity is shown even in its apparent object-relatedness and object-affectedness to be determined by immanent laws of its own being. This transcendental basis of consciousness is not understood by the finite object, which does not reflect upon the "productive imagination", that unconscious activity which posits the (apparent) object—but the great stimulus of Fichte's philosophy lay precisely in its claim to transcend "normal" consciousness in the name of an "absolute subject" that in its transcendental universality is subordinate entirely to its own laws.

A further important step was taken by Schelling, who—as it were—extended the sphere of Fichte's philosophizing to include the world of nature : the principle of an "activity returning into itself" is now to apply not only to human consciousness, but also to living and inanimate nature. The constitution of consciousness itself is pre-figured especially in the natural "organism", which as an element of self-centred life embodies the same essential structure as that of consciousness, even though itself it exists still on a pre-conscious level. Thus Schelling can say that spirit is a conscious form of nature, whereas nature is unconscious mind ("Geist ist bewußte Natur, Natur ist unbewußter Geist")—in which relationship it is not the distinguishing feature, but rather the continuity that is emphasized. For Schelling proceeds to work out a whole gradated system of self-evolving life that is continually raising itself to a higher power of itself, beginning with the lowest forms and cul-minating in the re-creation of the original undifferentiated unity in artistic creation (as he saw it in one period of his work at least— the "Romantic" period in Schelling was short-lived).

There are several important questions touched on here. First there is the new conception of nature, which becomes both a parallel to and a preliminary stage of consciousness (which element is lacking in Fichte). This means that the conscious and the uncon-scious, subject and object, are ultimately reducible to—in the sense that in reality they are but higher powers of—an absolute indifference, a state of undifferentiated unity. (Because of the con-stant recourse to this concept Schelling's philosophy of the period around 1800 is generally called "philosophy of identity"; but in one form or another such an "identity" is a basic Romantic pre-cept.) Because of the shift in emphasis (with respect to Fichte), however, the "intellektuelle Anschauung" is no longer inwardly directed (as with the Fichtean self-contemplation of reflective consciousness), but is as it were directed outwards, is the appre-hension of a unity of all being, a moment of ecstatic oneness with the universe. In this sense Hölderlin has also defined it as a state of "oneness with all that lives". This kind of Idealism thus partakes of a certain mystic quality—even if its ultimate unity, as Hegel puts it in scornful allusion to Schelling in his preface to the *Phenomenology of Mind*, might seem to be like the "night in which all cows are black". The point is, however, that such speculations enable the setting-up of a whole series of analogues between the various levels of the cosmic structure, since all such levels embody a single dialectical principle of self-finding through self-separation : "Romantic" medicine and "Romantic" psychology[6] are derivable largely from this general view, as also are the Romantic attitudes to the dream and the subconscious, which are widely regarded as manifestations of human belongingness to the totality of universal life, of which consciousness is a highly developed, but by no means fully emancipated form.

Another significant aspect of this view is the high evaluation, even glorification, of art that it implies. According to Schelling, the constant process of self-division and self-unifying that constitutes the structure of both nature and history is "closed" only in the activity of the artistic genius, which is both "conscious" (art is in a sense "applied" by the artist) and "unconscious" (his genius is in a sense given him, is beyond his control). In the work of art these two poles of being, which, though ever reunited, have ever been torn apart, are combined into a single and indissoluble whole. Thus art is the objectivization of the "intellektuelle Anschauung", the explicit realization of that ultimate unity of all things that can otherwise only be ecstatically and intuitively apprehended :

> For it is precisely that original ground of all harmony of the subjective and the objective, which in its original form could only be presented by the "intellektuelle Anschauung", that is completely removed from the subjective by the work of art and becomes quite objective.[7]

The work of art thus occupies a unique position, virtually at the pinnacle of the universe, in that it achieves conscious and objective representation of what was hitherto not present at any stage in harmonious completeness.

Seen in this light, art is not a "spontaneous overflow of powerful feelings", but is a product of self-consciousness, of "Besonnenheit", as much as of "inspiration". In other words, the Romantic ideal of art is a fusion of poetry and reflection, of literature and philosophy. One of the consequences of the view of Schelling just outlined is that art is "the only true and permanent organ and at the same time document of philosophy", as it can demonstrate "what philosophy cannot externalize, namely the consciousless in action and production and its original unity with the conscious".[8] In a similar sense, the fusion of literature and philosophy, that is, the production of a literature embodying philosophical reflection, formed one of the main Romantic objectives. As Friedrich Schlegel puts it : "All art is to become science ('Wissenschaft'), and all science is to become art; poetry and philosophy are to be united";[9]

"What can be done as long as poetry and philosophy are separate is done and complete. Thus the time has come to combine them".[10] Novalis expresses a similar thought when he finds in the conscious self-penetration of genius an absolute starting-point from which the whole of the world can be "moved" : "The point outside the world is given, and Archimedes can now fulfil his promise".[11]

A further sign of the Romantics' tendency to synthesize opposites is evident in their concern with defining their position within a more or less universal historical framework. The course of history tended to be seen as consisting of three stages, an original state of unity (a Golden Age), the intermediary stage of the present, where the dissonances of reflection are unresolved, and an anticipated stage of harmonization. These stages are of course actualized in various ways : not only Greece, but also the Middle Ages came to stand for the original statement of unity; Novalis' *Heinrich von Ofterdingen* is set in the Middle Ages, his essay *Europa* takes the medieval dominance of the Roman Catholic Church as its starting point. Indeed, the Romantics have often been accused of glorifying the Middle Ages and therefore looking backward rather than forward. In a sense, this may apply to certain writers belonging to a later stage of development, also to Wackenroder (and even Friedrich Schlegel was converted eventually to the Roman Catholic Church), but the characteristic Romantic attitude is to regard the Middle Ages as a precursor of a new "golden age" to come.

This emerges clearly from Novalis' essay *Europa*, in which he gives an historical account of the breaking down of the medieval unity, of the Reformation, Counter-Reformation, Enlightenment, French Revolution, seeing in each of these movements "notable crystallizations of the material of history", which have, however, tended to lose their creative impulse by becoming "fixed" into literal rigidity :

> Is the Revolution to remain merely the French Revolution, just as the Reformation remained merely the Lutheran Revolution? Is Protestantism, as a revolutionary movement, once more to become unnaturally rigid? Is one codified faith to be replaced by another?[12]

Against this tendency to coagulation Novalis sets a readiness to "learn" from history; the reader is referred to the set of connections that make up the whole context of history and invited to use the "magic wand of analogy" to re-interpret the present in the light of a kind of "intellektuelle Anschauung" of the "political self". In Novalis' view this must result in a new vision of wholeness, of the simultaneity of past, present and future, evinced rather in poetry than in organized religion. In the poetic proclamation with which the essay ends are combined an organic view of history and a post-French-Revolution spirit of poetic emancipation. Poetry thus gains a new dignity, in that it not merely *presents* the ideal to which all striving is directed, but is itself the means that principally enables such an ideal to be envisaged.[13]

Such a view is a further manifestation on the one hand of the Romantic emphasis of the continuity and homogeneity and thus of the ultimate unity of all things, on the other hand of the possibility of realizing this unity in a new and total creation. The view of nature as a kind of anticipatory analogue of human life is based upon such a presupposition. This applies also to other fields : thus the Romantics were concerned with showing that artistic genius was not something unhistorical and unique, but rather a more universal force raised to a higher power. In this sense, Novalis states that genius is "necessary for everything", what usually goes by that name is in reality "genius of genius". In other words, human perception and consciousness contain already a creative element, which, however, in the case of the artist is enabled to "coexist with the conscious will" (as Coleridge puts it in his rather derivative distinction between the primary and the secondary imagination) and is thus potentiated by reflection. It is misleading to speak in this context of "German theories of vegetable genius",[14] as it is precisely the "vegetable" element—the lack of a co-directing conscious will—that no longer applies to artistic creation. The tendency to regard the phenomena of human consciousness as the raising of the processes of nature to a higher power is shown in the various formulae such as "genius of genius", "poetry of poetry", that abound in Romantic writings : in such cases, artistic creation is shown as the self-surpassing of what has come into being through the process of history, but is at the same time endowed with the absoluteness of self-consciousness. In a sense, therefore, such motives echo the view of Schelling that poetry, as the objectivization of a totality that is not otherwise realizable, is the only adequate means of establishing the harmony of the world.

These general tendencies can now be illustrated more precisely with relation to particular writers. The concept of Romantic irony,[15] which represents a distinctive German contribution to Romantic theory, fits generally into the pattern already outlined. Its theoretical aspects were developed most fully by Friedrich Schlegel, who regarded his concept of irony as standing in some relationship to the irony of Socrates. It could be said that in each case the position of irony is an intermediary one, distinguishable both from the finite involvement that it relativizes (by mockery) and from the as yet unattainable transcendence that it hints at precisely by the act of freeing itself from the finite. Thus irony becomes a means of overcoming initial limitedness while still being engaged in a kind of "infinite approximation" to an ideal goal; Schlegel attributes to it "a feeling of the unresolvable opposition of the infinite and the finite, the impossibility"—but also the "necessity"—"of complete communication".[16] In that what is ironicized is thereby relativized, the use of irony suggests a "progression" beyond that which is actually presented or explicitly stated. This "indirect" progression is not an arbitrary device, but —according to Schlegel—a necessary process, in that transcendence is only possible by a constant rising above onself and that to which one is finitely bound : irony is "the freest of all licences, for by it one transcends oneself; but also the most strictly prescribed, for it is absolutely necessary".[17]

This applies in more than one way. It is related not only to the internal structure of the work itself, but also to the attitude of the artist to his own work, which latter therefore does not merely *embody* irony, but is itself an *object* of irony : for the self-transcendence of the artist is evinced in a self-distancing from the fiction of his work. Artistic activity thus becomes an "alternation between self-creation and self-destruction",[18] that is, an ever repeated self-positing that is constantly being relativized. From this stems the element of "destruction of illusion" that can best be regarded as one of the cruder manifestations of Romantic irony. In some writers, this destruction of illusion takes the form of the intrusion of the author into the action or narrative, in such a way that he does not merely comment on it, but also refers explicitly to the work as such, not just to the happenings presented in it. Or the (not altogether novel) device of a "play within a play" is adopted, for example by Tieck in his play *Der gestiefelte Kater* (*Puss in Boots*), which incorporates an audience as well as a performance.

But irony—for Schlegel—does not always take the form of such overt self-distancing from the object of one's own creation. He regarded Goethe's novel *Wilhelm Meisters Lehrjahre* as an outstanding example : a spirit of irony "hovers over the whole work", showing itself for example in the fact that the author "takes the persons and events so lightly, so capriciously, scarcely ever mentions the hero without irony and seems to be smiling down upon his masterpiece himself from an intellectual vantage point" ("von der Höhe seines Geistes").[19] But this does not prevent the work from being perfectly serious ("heiligster Ernst"); for the irony consists to a large extent in the sovereign completeness and

thoroughness of its design as a "completely organized and organizing work",[20] in which "every necessary part of the one and indi-
visible novel becomes a system in itself".[21] In Schlegel's view, one
gains the impression that the work is a representation of the
totality of human life, in which each element is at once independent and subordinate to the whole, has its "own independent
being" and is at the same time but "a small part of the infinite
world".[22] But this seeming self-representation of life is mediated
by the "freedom of a perfectly developed mind".[23] Thus irony
shows itself as the ability to transcend finite particularity in an
adumbration of the whole, as is clearly indicated in one programmatic passage :

> It is necessary to be able to abstract from all particularity, to
> comprehend the general without losing sight of the particular
> ("das Allgemeine schwebend zu fassen"), to survey a whole mass
> of material and grasp it in its wholeness, to investigate even the
> most hidden and combine the most disparate. We must raise
> ourselves above our own love and be able to destroy mentally
> what we worship; otherwise, whatever qualities we have, we
> lack feeling for the universe.[24]

From this it can be seen that for Schlegel irony has a direct
relationship to the presentiment of the totality of things : in this
sense it is "progressive" and one of the principal means of attain-
ing the "progressive universal poetry" that in one of his most
famous fragments he offers as a definition of Romantic poetry. In
another revealing definition, Schlegel calls irony an "indirect enthusiasm",[25] an indirect approximation to that ecstatic sense of
"oneness with all that is" that for so many writers of the Classical-
Romantic age constituted the nature of enthusiasm. This "universality" is for Schlegel the ultimate goal of Romantic poetry, which
is—through the mediation of reflection made necessary by historical development—to "reunite all the separate literary genres", to
be an "image of the age", presented in a series of "reflections" forever raising themselves—"as in an endless series of mirrors"—to a
higher power of themselves.[26] It is interesting to note that for
Schlegel the word "Romantic" in this connection seems closely
related to the form of the novel : "A novel is a Romantic book".[27]
For the novel, as the least regulated and most expansive of all
genres, would seem best fitted to accommodate this universality.

In his *Gespräch über die Poesie* Schlegel reveals a further dimension. If poetry ("Poesie") is not merely the word of the poet, but
is an element of all existence, if life itself is "the one poem of the
divinity",[28] then the work of the artist is in reality the reflective re-

creation of this ever-present divine element, is a partial objectivization of the ubiquitous "spirit of poetry" : "All sacred play of art is but a distant imitation of the infinite play of the world, the eternally self-constituting work of art".[29] In other words, Schlegel regards poetry (in its usual sense) as but an intensification, an organic development of the whole organized system of life, the recreation of this system in conscious production (this is essentially what he claims for *Wilhelm Meister*) : as the human being altogether is to nature, so is the artist to the human being. It is therefore not surprising that the *Gespräch über die Poesie* contains a plea for the creation of a "new mythology", for a form of art that would transfigure the whole of human existence, both in the autonomy of its self-consciousness and its supra-human, "mythical" basis.

In that irony—according to this view—is basically an integration of reflection upon a work of art with the work of art itself, it is a clear instance of that potentiation of creativity by reflection that forms one of the central impulses of Romanticism. It is closely related—as already indicated—to the very similar Romantic attitude to "criticism" : not only is criticism to embody a high degree of empathy, its objective is also—by transcending the work while still taking its starting point in the work—to raise the work, or at least that element of the universal force of "poetry" that is objectified in the work, to a higher power of itself. Thus Schlegel could refer to his criticism of Goethe's *Wilhelm Meister* as his "Über-Meister".

Various important connections exist between the Romantic writers and Hölderlin. Indeed, Hölderlin's novel *Hyperion* could in a sense be regarded as embodying essential aspects of the Romantic idea of potentiation through reflection. The complex narrative structure of this work is such that the whole novel, written in the epistolary form, consists of one long process of reflection upon a series of events that is already concluded, so that the structure of the novel is to be seen in terms of the developing attitude of the narrator to his own previous experiences; it culminates in his gaining a kind of total perspective upon the whole of his past life, a new vision of wholeness that finds its natural expression in poetic utterance. By the establishment and raising to a conscious level of a continuity of development between the narrated events, the simultaneous or immediately following reflections of the hero and his (much later) reflections as narrator, Hölderlin has given a new dimension to the epistolary novel and at the same time

created a work that embodies most fully the self-constituting unity
of "progressive" self-mediation.[30]

In the whole nature of his poetry—and clearly also in his poetic
theory—Hölderlin reveals tendencies relevant here. He regarded
consciousness of totality as the pre-supposition of his poetry, whose
"prophetic" nature it is precisely to present all temporal happenings
ultimately from the perspective of such an encompassing vision—
his poetic theory is concerned largely with the working out of the
modulations of a poetic mediation between the divine and the
human agent.[31] Thus in his essay *Über Religion* he regards poetry
as the means of establishing the "religious sphere" of communication between the human and the divine, and in his essay *Das
Werden im Vergehen* the function of poetry in establishing an
awareness of historical continuity precisely in times of change and
transition is analysed. The high seriousness of Hölderlin's odes,
elegies and hymns may separate him from his contemporaries, but
his situation of the "prophetic" utterance of the poet within the
whole process of history is such as to relate him to the Romantic
integration of poetry with the whole of historical development.
Just as Novalis—in his essay *Europa*—could envisage a coming
politico-religious harmony for which poetry provided a source of
inspiration, so could Hölderlin—much more expressly—regard his
poetry as a necessary preparation for the envisaged coming of the
gods. This whole view of poetry draws widely upon the speculative
impulses of Idealism and has its essential character largely in the
attempt to invest poetry with the capacity to relate human life with
the absolute and the divine, that is to say, to incorporate into it the
functions of philosophy and religion; this view is one of the most
fruitful consequences of the Romantic attempt to integrate reflection with poetic utterance.

It is noteworthy that whereas the concept of irony plays such
an important part in Friedrich Schlegel's view of poetry, it hardly
occurs at all in the writings of Novalis (Friedrich von Hardenberg);
indeed, he even seems to minimize its usefulness, as when in one of
his fragments he states that what Schlegel calls irony is in his view
but the characteristic of "genuine reflectiveness, true presence of
mind".[32] This points to an important difference in emphasis between the two writers. For Schlegel, irony is an expression of the
necessary incompleteness of "progressive universal poetry", is only
an "indirect" enthusiasm, whereas Novalis posits the possibility of
an intuitive grasp of totality, whereby the empirical self can be
raised to the "greater self—that is one and all at the same time" :[33]
"Man can at every moment be a suprasensual being".[34]

This characteristic bent of Novalis' thought can be illustrated by a brief reference to his dithyrambs *To Night*. He rejects the world of "light", of "day", in favour of the "night" : although the former informs the whole of earthly existence in "countless transformations", its sphere is circumscribed, spatially and temporarily, whereas night brings with it timelessness and permanence. From this it emerges that night is not merely a contrasting phase in the succession of light and darkness, but that "true night" is a world of inwardness—or of ecstasy—that apprehends a totality of being. That it is bound up with the motive of death is made evident particularly in the third of the six hymns, in which Novalis recalls the premature death of his fiancée Sophie von Kühn and alludes to the moment of ecstatic rebirth, when the "enthusiasm for the night" came over him and the whole of "earthly splendour" was dissolved together with the poet's sorrow, so that he felt himself taken up into an eternal reunion. A development similar to this quasi-mystical experience is enacted in other spheres : the turning to the night becomes fused with Christianity as a religion of death, the symbol of the cross being a "banner of victory" indicating the conquest of life. This view is also worked out historically (in the fifth hymn) : whereas for the world of antiquity death had been a frightening and incomprehensible force, the "New World" must learn to regard it as a kind of liberation and rebirth. Such an evaluation of night, of death, of love is a typically Romantic attitude. For Romantic art—as Hegel puts it—regards death no longer as "mere negation", but as one that "reverts to the affirmative, as resurrection of the spirit from its mere naturality and unfitting finitude".[35]

This idea of an "inner world" is made more precise by Novalis' concept of the "Weg nach innen", which is not so much a retreat from the external world as rather an encompassing of the external in its totality—in a totality that is externally never present : "In us, or nowhere, is eternity with its worlds, the past and the future". The external appears as a kind of "shadow world" that is to be transformed into a no longer deficient aspect of itself.[36] Such a transformation is anticipated by the "magic" power of the poet, his "art of freely manipulating the world of the senses".[37] The acquisition of such an ability is presented in Novalis' novel *Heinrich von Ofterdingen*, where the hero traverses various spheres of existence, embodied in the other characters of the novel. As Klingsohr puts it : "The land of poetry, the poetic Orient, has greeted you with its sweet melancholy; war has addressed you in its wild splendour, and nature and history have met you in the guise of a miner and a hermit", to which Heinrich adds "the divine phenomenon of love".[38] The accumulation of inner totality is—as indicated in the notes that are almost all that was completed of the second part of the work, with its sub-title "The Fulfilment" —finally such that Heinrich not only finds the "blue flower"—that famous symbol of Romantic longing (as it has become) that appears to him in the dream with which the novel opens and evokes in him his poetic longing—, but is able to pluck it and thus destroy the "spell" of the seasons to which the blue flower is still subject : "Heinrich destroys the kingdom of the sun"[39] and ushers in the new Golden Age. The novel is thus not only an account of the development of the poet to insight and maturity, it also presents the poetic anticipation of the complete transformation of the world.

In this sense, the path followed by Heinrich von Ofterdingen is not merely an "inward" one, but is as it were directed outward at the same time; or in terms of the basic precept of Novalis outlined above : the final attainment by the poet of consciousness of his poetic mission brings with it also the "magic" power to transform the world. This is of course not a naive presumption to unlimited power by the poet, but is based on the presupposition of an ultimate unity of the inner and the outer worlds, which allows the possibility of all things external being subordinated to an inwardly based activity that is however innately prefigured in the external world from the first : "the world must have an inborn tendency to accord with me—to be according to my will".[40] Or in more detail :

What is nature?—An encyclopaedic, systematic index or plan of our minds. Why should we rest content with the mere cataloguing of our treasures?—let us see them ourselves—and work upon them and use them in various ways.

The fate that oppresses us is the sloth of our minds. By extension and development of our activity we shall transform ourselves into fate.

Everything seems to be streaming in upon us, because we do not stream forth. We are negative, because we wish to be—the more positive we become, the more negative will the world around us become—until finally there will be no more negation, but we are all in all. *God wants gods*.[41]

Thus "fate and the mind are names for a single concept",[42] as Heinrich finally realizes; in that he becomes a mature poet ("Meister"), each of his actions is at the same time a "manifestation of the great, simple, unenfolded world—God's word".[43] With the acceptance of this point of view Novalis—as he himself recognizes—has taken up and developed, if with a somewhat different

emphasis, the doctrine of the essentially active and creative function of human consciousness put forward by Fichte : "Fichte has
taught—and developed—the active use of the organs of thought" ;[44]
Fichte's *Wissenschaftslehre*, as he says elsewhere, is "simply a
schematic outline of the inner nature of the artist".[45]

The working out of this theme—the awakening to consciousness (therefore the emphasis placed on "Besonnenheit") and the
consequent objectivization of the implicit unity of all things—has
important implications for the structure of the novel, in which all
seems to proceed without any sign of conflict or difficulty and
with predetermined ease and necessity. For Novalis is concerned
to show that not only does the "dream" become a "world", but
the "world" becomes a "dream", that the self-realization of the
poet is at the same time the self-poeticization of the world, so that
both are as it were co-operating to the same pre-ordained end.
With this is mind, Novalis introduces the motive of Heinrich's
dream, which—although he is at first unaware of it—anticipates
his future development; furthermore, Heinrich has the continual
sensation of having already known what he experiences at any
given moment—in other words, the course of his experience corresponds both to the inner laws of development of his own mind
and to the (seemingly) objective pattern of the world : it is both
internally and externally determined. When Klingsohr says that
"poetry breaks out everywhere in the proximity of the poet", that
Heinrich's companions have therefore imperceptibly become the
"voices" of poetry, that the "spirit of poetry" has been Heinrich's
constant companion and guide,[46] one must add that the spirit of
poetry is at the same time an integral part of the spirit informing
and unifying the whole of the world. Thus the poet, in whom this
identity is realized and raised to the level of consciousness, becomes
the "transcendental physician" of the world, poetry is the "construction of transcendental health", it achieves the "raising of man
above himself".[47] It is this demonstration of the poetically realized
consciousness of transcendentality that makes *Heinrich von Ofterdingen* one of the central works of German Romanticism and one
that illustrates most clearly the recurrent theme to which we wish
to draw attention.

It remains to relate briefly the aspect of Romanticism described
above to certain other developments of German literature that
fall within the general scope of Romanticism. To embark upon a
discussion of the applicability of such terms as "Early", "Middle",
"Late" and "High" Romanticism (not forgetting the "Satanic"
and the "National" varieties) would be to lapse into a mere

juggling with words; we wish now merely to indicate very briefly the general nature of the consistent and increasingly evident departure from the tendencies outlined above.

This is of course not to deny that there were elements of doubt and self-questioning present even earlier, or to assert that the whole of Romanticism is actuated by the over-riding optimism of Novalis. Ludwig Tieck might serve as an example here. In his well known tale *Der blonde Eckbert* human consciousness is depicted in terms of a falling away from the innocence of nature, and the restoration of the Golden Age (as symbolized by the song "Waldeinsamkeit") coincides with the destruction of human reason, which is unable to survive in a world where it is incapable of distinguishing fancy from reality, and in which therefore the "creative" power of the imagination reduces life to a substanceless dream. In others of his works—for example, in the novel *William Lovell*—Tieck illustrates some of the consequences of an extreme subjectivism that almost seems to degenerate into solipsism at some points. This implicit questioning of the autonomy of human consciousness, the revelation of its self-destructive implications, goes back in a sense, however, to the outwardly untrammelled power of subjectivity to fashion its own world, and reveals in this respect some of the basic characteristics of the phase of Romanticism that we have chosen to describe.

On the other hand, the dominant trends of the nineteenth century evinced themselves—generally speaking—in an opposition to Idealism, that is to say, in the growing awareness of the unmediability of those dichotomies that in Romanticism were susceptible of resolution in some kind of synthesis (even if in an "antithetical synthesis", as Friedrich Schlegel calls it). This trend is obvious in the course of post-Hegelian philosophical development : precisely the unreality of the claims of "Geist" to synthesize the direction of the world is a basic idea in the work of Feuerbach, Marx and others. (We shall illustrate a similar idea in the work of Kierkegaard.) The position of Schopenhauer, for whom the work of art could at best achieve a kind of release from the driving force of the "Will to live", which it was powerless to transform, reveals this shift of emphasis, indeed almost a reversal of the relationship of "Geist" to "Leben". A further stage of development was reached in Nietzsche, who regarded "Geist" as being "etwas am Leben". It is no accident that for Marx (and others) the world that had been "turned upside down" by Idealism had to be set back on its feet again. Leaving aside the question of which way the world should properly stand, one can see in this image the radical change that had taken place. The German

"Realist" literature of the second half of the nineteenth century
was characterized (much more than the corresponding writings in
other European languages) now by a spirit of resignation and
retreat, now by the ability to achieve an apparent mediation of
the unresolvable conflicts of the world only in a particular kind
of humour, which implies an awareness of its own impotence
(Keller and Raabe might serve as examples here).[48] The feeling of
powerlessness in the face of the conditioning forces of reality contrasts strongly with the Idealistic conviction of the transform-
ability of reality.

This shift of emphasis is already evident however in several
writers who are usually assigned a place in the Romantic movement
itself. Eichendorff is a case in point, especially as so many of his
motives, although they have penetrated to popular consciousness
so readily as almost to become Romantic "clichés", are unmistakably derivative from Novalis and Tieck. But the sense of affinity
with nature often takes on for Eichendorff the character of attraction by a daemonic, sinister force, whereas on the other hand the
transforming power of the poetic word is largely reduced to a
trivial embellishment of an existence that ultimately found its
only security either in bourgeois banality or in religion, and in
religion of a particularly traditional kind. To give one paradigmatic
example from the poem *Die zwei Gesellen* : of the two "Gesellen"
who go boldly and gaily forth into the world, one finally contents
himself with the ever so slightly circumscribed bliss of his "Lieb-
chen", his "Bübchen" and his "heimliches Stübchen", whereas the
other, who listens to the "thousand voices" of the "enticing sirens",
succumbs to the destructiveness of daemonic forces; and the poet's
conclusion does not mediate between these two poles, but reads,
plaintively and not very hopefully :

> Und seh' ich so kecke Gesellen,
> Die Tränen im Auge mir schwellen—
> Ach Gott, führ' uns liebreich zu Dir !

The narrative works of E. T. A. Hoffmann reveal likewise a
basically unresolved conflict. It has often been remarked that for
Hoffmann the world of the "Märchen" is continually brought into
pronounced contrast with an irredeemably mundane everyday
world, from which juxtaposition his humour and his irony largely
spring. The motive of creative genius seems here furthermore to
become closely associated with the scurrilous, even the morbid and
abnormal, the artist becoming not so much a representative figure
of humanity as a rather questionable exception.

The poetry of Heinrich Heine is also an instructive example

of the course of development undergone by Romanticism. In some of his poems, Heine seems to be taking up many of the already outworn clichés of Romanticism, which in his hands acquire a somewhat sentimental note; but on the other hand, his mocking irony continually breaks through and ridicules such traditional motives. The "irony" of Heine is thus not "Romantic" irony in the accepted sense, but is bitter and destructive, unable to establish a "progressively" mediating continuity, but rather directed against the pretentiousness of a falsely presumptuous imagination. His work represents therefore a transitional stage in the loss of that sense of unity that underlay the basic Romantic attitudes outlined above.

Finally, a revealing commentary on the displacement of emphasis in the question of irony is provided not only by Hegel, but also by Kierkegaard's criticism, which in view of his importance for modern thought is of particular interest. His thesis entitled *On the Concept of Irony* takes its starting point in an analysis of Socratic irony, which is then compared with that of the Romantic writers. Irony is defined as the "being-for-itself of subjectivity" ("das Fürsichsein der Subjektivität),[49] which in the case of Socrates was allied with the birth of subjectivity altogether : the self-constitution of subjectivity in the form of irony was a manifestation of estrangement from the "reality of substantiality", first effected by Socrates. This was "justified world-historically",[50] because at that moment of history the dissociation of subjectivity from the ground of its being was a necessary and inevitable development. With Romanticism, however, subjectivity rises "to a higher power of itself" and attempts to establish the oneness of its own being in the act of self-consciousness; the result of this attempt is however according to Kierkegaard merely "negative", in that the "infinite absolute negativity" (Hegel) of irony denies reality without being able to re-establish a connection with it. From this point of view, Kierkegaard rejects the legitimacy of Romantic irony.

In that Kierkegaard in his later works develops the idea of a necessary discrepancy between subjectivity and reality, so that the propositions "subjectivity is truth" and "subjectivity is untruth" stand side by side, he can be regarded as having formulated the objection to Romanticism that in any case the course of history has brought forth. But the historian of literature must of course differ from Kierkegaard's judgement, which itself has become historically relativized, and recognize that the potentiated subjectivity of Romanticism had indeed its "world-historical legitimacy". Romanticism is perhaps best regarded as the culmination of eighteenth-century thought, with its growing awareness of the creative power of subjectivity—not as a kind of anticipation of the "dissonances" of the modern age, with which it has comparatively little in common, but as the last and in a sense most ambitious attempt to establish the unity of the self and the world and—in another sphere—to demonstrate the unity of European culture. Precisely as such an attempt at a grandiose synthesis it gradually loses its legitimacy when through the course of development of the nineteenth century confronted more and more insistently with the barrier of unmediability between subjectivity and reality that its main effort was directed towards overcoming.

NOTES

1. Novalis: *Werke. Briefe. Dokumente.* Hrsg. von E. Wasmuth (Heidelberg 1953–57), I, pp. 128, 129, 130.
2. Cf. R. Wellek: "The Concept of Romanticism in Literary History", in R. W.: *Concepts of Criticism* (New Haven and London 1963), pp. 128–198.
3. Wellek, op. cit., p. 161.
4. A. W. Schlegel: *Vorlesungen über dramatische Kunst und Literatur,* Zweite Vorlesung.
5. G. W. F. Hegel: *Werke,* Jubiläumsausgabe; Bd 13, p. 121.
6. For a general treatment of such wider aspects of Romanticism, see e.g. R. Huch: *Die Romantik. Blütezeit, Ausbreitung und Verfall;* also W. Leibbrand: *Die romantische Medizin* (Leipzig 1899, 1902).
7. F. W. J. Schelling: *Werke.* Hrsg. von K. F. A. Schelling, 1856 ff, III, p. 628.
8. Op. cit., p. 627.
9. Friedrich Schlegel: *Kritische Schriften.* Hrsg. von W. Rasch (München n.D.), p. 21 (Kritische Fragmente 115).
10. Ibid., p. 98 (Ideen 108).
11. Op. cit., I, p. 336–7 (Blütenstaub).
12. Op. cit., I, p. 294.
13. Cf. W. Malsch: *"Europa", Poetische Rede des Novalis: Deutung der französischen Revolution und Reflexion auf die Poesie in der Geschichte* (Stuttgart 1965).
14. Cf. M. H. Abrams: *The Mirror and the Lamp. Romantic Theory and the Critical Tradition* (London 1960), pp. 201–213: "German Theories of Vegetable Genius".
15. Cf. I. Strohschneider-Kohrs: *Die romantische Ironie in Theorie und Gestaltung* (Tübingen 1960); also B. Allemann: *Ironie und Dichtung* (Pfullingen 1956).
16. Op. cit., p. 19 (Kritische Fragmente 108).
17. Ibid.
18. Ibid., p. 29 (Athenäum 51).
19. Ibid., p. 270.
20. Ibid., p. 268.
21. Ibid., p. 272.

22. Ibid., p. 264.
23. Ibid., p. 281.
24. Ibid., p. 268.
25. *Literary Notebooks 1797–1801*, Ed. H. Eichner, London, 1957, p. 134.
26. *Kritische Schriften*, p. 97 (Athenäum 116).
27. Ibid., p. 325.
28. Ibid., p. 284.
29. Ibid., p. 314.
30. Cf. L. Ryan: *Hölderlins "Hyperion". Exzentrische Bahn und Dichterberuf* (Stuttgart 1965).
31. Cf. L. Ryan: *Hölderlins Lehre vom Wechsel der Töne* (Stuttgart 1960).
32. Op. cit., I, p. 318.
33. Ibid., II, p. 454.
34. Ibid., I, p. 312.
35. Op. cit., p. 128.
36. Op. cit., I, pp. 310–311.
37. Ibid., II, p. 435.
38. Ibid., I, p. 132.
39. Ibid., I, p. 219.
40. Ibid., II, p. 441.
41. Ibid., II, p. 445.
42. Ibid., I, p. 193.
43. Ibid., I, p. 197.
44. Ibid., II, p. 144.
45. Ibid., III, p. 198.
46. Ibid., I, p. 132.
47. Ibid., III, pp. 2 and 18.
48. Cf. W. Preisendanz: *Humor als dichterische Einbildungskraft*, Studien zur Erzählkunst des deutschen Realismus (München 1963).
49. S. Kierkegaard: *Uber den Begriff der Ironie mit ständiger Rücksicht auf Sokrates* (Düsseldorf/Köln 1961), p. 262.
50. Ibid., p. 268.

BIBLIOGRAPHY

The following are some of the standard works on Romanticism (works listed in the footnotes are not repeated here).

W. Benjamin: Der Begriff der Kunstkritik in der deutschen Romantik. In: W. B.: *Schriften* (1955), 2, 420–528.
R. Haym: *Die romantische Schule* (1899).
R. Huch: *Die Romantik. Blütezeit, Ausbreitung und Verfall.* (1899, 1902).
H. A. Korff: *Geist der Goethezeit.* 3 (1940), 4 (1953).
R. Wellek: *History of Modern Criticism 1750–1950.* 2: The Romantic Age (1955).

Biedermeier

VII

Biedermeier

M. J. NORST

I

BIEDERMEIER, as a literary term, has no equivalent outside German literature. One assumes therefore that it either signifies a phenomenon peculiar to German literature, or that non-German criticism, less given to literary phenomenology, has failed to recognize the type and hence had no need for the label. A definition, one imagines, ought to settle the issue rapidly and neatly. And there precisely the difficulty begins. Is *Biedermeier* that attitude of mind which at times of social crisis urges a retreat into domestic cosiness; an attitude particularly pronounced amongst lesser writers in the first half of the nineteenth century? Grolman in 1935, Höllerer in 1958 interpret it in this way. Or is it, as Kluckhohn and Emrich see it, the dominant stylistic expression in the period 1820 to 1850? Or the name given to the literature of a historically defined period in Germany and Austro-Hungary, extending from 1815 to 1848 and including the work of all writers within the period : the literary equivalent of the political term *Restauration* as Majut and Sengle suggest? The critics quoted in each case span the whole period of *Biedermeier*-discussion and it is clear, that in the thirty years in which the term has been the subject of serious debate, the same degree of divergence of opinion has prevailed. Flemming diagnosed the problem quite accurately when he said :

> The dispute concerning its (i.e. *Biedermeier's*) definition strikingly demonstrates the acute lack of clarity and certainty, which in general characterizes literary history as a science, both with regard to its methodology and its fundamentals.[1]

It cannot be our aim here to provide a precise definition and so suggest a happy unanimity in usage, which, as we have seen, does not exist, nor to offer a quick remedy for the methodological uncertainty. What can be usefully done is to trace the history of the term and examine the concepts for which it has been called into service; to indicate the various ways in which *Biedermeier* is used today, suggesting some of the reasons for the conflicting usage;

and finally to consider the justification for such a term to label yet another German Literary Movement!

Biedermeier discussion has been bedevilled from the beginning by the conflicting associations which the word has conjured up and the value judgements which have attached to these. The starting point for any new and fruitful debate would certainly need to be the clear distinction between word and concept. To put it very simply one would first need to establish whether in the years 1815 to 1848 there existed amongst writers a community of thought and feeling, a homogeneity of expression or a confrontation with new problems which would become more meaningful if singled out from other groups or movements. And then, quite separately the vexed question ought to be taken up again : is *Biedermeier* the most appropriate term?

(a) Origin—humorous literary character

The origin of the word can be quickly traced and its history has been carefully documented by Majut and more recently by Williams.[2]

It was coined by Kußmaul and Eichrodt in 1853 and popularized in a series of poems published by them in the *Fliegende Blätter*. The first of these appeared in 1855 (Issue No. 493) as "Selected Poems of Weiland Gottlieb Biedermaier, Schoolmaster in Swabia". These poems as the introduction explains were parodies based on the rhymes of Friedrich Sauter, a Swabian village schoolmaster of the previous generation and "poet to boot". The series of parodies and originals was collected under the heading *Das Buch Biedermeier* and appeared as a section in Eichrodt's anthology *Lyrische Karrikaturen* in 1869 and again in Eichrodt's collected works in 1890. A few lines from Sauter's best-known effort *Kartoffellied*, a song of praise to Drake for giving us the potato, will serve to establish the type :

> Noch Eins ist mir erinnerlich,
> Schier hätt' ich es vergessen,
> Auch frische Häring lassen sich
> Zu den Kartoffeln essen.[3]

Majut has explained that the name was created in imitation of F. Th. Vischer's "Schartenmaier" and that word combinations with "maier" (farmer) were at the time a popular comic device. The old-fashioned spelling which was maintained for some time was presumably intended to heighten the comic effect. "Bieder" itself was beginning to lose caste. From its original meaning "appropriate", "necessary", it had developed by way of "useful" to "honest", "capable", "upright" but was by the mid-nineteenth century no longer unalloyed praise. It suggested, especially in combinations like "Biedermann"—-"decent but restricted in outlook, lacking in imagination". If we think of our own day and the play by Max Frisch, *Herr Diedermann und die Brandstifter*, it seems evident that the process of denigration has continued and that the idea of hypocrisy and self deception have become an integral part of the semantic complex.

The word then from the beginning suggested someone belonging to the lower middle class, clearly showing his rustic origin, simple, decent, home-loving, extremely limited and utterly prosaic : a figure of fun for the intellectual, the artist, the sophisticated city dweller. The parodies and the introduction make it quite clear that these were the qualities with which Kußmaul and Eichrodt invested their fictitious poet and that they understood their neologism in this way. Sauter stood as model for the :

> easily contented Biedermaier, whose small room, restricted garden ... and poor lot as a despised village schoolmaster modestly suffice to provide him with earthly bliss.[4]

The limited vision and passive acceptance, the respect for order and authority which make for contentment within the narrow confines of such a restricted sphere, and the unproblematic nature of such a life, provoke Kußmaul and Eichrodt a generation later to laughter which is at once gentle in its mockery and tinged with nostalgia for "the good old days". And the very act of parody introduces an element of condescension.

Originally then the word denoted this fictitious village schoolmaster-cum-poet and the emotive connotation linked a feeling of superiority with a certain nostalgia.

(b) Style in the applied and pictorial arts

The next development came when those made aware of a new concept chose to refer to it by the word *Biedermeier*. By the turn of the century the period immediately following the Napoleonic Wars was already being accepted as a well-defined stylistic unit, first by those concerned with interior decoration and the applied arts, later by art historians also. Folnesic's book published in 1903 bears the title *Rooms and Household Furnishings in the Empire and Biedermeier periods in Austro-Hungary* and the word, here freed of all pejorative associations, is used to distinguish the style of the post-Napoleonic era from that which preceded it. Folnesic provides a series of illustrations of furniture and furnishings and a catalogue containing detailed descriptions. The word *Biedermeier* is not defined nor in fact used in the descriptions and the illustrations do not extend beyond 1830. They make it clear, however, that there was indeed a change of style. Where Empire is characterized by straight lines, the use of marble and bronze for ornamentation and an air of aloof elegance, the later period stresses the rounded line, reduces ornamentation to the simplest of floral designs and exudes an air of genuine warmth and simple comfort. *Biedermeier* here denotes the style of a definite historical period, a style characterized by simplicity, functionalism, solid workmanship and a profound feeling for the unity which must exist between form and material.

The Centenary Exhibition of 1906 further emphasized the stylistic autonomy of these years, showing the fashion in dress, furniture, interior decoration and the other applied arts to be informed by the same spirit, distinguishing it both from the age of Napoleon and the later industrial age. *Biedermeier* when used in this way is today as neutral a designation as "Colonial" and people as readily order *Biedermeier* bedrooms as they insist on Colonial kitchens. The exhibition released a wave of enthusiasm for the age of the stage coach. Greater distance in time and the stylistic aberrations of the vulgarly ostentatious *Gründerjahre* had invested the simplicity of this earlier period (when money had been scarce) with a dignity and charm which evoked not merely nostalgia but real admiration. *Biedermeier* work was held up as an example to a factory age which had lost all sense of style.

Gradually *Biedermeier* was applied to the artists too—painters like Ludwig Richter, Moritz von Schwind, F. G. Waldmüller, Menzel and Spitzweg—and thus new associations began to attach to the term. Since the emphasis was on genre-painting the non-specialist came to regard the pictures primarily as illustrations of another age—the *Biedermeier* age. Idyllic scenes were accepted as photographic records of reality. The art historian used the term to distinguish a style which placed greater emphasis on the small details of everyday life; which stressed situation rather than action and therefore concentrated attention on the solid and the static against which the figures were significantly posed. In choice of material as well as in the representation of it *Biedermeier* paintings could be distinguished from those of the Romantics. If one compares C. D. Friedrich's *Riesengebirgslandschaft* which evokes a feeling of utter loneliness in an infinitely majestic and wild mountain scene with Ludwig Richter's *Lagerndes Volk im Gebirge* where the eye is immediately drawn to the figures at rest, above all the mother in her tender concern for her child, and where the mountains provide a natural counterpart to the human

scene, the change in outlook is very evident. In *Biedermeier* paintings, scenes of family life predominate : father at the piano with
his family gathered around him singing by the light of a single
candle; the family in quiet conversation about the dinner table;
two small boys, the elder with his arm placed protectively around
the younger, watching a cat and her kittens drinking milk from the
same saucer. Generally we are shown three generations together
sharing a moment's quiet pleasure. The curved line predominates
in table tops and lamps, in the brim of a hat or the curve of an
arm. The total effect is one of peace, safety and endurance and of
simple goodness. The tremendous danger of sentimentality in all
of this is obvious and only the best artists avoided it most of the
time.

Spitzweg's pictures, also classified as *Biedermeier*, are rather
different for though he also depicts small everyday happenings in
a small world, the characters involved are always slightly odd.
From the needy poet scribbling verses in bed under a torn
umbrella intended as protection against the leaking roof, to the
short-sighted Bookworm perched on his ladder in the library
doggedly reading about metaphysics in one book, while a second,
third and fourth are clutched in readiness between arms and legs,
Spitzweg has presented us with variations on the Eichrodt-
Biedermeier theme. We have a whole series of characters remote
from reality and therefore able to bear with equanimity the discrepancy between the ideal world of their imaginations and the
limitations of the physical reality. Their self-importance and eccen-
tricity make them ridiculous, their isolation makes them pathetic.
They are all related to the poor village schoolmaster who wrote a
hymn of praise to the potato and paid to have it published. Spitzweg gently satirizes the retreat from the larger social scene into the
private sphere, while painters like Richter glowingly affirm it.

(c) Cultural-historical Epoch

It is clear that the interest taken in the Exhibition and in these
painters would soon lead to an extension of the term to cover the
whole period. Meyer's *Konversationslexikon* of 1905 (6th edition)
already glossed the word as designating the period between 1816
and 1850 and in 1911 Max von Boehn's book entitled *Biedermeier
Deutschland von 1815–1848* appeared. The word occurs only in the
title not in the text of the book, but a perusal of the contents makes
it obvious that by *Biedermeier* Boehn simply understands the years
between the end of the Napoleonic Wars and the Revolution of
1848. He includes everything which in his opinion throws light on
the social and political conditions under which a German lived in

the Metternich era. It is interesting that he specifies German *Biedermeier* because as Folnesic's title showed, and as we shall see in the literary discussions, there has often been a tendency to see *Biedermeier* as a phenomenon peculiar to Austro-Hungary in the *Restaurationszeit*.

Boehn's book demonstrates that viewed against its political background *Biedermeier* emerges as a distinct period. Politically it can be defined by the Congress of Vienna in 1815 which attempted to expunge all changes since the French Revolution and by the Revolution of 1848 which demonstrated the folly of such an undertaking. The years between are characterized on the one hand by the extremely repressive measures taken by those determined to maintain the Old Establishment and on the other by the vigorous efforts of liberals and nationalists to secure the rights to which victory in the Wars of Liberation seemed to have made them heir. Till 1870 the history of Germany is the story of the struggle for unity and political freedom—with now one, then the other, predominating. After the Napoleonic Wars patriotic fervour brought the movement for unity to the forefront, but the murder of Kotzebue and the decrees of 1819 and 1820 which followed, put an end to overt nationalist activities. The issue of unity did not reappear in full force till after the failure of the 1848 Revolution though it remained alive in the economic sphere through the work of List. In the Austro-Hungarian Empire the nationalist movements did not seriously threaten the centralized system till after 1830, so that national unity or rather intra-national unity only became a vital issue there after 1848. Beginning in the 1820s then and gaining in vigour after the 1830 Revolution in France is the movement for political rights for the middle class. It is a struggle *against* the existing oppressive system with its censorship and inquisitorial methods and *for* new constitutional rights. The Carlsbad Decrees of 1819 and the *Wiener Schlußakte* of 1820 gave an impetus to the liberal movement and the political tension which resulted involved not merely "radicals" and "reactionaries" but also the non-radical and non-political elements. One needs to think only of the case of Jacob Grimm and the Protest of the Professors of Göttingen against the rescinding of the constitution in 1837.

Viewed politically and socially these were very turbulent times indeed and the clearest expression we have of the turbulence is in the writings of the Young Germans—Wienbarg, Gutzkow, Laube, Mundt—formed into a group only by the Federal Decree of 1835 which banned their writings. But whether like the Young Germans they believed in the efficacy of immediate and radical remedies; whether like Büchner, Hebbel, Heine and Grabbe they saw beyond the next revolution; or whether like the non-radicals Grillparzer and Stifter they dreaded revolutionary changes and looked for other remedies, all writers during this period reacted to the same given explosive situation. If 1820 to 1830 may perhaps be considered a period of relative enforced quiet, 1830 to 1848 is one of constant political unrest. It is also the period in which there is an unprecedented increase in literary production and in which the development of the mass reading public begins. Magill has shown that "the rate of increase has no parallel in the earlier or later history of German literature",[5] that in this period the number of publishing firms and of newspapers almost trebled and that lending libraries, reading circles and cultural societies both broadened the basis of the reading public and intensified the demand for books. Writers were no longer writing for an educated élite, the "common reader" had become a factor to be reckoned with.

The particular nature of the political struggle made the situation in Germany and Austria quite different from that in England or even in France. There is further the fact that the problems of industrialization were not an issue in Germany and Austria till later. Industrialization was a hope to some and a bogey to others, but, if one looks at the economic pattern of the time, not as yet a real force to be grappled with either in life or in literature. The problems, as we have seen, lay elsewhere. And again unlike his English and French counterpart it was the peculiar fate of the German writer to be deprived of any voice in politics at such a time.

Boehn in his book describes not the lull between two historical turning-points but the development which lead inevitably to the Revolution of 1848. It is evident that for him *Biedermeier* or *Beidermeierzeit* does not convey the idea of idyllic contentment but of struggle and violence.

A number of books of this type and of more general reminiscence followed and each of them attempted to eradicate the old associations with which as we have seen the word *Biedermeier* was linked. Houben called his book *Der gefesselte Biedermeier*,[6] stressing the severe censorship under which the writers suffered. Hermann in his *Das Biedermeier* published in 1913 warns :

> Only a decade ago nobody thought of *Biedermeier*, one simply referred to that period as *Vormärz*, that is as the years which saw the development of the revolutionary changes of March, 1848—and that period, which we today are fond of regarding as one of relaxed and rather charming slumber, of complacent satisfaction in a refined and cultivated way of

life ... indeed it was eminently political too! Politics exercised such power at that time that none could escape their influence.[7]

By the end of the first decade of this century the word *Biedermeier* had thus come to be used for a number of concepts which can be placed roughly under three headings. It could mean : a philistine attitude and a narrow range of artistic endeavour, a lack of intellectual curiosity, a sense of uncritical acceptance, an exaggerated concern with trivialities. It could also imply : domestic tranquillity and virtue : love of "real" things in a "real" world because they are a pledge of eternal harmony; in fact that state of innocence in which the German and Austrian *Bürger* was seen to live before the Fall of the Industrial Revolution—his sense of tradition, his social customs. Finally it could be used to express the idea of a period of violent political and social upheaval.

These we might term the three meanings of the word *Biedermeier* as they exist and are used even today. And to distinguish them more easily we can use three forms of the word to express these ideas—*biedermeierlich*; *Biedermeier*; *Biedermeierzeit*. As we shall see the controversy and confusion regarding its literary application depends mainly on which meaning of the word is accepted.

II

It was not until 1927 that any real attempt was made to suggest that the word had specific relevance for the literary historian. The years between the Congress of Vienna and the Revolution of 1848 had not in fact been seen as a special literary "period" at all. With very few exceptions (Wiegand in his *Geschichte der deutschen Dichtung*) literary histories which dealt in periods carved it up between Romanticism and Realism or treated it as a transition period between the two, explaining its characteristics in terms of what had gone before or was to come. Writers of the time were neatly disposed of as Classic or Romantic, Epigones or premature Realists.

The writers themselves were in a sense responsible for the view which later generations had of them as Epigones for they saw themselves in this light. It was after all one of them, Immermann, who in his novel popularized the word and presented his generation as one burdened by too great a heritage :

> We are, let us express the entire misfortune in one word, Epigones, and bear the burden which is the lot of all heirs. The great journeys into the realms of the spirit, upon which our fathers embarked from their huts and cabins, have provided us

with a store of treasures, which now lie about on every market stall.[8]

Stifter voices the belief of his whole generation when he sees himself as a humble follower of the great Goethe : "I am it is true no Goethe, but I am at least related to him"[9] and Grillparzer in his autobiography also remarks that aware though he is of the great gulf between them, he yet considers himself the best writer to have come after Goethe and Schiller. Each of the writers weighed himself against Goethe and Schiller and found himself and his fellows wanting. And the literary historians for the most part took them at their word and saw them as imperfect copies. Grillparzer in particular had to suffer under literary criticism which regarded him as a failed Classicist.

The only group of writers who from the beginning tended to be singled out were the Young Germans, who produced no literary masterpieces and with whom great writers like Heine, Büchner and Hebbel were sometimes loosely linked because of their political interests. The other writers neither formed themselves into groups nor were they seen as such by their contemporaries. They issued no clear aesthetic programme, were non-militant and seemed to possess no vital common factor which would justify their being regarded as a group or movement.

It was Kluckhohn, a specialist in the field of Romantic studies, who in 1927 first discussed the application of the term *Biedermeier* to literature in a talk significantly entitled *Fortwirkung der Romantik in der Kultur des 19. und 20. Jahrhunderts*.[10] This was followed by a spate of books and articles by Majut, Weydt and Bietak in a vigorous campaign to have *Biedermeier* accepted as a term with validity for the literary historian. In 1935 the literary periodicals *Deutsche Vierteljahresschrift* and *Euphorion* (then known in deference to the times as *Dichtung und Volkstum*) were devoted to a discussion of this problem. Musician, philosopher, English-specialist, art-historian all contributed articles aimed at building up the picture of an all-permeating Style, which as Kluckhohn expressed it, characterized :

this epoch ... the last relatively unified German cultural epoch, on which we today look back almost with a degree of envy.[11]

Kluckhohn wanted to apply the term only to those writers, who in their works most clearly embodied the qualities of a trend, which for him was the dominant one of the age, freely granting that other trends were also current at the time. Thus he very clearly separated the *Biedermeier* writers from the Young Germans for instance.

What had prompted his suggestion initially had been the awareness of a significant difference between the writings of Grillparzer,
Stifter, Immermann, Gotthelf and Raimund for example and
those of the Romantics, and a desire to free the former from their
nebulous existence as Post-Romantics. Majut put this in very
practical terms when he said :

> The recognition of an age as a period obedient to its own laws
> and separated from that which precedes and succeeds it, gener-
> ally begins with the use of a characterizing name.[12]

It is impossible to give here a full chronological account of all
the arguments but we can note the main lines, which, as has been
pointed out already, are in fact those still being followed today, in
some cases of course by the same people.

All critics then involved in the debate followed the same pattern.
They defined the term, distinguished *Biedermeier* from other movements (principally the Romantic), drew up a list of characteristics
both by way of illustration and as a justification for the definition
and finally listed the authors who fitted this scheme. Grolman
aptly if somewhat unkindly described this last procedure as "the
letting of rooms in the realms of cultural history".[13]

(a) Biedermeierlich

Those who interpreted the word in this sense either rejected the
whole category or at least recoiled in horror from the idea of
having any writer of stature included. Dünninger in discussing
Stifter declared : "It is impossible in my opinion to use the term
Biedermeier style to characterize literary things".[14] Sauer expressed
his indignation in a review of the first edition of the Merker-
Stammler *Reallexikon* in which *Biedermeier* was discussed, in the
following terms :

> in an age in which scholarship had only just begun to clear the
> tremendous chaos, anti-scholarship plunges everything into new
> chaotic disorder. In a rather unsatisfactory article, the time from
> 1815 to 1848 is degraded as "Literary *Biedermeier*". [15]

Biedermeier is seen as a label which lowers the prestige of those
to whom it is applied. Grolman explains that Jean Paul's Wuz,
Niebergall's Dummbach and Datterich are the epitome of *Biedermeier* and provides an enthusiastic defence of Stifter's great inner
courage and manliness in order to reject most emphatically the
notion that he might be called a *Biedermeier* writer. He summarizes
his position thus :

The concomitant circumstances are biedermeierlich but not the situation as a whole, and therefore now and again in the literature of the time, some of which is rather wide of the mark, this or that *biedermeierlich* element is to be found, clearly distinguishable from all else—but this does not capture the essence of the entire period, still less provide any useful guide to the entire literature of the epoch.[16]

It is clear that Höllerer in his *Zwischen Klassik und Moderne* understands *Biedermeier* in precisely the same way and for precisely the same reason refuses to allow Mörike to be thus degraded :

It is not difficult to list a great number of *Biedermeier* traits in Mörike. All of them together will, however, never suffice to allow one to label Mörike's work with a period term like *Biedermeier* with any degree of accuracy. One might equally well call Catullus a *Biedermeier* writer.[17]

Robert Minder in *Kultur und Literatur in Deutschland und Frankreich* puts it more picturesquely when in his defence of Mörike's poem *Der alte Turmhahn* he says :

Naturally Mörike cannot be blamed for the way in which his poem was misused particularly in the Goebbels era when it was held up as the prime example of the sincere and fervent German spirit. Mörike's *Biedermeier* sofa stands closer to Heine's mattress-grave and Oblomov's divan than to the honey-suckle covered retreat in the small rented garden of the average middle class citizen.[18]

The majority of those who reject the term entirely or would allow it only for the inferior literary productions of the time or the more unfortunate features of the great works have the Sauter-image before their eyes. It was the realization of this fact that caused Oscar Walzel to suggest the use of "geadelter *Biedermeier*"[19] a phrase too clumsy and pompous ever to gain acceptance.

(b) Biedermeier

Those who took their lead from Kluckhohn defined the term as the dominant but not the only trend in German literature between 1820 and 1850. They were, and still are, faced by the problem of defending the notion of a dominant literary trend against the evidence that in its own time at least it made practically no impression. There is simply no comparison between the effect that a book like Gutzkow's *Wally die Zweiflerin* had on the public of the time—it was probably the most widely read and discussed novel of its day—and the effect of a book like Stifter's *Witiko* which was read by scarcely anyone. Gutzkow's *Uriel Acosta* certainly attracted a larger and more responsive audience than Grillparzer's *Weh dem, der lügt*; and Herwegh's *Der Freiheit eine Gasse* for example, was undoubedly better known than any poem of Droste-Hülshoff's or Mörike's. Moreover, the writers were not even an influence on each other. Lunding has shown that Stifter, for example, was ignored or dismissed by Grillparzer, Droste-Hülshoff and Keller. While an individual writer may be neglected by his own age and find his true evaluation only later, the proposition that a "dominant" trend makes no impact on its own age is very different and would require elucidation.

What is seen to distinguish the writers generally grouped as *Biedermeier*—Gotthelf, Grillparzer, Raimund, Stifter, Droste-Hülshoff, Mörike—from other significant writers of the day, is essentially the non-political nature of their writing. They stressed tradition and moderation at a time when a revolution was in the making; they marvelled at the beauty and eternal order of God's universe, while their fellow writers fought desperately and angrily to remedy its present ills. This has lead to their being branded as "anti-liberal" and scorned for being "uncommitted" at a very critical moment in history; it has also brought the idyllic element in their writing into particular prominence. From their contemporaries, Hebbel and Keller, to the present day there are those who equate *Biedermeier* writing with *Biedermeier* paintings of the Ludwig Richter type, the tendency being to find the idyllicism of the painter more justified and therefore acceptable than that of the writer.

From 1933 to 1945 the *Biedermeier* writers were annexed for propaganda purposes and the distinction between them and the Young Germans was frequently drawn to stress the essentially Germanic, wholesome, optimistic character of the *Biedermeier* writers as against the "foreign", "dangerously decadent pessimism" of the Paris-orientated Young Germans and Heine. Here the emphasis was very definitely placed on the idyllic aspects but as these did not blend with the militarism of the times Trübner's *Deutsches Wörterbuch* feels impelled to append the following warning to the article on *Biedermeier* :

> But we today must apply to ourselves the dictum : the times of *Biedermeier* and of dreamy maidenhood are of course finally and forever at an end.

Modern criticism, partly by way of reaction, has stressed the "demonic" element in *Biedermeier*, the ambivalent nature of this idyllic state. Already Kluckhohn had remarked that the "serenity often grows out of the dark subsoil of melancholy".[20] Pascal, in speaking of Stifter's *Nachsommer*, so often cited as the most typical *Biedermeier* novel, refers to : "that gnawing uncertainty which always lowers on the horizon of this apparently soothing book".[21] So strong has been the modern reaction against the conception of *Biedermeier* as idyllic that Lunding already considers it necessary to issue a warning to those tempted to seek a solution in a "Sauter-*Biedermeier*" and "demonic *Biedermeier*" division !

Certainly these writers reacted to the critical climate of their day as violently as the Young Germans and though less obviously more profoundly. They lacked the Young Germans' optimism about the future; they lacked their faith in the value of quick political solutions; they therefore lacked their possibilities for vigorous action aimed at achieving realizable goals. Not one of them could have said with Hoffmann von Fallersleben :

> Ach ! ich bin zu früh geboren !
> Eine neue Welt beginnt.[22]

For them organic growth and the maintaining of traditional values were necessary conditions of worthwhile change and they looked towards a future which seemed to threaten chaos with an intense feeling of impending calamity. Immermann in his novel *Die Epigonen* has one of his characters say defensively that no one can blame him if instead of attempting to hold back the tide of materialism he lays claim to a small green island for himself and his family and tries to hold it as long as possible. Most of the writers conjure up this island. It is, however, at once refuge and fortress; it represents flight and challenge. If the world which they present as part of the cosmic order is so rational, so obedient to ethical laws, so free of dissension, it is because they feel a terrible need to defend ideals which are in danger.

The comparisons between the *Biedermeier* writers and their contemporaries have generally been drawn by those, who as we will see, would include both under the term. The shift in emphasis from the "idyllic" to the "demonic" picture of *Biedermeier*, used in the more restricted sense, has made it imperative for the distinctions between these writers to be reassessed.

Far more fruitful have been the distinctions drawn between *Biedermeier* writers and the Romantics. Much of this has come from studies of individual writers and has probably been the most valuable contribution which the whole *Biedermeier*-discussion has made. Beginning with Kluckhohn and Weydt the main differences in the attitude to the individual, to nature and to religion have been carefully analysed.

For the *Biedermeier* writer the ideal is no longer the genius or the great tragic hero, the individual who glories in his subjectivity —but the harmonious, well adjusted *Bürger*. Emotional displays of feeling, *Weltschmerz*, *Zerrissenheit* are no longer literary high fashion. For the Romantic cult of the individual, the *Biedermeier* writers substitute the cult of the community in which alone the individual can fully develop. The individual must be at peace with himself, all must be well in his relationship with his family, his community and with God. And it is possible to educate him towards this. The outward sign of the attainment of the ideal state is shown in his bearing. Like the medieval hero whose harmony gives "hôhen muot",[23] the *Biedermeier* hero is then described as "heiter"[24] which implies far more than good natured cheerfulness and has nothing at all to do with quietism or idyllicism. All that might threaten or endanger this precarious balance, all irrational or demonic forces must therefore be kept at bay. Artistically this is done by not allowing these forces to appear and thus presenting only the positive idea; or by showing them to have had disastrous consequences in the past. Thus passion, seen as egocentric and destructive, is eliminated in *Biedermeier* works unless it is required to serve as a warning.

In his attitude to nature, as Weydt has pointed out, the *Biedermeier* writer is also clearly distinguishable from the Romantic. Rejecting pantheism, man does not strive to lose himself in nature or to become one with it. Nature does not embody the Divine, it reflects it and thus acts as an example to man. There is constant detailed reference to the cultivation of nature with a proper understanding for what it demands. Most of the literary works show obvious delight in gardening, in gathering plants and stones and making collections where the individual pieces stand in meaningful relationship to each other. Weydt first drew attention to these characteristics in the works of Immermann, Mörike, Droste-Hülshoff and Stifter and coined the phrase *Sammeln und Hegen*[25] to describe a revealing trait which significantly enough he noted also in Storm's *Immensee*, Keller's *Landvogt von Greifensee* and in the work of Jacob Grimm, that is, in writers not normally recognized as *Biedermeier*.

The attention previously centred on the ego is now focused on the objective world, the objects within it and the relationship between them. The smallest things are cherished because they, as much as the large ones, derive their value from a fixed place in the cosmic order and bear witness to it. The *Biedermeier* attitude to the moving force within the cosmos owes more to the Age of Enlightenment and to Herder than to the Romantics. Both, as Bietak has pointed out, see the universe as essentially rational. There is evidence of a theistic but wholly undogmatic religious feeling and particular stress is given to ethics and to living "reasonably". Feuchtersleben's *Diätetik der Seele* (*Prescriptions for the Soul*) which was very popular and influenced Stifter considerably is in tune with this attitude and would not have found acceptance by the Romantics.

The value of the distinctions made between *Biedermeier* and Romanticism cannot be disputed and one can judge how necessary the term has become for this purpose by noting the frequency with which it is used in interpretations. This is particularly true in the case of Mörike where the transition from Romanticism to *Biedermeier* (used in this sense) is of great moment.

(c) Biedermeierzeit

Already Majut in 1931 had defined *Biedermeier* in very broad terms which included the Young Germans.[26] The period 1815 to 1848 was seen as a socio-political unit and the literature which it produced as *Biedermeier*, different from Romanticism on the one hand and Realism on the other. Friedrich Sengle also uses *Biedermeier* in this way—as the literary equivalent of the political term *Restauration*. It is obvious that the definition needs to be altered radically if the word is to be thus used. This approach, however, certainly has the advantage of illuminating various attitudes to the one set of circumstances.

Those who advocate this use of the term are concerned primarily with bringing out the connections between the literature of *Biedermeier* times and that of pre-Romantic times and distinguishing it clearly from Realism. They comment on the influences which, dormant in the Romantic era, were revived at this time. Particular attention is drawn to the links with the Age of Enlightenment— the stress on the rational, the great regard for the useful, which may even be confused with the good and the beautiful; the educational optimism; the belief in organic growth; pietism and lack of sectarianism. Comparisons are also frequently drawn between the Rococo forms and the delight in small genres, playful trifles and occasional verse which characterizes the period after 1815. Sedlmayr in his book *Verlust der Mitte* sees this as the most significant feature of the age.

The demarcation between *Biedermeierzeit* and Realism seems to be far harder to establish. The politically significant date 1848 is tacitly accepted as a convenient cutting-off point but little evidence is brought forward to reveal it as a necessary literary division.

Kölmel[27] attempts to show the marked difference between Gutzkow (seen as a *Biedermeierzeit* writer) and the Realists, Freytag, Schmidt and Ludwig. His findings suggest, however, that while their theories differ the works have much in common. Otto Ludwig in particular is seen as very close to the writers of the *Biedermeierzeit*. Certainly a novel like his *Zwischen Himmel und Erde* shows that one cannot reduce the difference to that between a transcendental and non-transcendental philosophy. The works of Stifter, Mörike, Droste-Hülshoff and Gotthelf very clearly reveal a belief in the transcendental; everything is at once itself and a reflection of the eternal. In the next generation much of the certainty has gone (one needs to think only of Storm, in many ways a *Biedermeier* writer) but there is no clear rejection of the transcendental. The difference is that between the generation which grew up with the ideas of Schleiermacher and Baader and the next generation which knew Feuerbach and Strauß. It was, however, left to the Naturalists to draw the radical conclusions.

Keller and Raabe are usually considered to be the writers who occupy a borderline position between *Biedermeier* and Realism and so one might reasonably expect them to reveal the characteristic difference most clearly. Yet this is scarcely the case. Martini sees the youthful Raabe as standing "within the cultural-historical precincts of literary *Biedermeier*"[28] and considers his *Abu Telfan* (1865–67) to be the beginning of his "realistic" period because he there depicts not the ideal, idyllic *Biedermeier* but narrow, restricting reality. Keller, originally seen by Weydt as a *Biedermeier* writer, resembles the later Raabe, in that he does not idealize the *Biedermeier* world and raise it to the status of a myth but mocks at its pettiness, unmasks its hypocrisy and reveals its inadequacies. His attitude reminds one of Spitzweg's though there is more bitterness in his laughter. Both Raabe and Keller attack what is *biedermeierlich* in their world but their positive values and style bear marked resemblance to that of the *Biedermeier* writers in the narrower sense of the word.

Chronologically the division between *Biedermeierzeit* and Realism presents many problems and invariably means doing violence to the work of those seen as the main representatives of *Biedermeier*, since much of it was published *after* 1848. Thus Mörike's *Mozart auf der Reise nach Prag* appeared in 1855; Stifter wrote the novels, from which characteristics of the *Biedermeier* style are most often derived, in the 'fifties and 'sixties (*Der*

Nachsommer, 1857; *Witiko* 1865–67); and Grillparzer's *Ein Bruder-zwist in Habsburg* appeared in 1872.

A radical division between *Biedermeierzeit* (viewed as a totality comparable with Baroque) and German Realism does not seem to be justified by style, content or chronology. The use of the term to cover the whole age does, however, allow the writers within the period to be seen more easily in relationship to each other and to the political and social conditions. Idealized family scenes in Büchner's *Lenz*, loving descriptions of a harmonious home and a cultivated garden in Gutzkow's *Daheim* on the one hand, and on the other a scene like the one in Raimund's *Der Alpenkönig und der Menschenfeind*, where the wretched conditions in the charcoal burner's hut are mercilessly exposed, show that the writers of the time, when they did exchange rôles, played them in the same way.

There are, however, considerable dangers inherent in this approach. By stressing the similarities between the revolutionary and the non-revolutionary writers, it conceals their far more significant differences and thus falsifies the picture. Furthermore, in order to prove the homogenous nature of the period, it is forced into exaggerating the differences between it and German Realism. Finally, there is of course the difficulty of the word *Biedermeier* and all its associations should all the politically active and radical writers be included.

III

We have seen how the term came into being and how its connotations varied according to context. Literary usage is linked with this, and those who use *Biedermeier* in the sense of *biedermeierlich* think primarily of Sauter; those who speak of *Biedermeier* take their lead from the art historians, though stressing in recent times the ambiguous nature of the idyllicism; those who think in terms of *Biedermeierzeit* share the views of the socio-political historians and stress the tension and violence of the period.

It is obvious, however, that *Biedermeier* as it stands is not wholly acceptable as a literary term and this is admitted even by its supporters. Jost Hermand in *Die literarische Formenwelt des Biedermeiers* is forced to admit :

In recent literary history the term *Biedermeier* is used comparatively rarely.[29]

This is borne out by those who might be expected to require the term most for purposes of classification. Compilers of bibliographies like *The Year's Work in Modern Languages* and *Germanistik* ignore it as do many literary historians. Killy in his anthology

Zeichen der Zeit Vol. 3 uses it as a chapter heading in the same way as he uses Freedom, The Arts and Death and includes extracts from Storm, Busch, Hebbel and Raabe which depict the Sauter world. Shipley's *Dictionary of World Literary Terms* quotes as *Biedermeier* writers Stifter, Keller, Raabe, Freytag and Mörike and characterizes the period as "complacent acceptance of the status quo", while Cassell's *Encyclopedia of Literature* rejects the term as unfruitful for critical distinctions. Part of the justification for the use of a term must certainly come from its general acceptance, and the fact that after almost forty years of discussion *Biedermeier* has not found this acceptance must lead one to question its validity.

Ought the term then to be rejected?. With considerable caution one would suggest that it should not. It has proved fruitful in showing different elements in Mörike; in freeing Grillparzer from his *Epigonentum*; in revealing essential qualities in the work of Stifter, Gotthelf, Droste-Hülshoff and Raimund. It has allowed a revaluation of the writings of Immermann, Uhland, Lenau, Rückert and others. It has thrown light on the late works of Goethe and Tieck. Moreover, it has made it possible to view Austrian writing more accurately. From the beginning *Biedermeier* was accepted in its Austrian context more readily than in its German one and even today the term is more commonly applied to Austrian literature than to German. Many characteristics of *Biedermeier* are frequently seen as features peculiar to the Austrian temperament—the retreat from social problems, the air of resignation, the concern with the apparently trivial, the dislike of disturbance. Since Romanticism was of less significance in Austria, it had proved unfruitful to try to see nineteenth century Austrian writers in terms of it and *Biedermeier* has made it possible for more meaningful connections to be made, notably with Rococo and with the Baroque theatre tradition.

But if the term is to be retained it must certainly be redefined and rehabilitated.

First the ambiguity would need to be resolved and *biedermeierlich* and *Biedermeier* seen as the negative and positive possibilities inherent in the attitude. Writers who attack the former could still believe in the ideals of the latter. This would also lead to a "neutralizing" of the term, a process not uncommon in terminology, one need think only of Baroque and Gothic, both of which began as denunciations and only gradually became neutral descriptions. The extension of the term to include the Young Germans and all other writers of the period does not seem practicable, the political term *Restaurationszeit* is, in any case, far more appropriate as a designation for this grouping.

A new approach to the description of the *Biedermeier* attitude and style is also needed. It has been a methodological error in the past to ignore the significance of the minor writers in indicating trends. We find particularly in *Biedermeier* studies that the characteristics have been abstracted from the works of perhaps four main writers, who then not surprisingly have been found to fit the description. Only if literary history is broadly based can terms such as *Biedermeier* serve any useful purpose as a descriptive dimension. It is then possible for the literary critic and historian to show how the individual deviates from the general pattern. No one writer will of course ever fit the pattern entirely, the minor writer rather more than the major.

The pressure exerted by the reading public which in the nineteenth century became a vital factor has also been disregarded. Already in 1912 Meyer in his *Die deutsche Literatur des 19. und 20. Jahrhunderts* found the development of a literary public in the 1820s to be a phenomenon essentially linked with the development of literary movements in the nineteenth century, yet *Biedermeier* studies of the past have not taken it into account.

Finally *Biedermeier* would need to be seen more clearly as part of the German Realist tradition. The socio-political situation did not change drastically in Germany after 1848. Industrialization was slow in coming, the Revolution of 1848 did not bring the desired changes in its wake, merely disillusionment and a renewed striving for national unity rather than political freedom. Martini has emphasized the social background of the German Realists by referring to the period after 1850 as *Bürgerlicher Realismus*, this holds equally well for the *Biedermeier* writers and distinguishes both from the Romantics. There is the same belief in *Bildung*, the same delight in social gatherings at home where music, poetry-reading and improvization play an integral part.

In literature there is much that links *Biedermeier* and the German species of Realism, so different from the French, English or Russian. They share an anti-Romantic desire for objectivity and a mistrust of the irrational. The tension between the ideal and reality is resolved by resignation, and this mood of "old age" which all *Biedermeier* critics beginning with Kluckhohn have noted, has recently been recognized as an essential characteristic of German Realism.[30] Provincialism is also a feature of both. Linguistically they both still draw on Goethe though there is a greater tendency to archaisms in the earlier period and greater use of dialect and colloquial speech in the later one. With regard to genres there is the same preference for story-telling whether in the form of narrative verse, the *Novelle* or the novel and yet the drama is considered to be the highest art form.

Differences do exist between *Biedermeier* and German Realism, the former has more faith in the possibility of achieving an ideal *bürgerlich* way of life, less awareness of its potential dangers; the latter is more conscious of its aims and proclaims them in programmatic statements. Both, however, represent a turning away from Romanticism and both are in turn rejected by the Naturalists who condemn them without regard for finer distinctions as idealistic Epigones.

The fact that it is not an international term has been brought forward as an argument against using *Biedermeier*. If, however, it helps to demonstrate that German Realism in all its form is very different from what is usually understood by the term, then this may well prove an advantage.

The term *Biedermeier* has had a confused history and since the only justification for a literary term is that it defines succinctly and associates broadly and meaningfully, it is, at the moment, of doubtful value. There is, however, an obvious need for this literary distinction and one can only hope that clarification may eventually lead to a general acceptance of the term and through it to a deeper understanding of the works its encompasses.

NOTES

1. Flemming, W. Die Problematik der Bezeichnung "Biedermeier", in: *G-RM*, N. F., Bd. 8, 1958, p. 384.
2. Majut, R., Das literarische Biedermeier. Aufriß und Probleme, in: *G-RM*, Bd. 20, 1932, p. 401 ff.
   Williams, C. A., Notes on the Origin and and History of the earlier "Biedermeier" in: *JEGP*, Vol. 57, 1958, p. 406 ff. Williams shows clearly that Kußmaul's rôle has been underestimated and that in fact he, rather than Eichrodt, can claim to be the inventor of *Biedermeier*.
3. I'd like to say just one more thing,
   It almost slipped my mind,
   A dish that's fit for any king
   Is fish and chips you'll find (freely adapted)
   Eichrodt, F. (ed.), *Das Buch Biedermeier*, 2nd ed. (Stuttgart, 1911), p. 16.
4. *Fliegende Blätter*, Vol. 21, No. 493.
5. Magill, C. P., The German Author and his Public in the Mid-Nineteenth Century, in: *MLR*, Vol. 43, 1948, p. 494.

6. *Biedermeier* in Chains.
7. Hermann, G., *Das Biedermeier* (Berlin, 1913), p. 6.
8. Immermann, K., Die Epigonen, in: *Werke*, Vol. 3 (Leipzig), p. 135.
9. Stifter in a letter to Heckenast, 13.5.1854.
10. "Further Influences of Romanticism on the Culture of the Nineteenth and Twentieth Centuries." The talk was delivered in Danzig on 7 October 1927 and printed in the *Ztf. für dt. Bildung*, Vol. 4, 1928, p. 62.
11. Kluckhohn, P., Biedermeier als literarische Epochenbezeichnung, *DVJs*, Vol. 13, 1935, p. 3.
12. Majut, R., Das literarische Biedermeier. Aufriß und Probleme, in: *G-RM*, Vol. 20, 1932, p. 401.
13. Grolman, A.v., *Biedermeier*-Forschung, in: *Dichtung und Volkstum*, Vol. 36, 1935, p. 312.
14. Dünninger, J., *G-RM*, Vol. 19, 1931, p. 173.
15. Sauer, A., *Euphorion*, Vol. 27, 1926.
16. Grolman, A.v., op. cit., p. 319.
17. Höllerer, W., *Zwischen Klassik und Moderne* (Stuttgart, 1958), p. 470.
18. Minder, R., *Kultur und Literatur in Deutschland und Frankreich* (Frankfurt, 1962), p. 52.
19. ennobled *Biedermeier*.
20. Kluckhohn, P., op. cit., p. 26.
21. Pascal, R., *The German Novel* (Manchester, 1956), p. 70.
22. Alas that I was born too soon!
A new world is in the making.
Fallersleben, H.v., *Unpolitische Lieder*, Vol. 1 (Hamburg, 1840), p. 162.
23. "hôhen muot" cannot be adequately translated. It implies inner harmony, a proper self-esteem and buoyant confidence.
24. serenely joyous.
25. collecting and cherishing. Weydt, G., Literarisches Biedermeier, in: *DVJs*, Vol. 9, 1931.
26. Majut, R., *Lebensbühne und Marionette. Ein Beitrag zur seelengeschichtlichen Entwicklung von der Genie-Zeit bis zum Biedermeier*. Germ. Stud. 100 (Berlin, 1931).
27. Kölmel, K., *Gutzkows Beurteilung der programmatischen Realisten Gustav Freytag, Julius Schmidt und Otto Ludwig* (Heidelberg, 1964). This is a preliminary investigation which is to be extended into a doctoral thesis. I am indebted to Prof. Sengle for allowing me access to it.
28. Martini, F., Der Realismus im 19. Jahrhundert und Wilhelm Raabe, *Dichtung und Volkstum*, Vol. 36, 1935, p. 280.
29. Hermand, J., *Die literarische Formenwelt des Biedermeiers* (Giessen, 1958), p. 3.
30. Martini, F., Spätzeitlichkeit in der Literatur des 19. Jahrhunderts, in: *Stoffe, Formen, Strukturen* (München, 1962).

168   PERIODS IN GERMAN LITERATURE

BIBLIOGRAPHY

Deutsche Vierteljahresschrift für Literaturwissenschaft und Geistesge-schichte, 13. Jahrg. Bd. 13 (Halle, 1935).
Dichtung und Volkstum, Bd. 36 (Stuttgart, 1935).
Flemming, W.: Die Problematik der Bezeichnung "Biedermeier", in: *G-RM*, N. F., Bd. 8, 1958.
Hermand, J., *Die literarische Formenwelt des Biedermeiers* (Giessen, 1958).
Majut, R., Der deutsche Roman vom Biedermeier bis zur Gegenwart, in: *Deutsche Philologie im Aufriß*, Bd. 2: Das literarische Biedermeier. Aufriß und Probleme, in: *G-RM*, 20 Jhrg. 1932.
Merker, P. and Stammler, W. (ed.), *Reallexikon der deutschen Liter-aturgeschichte* (Berlin, 1958).
Sengle, F., Voraussetzungen und Erscheinungsformen der deutschen Res-taurationszeit, in: *DVJs*, Bd. 30, 1956. Der Romanbegriff in der ersten Hälfte des 19. Jahrhunderts, in: *Festschrift für Franz Rolf Schröder* (Heidelberg, 1959). Stilistische Sorglosigkeit und gesellschaftliche Bewährung. Zur Literatur der Biedermeierzeit, in: *Formkräfte der deutschen Dichtung vom Barock bis zur Gegenwart* (Göttingen, 1963).
Williams, C. A., Notes on the Origin and History of the earlier "Bieder-meier", in: *JEGP*, Vol. 57, 1958.
This list merely attempts to select literature representative of the main points of view in the *Biedermeier* discussion.

Realism

VIII

Realism

JAMES M. RITCHIE

I

REALISM as a literary label has been applied to many different ages and authors. Since the 1930s a very special kind of Realism, namely Socialist Realism, has been the official literary doctrine of the Communist Party. Historically, however, Realism has come to be particularly associated with the literature of the second half of the nineteenth century. It is the nature of this Realism with which we are here concerned. In Germany literary Realism has been characterized as *bürgerlich* by some historians, while others prefer the term *Der poetische Realismus* as it was used by Otto Ludwig, for example, in his discussion of Shakespeare and Schiller and later taken over by Adolf Stern into his history of German literature.[1] And there have been other attempts besides "poetic" and *bürgerlich* to characterize the peculiar nature of German Realism. But whatever the qualifying epithet, Realism in some form is generally accepted as the main feature of the age. Theoretically it should be possible to be realistic about anything—the beautiful, the sordid, the past and the present, etc.—but a qualification like *bürgerlich* already indicates that in Germany, at least in the second half of the nineteenth century, literary Realism was very selective, focusing attention on the middle class rather than on the highest or the lowest social levels. Hence the "haute bourgeoisie" and Junker nobility, are to be found only in the latecomer Fontane, just as the lower depths of society, North German serfs and day-labourers, are not the normal concern of the so-called Realists. Similarly the qualification "poetic" should warn the modern reader who has been conditioned by twentieth century usage to expect from a work described as "realistic" a range of psychological and physical description calculated to shock, that the treatment will be rather different. Indeed any reader who approaches German Realist literature with his mind conditioned by such contemporary expectation of what "Realism" means, or whose ideas of Realism have been formed on an acquaintance with the works of European Realism, will be completely at a loss with German Realism. Here yet again Germany is apparently culturally out of step with the rest of Europe. As a result the German Realists are often quickly dismissed as inferior. Erich Auerbach in his famous study of the problem of *Mimesis, The Representation of Reality in Western Literature*, generously admits the merits of authors like Keller and Stifter, yet awards the honours to France :[2]

> In its grasp of contemporary reality French literature is far ahead of the literature of other European countries in the nineteenth century. As for Germany, or rather the territory where German is spoken . . . if we consider that Jeremias Gotthelf (born 1797) was but two years older and Adalbert Stifter (1805) six years younger than Balzac; that the German contemporaries of Flaubert (1821) and Edmond de Goncourt (1822) are men like Freytag (1816), Storm (1817), Fontane and Keller (both 1819); that the (comparatively) most noteworthy prose-fiction writers born roughly contemporaneously with Emile Zola—that is, about 1840—are Anzengruber and Rosegger : these names alone are enough to show that in Germany life itself was much more provincial, much more old-fashioned, much less "contemporary."

Becker in his vast compendium volume, *Documents of Modern Literary Realism* has practically nothing to say about German literature :[3]

> German participation in the realistic movement leaves much to be desired as far as both critical discussion and the works produced are concerned. Though there were during the middle of the century works of a certain importance in terms of their representation of everyday life, there was also a tendency towards what is called "poetic realism", which inclines towards the sentimental.

Time magazine (19 December 1960), in its review of the English translation of *Green Henry* (Grove 1960), was much more abrupt :[4]

> In the period in which Gottfried Keller was busy being the greatest Swiss novelist (*Der grüne Heinrich* was published in 1854) Tolstoy wrote *War and Peace*, Melville wrote *Moby Dick*, and Emily Brontë wrote *Wuthering Heights*.

These quotations reveal some of the embarrassment critics schooled on the great novels produced in France, England and Russia in this period felt towards the literature of German Realism which apparently failed to maintain itself at the European level it had achieved in the *Goethezeit* and sank into provincial obscurity. Inside Germany itself there was for a long time a tendency to see the second half of the nineteenth century in idyllic, harmonizing, panegyric terms as a pre-industrial peasant and small-town middle-class culture which contrasted favourably both with the French-inspired excesses of the Young Germans and with the so-called rootless big-city culture of the twentieth century. Yet even then it was generally admitted that literature had become marginal, peripheral. Germany in this period became world-famous for her science and philosophy, her music and song, rather than for her literary efforts. From the point of view of our problem this means quite simply that Germany was not successful in the form of the realistic novel which was so successful elsewhere. It remains to demonstrate to some extent why; also perhaps to offer a tentative defence of German Realism as it is, instead of condemning it for failing to conform with that of the rest of Europe.

II

In recent years literary critics have returned to a re-examination of the problem of Realism in German literature. Brinkmann has given an examination of how the term was used in contemporary and later German literary history before going on to a structural analysis of particular works. He questions the whole nature of the term and points out the obvious contradictions in its usage. What does Realism mean? Is it a philosophy (e.g. Feuerbach's materialism) expressed and formed in a work of art, or characteristics of style and artistic technique, or the use of particular objects, motifs, themes and so on? Other critics have been more historical. Silz, for example, points briefly to the *Goethezeit*, the Classic-Romantic era of about 1770–1830 characterized by the growth of Idealistic philosophy from Kant to Schelling, and continues, "broadly speaking, Classicism tended towards the idealized, generalized, and typical; Romanticism towards the unique, imaginary and supernatural".[5] Hence neither Classicism nor Romanticism was really concerned with reality and both were, he claims, subjective in their attitude to the world of things. He then goes on to show how historical developments in the nineteenth century inevitably brought about a greater concern for the issues of the day. Young Germany, which grew out of the economic and social repercussions of the Paris revolution on Germany, produced perhaps little of lasting literary value; yet it did bring literature closer to reality. Similarly the growth of railways, the beginnings of industrialization, the influence of the new journalism, the advances of the exact sciences, were of significance and "under the stress of these altered conditions, writers developed the element of realism which was already present in Romanticism". Yet this does not go far to characterize the nature of German Realism. When one reads the novels and *Novellen* of Keller, Storm, Raabe, Fontane and the others, one finds apparently no trace of all this—no railways, no industrialization, no scientific materialism—and (outside Switzerland) little or no politics. Hence if Realism means the tendency to direct the gaze towards empirically observable reality (*Mimesis*) as opposed to the idealistic art of Classicism and Romanticism, then already at this point Realism in Germany takes a different direction. Lukács as a Communist critic does attempt to show the relationship between political and social reality and the image of it presented by the Realists, but this proves an extremely difficult task and he is most successful with a politically conscious writer like the Swiss Gottfried Keller and least successful with a more typical German like Raabe. Switzerland had not experienced the catastrophe of the failed revolution of 1848 and a writer living in a great democracy like Switzerland could enjoy the feeling of identity with his people which was denied the crushed and beaten, isolated liberals of Germany. Lukács' sympathies are therefore with a democrat like Keller, or with others who, like Büchner, Heine and later Fontane, were on the path to an awareness of democracy. He does not concern himself with writers like Droste-Hülshoff and Gotthelf or Stifter who might with equal right have been described as the forerunners of the Realism of the second half of the nineteenth century. In fact, what was lacking for a long time was a general survey of nineteenth century literature from the point of view of Realism. Silz, Lukács, Brinkmann all restrict themselves to a series of separate studies of particular authors and works, without attempting to show any continuous historical development. They could argue with some degree of justice that the lack of continuity in their essays reflects the disjointedness in the development of German Realism itself; however, that a complete picture of the period is not only essential but also radically changes the whole image of German realistic literature has been conclusively shown by Martini's recent *Deutsche Literatur im bürgerlichen Realismus*.[6] Martini sets out to destroy the much-favoured image of German Realism as an essentially positive, healthy, optimistic age. 1848–49, the Year of Revolutions, is taken not only as the turning-point in the political life of Germany, but also as the literary watershed. Earlier writers, for example Gotthelf, who could be considered forerunners of Realism, are rightly felt to belong to a different generation from that which came to the fore after 1848. Some of them, for example Stifter, produced major works after 1848 yet their formative years were spent in the socio-religious acceptance world of the *Vormärz*, which put its characteristic stamp on their works. Claude David, the French literary historian, has also agreed to the advisability of seeing 1848 as the beginning of a new literary period. He produces an impressive list of reasons why this should be so.[7] Annette von Droste-Hülshoff dies in this year, Lenau shortly afterwards (1850). Heine has still eight years of life but in this time he composes only the poems of the *Romanzero*; in 1848 Grillparzer completes *Libussa*, his last tragedy; Mörike's work is also completed in all essentials, although the poet did not die until 1875. The last followers of Romanticism disappear, and at the same time the generation of the *Biedermeier* period also dies out. On the other hand the "littérature engagée" of the years preceding the March Revolution also suddenly ceases. Freiligrath emigrates to England, not to return to Germany for another twenty years. Herwegh also flees and his hymn to the young socialist movement, the *Arbeitermarseillaise* (1863), is composed abroad. There are still liberal writers—Keller, Spielhagen—but literature has now completely abandoned the militant element and has become discreet and subdued. The difference between a pre-1848 play like Hebbel's *Maria Magdalena* (1844) and the post-1848 rehabilitation of Authority and *Staatsräson* celebrated in *Agnes Bernauer* (1855) is typical of the deep division in the career of many nineteenth century writers. Wagner after the Revolution corrected the sense of the *Ring der Nibelungen*, putting a spirit of renunciation and asceticism in place of revolt. Similarly there was a change in the form as well as the ideas of the post-1848 period, which now tended to the "poetic" and the symbolic rather than the direct statement. This "poetization" of reality is he claims the characteristic trend in post-revolutionary Germany.

In what way then did writers like Keller, Storm, Raabe, Fontane, Meyer, who did not break in any sense radically with what had gone before—either with the Romantics, the Young Germans or the so-called *Biedermeier* writers—produce a literature which is clearly of the post-1848 period? This has been a major source of confusion regarding the German Realists. Not only was German Realism different from English, French and Russian Realism, particularly in the novel, but inside Germany itself there were no major *literary* upheavals to differentiate the Realists clearly from those who had gone before or even from their various contemporaries. The years following 1848 were years of great change in every sphere of German life. Great social and political developments were taking place; the middle classes were going through a period of ferment as they adapted themselves to their changing position in society; the growth of scientific materialism was making its impact on the industrial life of the nation, which was also catching up rapidly with the economic pace-makers like England; and politically the great "German Problem" which the Frankfurt Parliament of 1848 had failed to solve, namely the unification of Germany, was very much in the foreground. All this was happening, yet the modern reader naively expecting the literature of this age to mirror these events will be confused. German Realism is not naively mimetic. The German Realist was aware of all these problematic developments but far from any simple direct reproduction in literary terms of contemporary reality, one finds veiled reference, encapsulation and hints as the striking features of his presentation of them. Far from German Realism being good solid artifacts of an optimistic middle class, the age is in fact as Martini has characterized it : many-sided, problematic and contradictory. He presents a new image of an age markedly different from pre-1848 *Biedermeier* :[8]

> The picture of a multidirectional, contradictory age filled with change and crisis in which especially in literature antinomial, subjectivistic and centrifugal forces predominate. In these decades the disintegration of a firm, assured awareness of wholeness in the conditions of real life, in philosophy, in the sphere of aesthetic creation and the consciousness of the individual became dominant in form and content.

And indeed, one made aware of this process of disintegration, it is relatively easy to find contemporary expression given to the "contradictions" of the age. Constantin Frantz, for example, in an essay dealing with the problem of literature and political unity in the year 1865, writes :[9]

> If the contradiction really exists between the state disunity of Germany and the demands of reawakened national feeling, and if this contradiction begins to penetrate more and more into the general consciousness, then naturally the artists, the philosophers, and the men of learning will not remain unaffected by it either. Rather they too will feel compelled to work towards the solution of this great task; but by doing so there arises within them a divided interest, and an agitation which is detrimental to intellectual production, and indeed makes the creation of a classical work absolutely impossible. Witness of this is the literature of the day, which bears the mark of a feeling of dissatisfaction and contradiction writ large on its forehead.

Constantin Frantz has given an accurate description of the literature of his own age. Authors who attempted to deal directly in literary form with such problems as literature and political unity did fail disastrously to produce anything in any way approaching a classical work. It was no longer possible for the artist to withdraw into the world of his own ideas to see the absolute, the universal being, the real. The pull to participate in the movement of the age was not to be gainsaid, nor as a result could contact with the contradictions and general unsatisfactoriness of national conditions be avoided. No great works would be possible, claimed Frantz further, until the Germans achieved a satisfactory national constitution, which would give the genius a new basis to work on and, equally important, reawaken in the literary public that receptivity for works of a higher order which had practically disappeared. Here too Frantz was remarkably perceptive, for the nineteenth century German literary public did show unbelievably debased artistic preferences. As sociologists have pointed out, hardly any age has experienced such a thorough-going reversal of its critical judgments. The works which were welcomed with adulation in the nineteenth century and easily reached phenomenal numbers of editions are ridiculed today. Redwitz, Bodenstedt, Roquette, Scheffel—these were the authors really admired by the middle-class public, whereas the Realists Keller, Raabe, Storm and others, while they did enjoy some success, generally only succeeded in attracting a comparatively small circle of faithful admirers. In the age of Bismarck the *Bürger* showed little concern for great works of art. He had withdrawn from the world of ideals into the manageable world of business, science and technology in which he quickly showed his worth and changed the face of Germany as he had failed to do politically. Charlatan poets and artists satisfied his immediate needs for the "poetic". The German Realists meanwhile expressed growing awareness of the contradictions of the age not in radical representations of external reality, but in a "poetic", "inward" synthesis of the real and the ideal. *Innerlichkeit* must be accepted as one of the central characteristics of German Realism— indeed inwardness as much as anything is what makes German Realism "poetic". The German Realist does *not* show the social and historical world as it existed objectively. Rather is this world revealed as it was experienced and understood by the individual. German Realism is thereby never simply a mirror-image of objective reality, nor, however, is it a subjective speculation about reality. It is a complex and contradictory fusion of the subjective and the objective. Essentially at the heart of the matter is the isolated individual attempting to find coherence and order (*Zusammenhang der Dinge*) in the, for him, apparently increasing chaos of the modern world. For this he turned to what still seemed the constant, enduring values to be found in nature, the people, well-known and well-loved geographical areas, historical tales, cultural traditions, social and ethical values, etc. Yet the process of *Verinnerlichung* could never be allowed to go too far and here as elsewhere the German Realist tried to strike a happy medium. The attempt to combine the poetic and the real meant that the Realist could abandon himself neither to the objectively factual nor to the purely subjective. The balance to be struck between these two extremes is the essence of German Realism.[10]

> This literature of Realism is historically complete in itself at that point where it grew out of this strained and yet harmonizing polarity of being bound to objective reality while subjectivizing it, out of the coherence of the whole and the individual existence of the ego; where it experienced in this polarity the problematic nature of concrete human existence within the restrictions of this world.

But the literature of German Realism cannot be described simply in terms of the subject-object polarity without taking note of the one element which at once reveals the problematic nature of the age, namely *humour*. Indeed a recent study has taken humour as revealing the essential nature of the "poetic" in German Realism.[11] But already many years before, Bramsted had been aware of its importance and tried to tie it to the differing attitude to society of the "ethical" and the "aesthetic" writer.[12]

> The one frees himself from the pressure of social reality by biting satire, the other by soothing humour. The ethical writer wants to alter the world, the aesthetic writer only to contemplate it; the realism of the one is critical, that of the other poetical.

By this definition German Realism is aesthetic rather than ethical. Another examination of the humorous novel is largely in agreement with this interpretation of humour, while stressing once again the *Innerlichkeit* of the Realist.[13]

> The richness of the inner life of the humourist is such that it can embrace all contradictions and enable him to meet all men, good or bad, with understanding and sympathy and smile benevolently at their weaknesses and errors. He sees himself merely as a warrior for the essence against appearance, that is to say for the values of the inner life for the nature of the individual.

Martini stresses even more the "contradictions" of reality which humour makes apparent. Humour for him is a form of subjective release from the pressures of disillusioned reality, accepting life with all its disturbing elements while at the same time distancing oneself from it, revealing its contradictions while putting up with them with resignation, unmasking life while at the same time trying to be fair and find a tolerant compromise. The humour of the Realists ranges from the golden glow of Gottfried Keller to the tragi comic, the absurd and the grotesque, as in Raabe and Busch. But whatever the form, humour is a fundamental structural element in making the presentation of natural and historical reality "poetic".

It has been argued in general terms that as a type the Realist tends to the statistical norm, the social generality. He writes not of exceptional people (artists, leaders, prophets, poets, etc.) nor of the excitement of great art, grand passions, religious ecstasies. Fine rhetoric, pathos, elevated gestures, in fact any "excess" will be avoided, as the Realist concerns himself with commonplace people in everyday situations. This is certainly true of German Realist literature which becomes a literature of the intimate, the personal and familiar, the family, the neighbourhood, the province. The dangers of this are obvious and indeed the authors themselves were well aware of them. Was truth to outweigh poetry? This could not be allowed. Simple documentation and factual presentation of normal lives instead of the imaginative, impassioned presentation of exceptional ones could lead only to dullness, heaviness, slowness of tempo and boredom. Realism runs the risk of becoming trivial, recording the obscure lives of insignificant people incapable of expressing any thoughts or emotions even if they had them. Hence the German Realist attempted to avoid these pitfalls by giving not simply a presentation of something which really did happen, or really did exist. His work was still a fiction (*Dichtung*), but now a consistent fiction of the probable or at least possible, unlike Romantic tales which constantly deal with the impossible and the improbable. At the same time he attempted to give a *significant* picture, or not merely the real but also the ideal, i.e. that which reveals the real as meaningful. He could exploit the possibilities of the picturesque (e.g. local habits, customs, peasant costumes and tradition, etc.) to make his simple tales interesting in the same way as the Romantic exploited the exotic. Similarly his heroes are often curious "characters" rather than commonplace people. But basically it is this hint of meaning, this glimpse of significance behind the contradictions of the real world (*Zusammenhang der Dinge*) by which he hopes to raise his Realism above the mere documentation of random fact.

German literature, then, it can be said, suffers a considerable reduction in scope and range; the reader must leave behind the vast sweep of European Realism, leave behind the universal aspect of the *Goethezeit* and the *Restaurationszeit* and withdraw into a comparatively narrow and strangely quaint, old-fashioned world apparently unshaken by external events, political disturbance, economic change, philosophical or aesthetic speculation. But appearances are deceptive. A careful reading, a sensitive awareness of the characteristic process of *Verinnerlichung* reveal that the German Realist was aware of the paradoxes and contradictions of the age in which he lived and expressed them subtly in his own oblique manner. Nevertheless such oblique, discreet writing seems far removed from former glories. Now in the age of Realism German literature restricted itself to a concern with the German in his own regional setting, with all the force of popular and national traditions to draw on. Yet this in itself is one of the greatest contradictions of German Realism. The age which produced so many apparently endearing pictures of German village and small-town life with all their colour and richness was also the great Age of Emigration, in which hundreds of thousands of Germans tore up their roots in the hallowed tradition and left. There were writers in plenty to record the effects of this new *Völkerwanderung*, though it is normally not a theme treated by the major Realists directly :[14]

O sprecht! warum zogt ihr von dannen?
Das Neckartal hat Wein und Korn;
Der Schwarzwald steht voll finstrer Tannen,
Im Spessart klingt des Älplers Horn.

Wie wird es in den fremden Wäldern
Euch nach der Heimatberge Grün,
Nach Deutschlands gelben Weizenfeldern
Nach seinen Rebenhügeln ziehn!

Why did so many leave their native land if it had so much to offer? They left behind religious intolerance, political and economic restriction, land hunger, *Zunft- und Handwerkspedanterie* (Guild and Craft pedantry) to seek fortune and freedom in America. One must be careful not to be misled by Gotthelf and Keller, whose proud Swiss peasants and admirable guild craftsmen might easily perpetuate a picture of happy citizens and peasants which is in no way characteristic of Germany as a whole. Even Switzerland, as Gotthelf and Keller show, were exposed to the typical contradictions of the age (cf. *Geld und Geist*), while Germany, as Raabe with his wistful humour revealed, was still very much a *Bumsdorf* with no understanding whatsoever of the outside world. When

Leonhard Hagebucher comes home from imprisonment in Africa, then

> when confronted with this fabulous, strayed, out-of-hand, de-railed, uprooted, dislocated existence, German philistinism felt shaken to the core of its tax- and rate-paying, pew-letting, police-guarded and all-princely-authority-supervised, glorious security and expressed itself accordingly.[15]

Most of the nineteenth century Realists were *Bürger* born into the narrow world of provincial philistinism which they portray in their works with a mixture of love and rejection, and indeed *Verbürgerlichung*, i.e. the increasing influence of the middle classes on all spheres of life, the rise of the "prosaic" *Mittelstand* to economic if not political power, has often been put forward as a factor in the rise of Realism. The middle-classes, it is assumed, demand Realism, though in Germany, as has been seen, their real demand was for "poetic" idealization. In fact it is often extremely difficult to characterize this so-called process of *Verbürgerlichung*, just as it is difficult to recapture the nature of the German nineteenth century *Mittelstand*. Goethe had once called it the curdled milk which is left after the sour cream (the rich) has been skimmed off; but he probably came nearer to it in his remarks on German literature :[16]

> To it belong the inhabitants of small towns, of which there are so many well-situated and prosperous examples in Germany. All public servants, and their assistants, business people, factory owners and especially the wives and daughters of such families, also country parsons in their capacity as teachers of people in restricted but at the same time comfortable and morally re-warding circumstances.

After 1848 it became fashionable to address the craftsman class in town and country as *Bürger* : Bismarck indeed described such craftsmen as the very backbone of the middle classes and this adulation is exactly the kind of thing one finds in the works of the Realists who write tales of a master-slater (Otto Ludwig's *Zwischen Himmel und Erde*), a master-tailor, like Hediger in Keller's *Fähnlein der sieben Aufrechten*, or combmakers, as in the same author's famous story, though *they* come out of it all rather badly. The proletariat had yet to appear in the mass, hence the German Realist wrote not of the factory worker, the mechanical man of industrialization, but of the organic man-of-his-craft, not of the day-labourer but the settled *Bauer* (peasant), the organic man of the soil. He wrote of the age before the transformation of *Bürger* and *Bauer* into the ostentatious *Bourgeois*. Summing up towards the end of his masterly study, Bramsted has pointed to the limitations of the middle classes as the reason for the decline of German literature from the best standards.[17]

> The main experience, the central subject of most of these writers ... was formed by *Heimat* and class. Although occasionally they criticized these social factors, they could never rise superior to them. Therefore German literature of the nineteenth century after Heine lacked on the whole any European significance ... They thought in a middle-class manner, even when they lived somewhat bohemian lives, and they lived quite often in middle-class style, even when they did not think like commoners. This literary approach to the world could be polemicizing as with Spielhagen, proud as with Freytag, mellow as with Keller: it could be more aggressive as before 1870, or more condoning as after 1870; in any case it formed a striking feature of the fiction and of much of the poetry produced between 1830 and 1900.

Naturally it is false to think of the *Bürgerstand* of the nineteenth century as in any way a unified social group, and therefore capable of presenting a unified picture of itself. Here as elsewhere the contradictory nature of the age is apparent. The *Bürgerstand* was split down the middle by the contrasting forces of *Beharren* (permanence) and *Bewegung* (movement). "The ideal *Bürger* combined the two—he had both the *conservative* force of the aristocracy and the peasantry, and the *progressive* force of the town-dweller. The *Bürgertum* was at one and the same time expected to be a force for social and economic progress against the aristocracy and a force for permanence, order and moderation. Hence the *Bürger* tended to be politically liberal and progressive but with conservative tendencies. The balance between the two forces was obviously precarious."[18] The true *Bürger* (cf. Keller) was much distressed by the self-righteousness, vulgar ostentation and hypocrisy of the new bourgeoisie. Similarly if the world of the ideal *Bürger* became too narrow and confined he became a philistine (*Spieß-bürger*). Bramsted has characterized the essence of philistinism as follows :[19]

> conceited, self-satisfactory indifference, hostility to intellectualism, a limited horizon, such as were to be found throughout politically disunited Germany, and the numerous residential and petty towns. The prevalence of disintegrating individualism in towns was the result of the eighteenth century. The lack of a

central power and the tardy development of a public opinion supplied the fertile soil for German philistinism.

This is the world into which the German Realist leads his readers, yet unlike the French Realist (cf. Flaubert) the German rarely attacks philistinism with biting satire. In fact the absence of satire is one of the striking (negative) features of German literature. The German *bürgerlicher Realist* was more contemplative than aggressive; sadly and resignedly aware of inevitable change in the old world he loved, he could find solace neither in the reactionary state Christianity which the post-1848 restoration brought, nor in the aggressive critique of religion instituted by Strauß, Feuerbach and others. After 1848 there was no Christian literature of an artistic order and this is the greatest single difference between *Biedermeier* and Realism. Grillparzer, Gotthelf, Eichendorff were still writing from a Christian viewpoint, but they belong essentially to an earlier generation. Keller, Storm, Raabe and others were more moral than religious and with them an acceptance of the irrational, the ineffable, the fateful, took the place of orthodox faith. This too in a sense involved a limitation in the scope and range of their works. These Realists were concerned only with problems of life on this earth. For a philosopher like Feuerbach this did not necessarily entail loss. The reduction of God to an anthropomorphous extension of man himself could, he argued, result in an enhancement of the value of life on this earth, in the value of the real as distinct from the ideal world :[20]

Atheism sacrifices the world of ideal and fantasy for that of real life. Therefore atheism is positive, affirmative. It gives back to Nature and mankind the dignity which theism took away... Atheism is liberal, generous, tolerant; it grants every being its own will and talent, it rejoices deeply in the beauty of Nature, and in the virtue of man; joy and love do not destroy, they animate, affirm.

His simple claim was that life on this earth could be rich and good. But despite such affirmations of the positive advantages of atheism and a turn to reality, the result for many Realists who followed his teaching was a lingering sense of loss, a certain melancholy, the sadness of old men pondering on death, an ever-present awareness of the transience of all things.

III

Martini's history of the literature of *bürgerlicher Realismus* is essentially a history of literary forms. This proves a most illuminat-

ing approach to the period. Throughout the whole of the nineteenth century the drama and especially tragedy, was acclaimed
as the pinnacle of aesthetic perfection; yet in the second half of
the century the sense of the tragic was gradually lost and the drama
died. Where before 1848 Büchner and Grabbe had given expression
to a powerful tragic vision of existence, this survived only in Hebbel
and even today there is doubt as to how far his rather creaky intellectual constructions can genuinely be described as tragic. Certainly he has never become a figure of world drama like Büchner.
Various reasons have been suggested for the decline of tragedy in
the Age of Realism, and generally the finger of blame is pointed
once again at the *Bürger* who by his social-political situation had
been forced into an attitude of resigned, contemplative passivity
inimical to the very nature of drama which is based on action.
Further,

> the subjectivization of the language of literary forms, the trend
> towards the epic view of the world, the psychologization and
> relativisation of morals, the loss of metaphysical awareness, the
> acceptance of strict cause and effect in the interpretation of life
> processes—all this conflicted with the dramatic form. Last but
> not least, the liberal belief in development and progress was out
> of sympathy with the concept of tragedy.[21]

But if great tragedy disappeared there was an equal lack of significant dramatic production in other forms as well. Contemporary
revolutionary plays, historical dramas, political comedies, social
dramas, were produced in great numbers but were of poor standard. Only Anzengruber succeeded in writing significant *Volks-
stücke*. Only Wagner succeeded in producing the depth and scope
which was so noticeably lacking elsewhere. Opera for him was "the
regeneration of the whole, fundamental, simple and direct religious-
myth drama presenting the totality of man in epic expressive
form".[22] But significantly it is his music which is the true vehicle
of totality. The actual texts of his lyric-dramatic-epic operas
demonstrate all the weaknesses of the age.

In the same way as it is difficult despite Hebbel's *Maria Magdalena*, etc. to talk of the Realism of a declining form like the
drama, so too the lyric of the second half of the century is not,
despite equally massive production, the leading literary form. With
all the riches of the *Goethezeit* to choose from, it is noticeable here
again that the major forms (e.g. Ode, Hymn) are avoided and
the smaller or more narrative forms (e.g. Ballad) preferred. As has
already been suggested, the great lyrical works in Germany in the
nineteenth century were achieved outside the purely literary sphere

in the *Lied*, just as the opera took the place of the drama. In any event, the difference between the years before 1848 which had fostered the lyrical talents of Mörike, Heine, Platen and Lenau, Grillparzer and Droste-Hülshoff, and the years after 1848, is striking. The failure of the 1848 Revolution also meant the end of significant political lyrics, though Freiligrath, Herwegh and Heine were still writing. Realists like Keller, Storm and Fontane produced fine lyrical poetry and ballads but the lyrical appetite of the age was more easily satisfied by pseudo-poets like Geibel and the Epigones of the Munich Circle. Only C. F. Meyer, whose historicism, aestheticism and love of Romance forms and costumes brought him artistically very close to Geibel, Heyse and the Munich Circle, broke through to a new French-style plasticity and "produced some quiet restrained lyrics of great formal beauty in which the personal content is crystallized in an image rather than explicitly stated". This almost symbolic means of expression was to be the lyric of the future. But the ballad, verse-epic and shorter verse narratives were still the most favoured verse-forms as in the pre-1848 age of *Biedermeier*. The great successes of the age, as has been seen, were not the now cherished *Novellen* of the Realists, but Scheffel's *Der Trompeter von Säckingen*, Redwitz' *Amaranth*, Bodenstedt's *Mirza Schaffy* and Roquette's *Waldmeisters Brautfahrt*—historical, exotic, village and pseudo-cultural verse idylls which appealed to the contemporary taste for the "poetic".

But as Heine had recognized long before, this was to be the age of the prose narrative, not of verse. Throughout Europe the novel became the literary form of the age. Yet here again one is struck by the difference between the German novel of the second half of the nineteenth century and that of the *Goethezeit*. Gone now, for example, is the Romantic ideal of the novel as the expression of totality. Instead, as has been seen, the German novel withdraws to a smaller area of family life, the individual in his own neighbourhood or province. Great ideas, overwhelming passions, far-reaching concern for humanity in general, disappear. Instead of the common concern of the European novel, namely, action and event in the world of social reality, there is concern with the individual soul in its conflict with society. European literature outside Germany assumed the function of social criticism to an increasing degree corresponding to the development of a new cosmopolitan reading public. Writers in London, Paris, Petersburg rubbed shoulders with scientists and political leaders; they knew and influenced each other. Proudhon influenced the conception of Tolstoy's *War and Peace*; Turgenev's life touched upon that of Bakunin, Flaubert and Herzen.[23] Dickens was a parliamentary reporter.

Together they produced realistic novels with a social function, the intellectual food of an earnest and humanitarian public, novels which also became great works of art. Such social novels were attempted in Germany, mainly in continuation of the attempts of the Young Germans, but Gutzkow, Freytag and Spielhagen are not names one can seriously consider alongside Dickens, Disraeli, Tolstoy and Flaubert. The realistic social novel in Germany failed.[24] Clearly one can put forward political and sociological reasons for this failure—not least the lack of an intellectual and cosmopolitan centre like the great capitals, Paris and London, and the society corresponding to them. German *Dorf-* and *Kleinstadtgeschichten,* or novels in which the action takes place in a stuffy little *Residenz,* look very provincial and timid after the world of London, Paris and Petersburg. But one must remember that political and religious reaction following 1848 in Germany made all oppositional literature difficult, and besides, the still divided, particularized state of the country made it impossible to give a general picture of real life which would be "typical" for the whole of Germany. Apart from these reasons for the apparent failure of the German social novel there were more directly aesthetic reasons. Germany had no firm tradition of the novel as an accepted literary form as, for example, England had. The novel still tended to be discussed by critics like Hegel and Vischer as a debased modern form of the Homeric epic. Only the *Bildungsroman* like *Wilhelm Meister* or *Heinrich von Ofterdingen* seemed a true German form and that stressed once again the *inner* life of the passive, contemplative individual rather than giving an extensive portrayal of objective social reality as it impinges upon him. Further, it has been pointed out that the *Bildungsroman* by its very nature tended to concentrate on the past, leaving the hero on the threshold of his entry into the world— on the whole it does not show how, his education completed, he would cope with reality. In general it was accepted by critics and aestheticians that the drama and the epic were the realm of great deeds in the big world. In the novel the hero had to be "receptive" rather than active, suffering rather than doing, driven rather than driving, the dependent person exposed to and thereby revealing the fateful forces at work in the world or the society of the time. Little wonder, then, that the German novel of the nineteenth century has been accused of lacking in any serious representation of contemporary day-to-day social reality as it reflected historical developments, preferring the unchanging status quo, avoiding the ugly and keeping discussion at only a modest level, without probing too deeply. It has been accused of lingering too long among regional, provincial traditions, losing itself in the quiet of quaint little corners which were safe and German, and thereby failing to give a true picture of the age.[25]

It was heavily impregnated with the idyllic and the *Gutbürger-liche*, the lyrical and historical, the personal and the idealistic, the arabesque and the eccentric—a far cry from the determined surgery of Stendhal, Balzac and Flaubert.

The German social, historical, provincial novel and the *Bildungs-roman* tended to be "intensive" (as Ludwig put it) in the stress on the subjective element rather than "extensive" in portrayal of objective reality. A balance was struck between the hero and the world he lived in. First-person narratives, reminiscence techniques and framing tales became the preferred devices to produce this balance between the subjective and the objective, the individual and society, the intensive foreground and the related background. The novels of Raabe and Fontane have been subjected to consider-able critical reappraisal of late and have only gained in the process. Keller's *Der grüne Heinrich* is a significant work, as even *Time* magazine was prepared to admit. But even so well-disposed a critic as Roy Pascal leaves the Realist novels of "moral adaptation with-in the social sphere" with some doubts :[26]

> this limitation does not go without some spiritual impoverish-ment. From Gotthelf's world the great issues of modern life, its potentialities and subtle seductions are shut out. Raabe's intel-lectual vision is limited, and his conception of man's powers is modest and subdued. Fontane, with his robust commonsense, sidles away from tragic involvements. Neither of these two grapples with the fierce energies at work in modern society, and their tolerant humanism stops at accommodations which lack penetration and spiritual adventurousness.

But criticism of the path taken by the realistic German novel need not be entirely negative. While it is true that it reflects the general process of reduction to the idyllic genre-painting and indi-vidual character portrait in which the element of conflict is re-moved and subjective humour and a shrug of resignation take the place of action, nevertheless in general the German novel is being judged on the basis of a kind of Realism which is foreign to it. One must just simply accept the fact that the German novel is different, and that "the sphere of the novel cannot be reduced merely to social criticism and psychology, rather it can be just as open to problems of *Innerlichkeit* (inwardness)". Certainly this is the direction taken by the German Realist novel in its main forms.

It was the *Novelle*, however, not the novel, which was to prove

the appropriate form for German Realism and reveal its full poten-
tials. Apparently only in the smaller, not the larger, prose narrative
genre was great artistic production possible; only within a very
limited range could the desired synthesis be achieved : poetic presentation of reality. Many reasons have been suggested for the
success of the *Novelle*, e.g. that it was the form most suited to the
respectable middle-class journals of the age (Storm, Raabe and
others all wrote for such family newspapers), or that the fragmentary nature of the *Novelle*, which presents only a series of scenes or
episodes rather than the totality of events which may be expected
of the novel, was better suited to reflect the fragmented, dislocated
nature of Germany of that time and so on. Not that the actual
form of the *Novelle* was fragmentary. On the contrary the rather
loose form of the Young German and *Biedermeier* tale developed
after 1848 into a sophisticated and highly stylized literary genre.
While it was true, as Martini points out, that strict application of
dogmatic rules of form was avoided except by lesser talents like
Heyse, nevertheless the *Novelle* form was made "poetic" and
therefore aesthetically more acceptable than the novel, by extremely careful workmanship and solid manipulation of structural
elements like framework and reminiscence techniques, fictitious
story-teller, the chronicle form, careful use of leit-motifs and
symbols, anticipatory images, parallel plots, etc., which imposed
"poetic" form on the fiction of reality. In place of the extensive
epic panorama, one now has in the *Novelle* an intensive glimpse of
the intimate sphere, internal psychological crises and fateful
moments in the life of the individual. Once again this is the
characteristic process of *Verinnerlichung* and may mean a reduction in scope; but such veiled symbolic hints as to the irrational,
fateful forces of life, the "coherence of things" (*Zusammenhang
der Dinge*) was exactly what made real life "poetic" to the taste
of the age. The *Novelle* took reality only as a point of departure
to be treated artistically, selectively. Martini sees the modernity of
the *Novelle* in its openness to the problematic nature of life : man is
determined by forces beyond his control—change, fate, strange and
wonderful forces can break in at any time upon the most commonplace existence and throw it along completely different lines. Far
from being the didactic art form of a contented, idyllic, harmonious
middle-class world, the *Novelle* with its *Wendepunkt*, its concentration on the isolation of the individual, etc., is the perfect literary
expression of the "contradictions" of the age. Perhaps the most
significant achievement of the *Novelle* is the manner in which it
took over the rôle of tragedy. Indeed Bennett in his history of the
German *Novelle* went so far as to head one of his chapters "The

Novelle as a Substitute for Tragedy". The *Novelle* could be lyrical (as in the early works of Storm) but it was raised to the heights of the "poetic" by its approximation to tragedy.[27]

> the *Novelle* of our days is the sister to drama, and is the most deliberate form of poetic prose. Like drama, the *Novelle* treats the most profound problems of human existence. In order to be perfect, *Novelle* and drama alike demand one central conflict. The structure of the entire *Novelle* radiates from this nucleus, and this in turn demands the utmost conciseness and the rigid exclusion of all unessentials. Thus the *Novelle* demands of the poet the utmost that he can give.

Of course Storm's claims for the high artistry and tragic depth of the *Novelle* form need not be accepted without question. It can equally be argued that the very acceptance of the *Novelle* as a substitute for tragedy means a reduction in the scope of the tragic, which is now seen in terms of passive suffering or acceptance of the inevitable, an elegiac awareness of the transience of all values, the tendency to resolve the contradictions between the inner world of the individual and the external world of reality by resort to sentimentality, etc. Indeed it has been suggested that the *Novelle* might more fruitfully be compared with the melodrama than the drama, and such a comparison is in general agreement with Bennett's thesis of the *bürgerlich* avoidance of conflict, the placing of the stress on suffering which inevitably evokes not "fear and pity" but the more sentimental emotions. "Bennett's reminder of the *Novelle*'s nearness to the later, very epic *Leidensdramen* of the Naturalists shows the same awareness of the *Novelle*'s proximity to melodrama."[28]

However, the range of the nineteenth century *Novelle* of Realism is wide, embracing all the main forms already noted for the novel from the social, historical, regional to the idyllic, humorous, lyrical, balladesque and the ghost-story. The essential feature of the *Novelle* form was always the selection of the significant, the exclusion of the "unpoetic". It did not attempt to give a general picture of social reality and hence did not have to solve the insuperable difficulties of the German social novel which attempted to record a disunited and chaotic German society. Completely consistent and objective recording of reality was still felt to be inimical to a still generally accepted idea of what was *Dichtung*. While European Realism expressed itself in the cosmopolitan, social, humanitarian novel, often of vast range and scope, German Realism was most successful in the short, formalized, symbolic prose narrative. It is essential, however, not merely to record this difference (the limitations and restrictions of German Realism have been constantly stressed) but also to appreciate the extent to which within such restrictions literature of more than passing merit could be produced.

IV

Realism in Germany was no school or movement. The writers, as has been seen, were displaced from the centre of things by the successful politicians, businessmen, scientists and technologists who became the spiritual leaders of the country. Yet though they were pushed away they were rarely pushed out, rarely became outsiders or bohemians and generally found a profession which gave them a place in society. In fact their work represents an attempt, rare in German literature, to attain some kind of harmony between the poet and the *Bürger*, the artist and society. It was generally a despairing attempt, for there was still no German *Volk* with whom the writer could identify himself, no capital city to become the meeting-place, and so the melting-pot of the nation. Hence the Realist became an isolated figure, isolated not only in himself, but also cut off from his like-minded contemporaries in his own province in Germany, Austria or Switzerland. He was on the periphery, not at the heart.

A famous book on the literature of this period used the title *The Battle over Tradition*, and indeed tradition was a problem for the writers of the time. It is the problem of Keller's *Züricher Novellen*—on whom should one model oneself? Keller's answer is significant : [29]

> The only good "original" is the man who really deserves imitation! However, the only man really worthy of being imitated is the man who does whatever he has taken on properly and always produces a sound piece of work in his own sphere, even if this is *not* something totally unprecedented or of dazzling originality.

The originality, spontaneity, creative imagination of the Romantics is now suspect. The aim is now modest, the ideal attainable, the hero one who executes his joyful task assiduously, be it ever so humble. Instead of dealing with the problems of the outstanding individual, the artist, the leader, prophet and poet, or with the great world of art, love and religion, the Realist turned to more modest themes and heroes. However, he had gained considerably over the preceding generation. At least he was no longer crushed by the weight of tradition, as were the *Epigonen* born under the shadow of Goethe. He could select carefully from the riches of the past and build equally carefully on them. What were felt to be the subjective exaggerations of the Romantics and the Young Germans were consolidated into something more objectively binding. Pathos was avoided, satire disappeared, the "demonic", present even in Mörike and Stifter, was subdued. Novalis, Hölderlin, Kleist had little or no influence; the linguistic creativeness of Heine, Büchner, Grabbe was levelled off into a harmonious, accepted, written German with just enough dialect and colloquialism to give personal colouring. Always this meant careful workmanship, careful selection of scene and material, careful use of perspective of the story-teller, placing of leit-motifs, symbols, etc. This kind of "genre-painting", with fine details from still life, seems far removed from the tempests of Kleist and the pinnacles of Hölderlin; yet there was a gain in the expressiveness of the minute, the psychology of the overlooked in the intimacy of everyday life. This is the sensitivity of "the allusive, half-style of veiled expression and cryptic hints, muted sometimes to the point of silence, the indirect, masking narrative technique".[30] This was more than a reduction of German literature to the harmless, the idyllic, the philistine : it was an attempt by the Realists to bring together the conflicting elements of the age to which they were heirs, it was an attempt to arrive at a new synthesis of all that had gone before. Only Goethe was felt to have achieved the desired balance and it was he who was proclaimed the exemplary Realist. The famous passage in Keller's *Der grüne Heinrich* is sufficient testimony to the love of reality and the awareness of its "coherence and depth" which Goethe's works were felt to impart :[31]

I felt a pure and simple pleasure such as I had never known before. It was his love, giving itself up completely to everything that existed and was organically complete, a love which honours the right and significance of every single thing and feels the coherence and depth of the world.

This too marks a difference between pre- and post-1848. The Young Germans and others had been the *Goethefeinde*, but now this conflict too is over, so much so in fact that one critic has claimed that the whole of the Age of Realism is characterized by the style of the older Goethe. The Realists, it is argued, created no new style, they all in a sense spoke Goethean. Certainly all wrote an extremely literary style.

Whereas the language and style of the years up to 1848 had shown considerable experimentation, now it all becomes more conservative, more toned down (*ausgeglichen*). Whereas it was true there were less incoherent and unfinished torsos, and the care and polish expended were to be commended, theirs was the care and steadiness of the careful workman following the rules of his guild, the work of the artisan craftsman rather than the inspired artist. Compared with Classicism and Romanticism there was a decline in linguistic power into formalistic traditionalism.[32]

And whereas the *Goethezeit* had been influenced by the great works of world literature and the influence of France up to 1848 had been extremely strong, after the Revolution there is a sudden narrowing to national sources. True, the historical novel came under the influence of Walter Scott, Dickens left his mark particularly on minor Realists like Ludwig, Freytag, Reuter and Auerbach while Turgenev was known to Storm and Fontane; but generally speaking the German Realists were unaware of their great European contemporaries Flaubert, Tolstoy, Dostoyevsky and others, and remained unaffected by them stylistically. Hence German Realism is not merely non-European, it is markedly "German". On the whole the German Realists were inarticulate about their art, reluctant to engage in wide-ranging discussions of the problem of mimesis and unwilling to work out a consistent Realist aesthetic. It was part of the "anachronism" of German cultural development that the Marxist critique of society made little or no impact on the German Realists of the post-1848 period and was to remain without influence till the real *Gründerzeit* in the age of Naturalism. Feuerbach, who was the most influential thinker of this time, looks very shallow when compared with Marx, while Vischer was a professional academic philosopher who never had the wider impact, comparable with the belated influence exercised by Schopenhauer, the philosopher of pessimism and Nirvana on Raabe, Wilhelm Busch and others.

Yet despite the unmetaphysical, aesthetically uninterested nature of German Realism it cannot be dismissed as trivial. It must give us pause to remember that titanic figures like Wagner and Nietzsche considered Keller great; that the impact of the Realists on traditionalist twentieth-century writers has been considerable; and that the art of Thomas Mann derives directly from the themes and techniques of Raabe, Storm and Fontane and seems inconceivable without them. Above all the Realists captured in poetic form a life still lived in nature, a patriarchal regional community with old-style costumes. They deployed the arts of the regional and historical tale to lend dignity, distance and thereby poetry to the folk-lore, traditions and national heritage of the German lands, allowing humour to cast its golden glow over the discrepancies of reality. They stood at the heart of a society in flux clinging to values that were fast being swept away.

Always at the heart of the works of the Realists is the awareness of TIME, for essentially they were concerned not to record reality as they saw it, but to preserve the ideal image of the old world before it disappeared for ever.[33]

NOTES

1. See the chapter "Der poetische Realismus" in the section "Shakespeare und Schiller" of Ludwig's *Dramatische Studien*. Brinkmann reminds us that Ludwig did *not* invent this term: "Die irrige Meinung, Otto Ludwig habe die Formel 'Poetischer Realismus' geprägt, hält sich übrigens bis heute unverwüstlich. Daß sie schon bei Schelling ('Vorlesungen über die Methode des akademischen Studiums' 1802, Schellings Werke, hrsg. v. Manfred Schröter, München, 1927, Bd. 3, S368) steht und von dort offenbar durch Ludwig übernommen wurde, scheint weithin unbekannt geblieben zu sein." Brinkmann, *Illusion und Wirklichkeit* (Tübingen, 1957), pp 3–4.
2. Erich Auerbach, op. cit., p. 516.
3. George J. Becker, op. cit., p. 12.
4. Issued in England by John Calder, who has also published a translation of Keller's *Martin Salander*.
5. Walter Silz, *Realism and Reality* (Chapel Hill, 1954), p. 11.
6. Fritz Martini, *Deutsche Literatur im bürgerlichen Realismus* (Stuttgart, 1962).
7. Claude David, *Von Richard Wagner zu Bertolt Brecht*, Eine Geschichte der neueren deutschen Literatur, Fischer Bücher des Wissens, No. 600, pp. 11–12.
8. Fritz Martini, op. cit., p. 3.
9. Constantin Frantz, "Literatur und politische Einheit" in *Die Wiederherstellung Deutschlands* (Berlin, 1865), quoted from *Zeichen der Zeit*, Bd. 3., Fischer Bücherei, 276, p. 24.
10. Fritz Martini, op. cit., p. 76,
11. Wolfgang Preisendanz, *Humor als dichterische Einbildungskraft*, Studien zur Erzählkunst des poetischen Realismus (München, 1963).
12. Ernest Kohn Bramsted, *Aristocracy and the Middle Classes in Germany*. Social Types in German Literature 1830–1900 (London, 1937), p. 5. This excellent book has just been reissued by the University of Chicago Press, 1965.
13. Anna Krüger, *Der humoristische Roman mit gegensätzlich verschränkter Bauform* (Limburg/Lahn, 1953), p. 12
14. O speak! why did you move away?
    The Neckar Valley has wine and corn;

The Black Forest stands full of dark pines,
The mountain horn echoes across the Spessart.

In those foreign woods
How you will long for the mountain greenery
of the homeland
Germany's golden wheat fields
The slopes of the vine-yards.
from Ferdinand Freiligrath's poem *The Emigrant* in "Die Aus-
wanderer", Gedichte von Freiligrath, Stuttgart und Tübingen, 1848.

15. Wilhelm Raabe, *Abu Telfan: Sämtliche Werke*, Band 7 (Freiburg
    und Braunschweig, 1951), S.38.
16. Goethe, Aufsätze und Rezensionen zur deutschen Sprache, Literatur,
    Musik und Ästhetik. In *Gesamtausgabe der Werke u. Schriften*
    (Cotta, Stuttgart), vol. 15, ed. W. Rehm, p. 653.
17. Ernest K. Bramsted, op. cit., pp. 333–34.
18. J. M. Ritchie, The ambivalence of "Realism" in German Literature,
    Orbis Litterarum, Vol. XV. No. 3/4, 1961. p. 200–17.
19. Bramsted, op. cit., p. 217.
20. Ludwig Feuerbach, "Die Nichtigkeit des Gottglaubens": Dreissigste
    Vorlesung: Vorlesungen über das Wesen der Religion (Stuttgart,
    1908), S354–358, quoted from *Zeichen der Zeit*, Bd. 3, Fischer
    Bücherei, 276, p. 366.
21. Martini, op. cit., p. 117.
22. Martini, op. cit., p. 191.
23. Robert C. Binkley, *Realism and Nationalism 1852–1871* (New York
    and London, 1935), Chapter iii, "Realism and Materialism".
24. J. Dresch, *Le roman social en Allemagne de 1850 à 1900* (Gutzkow,
    Freytag, Spielhagen, Fontane), (Paris, 1913), also Pierre Paul Sagave,
    Recherches sur le roman social en Allemagne (Aix-en-Provence, 1960).
25. H. H. Remak, The German Reception of Realism, *PMLA* LXIX,
    1954, p. 417.
26. Roy Pascal, *The German Novel* (Manchester University Press, 1956),
    p. 299.
27. *German Narrative Prose*, ed. Dr. E. J. Engel (London, 1965), Vol. I,
    p. 332.
28. J. M. Ritchie, Drama and Melodrama in the Nineteenth Century
    Novelle, *Aumla* No. 19, May 1962, p. 86.
29. *German Narrative Prose*, ed. Dr. E. J. Engel (London, 1965), Vol.
    I, p. 289.
30. Martini, op. cit., p. 113.
31. Quoted from Wolfgang Kayser, *Die Wahrheit der Dichter*, Wand-
    lung eines Begriffs in der deutschen Literatur, Rowohlts deutsche
    Enzyklopädie, No. 87, p. 118.
32. Martini, op. cit., p. 103.
33. J. M. Ritchie, The Ambivalence of "Realism" in German literature,
    Orbis Litterarum, Vol. XV. No. 3/4 (1961), p. 217.

SELECT BIBLIOGRAPHY

Auerbach, E., *Mimesis* (Bern, 1946), English edition (Princeton, 1953).

Becker, G. J., ed., *Documents of Modern Literary Realism* (Princeton, 1963).

Bramsted, E. Kohn, *Aristocracy and the Middle Classes in Germany. Social Types in German Literature 1830–1900* (London 1937, 2nd edition University of Chicago, 1965).

Brinkmann, R., *Wirklichkeit und Illusion* (Tübingen, 1957).

Demetz, P., *Formen des Realismus: Theodor Fontane* (München, 1964).

Greiner, M., *Zwischen Biedermeier und Bourgeoisie* (Leipzig, 1953).

Lukács, G., *Essays über Realismus* (Berlin, 1948). *Deutsche Realisten des neunzehnten Jahrhunderts* (Berlin, 1951).

Martini, F., *Deutsche Literatur im bürgerlichen Realismus 1848–1898* (Stuttgart, 1962).

McClain, W., *Between Real and Ideal* (Otto Ludwig) (University of North Carolina Press, 1963).

Preisendanz, W., *Humor als dichterische Einbildungskraft. Studien zur Erzählkunst des poetischen Realismus* (München, 1963).

Ritchie, J. M., The Ambivalence of "Realism" in German Literature, *Orbis Litterarum*, Vol. XV. No. 3/4 (1961).

Silz, W., *Realism and Reality. Studies in the German Novelle of Poetic Realism* (University of North Carolina Press, 1954).

Naturalism

IX

Naturalism

G. SCHULZ

I

Zola, Ibsen, Leo Tolstoi,
eine Welt liegt in den Worten,
eine, die noch nicht verfault,
eine, die noch kerngesund ist!

Klammert euch, ihr lieben Leutchen,
klammert euch nur an die Schürze
einer längst verlotterten,
abgetakelten Ästhetik :
unsre Welt ist nicht mehr klassisch,
unsre Welt ist nicht romantisch,
unsre Welt ist nur modern!![1]

THESE provocative lines are part of a longer poem with the significant title *Zwischen Alt und Neu*, now included in a collection of verse called *Das Buch der Zeit. Lieder eines Modernen*.[2] The author of this book of contemporary "songs", which was first published in 1886, was Arno Holz, twenty-three years old and almost unknown, but soon to become one of the leading figures of German Naturalism. The word "Modern" was fashionable at that time, and the term *Die Moderne* was coined to define a whole era and a new generation of writers and artists, who despite their diverging views all claimed to be just this. All that united them under this banner was the common feeling that great changes had taken place in Germany as well as in other countries during the past few decades. The industrial revolution and in its trail modern capitalism had spread all over Europe. New political and social problems arose. Science had made far-reaching discoveries. Charles Darwin's theories of the "Origin of Species by Means of Natural Selection", the utilitarianism of John Stuart Mill and Herbert Spencer, also Hippolyte Taine's positivistic philosophy of art contributed considerably to a new rationalistic, anti-metaphysical interpretation of the world. But German literature, so far, had taken no notice of these changes. In France Flaubert, the

Brothers Goncourt, Zola, in Russia Dostoyevsky, Turgenev, Tolstoy, in Scandinavia Strindberg and Ibsen, all tried to reflect realistically in their works what had happened both inside and outside the human mind after the far-reaching political, economic and intellectual revolutions of the past sixty or seventy years. In Germany, however, literature was not a matter of public interest. After the foundation of the Empire in 1871, Germany developed rapidly into a modern industrial country, but her cultural achievements lagged behind those of her neighbours. No important writer, who could be compared with Zola, Ibsen or Tolstoy, had emerged since the end of the classical period. Thus it was the avowed intention of the young "Moderns" to bring German culture up to date, and to establish a German national literature which need not blush when compared with its French or Russian counterpart.

It is difficult to tell whether this intention was the actual stimulus for the young generation of writers, or whether in the first instance it was their determination to give expression to a new reality and discard a false, outdated romanticism. In other words : it remains doubtful whether their endeavour arose from some secondhand literary incentive or whether it represented the genuine creative urge of the artist to give his own vision of the world. The former is more probable, as German Naturalism started with a theoretical prelude of considerable length. There is also little originality in its first productions and little understanding of the social, political and economic background. This lack of comprehension is partly due to the fact that its originators were considerably less talented than they sometimes believed. On the other hand one cannot blame them altogether for their failure to interpret and reproduce artistically a situation more complex and confusing than in any other European country.

Germany joined the family of European industrial nations only very late. Her division into many small states and petty dynasties after 1648 had considerably hampered social and political progress throughout the seventeenth and eighteenth centuries. The failure in 1848 to establish at least a constitutional monarchy and to obtain for the rising middle-class political rights and influence had further retarded Germany's progress. Everything usually linked with the first stage of the industrial age—large cities with their huge, gloomy and noisy factories, dilapidated living quarters to house the army of industrial workers in misery and poverty, workers' organizations and trade unions to fight for the rights of the proletariat—all this really developed in Germany only after 1871. And it took another ten years or more before literature and

art began to take notice. When Holz, in the opening poem of his
Buch der Zeit, says :

Already, the ghost of the social question rears its red and ugly
dragon's head out of darkness and distress . , ,[3]

he points, eight years after Bismarck's Anti-Socialist Law, to one
of the main problems of his time. Bismarck's law, which banned
for almost twelve years all activities of the Social Democratic
Party and its many affiliated organizations without formally ban-
ning the party itself, marks the difference which existed between
Germany and most of the other western European countries. After
more than three centuries Germany had become a united nation,
its political influence and economic strength were growing rapidly,
but on the other hand social problems of such severity arose that
the prevailing system of government was unable to cope with them
adequately. Bismarck's *Reich* always remained a hybrid. Its constitution denied Parliament any direct influence on the government, and the function of the elected representatives of the people
was reduced to expressing approval or ineffectual protest. Bismarck
based the new German empire on his own strong personality and
on the political support of the Prussian nobility. No doubt the
introduction of compulsory insurance for workers against sickness
and incapacitation was progressive and a considerable contribution
towards their social security. But Bismarck regarded all their
representatives and organizations as potential enemies of the nation
thus denying them political responsibility and in effect preventing
the growth of a German nationalism, which would embrace the
whole of the nation.

The literary situation was just as hybrid as the political scene.
The heroes of the day were writers such as Emanuel Geibel, Paul
Heyse, Felix Dahn, Viktor von Scheffel, Gustav Freytag and Ernst
von Wildenbruch who, partly with pomp and splendour, partly
with refinement and sublimity, partly also with crude heroism and
false historicism served more or less as scene-painters for the
political stage of the Bismarck empire and the *Gründerzeit*. Other
writers such as Fritz Reuter and to some degree also Theodor
Storm had withdrawn into provincialism after the failure of the
1848 revolution. Gottfried Keller and Conrad Ferdinand Meyer
lived on the periphery of the German speaking area and despite
their high literary standing did not reach a wider German public.
Wilhelm Raabe was known only to a small and esoteric community,
and Theodor Fontane's great novels were still to be written. Thus
the literary scene in Germany was virtually without any talents
who could be even remotely compared to the great writers in

France, Russia or Scandinavia. Above all the German public was too concerned with material prosperity and welfare to worry about cultural matters.

Under these circumstances young writers such as Arno Holz, Heinrich and Julius Hart, Hermann Conradi and Karl Henckell, Karl Bleibtreu and Michael Georg Conrad, to mention only the most important names of early German Naturalism, found themselves in a very complicated and precarious situation. Nearly all of them were born in the decade between 1855 and 1864. They had been children when Bismarck had forged the German empire out of "blood and iron", and had witnessed the rise of their backward and tardy confederation of states to a world power. They belonged to this new nation and wanted to give it what it still lacked : a national literature that would break away from stale convention and aesthetic playing with words. In an open letter to Bismarck the brothers Heinrich and Julius Hart wrote in 1882 :

> Eleven years have now passed since the new Empire arose out of the chaos of the great war. Who does not remember with sadness the enthusiasm of those days when in all spheres men hoped for the highest, expecting to reach it over night by storm. Literature, too, was to enter upon a new golden age; national epics, national dramas, national theatres were expected from one day to the next. Disillusionment soon followed, for it had simply been forgotten that the old, the established and the settled would not suddenly be illuminated by a new light and change their style and ideals but that, rather it would be necessary first of all for a new generation to grow up, whose spirits had been tempered and forged by the influence of the powerful events around them.
>
> Now, however, the time has come, for this younger generation to step forward—whether it will accomplish anything, remains to be seen—but it is there, knocking at the door.[4]

But the doors were not thrust wide open, when the young generation knocked. The social and political contradictions began to impinge on literature. Writers who wanted to free themselves from the aesthetic conventions of a by-gone time, who were resolved to show reality as they saw it, could not close their eyes to the shocking social conditions under which the majority was forced to live, and soon found themselves in opposition to their country and to a government that not only tolerated conditions unworthy of human beings but also watched with suspicion, every attempted criticism. Thus in German Naturalism we find many contradictory opinions, doctrines and convictions. National pride blends with the longing for an international brotherhood of all men. The optimism of the founders of a new era of literature merged with the pessimism that derives from the spectacle of millions deliberately deprived of the wealth they create by the work of their own hands. The official spirit of progress seems to be utterly false; injustice and untruth appear to dominate everywhere.

> Die Zeit ist tot—die Zeit der großen Seelen—
> Wir sind ein ärmlich Volk nur von Pygmäen, . . .
> Die sich mit ihrer Afterweisheit frevelnd blähen
> Und dreist sich mit der Lüge Schmutz vermählen—[5]

says Herman Conradi in one of his contributions to Wilhelm Arent's anthology *Moderne Dichtercharaktere* (1885).

Realism and idealism, pessimism and optimism, objectivity and subjectivity, collectivism and individualism—all these and more can be found in the many articles and pamphlets, poems and stories, novels and dramas of this generation of young writers. What unites them is their claim to be "naturalists", "realists", seekers of the truth, and enemies of falsehood and gloss. For the rest their views are as changeable and erratic as the views of any young people. Naturalism in Germany is therefore no unequivocal movement which can be clearly described, but an interlacing of different tendencies and trends which have as common denominator solely the intention of turning away from the conventional literature of the 'seventies and representing accurately and veraciously what is seen as a new reality.

II

Since Emile Zola in the preface to his novel *Thérèse Raquin* referred to

> le groupe d'écrivains naturalistes, auquel j'ai l'honneur d'appartenir,[6]

there have been definitions and explanations of Naturalism galore. But they remain as contradictory and manifold as the whole movement itself. What makes it so difficult to see a common factor in such definitions is the fact that they start from completely different points. The 'seventies and 'eighties of the nineteenth century, particularly in Germany, are a time of fermentation and considerable changes, which affect not only the political, economic and social spheres, but also involve science and technology, psychology and philosophy, art and aesthetics. Some of the young revolutionaries use the term Naturalism in a narrow artistic sense only, others, give it a wide, almost boundless meaning. For some, Naturalism is limited to the discussion of social problems or to the criticism of old and superseded values, for others it signifies a literature that is to establish entirely new values and ideas. But all believe that the only hope for a literary renaissance lies in abandoning false and out-lived ideals in favour of the paramount and pressing questions of the present and the future.

> We, that is, the *young generation*, of the rejuvenated, united, great fatherland, want poetry to become once more a shrine, a sacred place of pilgrimage for the people,[7]

proclaims Karl Henckell. And in this sense only—signifying *this* "young generation" of writers between 1880 and the end of the century, their ideas and their works—will the terms "Naturalism" and "Naturalists" be used in the following pages.

The young Naturalists came together and discussed their views and works in circles and groups with fluctuating membership. Two main centres stand out clearly : *Munich*, the capital of Bavaria and largest city in southern Germany, a traditional centre of art and music; and *Berlin*, the capital of the new Empire and a big and rapidly developing modern industrial city. The centre of the Munich circle was Michael Georg Conrad, who settled there in 1882 after years in Switzerland, Italy and Paris. The radius of this circle was the periodical *Die Gesellschaft*, the first number of which appeared on 1 January 1885, and the periphery consisted of writers such as Conrad Alberti, Otto Julius Bierbaum, Karl Bleibtreu, Hermann Conradi and Wolfgang Kirchbach, to mention only some of the main figures; for almost all contemporary writers of distinction contributed to *Die Gesellschaft* during the eighteen years of its existence, including those (e.g. Liliencron and Dehmel), who stood outside the general trend of Naturalism. Conrad opened his periodical with a programmatic declaration :

> Our GESELLSCHAFT will spare no pains to oppose the prevailing piteous shallowness and weakness of the literary, artistic and social spirit, with its antithesis, namely strong, manly achievements which will effectively combat the current demoralising deceitfulness, romantic shamming and debilitating fantasies. We declare war on the expedient idealism of the philistines and on the puritanical white lie of the old clique and party system in all spheres of modern life.[8]

The tendencies are clear from this beginning. Conrad in his various articles and essays demands :

Faithful presentation of life to the strict exclusion of the romantic element.[9]

Art was to become a branch of science :

There is no truth outside science.[10]

Zola, whom Conrad had met in Paris, was for him the "Grand Master" of modern literature, and Naturalism an international movement rather than the starting point of a new national literature, as the Brothers Hart and some of their friends in Berlin maintained.

Opposition to Conrad's Zola-worship soon arose. Karl Bleibtreu, from 1889 co-editor of *Die Gesellschaft*, published his book *Revolution der Literatur* in 1886, in which he denounces the Naturalists as "callow youths" and calls for "true realism" as a higher form of literary expression. He does not oppose faithful reproduction of reality, but he wants to include the romantic, i.e. idealistic element as well :

The new poetry will consist of so blending Realism and Romanticism that the naturalistic truth of dry and expressionless photography merges with the artistic liveliness of ideal composition.[11]

Conrad was broad-minded enough to tolerate contradictory opinions within his periodical, and when in 1889 Conrad Alberti published his *Zwölf Artikel des Realismus* in *Die Gesellschaft*, it became almost a stronghold of opposition to the *konsequenter Naturalismus* and radical "Zolaism" of some members of the Berlin circle.

Berlin had already become a centre of literary revolution a few years earlier. In 1877 the brothers Heinrich and Julius Hart had arrived in the new capital, and from 1882 to 1884 they published their *Kritische Waffengänge*. At first they laid a much stronger emphasis on the foundation of a German national literature than Conrad did in the more cosmopolitan Munich. The new art, the Harts claimed, had to come

from the soul of the Germanic peoples,[12]

but it had, of course, to be a faithful reproduction of reality and also observe the recent achievements of science, medicine and psychology. Yet, the final aim was the "Naturalism of the genius", and the modern poet

. . . will at the same time be a prophet, striding ahead of his weary struggling contemporaries like Tyrtaeus and keeping the goal visible before them, so that they do not slacken and lose enthusiasm.[13]

In the 'eighties the Brothers Hart gathered about them almost all important figures in the literary revival of those years, either in person or as contributors to their *Berliner Monatshefte*, a short-lived periodical which they published from April to September 1885. In their Berlin flat the idea of editing the anthology *Moderne Dichtercharaktere* was conceived; Arent, Conradi, Henckell, Kretzer, Holz and Hartleben were among their regular guests, and they also became foundation members of a literary club which gave itself the laconic name *Durch*. The most important function of this club was not so much the establishment of new literary programmes, as the fact that the discussions and arguments served as stimulus for the only two authors of German Naturalism whose work really survived all tides of literary taste and fashion : Arno Holz and Gerhart Hauptmann. Other members of *Durch* were Holz' friend and collaborator Johannes Schlaf, the Scottish-born John Henry Mackay, the socialist intellectual and writer Bruno Wille, and, as guest, Wilhelm Bölsche who in his *Die naturwissenschaftlichen Grundlagen der Poesie* (1887) had hailed modern science—Darwinism, genetics and the theory of environment—as the basis of human thought and ideas, and established art as a scientific experiment. Several of these writers frequently met in Friedrichshagen, an eastern suburb of Berlin near the Große Müggelsee, where Bölsche and Wille had their houses. Later the Brothers Hart too settled there, and Hauptmann lived only a few miles away in Erkner. It was in this beautiful, quiet scenery of lakes, gardens and pine-forests that one day in summer 1889, Hauptmann, as Bruno Wille reports,

lay next to Bölsche and myself among some juniper bushes in the forest and read us his newly completed drama "Vor Sonnenaufgang". We were carried away by it and I had the impression that the dawning day of its title heralded a new and worthy era of moral culture and at the same time of literature.[14]

The gap between theory and practice in German Naturalism had begun to close.

Hauptmann came at the right time[15]

remarks Heinrich Hart in his memoirs. In April 1889 the *Freie Bühne* had been founded in Berlin, where after the model of the *Théâtre libre* in Paris, controversial modern plays, mostly banned by the censors, were to be staged in private performances. It had no permanent ensemble or theatre. The performances took place on the best stages of Berlin and started at noon on Sundays. The cast consisted mainly of famous actors who made themselves available as pioneers of a new literature. The *Freie Bühne* opened on 29 September 1889 with Ibsen's *Ghosts* and closed with the performance of Zola's *Thérèse Raquin* on 3 May 1891.[16] But its end did not mean defeat. By this time the ban was broken, and public theatres had taken modern plays into their regular repertoire. However, to circumvent censorship special performances of the *Freie Bühne* were also staged later, for instance in the case of Hauptmann's *Die Weber* in February 1893. Despite various feuds between its members and also despite rival enterprises by Bleibtreu, Alberti and Wille, the *Freie Bühne* marks the climax of German Naturalism. With its end the movement began to decline.

The history of Naturalism in Germany can be divided into three periods : a mainly theoretical prelude from 1882 to 1888, a short culmination period between 1889 and 1892, and, finally, a period of gradual dissolution and secession, until by the turn of the century other literary modes, Neo-Romanticism, Impressionism and later Expressionism, had begun to dominate the scene.

In the literary production of the first period novels and poetry prevailed. Most of the novels of early German Naturalism were written in an attempt to put Zola's theory of the *Roman expérimental* into practice in Germany and to follow the great example in his *Rougon-Macquart* cycle. Kretzer's novels, the first of which, *Die beiden Genossen*, appeared in 1880, can be mentioned in this context, although Kretzer owes as much to the traditional German Realism of the nineteenth century as he owes to Zola; the same applies to Sudermann with his *Frau Sorge*. Michael Georg Conrad planned a series of ten novels on contemporary Munich, but completed only three volumes. There were also several attempts by Bleibtreu and Alberti, but they are only of historical interest. This is also true of most of the poetry of this period, which flourished as the immediate expression of individual protest against stale and antiquated conventions. The stress in all these works was on content rather than on form. The national pride of the new empire, the rising problems of the industrial revolution, and the vigour of a young generation sought artistic expression regardless of formal means and techniques.

This changed with the foundation of the *Freie Bühne*, with the publication of Holz' and Schlaf's *Papa Hamlet* and with the early plays of Gerhart Hauptmann. Although a "Sketch" in prose, *Papa Hamlet* with its short scenes and its dialogues came very close to the dramatic form, and the brief triumph of German Naturalism between 1889 and 1892 was almost entirely a triumph of the stage. Apart from Hauptmann's works—the first version of *Die Weber* was finished in 1891—there were Holz' and Schlaf's *Familie Selicke*, Halbe's *Eisgang* and *Jugend*, Sudermann's *Die Ehre*, *Sodoms Ende* and *Heimat*, Schlaf's *Meister Oelze* and Hartleben's *Angele*. Of these, too, only a few have survived, but it is usually with these works that Naturalism in German literature is associated, and this with some justification. If the works of the first period were interesting because of their new content, then it was now a new form, a new language and style that gave these works novelty and modernity.

The shifting of interest from content to form was not solely a reflection of greater artistic maturity in the authors concerned. It also depended—as later the decline of Naturalism—on changes in the political and social situation of Germany. In 1888 the young Emperor William II ascended the throne, in 1890 Bismarck was dismissed, and the Anti-Socialist Law was repealed. Social problems did not cease to exist, but at least they became less pressing than before, and at first the young monarch with his vital personality and his promises inspired new hope. These hopes, however, were soon disappointed not only because of incidents such as William's protest against the public performance of Hauptmann's *Die Weber* —he cancelled his permanent seat in the *Deutsche Theater*—but also because of his one-sided preference for historical plays which were to serve as a background to his own heroic ambitions. With the year 1893 Naturalism as a dominant literary movement had virtually come to an end in Germany. Two months after the première of Hauptmann's *Der Biberpelz* on 21 September 1893 his "Traumdichtung" *Hanneles Himmelfahrt* was performed in Berlin; it was the author's tribute to the rising tide of Neo-Romanticism— in the same year as Hofmannsthal published his *Der Tor und der Tod*.

As Hauptmann's example shows, Naturalist themes and modes of expression did not disappear altogether and overnight. Later plays like his *Fuhrmann Henschel* (1898), *Michael Kramer* (1900), *Rose Bernd* (1903) and *Die Ratten* (1911) all have their roots in this movement, technically as well as in subject matter. There are also Paul Ernst's one-act plays *Lumpenbagasch* and *Im Chambre séparée* (1898), Holz' *Sozialaristokraten* (1896), Hartleben's *Rosenmontag* (1900), Halbe's *Der Strom* (1903), and novels such as Helene Böhlau's *Rangierbahnhof* (1896), Bierbaum's *Stilpe* (1897) and Else Jerusalem's *Der heilige Skarabäus* (1909), all of which belong to the aftermath of Naturalism in German literature. But by this same time the Nietzsche cult was spreading, Frank Wedekind's first plays were being performed, George's exclusive *Blätter für die Kunst* and the early poems of Rilke, Dehmel and Hofmannsthal were appearing, Schnitzler was writing his *Reigen* and Thomas Mann his *Buddenbrooks*. By and large Naturalism was being succeeded by

a mysticism of the nerves

as Hermann Bahr predicted in 1891. But Bahr also found that things would never be the same again :

Now it will become obvious, that, although we are basically too psychologically inclined to be satisfied with objective Naturalism for any period, we have, however, been under the influence of Naturalism too long already, ever to be able to return to the old psychology.[17]

However, it was not in the field of psychology alone that Naturalism had exerted its influence.

III

The first act of regeneration which Naturalism brought to literature was the introduction of a reality which so far had not been treated by writers in Germany : the world of technology and science, the social problems arising from the growth of modern capitalism, the miseries of the poor and of the outcasts of society. Thus Arno Holz, addressing his age, claims :

Mir schwillt die Brust, mir schlägt das Herz
und mir ins Auge schießt der Tropfen,
hör ich dein Hämmern und dein Klopfen
auf Stahl und Eisen, Stein und Erz.

Denn süß klingt mir die Melodie
aus diesen zukunftsschwangern Tönen;
die Hämmer senken sich und dröhnen :
Schau her, auch dies ist Poesie![18]

All this is only the invitation to write new and different poetry, it is not yet modern poetry itself. Holz' poems are traditional in their form and expression, and they only touch the surface of the actual problems. The true dilemma of the artist in a technical age is demonstrated more clearly in a short piece of lyrical prose, *Eine Frühlingsnacht*, which Hermann Conradi first published in 1888. One night in May a young poet has kissed a girl to whom he has been devoted for a long time. The experience has opened his eyes and mind to the beauty of this night in spring, and he leans out of the window. The beams of moonlight play on the roofs, he smells the sweet scent of violets and hears the whispering of the wind, and he is deeply, happily moved by something inexpressible, enigmatic, unknown within himself—until gradually reality regains the upper hand :

> Cool and damp, the night air caressed his forehead. He became calmer, more sober. The submerged workaday world rose up again, and the kiss, which he had given that evening to a beautiful girl he loved, seemed suddenly less sweet. He found it almost flat and the old indifference gained the upper hand again. He caught himself thinking all kinds of rather crude thoughts. Finally, it even occurred to him, that he was actually only seeing these moonlit roofs because a chemical process had taken place on his retina. And he laughed loudly into the night . . .[19]

This process of disillusionment, which Conradi here describes, illustrates clearly the dilemma in which many of the young literary revolutionaries and innovators found themselves with their demand for a realistic, scientific approach towards nature and man. In their hearts they were still Romantics, enthralled by the magic beauty of nature and all its "props"—nightingales and moonlight, forest murmurs and the seductive scent of flowers. But science had reduced this magic to something measurable and comprehensible, and destroyed its sentimental value. Thus to be "modern" meant also to be unsentimental, rational, matter-of-fact.

This contradictory attitude towards nature goes through the whole of German Naturalism. Even in some of the most progressive, realistic and "modern" works the longing for an idyllic past is detectable and betrays the fact that the writers' ties with the past were much stronger than they were willing to admit even to themselves. The modernism of the Naturalists is hybrid—like the whole movement, and *Zwischen Alt und Neu* the title of the poem by Holz, also describes precisely the place of Naturalism within the history of German literature. Holz' work is characteristic of this split between emotional bonds and the urge to be modern, truthful and realistic. The same poet who draws attention to the poetic qualities of steel and iron, of machines and factories, nevertheless opens his *Buch der Zeit* with the following lines :

> Weit hinter mir liegt die Millionenstadt,
> ihr wildes Leben hielt mich wild umkettet,
> nun aber hab ich, ihrer Wüste satt,
> in meine grüne Heimat mich gerettet ![20]

Again and again this idyllic trend can be found in his poetry, whether he talks about *die süße Schönheit dieser Allnatur*[21] or simply stammers *Natur! Natur!*[22] It is nature before and outside all human society which offers refuge to the modern poet tired of his modernity. He realizes that the blue flower of Romanticism has withered, but realizes it with sadness and longing.

> Zwar mein Kopf hat sich schon längst
> radikal emanzipiert;
> doch in meinem Herzen blühn noch
> alle Blumen der Romantik![23]

Thus modern capitalism, industrial and city life, social wrongs and brutalities are often criticized from a position outside and beyond society, a position which is typical of the many contradictions found throughout German Naturalism. This "escapism" is one of its basic weaknesses which to a greater or less extent can be observed from the first beginnings right through to the end. Else Jerusalem, in her novel *Der heilige Skarabäus*, takes the same point of view as Holz, Conradi and others. In this book the management of a city brothel under various owners is described at great length. Undoubtedly the story has literary merits and avoids the tearful sentimentality of other books of this kind, but in the end it is mainly the "capitalization" of this profession to which the author objects. Much of Max Kretzer's work is of the same nature. Lack of understanding, discrimination and differentiation characterize the social criticism of German Naturalism.

The "red dragon's head" of the "social problem"—as Holz said —was the main topic of Naturalism. Man is no longer free in his decisions, but is conditioned by the *milieu*: the hereditary taints with which he was born, and his early social environment. That he cannot escape from this, was one of the main revelations of science and philosophy in the second half of the nineteenth century. *Milieu* became as popular a catch-word as *modern*, and the effect of *milieu* theories on literature can hardly be overestimated. Usually, one associates with the word *milieu* the large industrial cities—Berlin in particular—with their slums full of poverty and squalor, their sooty factories and noisy, narrow streets. This, however, is not the complete picture, as the reflection of *milieu* on literature was not limited to the most obvious symptoms and deficiencies of capitalism. A large proportion of Naturalist literature is set in the country, and it is often here that the influences of hereditary factors become more clearly visible than in the city slums of a proletariat which virtually had no past. One has only to think of Gerhart Hauptmann's first play *Vor Sonnenaufgang*, where he shows the disastrous effects of alcoholism on a family of newly rich peasants in Silesia. Other examples are Max Halbe's successful play *Jugend*, Sudermann's novel *Frau Sorge*, and also the gloomy atmosphere of Johannes Schlaf's *Meister Oelze*. The healing power of a simple life away from the big cities and closer to nature, seems to be no longer effective.

In the cities the problems of the industrial age are perhaps more clearly visible, because it is here that social contrasts clash with full violence. There are various standard types of "settings" for the conflicts and tragedies of Naturalism. The best known is, perhaps, the *Mietskaserne*, the large slum block of flats which houses the outcasts of society as well as the workers and their families. From Kretzer's early novels to plays such as Hauptmann's *Die Ratten* this is the setting for many novels and dramas. Often the squalid dwellings of the poor are huddled together in the backyards of the stately homes of the rich, and *Vorderhaus* and *Hinterhaus* symbolize the social distinctions.

Class division is a powerful motivating force. Often social contrasts appear rather over-simplified as in Sudermann's *Ehre*, often they are highly differentiated as in Hauptmann's *Die Weber, Der Biberpelz* or *Die Ratten*. But differentiated or not—the division between the haves and the have-nots remains a basic divergence of the time. Human ideals and relations are reduced to a money problem, because there are always those who can buy—not only the luxuries of an easy life, but even the daughters of their employees. It is this last aspect, on which Naturalism dwells a great deal, and it is the fate of the victims rather than the immorality of the seducers which predominates. This does not mean that only one side is represented, but it is quite obvious that the main interest and, of course, sympathy of Naturalism lies with the lowly, the poor and humiliated. This sphere as well as that of the lower-middle classes and the artistic bohème the authors knew best from their own experience; they sometimes took great pains to study the *milieu*, particularly by frequenting taverns, restaurants, cabarets and theatres. But the higher they reach in the social system the vaguer their descriptions become. For Naturalism reality in most cases means reality of the proletariat and the middle class. In this the authors are captives of their own milieu theories.

Outcasts and asocial elements—the *Lumpenproletariat*—as the most controversial victims of a rotten social system are their favourites. For obvious reasons this category is often represented by the prostitute, for a long time taboo in literature, but since Edmond and Jules de Goncourt's *Germinie Lacerteux* (1864) and Zola's *Nana* (1880) a figure which most flagrantly shows human degradation through social iniquity, and thus also appeals to our compassion. Karl Henckell concludes his poem *Die Dirne*:

Heißa, heißa, hopsassa!
La la la . . .
Hopsassa!
Schöner grüner,
Schöner grüner Jungfernkranz!
— — Mir wird schlecht.—
Hunger—Brot! Brot!
Liebste für'n Lumpengeld,
Ist doch 'ne elende Welt!—
O läg ich tot . . . ![24]

Everywhere we find the same half sentimental, half businesslike attitude. In one of Conradi's stories a girl has to earn a living in this way not only for herself, but also for her parents who in their desperate situation have no choice but to accept the "blood money" to buy "a few rolls, a handful of coal, a morsel of meat, a pound of flour. . . ." In Paul Ernst's one-act play *Im chambre séparée* girls of thirteen or fourteen are employed to entertain the guests of a "Chantant", although they would still prefer to play with their dolls.

The actual labourers, those toiling in front of the blast furnaces or in the city abattoirs, are represented to a much lesser degree than the *Lumpenproletariat*. Indeed the deepest insight into the hardships of the workers is given by a work, in an historical setting, Hauptmann's *Die Weber*, the best play produced by German Naturalism. The struggle of the emaciated weavers for their bare existence is seen by Hauptmann as part of mankind's far greater, and always futile, attempt to rise above its limitations and to free itself from sufferings which seem not only to be imposed on it by social circumstances but apparently are its eternal fate. It has often been maintained that Hauptmann's play has no political slant. This is correct in so far as it certainly is not an illustration of socialist or communist party programmes. To deny, or, at least ignore, on the other hand, Hauptmann's deep sympathy with the oppressed, and his contempt for those who ruthlessly exploit their power and superior position, is to distort obvious facts.

A great variety of characters and true-to-life types can be found within the various strata of the middle-class, particularly the intellectuals, public-servants and also the craftsmen of the lower middle-class. Hauptmann's *Friedensfest, Einsame Menschen, Kollege Crampton*, Sudermann's *Sturmgeselle Sokrates*, Holz' *Sozialaristo-*

kraten, to mention only some of the better known works, all deal with problems of the German middle-class at the turn of the century, a middle-class deprived of political activity and efficacy, excluded from any influence on current affairs, and involved in domestic quarrels or adjusting their old ideals to the new reality. The manager types, the business magnates of the growing and expanding industry, the masters of machines and factories, of trusts and banks are only occasionally represented, and then not convincingly. Similarly the actual "ruling classes", the *Junker* and the military caste, appear only rarely. Hartleben's *Rosenmontag* is the only play that is devoted entirely to the antiquated and inbred morals of such an important institution as the army in Wilhelminian Germany.

Without any doubt the type most dear to the hearts of the Naturalists was the artist in his many different guises as singer and actor, sculptor and painter, poet and journalist. In this milieu the authors themselves were at home, and a considerable number of *Künstlerdramen* and *Künstlerromane* was written between 1889 and the turn of the century. The common denominator of all these works, whether tragedies or comedies, is the observation that the artist has become an outsider incapable of shaping public opinion and influencing public affairs. The spirit of early Naturalism, which once induced the Brothers Hart to write an open letter to Bismarck, was replaced by the tendency towards individualism and self-irony, which was latent already in some of the first publications of Conradi and Holz, of Henckell and Bleibtreu.

The utilitarianism and pragmatism of the middle class had proved stifling and hostile to any form of artistic expression, but the bohemian attitude too, once adopted in protest against philistinism, now appeared just as illusory and false. The whole concept of art and the artist was subject to changes which, although brought about by the shifting economic and social structure of the *Reich*, nevertheless also indicated a crisis of far deeper consequences. These artist-tragedies are neither merely personal cases nor cases of social injustice towards exceptional beings. They are symptomatic of a crisis in the intellectual structure of the whole period and indicate the changing place of art and the artist in a technical age. It is this transitional position of the artist between the concepts of the nineteenth and twentieth centuries that makes these plays and novels so important and interesting. What may appear outwardly as the clash between generations, as in Hauptmann's *Michael Kramer* is in reality also an indication of this crisis. The artist's function seems to be reduced to the questioning of existing values, and thus an older generation with a traditional concept of

the authority and mission of art must necessarily fail to understand
the dilemma of the rising generation. Only when Arnold Kramer
is dead, does his father begin to recognize the true genius of his
son. Michael Kramer has devoted years of solitude and solemnity
to a painting of Christ the Saviour. But he has failed, although
with greatness. Arnold, on the other hand, only saw and drew the
grotesque and ugly faces of the selfrighteous barbarians around
him—his world consisted of *Fratzen*, but they were the reality in
which he had to live. By exposing their ugliness and inhumanity
Arnold has revealed himself as the true artist. Before the open
coffin the father has to admit his failure; all his values and aims
have collapsed under the impact of his son's life, work and death,
and what remains for him is an open question :

> Where are we to land up, in what direction are we drifting?
> Why do we sometimes shout joyously into the unknown? We
> little men, abandoned in a frightful world? As if we knew where
> we were going?[25]

"But the spirit of our age is a spirit of enquiry," says Holz in his
Buch der Zeit, where he also speaks of the "old universal scholar,
Dr. Doubt".[26] It is in the effort to question established and largely
superseded values that the Naturalists achieved their greatest
success, although they often spoiled it with the attempt to create
new rules and values which necessarily had to be vague and
general.

The inadequacies and shortcomings in the morals of an entire
age are first visible in discrepancies and clashes between the public
and the private spheres, and particularly in the relations between
the sexes. In Paul Ernst's one-act-play *Die schnelle Verlobung* Herr
Schmelzer, a merchant, remarks to his wife about their daughter
whom they want to marry off as soon as possible :

> If we don't sell her now, two, three years from now it will be
> too late; the best we can expect then is a widower with a few
> children . . .[27]

The bond between husband and wife has been reduced to a monetary relationship, love and marriage exist in two completely
separated spheres. This theme goes right through German Naturalism just as it played a major rôle in the realistic literature of the
nineteenth century. One has only to think of Balzac's or Maupas-
sant's novels, and also later of Fontane's *Frau Jenny Treibel*
(1893). But the contribution of Naturalism differs from that of the
older generation. Tragedy or tragi-comedy are mostly permeated
by an ethical relativism or even cynicism which was not found to

any marked degree in the works of either Balzac or Fontane. There is as much irony in the title of Hauptmann's *Einsame Menschen* as there is in that of his earlier *Das Friedensfest, eine Familien-katastrophe*; family bonds and ties have loosened in the same way as the relations between man and woman deteriorated under a social system that replaced ethical values by monetary ones.

Perversion of natural human relations, perversion of human values, of moral and religious institutions, of justice and law—a long catalogue of examples for this could be given from Naturalist literature. The church and its representatives are frequently assaulted, the tone ranging from mild satire as in Hartleben's story *Vom gastfreien Pastor*, where an honest country parson unknowingly lodges in a city brothel, to bitter attacks such as Conrad's *Warum Pastor Hüpfebein heiraten mußte*, parts of Kretzer's *Das Gesicht Christi* or, in particular, a number of poems in Holz' *Buch der Zeit*. The ultimate stage of depravation, of human corruption and degeneration appears under the image of "animalization"— *Vertierung*. As Kandidat Wendt in *Die Familie Selicke* observes :

> Men are no longer what I considered them to be! They are egoistic! Brutally selfish! They are no better than animals, cunning beasts, prowling instincts, which fight one another, blindly striving for dominance to the point of mutual destruction. All the beautiful ideas which they dreamt up, of God, love and ... oh, that's all rubbish![28]

Or Michael Kramer, facing his dead son :

> See, there lies a mother's son! What cruel beasts men are![29]

In the description of human humiliation and degradation Naturalism achieved its most convincing works. Man here is exposed to forces which he cannot control, an animal, driven by its desires; a machine, an object in the hands of other powers :

> Stahl und Eisen, Blut und Dampf,
> rollen, donnern, sieden, zischen,
> und ein Wehruf gellt dazwischen :
> Dieses Leben ist ein Kampf![30]

But all this is not merely applied Darwinism and should not be interpreted as social criticism alone. Here man is shown in a situation of complete hopelessness, lost in a world which he does not understand and over which he has no ultimate control : he is exposed to incomprehensible forces, a hunted animal unable to recognize the hunter, who appears in so many disguises. One of his masks is chance. Or there is "fate", disguised, for instance, as the merciless river which exercises its almost magic influence on the people living on its banks, as in Halbe's *Der Strom*. There are the dark forces of inheritance, the inescapable prison of the milieu, the devastating sexual urge—and to all this man is helplessly subject,

There's something deep down in man . . . the will is no more than a straw,[31]

says Wilhelm Scholz in Hauptmann's *Das Friedensfest*, and thereby firmly characterizes a situation which since then has often been called "modern". It is a world without any solid, unshakeable values, a world finally also without God. This may be said to be the most important contribution of the Naturalist generation towards the development of modern literature. Some of its works will survive although they may have lost their immediate impact and although their philosophy has been superseded. But in the plays of the young Gerhart Hauptmann, in some poems by Holz and, perhaps, Conradi, in *Papa Hamlet* and *Meister Oelze*, a human crisis is revealed which so far had hardly been recognized in literature. It has become the task of the twentieth century to fathom and interpret this crisis.

IV

There can be no doubt that German Naturalism would not have been possible without the stimulus it received from the outside—from France and Scandinavia in particular. At the same time Naturalism represented the attempt to establish a new national literature in Germany, worthy of her great literary tradition. Thus, this rather ambiguous situation led, on the one hand, to mutual accusations of *Ausländerei* by the various literary groups and factions, and, on the other to the search for models and forerunners in the history of German literature. Revolutionary and transitory movements such as *Sturm und Drang* and *Junges Deutschland* offered themselves as most suitable for this purpose; Büchner, Grabbe, Heine and J. M. R. Lenz were discovered or re-discovered and raised above Goethe and Schiller. But favour and disfavour were not distributed evenly. In particular, reference in Naturalist literature to Goethe's personality and work is a composite of reverence and scepticism. After all, Goethe remained the classical poet who had poured his profound knowledge of man and reality into an abundance of forms that made his work unique and virtually unsurpassable.

If Naturalism ever wanted to become a new classical period of literature it could do so only by creating new and original forms for the expression of its new and original ideas. The literary work produced by German Naturalism during the eighties had almost entirely failed to achieve this; but new epic, lyric and dramatic forms did evolve. Holz' and Schlaf's collection of stories *Papa Hamlet* in 1889 was the first genuinely new form of literary expression attempted. Arno Holz later described it in his book *Die Kunst : ihr Wesen und ihre Gesetze* (1891). His immediate predecessor was Zola with the famous definition :

> Une oeuvre d'art est un coin de la nature, vu à travers un tempérament.

Holz' own formula is $Kunst = Natur - x$, and he interprets it thus :

> Art has the tendency to be nature again. It does so in accordance with the respective conditions of reproduction and their application.[32]

x thus represents the restrictions and limitations to which the artist as a human being necessarily is exposed. This formula comprises what has since been called *konsequenter Naturalismus*, and the "consequences" become most obvious when seen in the light of the actual literary works produced in accordance with this theorem. From a traditional point of view, *Papa Hamlet*, for instance, could be described as the tragic story of the depravation and misery of the once great Hamlet-actor Niels Thienwiebel and his family; the tragedy ends in the murder of his little son Fortinbras and in the death of the hero. But Holz and Schlaf call their story a *Skizze* : what seems to matter to them is the character of the hero rather than his actions, and the plot is of importance only in so far as it helps to reveal the character. Other factors predominate : the background, the milieu by which man and his actions are conditioned, and the speech through which man reveals himself to his fellow creatures. The minute description of the milieu blends with "naturalistic" recordings of human dialogues :

> "Hä? Was? Was sagste nu?!"
> "Was denn, Nielchen? Was denn?"
> "Schafskopf!"
> "Aber Thiiienwiebel!"
> "Amalie! Ich ..."
> "Ai! Kieke da! Also döß!"
> "Hä?! Was?! Famoser Schlingel! Mein Schlingel!
> Mein Schlingel, Amalie! Hä! Was?"[33]

This has been called *Sekundenstil,* and it represents the attempt to bring literature as close to "nature" as possible by recording reality photographically and phonographically second by second. But Holz should not be misunderstood. Absolute photographic truth was never his ideal, and he was certainly aware that the artist will not be able to reproduce nature and reality in their totality. He has to limit himself to sections of it, but with as much impartiality as possible. This attempt to be impartial is the source of the demand for faithful reproduction of the milieu, the detailed description of background and personal appearance as well as the use of slang and dialect. At the same time the impartiality of the artist towards his subject-matter marks his position in a world in whose values he no longer believes although he is unable to postulate new ones. He claims merely to record facts. He does not apportion guilt or blame.

The impact of such ideas was greatest on the stage. Drama is a slice of life, an interplay of acting characters, not a constructed plot. This implies that the end often has to be left open—most conflicts in real life do not end with a pathetic death scene, but with compromise and a question mark. The structural weakness of such premises is clearly visible in a play such as *Familie Selicke* written in accordance with this theory. Despite some moving scenes and convincing characters the play as a whole does not come to life, and remains boring and undramatic. A true reproduction of reality does not automatically result in a good play, and *Familie Selicke* is a failure not simply because its authors lacked talent but also because they lacked insight into the essence of dramatic art. The possibilities as well as limitations of Holz' theories come fully to light when confronted with a work of genius : Gerhart Hauptmann's *Die Weber*. Here too milieu is described in minute detail, the language of the weavers—at least in the first version of the play—is recorded with almost phonetic accuracy, and the famous ending, the death of old Hilse, is as accidental and arbitrary as life itself. The play as a whole seems to be the best illustration of Naturalist theory. It also shows that neutrality and impartiality is the only possible artistic attitude in a time where all values have become relative. What the poet, the artist can convey is part of mankind's endless struggle towards a better and more humane existence, a struggle which very often may result in tragedy, but which has to be accepted as our fate, although we do not understand it. One is reminded of Michael Kramer's last words in Hauptmann's play : "Where are we to land up, in what direction are we drifting?" It is with this scepticism and agnosticism that the revolutionary fervour of Naturalism finally ends. One could call *Die Weber* the culmination of this movement, but at the same time this play in its vivid expression of human suffering stands, like all great literature, high above literary theories and schools.

Arno Holz also applied his theory of consistent Naturalism to poetry and spent more than twenty years on this formal experiment. Nature in its totality was to him the only proper subject for poetry, at least as much of it as one single author could grasp, and for this purpose the conventional forms were unsatisfactory. In any case forms should not be imposed on the subject matter of the poem, every individual theme demanded its own specific form, and thus patterns of rhyme, metre and stanza were no longer valid. To Holz the line was the only acceptable unit for poetry, and rhythm its proper force. Thus he aimed at

... lyric poetry which renounces any creation by means of words of music as an end in itself and which is carried solely by a rhythm that is given life only by what that rhythm expresses.[34]

Holz arranged his lines and poems around their central axis, and by an effusion of words tried to render the true "nature" of his subject, as accurately as possible, e.g. a bed inviting for love :

Ein
löwenpratzig ... ein löwenklauig, ein ... löwentatzig
tiefes ... breites,
niederes,
karfunkeldämmerflimmerüberblutetes,
rubinampelscheinschimmerüberflutetes,
duftend, dampfend,
sinnberauschend, sinnbetäubend,
sinnumnebelnd
weihrauchbeckenwolkenumwirbelglutetes,
seidenweiches,
seidenwonniges, seidenwohliges,
seidenwogiges,
seidenwiegiges, seidenschmiegiges,
seidenkühliges, seidenüppiges, seidenpfühliges
... Purpurlager ...[35]

This is but a very modest example of what makes the final version of his *Phantasus* an orgy of words, a free and uninhibited playing with the particles of the language that goes far beyond the theory from which Holz started. Yet, even these verbal experiments in *Phantasus* are symptomatic of the literary period during which they were begun. In 1901 Hofmannsthal wrote his famous *Brief des Lord Chandos*[36] in which he gave expression to a linguistic crisis which had been latent for some time. The modern German language originated in the eighteenth century and was moulded by Gottsched and Lessing, Klopstock and Herder, Goethe and Schiller, Hölderlin and Kleist. But their language could no longer suffice for a young generation confronted with an altogether different reality. Various attempts were made to renew and replenish it. In Holz' *Buch der Zeit* we find words such as *Mietskaserne, Armenhilfsarzt, Zeitungsfrau, Trottoir, Maschinenraum, Fabrik, Mansardenwohnung, Retourbillett* or *Hinterhaus*, which hitherto hardly could have had belonged to the vocabulary of a poet. This crisis becomes even more obvious in the many ironical quotations, particularly from the works of Goethe and Schiller, which point to the continual difference between ideal and reality. But perhaps the best and most extreme expression of this crisis is the speechlessness which we encounter again and again in Hauptmann's plays. At the peak of an emotional disturbance his characters are overwhelmed by the incomprehensible whole of life, and human language fails altogether, as for instance, in the reconciliation scene between father and son in *Das Friedensfest*.[37] Of this *Sprachkrise* Naturalism gave the first indication, and it is here that some of the most interesting aspects of this period are concentrated.

What once shocked contemporaries—that prostitutes and thieves, criminals and social outcasts were shown as victims of a self-righteous society and thus could become heroes of literary works—can no longer shock audiences dulled by a much franker treatment of sex and crime than any Naturalist dreamt of. And the *Sekundenstil* of Holz and Schlaf has proved as transitory as the whole period. Naturalism certainly did not achieve what it set out to create, a new classical age of German literature. The weaknesses of Naturalism, its theory and practice, have been discussed many times, and it is not necessary to repeat the arguments and accuse these writers of the deficiencies of their theoretical position and the wrongness of their conception of art. Naturalism is literature in a time of crisis and transition. The influence it exerted on the future development of German literature points in many directions. Expressionism in form and content owes much to the experiments of Holz and to his "poetry of the big city". Much of *Heimatkunst* is already inherent in the works of Halbe and Sudermann, and elements of Neo-Romanticism, Impressionism and the Nietzsche cult can be traced as far back as the early days of Naturalism. Probably its greatest achievement, however, is in the fact that in its later works German Naturalism assigned to the artist an entirely new position, both in relation to society and to his own work. The spirit of the age had become a spirit of enquiry, as Holz said. The writer was no longer the missionary and priest of a new idealism, but the sceptical recorder of an unfathomable and enigmatic reality. From here streams of influence merge with the whole literature of the twentieth century. Hermann Bahr seems to be right when he says in his book *Die Überwindung des Naturalismus* (Beyond Naturalism) (1891):

Naturalism is either an interval to allow the old art to revive or an interval in which to prepare for the new; either way it is only an entr'acte.[38]

NOTES

1. Arno Holz, *Werke* (Hermann Luchterhand Verlag, Neuwied/Berlin, 1961–1964), vol. V, p. 302.
   Zola, Ibsen, Leo Tolstoy,
   a (whole) world lies in those names,
   one (which has) not yet rotted,
   one which is still healthy to the core!

   Cling, you dear people,
   Do cling to the apron strings
   of a long dissipated,
   dismantled aestheticism:
   our world is no longer classical,
   our world is not romantic,
   our world is only modern!
2. Holz' poem *Zwischen Alt und Neu* was first published in the revised edition of his *Buch der Zeit*. The 1886 edition does not include it, although it was probably written at that time.
3. Holz, *Werke*, vol. V, p. 15.
4. Erich Ruprecht (ed.) *Literarische Manifeste des Naturalismus 1880–1892* (Stuttgart, 1962), p. 24.
5. Hermann Conradi, *Gesammelte Werke* (München/Leipzig, 1911), vol. I, p. 17.
   The age is dead—the age of great souls—
   We are nothing but a miserable pygmy people
   Who blasphemously parade their puny knowledge
   And impudently marry with the filth of falsehood.
6. Quotation cf. Albert Soergel, *Dichtung und Dichter der Zeit* (Voigtländers Verlag, 20th ed., Leipzig, 1911), p. 20.
7. In his introduction to *Moderne Dichtercharaktere* (1885), cf. Ruprecht, p. 48.
8. Ruprecht, p. 56.
9. Ruprecht, p. 59.
10. Ruprecht, p. 61.
11. Ruprecht, p. 83.
12. Ruprecht, p. 22.
13. Ruprecht, pp. 34 and 37.

14. Bruno Wille, "Erinnerungen an Gerhart Hauptmann und seine Dichtergeneration", in : Walter Heynen (ed.), *Mit Gerhart Hauptmann* (Berlin, 1922), p. 106.
15. Heinrich Hart, *Gesammelte Werke* (Berlin, 1907), vol. III, p. 74.
16. On 20 October Hauptmann's *Vor Sonnenaufgang* followed, causing a theatre scandal in April 1890, after plays by Björnson, Tolstoy and others, Holz' and Schlaf's *Familie Selicke*, and in June Hauptmann's *Friedensfest*. The second season brought, amongst others, Hartleben's *Angele* in November 1890 and Hauptmann's *Einsame Menschen* in January 1891. Cf. Lee Baxandall, "The naturalist innovation on the German stage: The Freie Bühne and its influence", in: *Modern Drama*, Lawrence (Kansas), vol. V (1963), No. 4, pp. 454–476.
17. Ruprecht, pp. 251 and 243.
18. Holz, *Werke*, vol. V, p. 26.

> My breast swells, my heart beats
> And tears spring into my eyes,
> When I hear your hammering and your beating
> Upon steel and iron, stone and ore.
>
> For the melody of these portentous
> Notes sounds sweet to me;
> The hammers fall and boom :
> Behold, this too is poetry !

19. Conradi, *Gesammelte Werke*, vol. III, p. 257.
20. Holz, *Werke*, vol. V, p. 7.

> Far behind me lies the metropolis
> Its wild life held me wildly chained
> Now, however, tired of its wilderness
> I have escaped into my green homeland.

21. Holz, *Werke*, vol. V, p. 10.

> The sweet loveliness of all-embracing nature.

22. Holz, *Werke*, vol. V, p. 243.
23. Holz, *Werke*, vol. V, p. 309.

> It is true my mind is long since radically emancipated but all the flowers of Romanticism still blossom in my heart.

24. Walther Linden (ed.), *Naturalismus* (Leipzig 1936), p. 114, in: *Deutsche Literatur. Sammlung literarischer Kunst- und Kulturdenkmäler in Entwicklungsreihen.*

> Heissa, heissa, hopsassa !
> La La La
> Hopsassa
> Lovely green,
> Lovely green virgin's garland !
> I feel ill.—
> Hunger—Bread ! Bread !
> A sweetheart for a paltry sum,
> 'tis a miserable world !—
> Oh, if only I were dead. . . . !

25. Hauptmann, *Das gesammelte Werke* (Berlin, 1942), vol. III, p. 442.
26. Holz, *Werke*, vol. V, pp. 17 and 12.
27. Paul Ernst, *Dramen I* (München, 1932), p. 93.
28. Linden, *Naturalismus*, p. 227.
29. Hauptmann, *Das gesammelte Werk*, vol. III, p. 439.
30. Holz, *Werke*, vol. V, p. 258.
    Steel and iron, blood and steam,
    Roll, thunder, seethe and sizzle,
    And a scream of pain shrieks between:
    "This life is a battle!"
31. Hauptmann, *Das gesammelte Werk*, vol. I, p. 411.
32. Ruprecht, pp. 3 and 211, cf. also Holz, *Werke*, vol. V. Kunsttheor-
    etische Schriften, p. 16. It is probably worth noting that Goethe once
    said to Riemer: "In der *Natur* ist alles was der Mensch hat und
    noch ein Inkommensurables, ein x, was *er* nicht hat; der *Mensch* hat
    alles was die Natur hat und noch ein Inkommensurables, was sie
    nicht hat; kommen nun alle beide zusammen, so muss etwas ganz
    Vortreffliches entstehen." Cf. Friedrich Wilhelm Riemer, *Mitteilungen
    über Goethe*, ed. Arthur Pollmer (Leipzig, 1921), p. 341.
33. Linden, *Naturalismus*, p. 126.
    "Eh What? What do you say now?"
    "What's the matter, Nielchen? What is it?"
    "Blockhead!"
    "But Thiiienwiebel!"
    "Amalia! I . . ."
    "Oh! Look at that! What do you know!"
    "Eh?! What?! What a rascal! My boy! My boy,
    Amalia! Eh! What?"
34. Holz, *Werke*, vol. V, Kunsttheoretische Schriften, p. 67.
35. Holz, *Werke*, vol. I, p. 68. This experimental poetry is untrans-
    latable.
36. Hugo von Hofmannsthal, *Ein Brief*, in: *Ausgewählte Werke in zwei
    Bänden,* ed. Rudolf Hirsch (S. Fischer Verlag, Frankfurt/M.), vol.
    II.
37. Hauptmann, *Das gesammelte Werk*, vol. I, p. 413 f.
38. Ruprecht, p. 251.

BIBLIOGRAPHY

Anthologies

Walther Linden (ed.), *Naturalismus* (Leipzig, 1936) (Deutsche Literatur.
  Sammlung literarischer Kunst- und Kulturdenkmäler in Entwicklungs-
  reihen. Reihe: Vom Naturalismus zur neuen Volksdichtung, Band 1).
Artur Müller and Hellmut Schlien (eds.), *Dramen des Naturalismus*
  (Emsdetten/Westfalen, 1962).
Erich Ruprecht (ed.), *Literarische Manifeste des Naturalismus 1880–1892*
  (Stuttgart, 1962).

General Literature on German Naturalism

Jethro Bithell, *Modern German Literature, 1880–1950,* 3rd edition (London, 1959).

Richard Hamann and Jost Hermand, *Naturalismus* (Berlin, 1959).

Adalbert von Hanstein, *Das jüngste Deutschland* (Leipzig, 1900).

Georg Lukács, *Deutsche Literatur im Zeitalter des Imperialismus* (Berlin, 1946).

Fritz Schlawe, *Literarische Zeitschriften 1885–1910* (Stuttgart, 1961).

Hans Schwerte, Der Weg ins Zwanzigste Jahrhundert, 1889–1945, in: *Annalen der deutschen Literatur,* ed. H. O. Burger (Stuttgart, 1952).

Albert Soergel, *Dichtung und Dichter der Zeit,* 1st edition (Leipzig, 1911); completely revised edition by Curt Hohoff, Vol. 1 (Düsseldorf, 1961).

Special Studies

W. R. Gaede, Zur geistesgeschichtlichen Deutung des Frühnaturalismus, in: *Germanic Review,* Vol. XI (1936), pp. 196–206.

W. Kayser, Zur Dramaturgie des naturalistischen Dramas, in: *Die Vortragsreise.* Studien zur Literatur (Bern, 1958), pp. 214–231.

H. Motekat, Absicht und Irrtum des deutschen Naturalismus, in: *Experiment und Tradition.* Vom Wesen der Dichtung im 20. Jahrhundert (Frankfurt/M., 1962), pp. 20–31.

W. H. Root, German Naturalism and its literary predecessors, in: *Germanic Review,* Vol. XXIII (1948), pp. 115–124.

B. E. Schatzky, Stage setting in naturalist drama, in: *German Life and Letters,* N. S. Vol. VIII (1954–5), pp. 161–170.

H. Schwerte, Deutsche Literatur im Wilhelminischen Zeitalter, in: *Wirkendes* Wort, Vol. XIV (1964), pp. 254–270.

The Turn of The Century

X

The Turn of The Century

B. COGHLAN

O NE aim of this volume is the analysis of literary labels; not only the wording but also the adhesive properties of the gum in all critical climates. At the starting-post represented by the turn of the century a number of likely looking contenders foregather : Impressionism, Neo-Romanticism, Decadence and Symbolism make up a formidable quartet. If we abandon the first metaphor abruptly and labour the second, it may seem that the dark horse with the staying power will be found wearing the dun colours of *Sprachkrise*.[1] This essay may help to show that more spectacular—and already traditional—terms such Impressionism or Decadence are at best terms of convenience and rather limited in their application. At worst they may be downright misleading. It is easy to see how they arise. In the first number (1892) of *Die Blätter für die Kunst* Stefan George writes :

A poem is not the reproduction of a thought but of a mood ... We do not desire the invention of stories but the reproduction of moods; not reflection but presentation; not entertainment but *impression*.[2]

One is impressed by the *ex cathedra* tone of self-evident truth; obviously this is what George intends to do in his own work and to encourage in others. Naturally, perhaps, one starts looking for proof of his ambition in works written not only close to this date but well after it too. Only one sin ranks higher in the mind of the reading public than an author's failure to develop : his wrong-headed insistence on doing anything different from what he did in his early work. Hofmannsthal is not the only author to be tarred with the brush used in his juvenilia. George's definition, moreover, is simple and concrete; and correspondingly attractive. And it seems to set up a convenient antipole to the anything but Impressionistic goings on up north—in *Die Weber* for example—at the same time.

So one looks for proof; and it seems to be easy to find. One lays firm critical hold of the youthful Hofmannsthal, processes, let us say, *Der Tod des Tizian* (1892) and drives a firmly classifying pin through the poetic head of this particular butterfly :

Er hat uns aufgeweckt aus halber Nacht
Und unsre Seelen licht und reich gemacht
Und uns gewiesen, jedes Tages Fliessen
Und Fluten als ein Schauspiel zu geniessen,
Die Schönheit aller Formen zu verstehen
Und unsrem eignen Leben zuzusehen.[3]

What could be more "decadent" than this group of effeminate youths intoning a dithyramb to the old superman? And the idiom and diction of "neo-romanticism" are there in full Swinburnian spate. There too, it seems, is the tail-end (overgrown, over-refined, exhausted and narcissistic, febrile in its sensitivity), of mid-century *Historismus* : flight into the past, the overblown ripeness of the late Renaissance ... Hofmannsthal himself pours fuel on the "decadent" flame when he defines modernity as old furniture and young nervosities. "Ripened early, sensitive, sorrowful", as he wrote in the prologue to Schnitzler's *Anatol.*

The idea of pole and antipole in literature at the turn of the century can be expressed in a number of deceptively clear-cut ways : brash, forward-looking Berlin, lush, melancholy, backward-looking Vienna; Hauptmann on an alcoholic, heredity-ridden, indignant rampage,—Hofmannsthal losing himself in the snows of yesteryear while Schnitzler dissects the psyche of a decadent culture. If it were as easy as this one could cite Musil's witty account of the prevailing mood and leave it at that :

Walter and he had been young in that now vanished time, shortly after the turn of the century, when a great many people were imagining that the century too was young ... Nobody knew exactly what was on the way; nobody was able to say whether it was to be a new art, a New Man, a new morality or perhaps a re-shuffling of society. So everyone made of it what he liked. But people were standing up on all sides to fight against the old way of life. Suddenly the right man was on the spot everywhere; and, what is so important, men of practical enterprise joined forces with the men of intellectual enterprise ... The Superman was adored, and the Subman was adored; health and the sun were worshipped, and the delicacy of consumptive girls was worshipped; people were enthusiastic hero-worshippers and enthusiastic adherents of the social creed of the Man in the Street; one had faith and was sceptical, one was naturalistic and precious, robust and morbid; one dreamed of ancient castles and shady avenues, autumnal gardens, glassy ponds, jewels, hashish, disease and demonism, but also of prairies, vast horizons, forges and rolling-mills, naked wrestlers, the uprisings of the slaves of toil, man and woman in the primeval garden, and the destruction of society ... If that epoch had been analysed, some such nonsense would have come out as a square circle supposed to be made of wooden iron; but in reality all this had been blended into shimmering significance. This illusion, which found its embodiment in the magical date of the turn of the century, was so powerful that it made some hurl themselves enthusiastically upon the new, as yet untrodden century, while others were having a last fling in the old one, as in a house that one is moving out of anyway, without either one or the other party feeling that there was much difference between the two attitudes.[4]

Musil's account is valuable, however, in that it shows how all involved regarded themselves as equally "modern". Terms such as Impressionism are satisfactory enough if they help to describe a technique, the "how" of writing. Neo-romanticism can work its passage if it is limited to describing a stylistic device in, say, the young Hofmannsthal, or Rilke in his Prague and Bohemian poems. When such a term is extended to cover other important features of fin de siècle literature such as the many aspects of traditionalism, conservative hankering for the past, the literary expression of the new psychology, then it becomes so approximate as to be meaningless or at best only incidentally accurate. Put it another way: yesterday's decadence—another loaded term—may be tomorrow's truth. The angry response to Ibsen is a case in point: angry denial of truth and "right-minded" accusation give way to a more or less sober acceptance of reality revealed. One can object to the term Impressionism for comparable reasons. Thanks to its use in connection with painting the word carries associations of something fleeting, an evanescent sight, sense or mood. In literature the term is extended to take in the depiction of highly subjective moods and involuntary or instinctive response to all manner of stimuli. That this can lead to subtlety for its own sake, to a "decadent" playing with feelings and states of mind, is fairly obvious. It is perhaps this somewhat sensational or titillating quality in literary "Impressionism" which has stuck to its name at the expense of other and, as we shall see, perhaps more significant qualities in literature at the turn of the century in which these same subjective techniques are also used to striking but more durable effect.

Possibly the most serious objection to any of these more or less traditional terms is that they do not convey the sense of newness and of a fresh start which typifies much of the writing which will be considered in the course of this essay. And both newness and freshness were sorely needed. Like modern Australia, Wilhelminian Germany seems to have been an old men's society; and late Habsburg Vienna no less. When, in *The Lucky Country*, Donald Horne writes "And the dominance of old ideas and ageing men has led to a lot of imitation in younger generations",[5] one recalls Stefan Zweig's picture of his childhood world :

> Young people, who always instinctively desire rapid and radical changes, were . . . considered a doubtful element which was to be held down . . . for as long a time as possible . . . the various age groups were valued quite differently from what they are today . . a man of thirty was regarded as an unfledged person, and even one of forty was barely considered ripe for a position of responsibility . . . So arose the situation . . . that youth was a hindrance in all careers, and age alone an advantage . . . Men wore long black frock coats and walked at a leisurely pace, and whenever possible acquired a slight *embonpoint*, in order to personify the desired sedateness; and those who were ambitious strove, at least outwardly, to belie their youth, since the young were suspected of instability . . . All those qualities which today we look upon as enviable possessions—freshness, self-assertion, daring, curiosity, youth's lust for life—were regarded as suspect in those days that only had use for "substance".[6]

In more aggressive mood one thinks back to Nietzsche's roistering onslaught on the "es ist erreicht" mentality just a few years after the unification of Germany in 1871 :

> . . . for I can see how everyone is convinced that we no longer need any struggle, any such bravery at all; on the contrary, we are told, nearly everything has been arranged as nicely as possible and in any case everything necessary has been discovered or done long since : in short culture's best seed has in part been sown, in part it is already sprouting well—and here and there, indeed, blooming luxuriantly. In this sphere one sees not only satisfaction but joy and ecstasy. I sense this ecstasy and joy in the unprecedentedly confident behaviour of German newspapermen and of those fabricators of novels, tragedies, songs and histories : for these people visibly form a very cohesive society which seems to have organized a conspiracy, namely to take control of those hours of idleness and digestion which for modern man constitute his "cultural moments", and catching him in these moments they stun him with printed paper. At the present time, since this war, this society has a monopoly of happiness, dignity, self-confidence; after such triumphs of German culture

it feels itself not only sanctioned and confirmed but nearly sacrosanct . . .[7]

Certainly one of the most remarkable features of unified Germany, and it is not creditable, is the way in which its literature and theatre were dominated by the old and ageing. Where new ideas do emerge, where some sense of the condition of modern man is to be found, is largely in the late work of the few old men who see beyond the surface of this "great but essentially mendacious century"[8] (as a German journalist put it on the occasion of Wagner's sesquicentenary): Fontane in his Prussian dialogue which reveals character and condition without recourse to explanatory comment; Keller in *Martin Salander*; Storm in *Ein Bekenntnis* and perhaps most of all in "Geh nicht hinein":

> Vor wenig Stunden noch
> Auf jenen Kissen lag sein blondes Haupt
> Zwar bleich von Qualen, denn des Lebens Fäden
> Zerrissen jäh; doch seine Augen sprachen
> Noch zärtlich, und mitunter lächelt' er,
> Als säh er noch in goldne Erdenferne.
> Da plötzlich losch es aus; er wusst es plötzlich
> —Und ein Entsetzen schrie aus seiner Brust,
> Dass ratlos Mitleid, die am Lager sassen
> In Stein verwandelte—er lag am Abgrund;
> Bodenlos, ganz ohne Boden.—"Hilf!
> Ach Vater, lieber Vater!" Taumelnd schlug
> Er um sich mit den Armen; ziellos griffen
> In leere Luft die Hände; noch ein Schrei—
> Und dann verschwand er.
> Dort, wo er gelegen,
> Dort hinterm Wandschirm, stumm und einsam liegt
> Jetzt etwas—bleib! Geh nicht hinein! Es schaut
> Dich fremd und furchtbar an; für viele Tage
> Kannst du nicht leben, wenn du es erblickt.
> "Und weiter—du, der du ihn liebtest—, hast
> Nichs weiter du zu sagen?"
> Weiter nichts.[9]

Such realism and percipience are rare, however; we seem to be confronted here with a complacent society getting the books it deserves as well as the government. Nevertheless, it is remarkable that apart from Nietzsche and the few examples given here there does not seem to have been much overt realization of what was happening to the twin souls in the human breast about which Goethe had been concerned several generations earlier. If one thinks back only as far as Droste-Hülshoff and Mörike the falling-off is striking.

And then, quite suddenly it seems, the picture changes. It is as if a whole new generation takes over. Rarely can Walter Bagehot's dictum have been so strikingly confirmed :

> Generally one generation ... succeeds another almost silently; at any moment men of all ages between thirty and seventy have considerable influence; each year removes many old men, makes others older, brings in many new. But sometimes there is an abrupt change. In that case the affairs of the country are apt to alter much, for good or for evil; sometimes it is ruined, sometimes it becomes more successful, but it hardly ever stays as it was.[10]

By 1890, indeed, there was every certainty that far from staying as it was, German literature would never be the same again. Most of the reputations which have dominated the German scene over the past half-century and more were made in the fifteen years or so between the late 'eighties and the early nineteen-hundreds : Hauptmann, George, Hofmannsthal, Mann, Rilke. All of them were young men, none over thirty, when their first effective blows were struck. Consciously (George) or unconsciously (Mann), overtly (Musil, *Törless*) or by implication (Hofmannsthal, *Märchen der 672. Nacht. Der Tor und der Tod*) they questioned or contradicted the values and poked around behind the façade of the society in which, with Musil's Ulrich and Walter, they grew up.

Perhaps one should recall the realities; and it will be only fair if we move right outside "literature" to illustrate them. Albert Schweitzer, an exact contemporary of Mann and Rilke, has this to say of the *fin de siècle* :

> So many symptoms forced me to conclude that our proud and industrious race was intellectually and spiritually tired. It seemed to me that people were persuading themselves that previous hopes for the future of mankind had been too exalted and that we should have to limit ourselves to striving for what was within reach. The watchword *Realpolitik*—applied to all topics—really meant that a short-sighted nationalism was approved and a pact made with forces and tendencies which had previously been fought because they were the enemies of progress ... Towards the end of the century people reviewed the past and tried to evaluate its achievements in all spheres of activity. They did this with an optimism which I found quite incomprehensible. Everywhere people seemed to assume that we had not only ad-

vanced in knowledge and inventiveness but that in a spiritual and ethical sense we had likewise reached a standard never reached before and never to be lost in the future. It seemed to me, however, that in our intellectual and spiritual life we had not only failed to surpass bygone generations but that in many respects a good deal of their achievement was running away between our fingers.[11]

Schweitzer notes what might be called a middle-aged quality in the *Zeitgeist*. Perhaps, ironically enough, the most striking feature of the writers with whom we are concerned in this essay—Impressionists, so-called Neo-Romantics, or at any rate non-Naturalists in any strict sense—is the mellow reflectiveness (Hofmannsthal, Rilke) or masterfully oracular tone of obvious truth revealed (George) with which these young men reflect on their and the human condition generally. For both tones are usually attributes of age. On the face of it it would seem as if the new writers were beating the *Zeitgeist* by joining it. It would be facile to say that they had nothing to be ecstatic and youthful about. Neither had Shelley, but his poetry, one might think, is clearly the work of a young man. Probably the clue to the situation is to be found in the sense of time and epoch. There has been a good deal of talk in recent years about *Spätzeitlichkeit*[12] in which one sometimes forgets—the realization is far from new—that every age is at the same time child, mature man and woman, and ripe or senile old age. But, as the Marschallin might say, "the difference is in the 'how' ".[13]

The "difference" to be noted in young writers at the turn of the century is their unusual acuity of language which is often combined with remarkable beauty and evocativeness. And then there is the probably unprecedented degree of self-awareness, the ultimate stage, one might think, in historical feeling, of oneself as part of history : a feature of the nineteenth century which caused Killy to give the title of *Das historische Jahrhundert* to the volume of his *Lesebuch* which covers the years 1832–1880. But now, around the turn of the new century, instead of oneself and one's epoch as the proud culmination[14] there is the sense of alienation from the age, of the age as hostile and wearing many masks, none of them wholly representative and concealing no one definable identity. Hofmannsthal's comment on Basilius (in *Der Turm*) is quite revealing, especially when we recall how much of the old epoch was deliberately embodied in this figure :

The act ... contains a good deal that is very palpably mimetic : on the one hand the ceremonial, on the other the ... violent action which lies in wait from the beginning and finally breaks forth. As to details · I am sure that in the case of the King at least, I have not weakened at any point his conscious regal allure. Indeed he is almost terrifying because one cannot guess at all what sort of man breathes behind this mask. But that is as it should be.[15]

It is good to emphasize this sense of isolation and alienation at the present time when the "disinherited mind", "der unbehauste Mensch" and the "discontinuous personality" are such markedly modern concepts; for here, around 1900,[16] are the signs and symptoms large and plain. Perhaps the most horrifying aspect of a coldly horrifying book, Musil's *Törless* (1906), is the way in which the outside world does not penetrate the private obsessions of the tight little group at the school. For there does not seem to be any relevant outside world. At least as striking is the loneliness of Hanno Buddenbrook. It is possible not to take Mann's rather dated association of artistry with bourgeois decline too seriously, or at least as not all-explanatory. What at all events is perhaps more savagely memorable is Hanno's remoteness from the safe and solid world which surrounds him. Where it does intrude, the familiar world is hostile; the private realm has primacy, but the mind is no kingdom in Blake's sense. Emphasis on this move *inwards*, a complete change of vantage-point, is perhaps more important in a study of some so-called "Impressionists" than further discussion along the more traditional lines typified, for example, by Albert Roeffler a generation ago[17] and latterly by Fritz Sommerhalder in his Zürich (ETH) inaugural lecture.

A certain concentration on the "subjective", "moodful", "subtle" aspects of literary Impressionism is legitimate so long as it does not ignore the pressure which drives a writer to create in this way. "Pressure", indeed, is the key-word here : what J. B. Priestley, describing Ibsen, calls the "terrific pressure from within, finding some relief in his art, that compelled him to reveal ... to suggest to his audiences the misty and often sinister borderland between consciousness and the unconscious, turning himself into a prophet ... of the depth psychology that was soon to invade the clinics, a Freudian before Freud, a Jungian before Jung".[18]

With this in mind one might generalize and say that common to most major writers around the turn of the century is the ability to reveal, in prose narrative, verse or drama, this new-old inner dimension of the personality, a landscape of the soul with its beautiful and horrifying heights and depths :

Wo ist zu diesem Innen
ein Aussen? Auf welches Weh
legt man solches Linnen?
Welche Himmel spiegeln sich drinnen
in dem Binnensee
dieser offenen Rosen....[19]

It is strange and a little amusing to reflect that this awareness of
"something far more deeply interfused" often led to some kind of
Sprachkrise, some kind of doubt in the ability to communicate.
One says amusing because this crisis is often expressed in language
of the greatest clarity and aesthetic appeal. Hofmannsthal's *Ein
Brief* (the Chandos Letter) is the classic example of such "decadent" disintegration :

> My spirit forced me to see everything ... in uncanny close-up :
> just as when I once saw a piece of the skin of my little finger
> under a magnifying-glass—and it looked like a field lying fallow
> with furrows and ridges—so it was now with men and their
> actions. I could no longer embrace them with the simplifying
> eye of custom and habit. Everything fell apart; and the parts
> broke into smaller parts; and nothing could be grasped any more
> by any one single concept. Individual words swam around me;
> they ran together into eyes which stared at me : and I, in turn,
> am forced to stare at them. They are whirlpools, and gazing
> down into them makes me giddy; and they turn and twist un-
> ceasingly, and passing through them one reaches only empti-
> ness.[20]

But it is easy to beg the question. The fact that Hofmannsthal
can "startle this dull pain, and make it move and live", that George
can give precise expression and oratorical vigour to his dilemma
("Ich wollte sie aus kühlem eisen/Und wie ein glatter fester streif,/
Doch war im schacht auf allen gleisen/So kein metall zum gusse
reif".)[21] neither vitiates nor solves the problem. For the writer here,
in his awareness of isolation, is acting as a representative, a *Stellvertreter* for his time. He is, to echo Hofmannsthal's famous *mot*,
a seismograph,[22] and a seismograph reacts involuntarily, recording
the nature of the disturbance irrespective of any feelings which the
affected or reacting body (celestial or otherwise ...) might have.
Perhaps Rilke's final expression of this state of being is the most
acute of all :

> O Leben, Leben : Draussensein.
> Und ich in Lohe. Niemand der mich kennt ...[23]

What has been lost is any sense of meaningful human society; and probably any real belief in values and existence beyond it. The crudely sociological yardstick of interpretation—what Lukács calls "vulgar sociology"—is not needed to help us note the dominant conviction that social ties are a chimera. This expresses itself in various ways : in Hofmannsthal's deep concern with "Bindungen" :

> —but in the middle of being thrown hither and thither, dazed and in fear of death, we are also aware of, and we know that there is also a Necessity which chooses us from one moment to the next, which comes so quietly, so close to our hearts and yet cuts keen as a sword. Without that there would have been nothing you could call a life at the front but only men dying in heaps like brute beasts. And the same Necessity runs between men and women as well—where that exists, there is a having-to-come-together, and forgiveness and reconciliation and a standing-by-one-another. And here is a place for children, and here is a marriage and a sacrament, in spite of everything.[24]

This concern may on the other hand take a rather negative form as in George's description of his technique as "barbed wire to keep out the uninitiated"; or it may take the form of concrete depiction of the illusoriness of any social forms—would anyone claim today that in *Buddenbrooks* Thomas Mann was writing only about his own specific class of society?[25]—or it may find expression in Rilke's painful awareness of isolation.

It is good to be clear about one thing, however : this is not "decadence", neither is it nihilism. Time was when it was fashionable to speak of early Hofmannsthal, Rilke fairly generally and George *in toto* in terms of escapism, Neo-Romantic flight into history ("sinking Renaissance", etc.[26]) or the luxuriant labyrinths of the poet's over-refined personal world.—It is probably superfluous to remark that Hofrat Behrens was not in love with tuberculosis and Hofmannsthal approved neither of Claudio nor of the rich man who meets such a miserable end in *Das Märchen der 672. Nacht*. Often, however, the sad thing about such art is the fact that the more acute and comprehensive the depiction, the more removed from the people who could most profit by it the work becomes, a fact which has far-reaching implications to which we shall return later. *Der Turm* and the *Duineser Elegien* are cases in point. It is hardly likely that either will ever become exactly popular or even part of a vaguely but affectionately perceived national property in the manner of *Faust* or *Hamlet*.

The temptation, natural enough in itself, is for the seismographic writer to jump off his reactor and turn to programme-making. When this happens the dangers are great even though the results may still be artistically acceptable. George's *Das Neue Reich* and the climax to the fifth act of *Der Turm (I)*, neither of them free from a certain strenuous tone, are at least candidates for debate in this context.

Even, however, as one postulates the isolation of the artist a curious paradox emerges. It is rather encouraging. To define it we have to retreat a fair way into the nineteenth century. Reflecting in general terms it is probably true to say that no writer since Goethe (and, in a different sense, Heine) had really reached across the various provincial, regional, denominational and national barriers of the German-speaking lands.[27] The concept of the "Nation" in Fichte's sense or—and Hofmannsthal would shudder at the proximity![28]—in the way the term is used in *Das Schrifttum als geistiger Raum der Nation*, does not seem to have evoked much response other than from relatively ephemeral writers in the days of, for example, The Young Germans or the 1848 revolution. Grillparzer might be seen as a shining exception, but his social-political menu is generally framed in the yellow and black of Habsburg Austria. Apart from him, if one passes the major figures in review before the inward eye one will probably tend to see them rather against the background of their region : Keller/Zürich, Mörike/Swabia, Storm/Schleswig-Holstein, Raabe/Brunswick, Fontane/Berlin : and so on. Not that these important writers are apostles of *Heimatkunst*. But the presence and importance of the *genius loci* are undeniable. With the writers under discussion here, however, the picture is rather different even though the temptation to explain them away in terms of regional origins, environment, allegiance, etc. is considerable : for, oddly enough, most of them came from the periphery of the German area and most of them had to do with languages and cultures other than their own as a result : Mann/Lübeck, Hofmannsthal/Vienna, George/Rhineland (with Lorraine peering over his ancestral shoulder), Rilke/Prague. And, of course, all of them bear the stigma or charisma, as Hofmannsthal would say, of their origin, even the seemingly rootless Rilke.[29] For all of them, however,—and this is a significant move forward in German literature—the wider stage of Germania loomed large in their awareness. Rudolf Borchardt's characteristically aggressive definition of the difference between George and Hofmannsthal seems to imply this :

> Both great reformations developed as the constellation of their time demanded. The shadow of force and violence lies across George's creation, the shadow of sorrow and brevity across

Hofmannsthal's : ... the one burst forth volcanically, the other unfolded naturally; revolution and restoration, heroic violence and heroic inheritance ... in the one a superforce, in the other a simple strength. On the one side the wild gardener tore the rotten tree up by its roots and threw it away ... On the other the patient gardener ... cultivated the new stem ... from what was old and almost dead ...[30]

In a complex geological metaphor Borchardt goes on to describe how George emerged from the "arbitrary, molten fluidity" of Germany before the unification and how as he burst forth he created— and actually became—"national rock". Hofmannsthal, however, is for Borchardt a natural, inevitable manifestation, the product of a continuous unfolding process in an organic, spiritual-intellectual conformation ("eines geistigen Erdinnern") : the allusion to Habsburg Austria is fairly obvious. One does not, perhaps fortunately, have to pursue Borchardt's rather tortured metaphor nor share his exaggerated enthusiasms to see that with both George and Hofmannsthal we are not far from the idea of the poet as some kind of national preceptor.

To say that George was a self-conscious prophet is hardly new; and such phrases as "Statthalter of the German spirit" (Curt Hohoff) have been applied to Hofmannsthal for many years. But there was a world of difference between the two preceptors in the way in which they approached their self-appointed task; and Borchardt's account is not really exhaustive. Borchardt, indeed, does make it rather easy for himself : his polarities, while apparently comprehensive and certainly attractive in an emotional way, do not allow for the honest search, the "expressions of uncertainty, misgiving, doubt and even of world-weariness and despair"[31] which preceded the emergence of George, the exclusive master with his aura of incense, acolytes and Maximin ... Neither does Borchardt take in the sober, harder, yet in some ways more gentle and certainly more realistic George described by Hans Brasch at the end of the war (1918) :

> ... with melancholy pride he accepted our new, humiliated position in Europe. Now, for the first time, it seemed to him that the road was clear for the new, poor, naked German human being ... neither did he withold respect for many of the new leaders of the people, for they were simple and without show ... Now, for the first time in centuries, he saw the possibility of a sober, simple freedom for Germany, in which men could speak to and stand by each other.[32]

We are confronted here with at least one significant paradox in Stefan George; and it bears on his influence and ultimate value as a preceptor. On the one hand he searches unceasingly in his verse for purity, for crystalline lucidity, for what is "schlicht". It is remarkable how often the paradox-image of cold fire dominates one's mind when reading some of his best verse. Controlled intensity, warmth which never loses its austere chill is the prevailing tone :

> Wer je die flamme umschritt
> Bleibe der flamme trabant!
> Wie er auch wandert und kreist :
> Wo noch ihr schein ihn erreicht
> Irrt er zu weit nie vom ziel.
> Nur wenn sein blick sie verlor
> Eigener schimmer ihn trügt :
> Fehlt ihm der mitte gesetz
> Treibt er zerstiebend ins all.[33]

And then there is the sense of precision, of objective statement, concrete depiction, the cool clarity of sharply outlined images succeeding each other in calm procession :

> Du schlank und rein wie eine flamme
> Du wie der morgen zart und licht
> Du blühend reis vom edlen stamme
> Du wie ein quell geheim und schlicht
>
> Begleitest mich auf sonnigen matten
> Umschauerst mich im abendrauch
> Erleuchtest meinen weg im schatten
> Du kühler wind du heisser hauch . . .[34]

And yet : for all the icy control there does seem to be an undertow of emotional passion; there are chain-reactions of association; hectic heroic overtones in terms such as "das wahre sinnbild" fastened to "das völkische banner"—which can scarcely be conveyed by translations such as "true sign or symbol" and "people's banner". It is strange how often one's mood, even as a non-German responding unwillingly or at least slowly and only by empathy, changes from dispassionate calm to something approaching exhilaration at—what?—at something vague, which is to come, something "zukunftsträchtig" . . .

> Er führt durch sturm und grausige signale
> Des frührots seiner treuen schar zum werk
> Des wachen tags und pflanzt das Neue Reich.[35]

One can well believe Heiseler, himself an impressionable youth when these verses were written, who describes the effect of this as follows :

> In the 'twenties and 'thirties these verses passed from mouth to mouth as a sign of hope for Germany. They have been interpreted as according with the National Socialist movement; and the National Socialists did in fact lay eager claim to them ... And it was not only deception or self-delusion on the part of those who hoped ... Much of the hopeful ... surge of those years found a voice in George's work; much too of other, darker stirrings within the age. Certainly, George himself, with his sober eye for political realities, recognized the impure fanaticism of the Hitler movement from the start—and despised it ... But that does not change the fact that even men of his inner circle— in their youthful zest—thought differently.[36]

It is absurd to make George "responsible" for any aspect of National Socialism; but his cool rhetoric might well have had a dangerously utopian effect on people unused to responding or thinking in precise political or social terms. A prominent Social Democrat of the 'twenties is reported to have said rather wearily that it was difficult to get people excited about milk-prices; but they were after all the realities. George is perhaps too often too exciting, in the quite literal meaning of the word; the sense of disappointment as one returns to the sober world of everyday reality may place too great a strain on young men in a hurry and older men frustrated by their own disillusionment. Marginally—and it is an odd thought—one might wonder at George's deliberate revival of such emotive archaisms as "du blühend reis" and ask in what essential way he, a reformer of the language and creator of a "new" poetic idiom, differs from, say, Wagner in *Die Walküre* or many a lesser nineteenth century medievalizer. . . . Is the difference one of kind? Or is it, as one might suspect, more one of degree and subtlety in application?

In Hofmannsthal's case—and Hofmannsthal was rather more balanced both personally and artistically—the picture is a little more clear. An interesting and productive polarity can be seen : between the Chandos Letter and *Briefe des Zurückgekehrten*. The latter have been curiously under-estimated or at least neglected. Certainly *Chandos*, as we have seen and as has been shown very conclusively elsewhere,[37] conveys the personal dilemma implicit in the attempt to communicate at a time when the old baroque antithesis of *Sein und Schein* (appearance and reality) is so huge and shattered into so many fragments as to be inexpressible. What

Hofmannsthal is lamenting here seems to be the vain pursuit of that kind of language to which Rilke aspires :

> ... thus one often finds oneself at variance with the external behaviour of a language and intent on its innermost life, or on an innermost language, without terminations, if possible—a language of word-kernels, a language that's not gathered, up above, on stalks, but grasped in the speech-seed. Would it not be in this language that the perfect Hymn to the Sun would have to be composed, and isn't the pure silence of love like heart-soil around such speech-seeds? Oh, how often one longs to speak a few degrees more deeply... one gets only a minimal layer further down; one's left with a mere intimation of the kind of speech that may be possible *there*, where silence reigns.[38]

But *Chandos*, after all, is expressed in personal terms even though the wider social implications may be clear enough. In *Briefe des Zurückgekehrten* Hofmannsthal takes on the guise of a returning expatriate business-man. This is in itself a rather far cry from the still somewhat exclusive and aristocratic disguise which he had donned for the Chandos Letter. And in *Briefe des Zurück-gekehrten* he takes as his text the wider scene of Germany as a whole :

> When I came home I thought I'd see how they lived... They're rich and they are poor and you bump into the poor or into the rich and neither gives a pure sound... They have an upper and a lower, a better and a worse, a coarser one and a refined one, right and left, those for and those against, and bourgeois rules and rules for the nobility : but nothing adds up—there's something missing. I can't give you the artistic phrase for it, but it's something that's in the English character—grandiose and complex as it is; and it's in the Maori character—childlike and artless as that is : it's the ability to form a community.[39]

Perhaps the most striking aspect of these letters, however, is the way in which Hofmannsthal peers behind the glittering façade of Hohenzollern Germany at the turn of the century and in doing so points to the dissociation of personality, noted earlier in the present essay, which is for him the cardinal element in the moral decline of the nation :

> ... for in actual fact nothing that they do really speaks for their whole character; their right hand truly does not know what their left hand is doing; what they think in their heads does not correspond to what their hearts say... the façade does not correspond to the back stairs... nor their public affairs to their

private lives. That is why I am telling you that I cannot find them anywhere, neither in their gestures nor in their actual speech; because their whole being is not in any one of these things . . .[40]

Thus personal and social factors are brought together; or rather what Hofmannsthal sees as a great falling-off in the nation is for him the projection writ large and multiplied a million times of an individual failing. To counter this he sets up the image of an older attitude to life. He recalls an ancient folder of Dürer's etchings, familiar to him since childhood. He remembers how often, in a childish way, he had measured reality against the clear, firm attitude to existence which seemed to emanate from these scenes of common life :

Everything in those old pictures was different from reality : but there was no gap between the two. That old world was more pious, more exalted, milder, bolder, more lonely. Their tools were not the same; their dress was strange and their gestures were larger than life. But there were very deep—I don't know how deep—qualities in their character, something behind the gestures : their relationship to nature, or if I may say it in such dry words, their attitude to life : how far it is opposition, how far submission, where rebellion is proper and where surrender, where equanimity and a dry retort and where high spirits and jollity : this essence, this reality behind everyday appearances, this quality which is forced out of men by the simple deeds of everyday life just as sweetness and coarseness are forced from the bark and branches of a tree . . .—this quality : my world, as those old pictures know, as I know now and knew then, has this quality. For there was some force within me that made me measure reality against it; and almost without realizing it, I measured everything against that terrifying exalted, black, old magic world; I tested everything on this touchstone to see whether it were gold or just a poor gleam of yellow.

And now I drag the great Germany and the Germans of today before this judgement seat of my childish fancies, from which, in my inmost self, I could not get free, and I see that they do not pass the test; and I can't get over it.[41]

Hofmannsthal's personal, moral precept is simple, direct and demanding :

As I've said, there's almost nothing of the theoretical in me, as good as nothing. Nevertheless, I have one or two phrases, aphorisms, or whatever you call them . . . The whole man must move at once : there you have one of the great truths ... I don't quote it often, but it's always present in me somewhere. With such truths—I don't think there are many of such strength and simplicity—it's the same as with that mechanism which you have in the inner ear—little bones or little reacting spheres; they tell us whether we're in equilibrium or not. The whole man must move at once.[42]

If we dwell on Hofmannsthal it is because in his concern for society he neither neglects the fallible and all too human individual as its mainspring, nor does he fall into mere exhortation or ideology. At the same time, while stressing individual values and personal responsibility—as he also did later in the Marschallin and Hans Karl—he usually has the wider, social picture firmly in view. It is one thing to save your own soul; it is more important that in saving it you help others to save theirs : "but now this zone of loneliness isn't there any more; now my love is distributed everywhere, even if as yet in a very unsatisfactory way; but distributed all the same— ...."[43] It is perhaps this wider concern that distinguishes his attitude from Rilke's equally gentle approach to the idea of the poet as guide and preceptor :

Art cannot be helpful through our trying to help and specially concerning ourselves with the distresses of others, but in so far as we bear our own distresses more passionately, give, now and then, a perhaps clearer meaning to endurance, and develop for ourselves the means of expressing the suffering within us and its conquest more precisely and clearly than is possible to those who have to apply their powers to something else.[44]

Few writers, in fact, point up more than Rilke the growing isolation of the writer : "Wer, wenn ich schriee, hörte mich denn ...?"[45]—Who indeed? For Rilke reminds one very much of the princely pilgrim under the stairs of his own house in Hofmannsthal's *Der Dichter und diese Zeit* :

... and he returned, but before he crossed the threshold, he was commanded to enter his own house as an unknown beggar and to live where the servants might tell him. The servants gave him a place under the stairs, where the dogs sleep at night ...
This act of dwelling unrecognized in one's own house, under the stairs, in the darkness, with the dogs : a stranger and yet at home; like one who is dead, as a phantom in everyone's mouth, a commander of their tears ... without any rank or position in this house, with no service, no rights, no duties save to be idle

and lie there and weigh up all these things day and night within oneself, and to live through great sorrows and great joys . . . He, however, he who lies like a ghost in the darkness, possesses all these things : for each of them is an open wound in his soul . . . —this act of dwelling there unrecognized is nothing but a symbol . . .[46]

We spoke earlier of *Sprachskepsis* and difficulty of communication; paradoxically, it was noted, those who suffer from *Sprachskepsis* are most adept at expressing it; the most beautifully eloquent are the most consciously tongue-tied. No one will ever say that Rilke was tongue-tied. But *Sprachskepsis* in him takes on another form as he gets older. And in this he is a very representative modern figure. It is one thing for George Steiner to see Rilke as part of a great old tradition :

> The difficulties are immense. The younger German writers feel themselves profoundly estranged from the classic achievements of modern German literature. Composed in an idiom and sensibility radically different from that of the war years or the present, the work of Thomas Mann, of Musil, of Rilke is often remote. It stands in an aura of sepulchral glory.[47]

One offers no counter-claim. Of course Rilke's roots in an older tradition are obvious. So are Schönberg's; and apparently Picasso can draw like an angel or Michaelangelo. But Rilke, like Schönberg and Picasso, points forward to the present, not into the past; neither is he marooned in his own age. For Rilke is curiously "modern" in this : however attractive and accessible his work may have been when he was younger, the poetry of his middle-age and ultimate maturity does not get across to any but the initiated reader; the cognoscenti who scarcely need converting. If tempted to doubt this rather low assessment of his general appeal one can only, pedantically but truly, fall back on the experience of intelligent and not insensitive university students trying to read him at sight and for the sheer enjoyment or appreciation to be gained from it. And Rilke was aware of this gap between his language and his readers—real and imaginary. He was only too painfully aware of the way in which his comprehensive vision of the world was not reflected in their minds :

> Er lag. Sein aufgestelltes Antlitz war
> bleich und verweigernd in den steilen Kissen,
> seitdem die Welt und dieses Von-ihr-wissen,
> von seinen Sinnen abgerissen,
> zurückfiel an das teilnahmslose Jahr.

Die, so ihn leben sahen, wussten nicht,
wie sehr er *Eines* war mit allem diesen,
denn dieses : diese Tiefen, diese Wiesen
und diese Wasser *waren* sein Gesicht . . ,[48]

Rilke indeed seems to mark the point of no return. Like the notes to *The Waste Land*—or rather the necessity for them—he epitomizes the isolation of the modern poet : the poet who has so much to give but, as in the *impasse* in Bergman's *The Silence*, cannot make the necessary contact. Rilke's seismograph continues to react to the last and a few are there to record its tremors. But he represents the end of the line. And it is a long way back to the time when Hofmannsthal could publish the Chandos Letter in the daily press.

In a way it might be thought a pity that Rilke has probably had a greater influence amongst the upper échelons of the intellectual élite than Hofmannsthal. For Hofmannsthal generally tried—not that he succeeded anything like consistently—to reach and affect people. He rarely forgot that the poet, however complex his vision of the world, is as nothing if he stays in the void. But perhaps Rilke is more typical. If he finds the realities of existence too complex for expression in terms that are generally accessible he is at one with the more significant of his present-day successors : Celan, Bachmann . . . And with this difference, as Holthusen and Kemp pointed out some years ago :

If we want to try to say something about the consciousness of the younger and of the most recent generations, then the first point to strike us is this : there are no longer any "world systems" in lyrical form; the old determination to set up great plans for a theory of life and existence in general—in the sense of Rilke and George—has abdicated . . . We might say that the contemporary poet has no opinion on the scene as a whole; neither is he inclined to feel responsible for the world as such or to lay claim to the office of representative for humanity in the manner of the author of the *Duino Elegies* . . . His (i.e. the contemporary poet's) interest is kindled by the invincible resistance of the external world, and wherever he senses its secret decay and dissolution . . . he is satisfied if he can win for himself a little piece of security in four verses and three feet of reality as a basis for existence. The prevailing atmosphere is remarkably reminiscent of that which followed the Flood.[49]

Contemporary lyric poetry is not within the brief of this essay; otherwise one might take up arms against some of the more quietistic implications in this assessment. Indeed, with an angry Enzensberger clamouring, not at all like Rilke addressing the angels, to be heard, one would have no choice. But the central point is clear : the reluctance of poets today to set up or embrace any "total view" of existence.

And this indeed accounts for the preoccupation here with figures such as George, Hofmannsthal and Rilke. The more colourful "Neo-Romantic" aspects of these and other writers might have proved a more attractive proposition—superficially at least. And one might well have portrayed what was after all a high-water mark in the more recent German theatre. If, however, we are to select any one strand as being more significant, of most lasting value than any other, then it may perhaps be found in this attempt—sometimes confident, sometimes arrogant, sometimes reluctant and hesitant—by major creative artists to show the ailments of their age and to guide their contemporaries. Necessarily this leads us well beyond the turn of the century. For all the men discussed here made their reputations at an early age and came to final maturity only within the living memory of many people still alive today. But the tools were fashioned and the awareness dawned during the decade which has been characterized—not inaccurately but incompletely—as "decadent" or merely "naughty". In piercing the shams and dubious traditions, the extrovert *Epigonentum* of Wilhelminian Germany these artists, wittingly or unwittingly, looked ahead to dilemmas and *impasses* which we recognize as our own. Of them one can often say what Ernst Jünger said of *Auf den Marmorklippen* when reading it shortly after its completion :

> Already certain features were developing which had not occurred to me while I was writing the work and which were nevertheless quite clear to me now. Thus the author's creations separate themselves from him and continue to grow in places which he does not know. But for this to happen there has to be something elemental, something unformulated in the language itself; otherwise everything withers away.[50]

Perhaps, most of all, the writers discussed briefly here bear out the truth of Rudolf Borchardt's reluctant admission :

> On the other hand this epoch does not give rise to any thought, object or individual without stamping it invisibly and inevitably with its own terrible sign.[51]

NOTES

N.B. For prose and poetry quoted in the text published translations have been used as far as possible; prose translations are printed in the text; in the case of poetry the original is printed in the text, the translation in the notes. Where no translation was available the author's own version has been given; in such cases the notes refer to the German original.

1. *Sprachkrise:* literally a "crisis in language", i.e. a pessimistic questioning of the power of language to communicate. Sometimes the term *Sprachskepsis* (scepticism towards language) is used.

2. Transl. E. K. Bennett. See Bennett, *Stefan George* (Cambridge, 1954) p. 23.

3. Literally: he has awoken us from our twilight state ("half night") and made our souls rich and bright; and he has shown us how to enjoy the ebb and flow of each day as a dramatic spectacle, how to understand the beauty of all forms, and to be spectators of our own lives.

4. *The Man Without Qualities* (London, 1953), vol. 1, pp. 58–9.

5. *The Lucky Country*, Penguin (Australia, 1964), p. 216.

6. *The World of Yesterday*, Hallam Edition (London, 1953), pp. 34–5.

7. *Unzeitgemässe Betrachtungen. Erstes Stück, Werke,* 3 vols., ed. Karl Schlechta (Munich, 1954), vol. 1, p. 138.

8. "dieses grosse, verlogene Jahrhundert".

9. Just a few hours ago
his blonde head lay on that pillow;
pale, indeed, with pain, for the threads of life
snap suddenly; but his eyes still
spoke tenderly, and from time to time he smiled,
as if he could still see into life's golden distance.
Then suddenly it went out; he knew it, suddenly
—and terror screamed from his breast,
so that those at his bedside, helpless,
were turned to stone—he lay at the chasm's edge,
below him nothing, nothing at all.—"Help!
Oh Father, dear Father!" Wildly
his arms beat around him; aimlessly
his hands seized the empty air; another cry—
and then he vanished.   There, where he lay,
there behind the screen, silent and lonely lies
something—wait! Don't go in. It will
look at you strangely and terribly; for days
you won't be able to live if you've seen it.
"Well then—you who loved him; haven't
you anything else to say?"
Nothing else.

10. Quoted by Donald Horne, *The Lucky Country*, op. cit., p. 215.

11. *Selections from Albert Schweitzer* (London, 1953), p. 45.

12. The idea that a period or epoch is "late" in a cultural sense: late with the connotation, perhaps, of aged, even decadent, e.g. late Rome, late Habsburg, etc. See *Spätzeiten und Spätzeitlichkeit.* Vor-

träge gehalten auf dem II. Internationalen Germanistenkongress 1960 in Kopenhagen. Hrsg. im Auftrage der Internationalen Vereinigung für Germanische Sprach- und Literaturwissenschaft von Werner Kohlschmidt (Bern und München, 1962), p. 176

13. "Und in dem 'Wie' da liegt der ganze Unterschied—." Hofmannsthal, *Der Rosenkavalier*, Act I. *Lustspiele I* (Stockholm, 1947), p. 331.

14. Jakob Burckhardt's definition of this attitude would be hard to excel for clarity and brevity: "Our extreme and really rather ridiculous egoism considers as happy those epochs which have anything in common with our own ... Just as if the world and its history existed for our benefit. Everyone sees his own times as the fulfilment of all times past, and not simply as one of many passing phases." See *Weltgeschichtliche Betrachtungen* (Stuttgart, 1918), p. 262.

15. *Hugo von Hofmannsthal—Carl J. Burckhardt: Briefwechsel* (Frankfurt, 1957), p. 99.

16. To illustrate this assertion by reference to *Der Turm* is at first sight unjustifiable: the first book edition of *Der Turm* did not appear until 1925. On the other hand it is worth recalling that Hofmannsthal had been concerned with the theme as early as 1902 when he wrote a free adaptation of parts of Calderón's *La vida es sueño*. Some critics place his interest in the idea as far back as 1897. Certainly, if one considers the content of *Das Salzburger Kleine Welttheater* (1897) such an assertion is at least tenable. For an outline of the genesis of *Der Turm*, see either Jakob Laubach, *Hugo von Hofmannsthals Turm-Dichtungen, Entstehung, Form und Bedeutungsschichten* (Fribourg, 1954), or the present writer's *Hofmannsthal's Festival Dramas* (Cambridge, 1964), pp. 184–5, 298–302.

17. Albert Roeffler, *Bilder aus der neueren deutschen Literatur* (Frauenfeld/Leipzig, 1933).

18. *Literature and Western Man*, Mercury Books no. 31 (London, 1962), p. 231.

19. Where for this inner's waiting
    an outer? What pains partake
    such lawn's alleviating?
    What heavens are contemplating
    themselves in the inland lake
    of these wide-open roses...
    Transl. J. B. Leishman, *New Poems* (Rilke, *Neue Gedichte*), (London, 1964), pp. 264–5.

20. *Prosa II* (Frankfurt, 1951), p. 14.

21. I wanted it to be of cool iron and like a smooth, firm fillet; but in all the seams of the mine there was no metal ready to be cast.
    Die Spange, transl. E. K. Bennett, op. cit., p. 59.

22. "Der Dichter und diese Zeit", *Prosa II*, op. cit., p. 286.

23. O life, life: out there. (Literally: "being outside", even "shut out".) And I in flames. No one who knows me...
    "Letzte Verse" (Val-Mont, December 1926), *Gedichte 1906–26* (Wiesbaden, 1953), p. 637.

24. *Der Schwierige*, Act II, Sc. x, trans. Willa Muir, *Hofmannsthal Selected Plays and Libretti*, ed. Michael Hamburger (London, 1963/ 64), p. 746.
25. This unconscious or seismographic element is finely described by Ernst Jünger who tells how, on finishing the fair-copy ("Reinschrift") of *Auf den Marmorklippen*, he discussed his work with his brother Friedrich Georg: "Already certain features were developing which had not occurred to me while I was writing the work and which were nevertheless quite clear to me now. Thus the author's creations separate themselves from him and continue to grow in places which he does not know." *Gärten und Strassen*, entry for 12 August 1939, *Werke*, vol. 2, *Tagebücher II* (Stuttgart, n.d. [1962]), p. 67. Hofmannsthal describes a comparable experience in *Das Salzburger Grosse Welttheater*: "I think that in this—as is always the case in the apparently instinctive actions of an artist—a hidden plurality guided my hand." "Das Salzburger Grosse Welttheater in der Collegienkirche zu Salzburg, 1922." In *Festspiele in Salzburg* (Frankfurt, 1952), pp. 45–6.
26. Stage direction in Hofmannsthal, *Gestern* (1891), *Gedichte und Lyrische Dramen* (Stockholm, 1946), p. 207.
27. "A German cabinet-maker, who was hammering away in the living-room of the Swiss *Grüner Heinrich*, broke his silence and said: 'The great Goethe is dead.' Literature's reputation was so great in the eyes of the common man that he really sensed the dividing lines between two epochs which was drawn by this death." Walter Killy, ed., *Zeichen der Zeit, ein deutsches Lesebuch*, vol. 3, *Das historische Jahrhundert*, Fischer Bücherei 276 (Frankfurt, 1959), p. 11.
28. See Carl J. Burckhardt, *Erinnerungen an Hofmannsthal und Briefe des Dichters* (Munich, 1948), p. 27: "On one occasion he read Fichte's *Reden* with a good deal of distaste; afterwards he talked about a blind and boastful ethos, feverishly heightening the sense of self. He called it false—and provincial."!!
29. See, for example, Carl J. Burckhardt, *Ein Vormittag beim Buchhändler* (Basel, 1951), pp. 10, 19, 26, 42.
30. "Hofmannsthals Lehrjahre" (1930/1954), *Gesammelte Werke in Einzelbänden, Prosa I* (Stuttgart, 1957), p. 149.
31. E. K. Bennett, *Stefan George*, op. cit., p. 45.
32. Quoted by Bernt von Heiseler in "Stefan George", *Lebenswege der Dichter. Vier Beiträge* (Gütersloh, 1958), pp. 180–1.
33. Who once has circled the flame
    Always shall follow the flame!
    Far though he wander and turn:
    Never too far from the goal
    While he is reached by the light.
    But when he loses its gleam,
    Duped by a flash of his own:
    Law of the centre he leaves,
    Shattered and driven through worlds.

Transl. Carol North Valhope and Ernst Morwitz, *Stefan George: Poems* (London, 1944), p. 211.

34. You flawless as a flame and slender,
You flower sprung from Crown and Spear,
You as the morning, light and tender,
You secret as a spring and clear,

Companion me in sunny meadows,
Entremble me in evening haze,
You shine upon my path through shadows,
You cool of wind, you breath of blaze.
Transl. Valhope and Morwitz, op. cit., p. 245.

35. Through tempests and the dread fanfares of dawning,
He leads his tried and faithful to the work
Of sober day and founds the Kingdom Come.
Transl. Olgo Marx and Ernst Morwitz, *The Works of Stefan George* (Chapel Hill, 1949), p. 297.

36. Op. cit., p. 192.

37. Notably by Herman Broch, "Hofmannsthals Prosaschriften", *Neue Rundschau*, 2/1951, pp. 1–30. See also Introduction (in translation by J. P. and Tania Stern) to *Selected Prose* (of H. v. H.) (London, 1952).

38. Quoted by J. B. Leishman, *Rainer Maria Rilke: Duino Elegies* (transl. J. B. Leishman and Stephen Spender), 3rd ed. (London, 1948), p. 20. The passage is part of an unpublished letter to Nanny Wunderly-Volkart, February 1920. See J. R. von Salis, *Rainer Maria Rilke: The Years in Switzerland* (transl. N. K. Cruickshank) (London, 1964), pp. 211, 310.

39. *Prosa II*, pp. 336–7.

40. Op. cit., pp. 332–3.

41. Op. cit., pp. 340–1.

42. Op. cit., pp. 323–4.

43. Letter to Dora von Bodenhausen, 27 October 1911. *Hugo von Hofmannsthal: Eberhard von Bodenhausen: Briefe der Freundschaft, 1897–1919* (Düsseldorf, 1953), p. 128.

44. Noted by J. B. Leishman as "jotted down on the writing-pad which contains the draft of the last two Elegies to be written, the Tenth and the Fifth". Op. cit., p. 16.

45. Opening line of the *First Elegy*.

46. *Prosa II*, pp. 280–1. "Symbol" is not really satisfactory as a translation of the last word ("Gleichnis") which has suggestions of "parable", "simile", etc.

47. "Language out of Darkness." *The Listener* (London), vol. LXXII, no. 1843, 23 July 1964, p. 123.

48. He lay. His high-propped face could only peer
in pale refusal at the silent cover,
now that the world and all this knowledge of her,
torn from the senses of her lover,
had fallen back to the unfeeling year.

Those who had seen him living saw no trace
of his deep unity with all that passes;
for these, these valleys here, these meadow-grasses,
these streams of running water *were* his face...
Transl. J. B. Leishman, *New Poems*, op. cit., p. 79.
49. Hans Egon Holthusen and Friedhelm Kemp, eds., *Ergriffenes Dasein: Deutsche Lyrik des zwanzigsten Jahrhunderts*, 7th ed. (Munich, 1959), pp. 393–4.
50. See note 25.
51. "Rede über Hofmannsthal" (1902/5). *Ges. Werke in Einzelbänden, Reden* (Stuttgart, n.d. [1955 or 1956]), p. 56.

SELECT BIBLIOGRAPHY

The list which follows makes no claim to comprehensiveness. In the hope of encouraging further discussion, however, an attempt has been made—*inter alia*—to include works of widely differing and even opposing views (e.g. Soergel-Hohoff—Hamann-Hermand—Lukács), to include some works of a more general, informative kind, and to suggest a few books in English especially for the benefit of those whose knowledge of German is limited.

Alewyn, Richard: *Uber Hugo von Hofmannsthal*, Göttingen, 1958.

Alker, Ernst: *Die deutsche Literatur im 19. Jahrhundert (1832–1914)*, 2nd ed., Stuttgart, 1962.

Allemann, Beda: *Zeit und Figur beim späten Rilke: ein Beitrag zur Poetik des modernen Gedichtes*, Pfullingen, 1961.

Bassermann, Dieter: *Der späte Rilke*, Munich, 1947.

Bennett, E. K.: *Stefan George*, Cambridge, 1954.

Bithell, Jethro: *Modern German Literature*, 3rd ed., London, 1961.

Broch, Hermann: *Hofmannsthal und seine Zeit: eine Studie*, Munich, 1964.

Buddeberg, Else: *Rainer Maria Rilke: eine innere Biographie*, Stuttgart, 1955.

Butler, Eliza Marian: *Rainer Maria Rilke*, C.U.P., 1941.

Coghlan, Brian: *Hofmannsthal's Festival Dramas*, C.U.P., 1964.

Duwe, Wilhelm: *Deutsche Dichtung des 20. Jahrhunderts*, 2 vols., Zürich, 1962.

Friedmann, Hermann and Mann, Otto, eds.: *Deutsche Literatur im XX. Jahrhundert*, 2nd ed., 2 vols., Heidelberg, 1961.

Fuerst, Norbert: *Phases of Rilke*, Bloomington, 1958.

Gray, Ronald: *The German Tradition in Literature, 1871–1945*, C.U.P., 1965.

Gundolf, Friedrich: *George*, Berlin, 1920.

Hamann, Richard and Hermand, Jost: *Impressionismus*, Berlin, 1960.

Hammelmann, Hanns A.: *Hugo von Hofmannsthal*, London, 1957.

Hildebrandt, Kurt: *Das Werk Stefan Georges*, Hamburg, 1960.

Holthusen, Hans Egon: *Rainer Maria Rilke: a study of his later poetry*, transl. J. P. Stern, Cambridge, 1952.

Jens, Walter: "Der Mensch und die Dinge. Die Revolution der deutschen Prosa", in *Statt einer Literaturgeschichte*, Pfullingen, 1957, pp. 59–85.

Kluckhohn, Paul: "Die Wende vom 19. zum 20. Jahrhundert in der deutschen Dichtung", *Deutsche Vierteljahrsschrift*, 29, 1955, pp. 1–19.

Lukács, Georg: *Deutsche Literatur im Zeitalter des Imperialismus*, Berlin, 1945.

Mason, Eudo C.: *Rilke*, Edinburgh, 1963. *Rilke, Europe and the English-speaking world*, C.U.P., 1961.

Morwitz, Ernst: *Kommentar zu dem Werk Stefan Georges*, Munich, 1960.

Motekat, Helmut: *Experiment und Tradition*, Frankfurt/Bonn, 1962.

Norman, F., ed.: *Hofmannsthal: studies in commemoration*, London, 1963.

Oswald, Victor A.: "The old age of Young Vienna", *Germanic Review*, 27, 1952, pp. 188–99.

Rey, William H.: *Weltentzweiung und Weltversöhnung in Hofmannsthals Griechischen Dramen*, Philadelphia, 1962.

Shaw, Priscilla Washburn: *Rilke, Valéry and Yeats, the domain of the self*, New Brunswick, 1964.

Salis, Jean Rodolphe von: *Rainer Maria Rilke, the years in Switzerland: a contribution to the biography of Rilke's later life*, transl. N. K. Cruickshank, London, 1964.

Soergel, Albert and Hohoff, Curt: *Dichtung und Dichter der Zeit. Vom Naturalismus bis zur Gegenwart*, Vol. 1, Düsseldorf, 1961.

Sommerhalder, Hugo: *Zum Begriff des literarischen Impressionismus*, Inaugural Lecture, Zürich, 1961.

Wood, Frank Higley: *Rainer Maria Rilke: the ring of forms*, Minnesota, 1958.

An excellent guide to critical literature on the period 1880–1950 is Martini, Fritz: "Deutsche Literatur zwischen 1880 und 1950. Ein Forschungsbericht", *Deutsche Vierteljahrsschrift*, 26, 1952, pp. 478–535.

Expressionism

XI

Expressionism

H. MACLEAN

FOR a considerable time Expressionism has been seen as a part of a general literary revolution, which took place before and after the turn of the century. It was a revolt against traditional concepts, against values as typified in classical and romantic thinking, against the notion of man as central figure in a stable universe and against schematic and objective art forms. The differences separating Expressionism from Naturalism on the one hand and from Neo-Romanticism on the other may be regarded as more a matter of variable emphasis than outright opposition. The Expressionist shared with the Naturalist his sympathy for misery and poverty, his indignation about social evils, but not his rôle of recorder and analyst of the human situation. Like the Naturalist, he noted the vulnerability and helplessness of man in his material environment, but felt more directly involved in the need to extricate him from his spiritual plight and give him new hope and new faith, or at least an awareness of his degraded condition. And he also made full use of the naturalist extension of theme and vocabulary to include the hitherto unacceptable in art, the technical, the ugly, the sordid and the diseased, but was not inclined to investigate causes and determining factors.

The Expressionist showed marked similarities with the Neo-Romantics, accepting "but in each case with a difference, the cult of the irrational, the representation of the dream-world, the application of the symbols, and the heightening of the emotional effect to the point of ecstasy".[1] The difference consisted mainly in the rejection by Expressionism of the more passive and restrictive aspects of Neo-Romanticism, its aestheticism, its tendency to look backwards into the past, to use legend and fairy-tale, to create a hermetic world from which reality and vulgarity are excluded. Even the most withdrawn of the writers included under the Expressionist collective, poets such as Georg Trakl and Else Lasker-Schüler, cannot shield themselves from the intrusive reality of modern mass urban living.

All these points have been made many times and they remain, by and large, valid. But they do not stress the burning sense of difference, the violent reaction against the dominant and fashion-

257

able art forms of the day, which the young generation of writers and artists felt and expressed increasingly during the first decade of the twentieth century. Naturalism and Impressionism loomed in avant-garde circles as bigger bogeys than the comfortably bowdlerized ideas of romantic literature taught in school and home. What distinguishes the beginnings of Expressionism is the emergence of a more aggressive and emotional attitude towards art and life, or even more, the will to total dedication and absorption of the whole personality and mind into the work of art. It was in the visual arts that the new attitudes asserted themselves first, and most confidently and aggressively. Painters such as Kirchner, Pechstein, Schmitt-Rottluff and Nolde, who formed the *Brücke* group in 1905, turned away from the passivity and delicacy of Impressionism and took as their model, both technically and emotionally, artists such as van Gogh and Munch. For it is the most prominent of van Gogh's characteristics that his whole personality blazes out of the canvas and that he fascinates and repels at the same time. The Expressionist writer and painter was never so insulted as when his work was regarded coolly and indifferently, or worse, when it was simply "enjoyed" as entertainment.

It was from France that the main impetus came. The primitive themes of the south seas and negro art have as a corollary the suggestion of dynamism and surge of basic emotion which sweeps aside the sophistication of civilized controls and techniques. The *Fauves*, established also in 1905, made use of pure elementary colour, which, together with the disruption of realistic space concepts, are echoed and developed with greater emotional intensity in the works of *Die Brücke*, and in the *Blaue Reiter* school, which provided a highly articulate and theoretical backing to experimental work in art, and by a natural extension, to writing. The links between the visual arts and writing were particularly strong in the period before the First World War and parallels between painting and literature both in theme and technique, have been drawn.[2] The closeness of the link is, however, most convincingly demonstrated by those, such as Ernst Barlach, Alfred Kubin and Oskar Kokoschka, who achieved considerable standing in both fields. All three are better known as artists than as writers, but Barlach and Kokoschka especially have enjoyed an increase in their literary reputations over recent years. It was from the visual arts too that the term "Expressionism" derived and it was to French artists that it was first applied. It appears not to have been used by the French themselves, but to describe a group of French artists, among them Braque, Dufy, Picasso, Vlaminck, who were represented in the exhibition of the Berlin Secession in the early summer of 1911.[3] In the August number of *Der Sturm* in the same year Wilhelm Worringer used the term, and from that point it gradually gained currency. Yet it was at first assumed to apply exclusively to painting and was suspect in the literary world until after the beginning of the war.[4] Indeed, despite its fashionable popularity from 1916 until the middle 'twenties, the term "Expressionism" has remained suspect to the present day.

It was in 1910 that the literary groups, no less aggressive or radical than the painters, began to form around clubs and journals. *Der Sturm* was founded in 1910 by Herwarth Walden who claimed more or less exclusive rights to the literary revolution and published in 1912 the German translation of the fierce Futurist manifestos written by Marinetti in 1909. Franz Pfemfert's *Die Aktion*, founded a year later as a rival to *Der Sturm*, was as provocative as the title indicates, and the founding of these two journals was followed by a whole host of new publications. Enthusiasm was colossal. In *Die Aktion* of 1913 a new age of poetry was announced, only half facetiously, which would change the tempo of the lives of bakers, tramwaymen and stock-brokers who, in capital letters, "hate everything which is not poetry".[5] Some of the greatest talents remained isolated—Georg Trakl, Gottfried Benn, Franz Kafka, to name the most considerable—but most were unwilling to reserve their work for the select appreciative few. Literary clubs, *Der Neue Club* (1910), *Das Neopathetische Cabaret* (1910), *Gnu* (1911), sprang into being, and in numerous coffee-houses and halls up and down the length and breadth of the country writers and critics and a frequently bewildered, sometimes hostile, sometimes appreciative public met to hear and discuss the literary productions of an army of young writers whose numbers, fed by unrivalled opportunities for publishing, were increasing at a rate hitherto unknown in Germany.

The intrusion of the Futurist manifestos on the German scene in 1912 can be seen, superficially at any rate, as supporting the intentions of the German writers and giving them direction and cohesion. Marinetti claimed that speed, power, efficiency and aggressiveness were the prime needs of the future. He took up an extreme, unambiguous position by praising the city and the machine as the chief instruments in both the social and the aesthetic revolution, which would overthrow existing patterns and make a complete break with the past. But the Italian theorists not only noted the displacement of man from the centre of things, they drew the conclusion that, since he was dominated by museum, library and fixed thought patterns implanted in him by past ages, he must also be excluded as a subject for painting and literature.[6] "The pain of a man is just as interesting for us as the pain of an electric torch which suffers from a spasmodic twitching."[7] The age of humanism was dead and man reduced to the level of material things.

Marinetti was fêted when he spoke in Berlin in 1912 and it would be false to underrate the stimulus which the Futurists gave to the more experimental groups, especially to the group centred around *Der Sturm*. But although they were presented with a novel clarity and precision which made its own impact, the content itself of the manifestos was not unfamiliar to the Germans, as Alfred Döblin pointed out at the time in an open letter to Marinetti: "Marinetti, you are not saying anything new to us; I may say : you embrace our cause."[8] Moreover there were clearly differences. The Germans did not accept the Futurist doctrine in its entirety. Those of them who could lay claim to a defined political attitude were leftist and ignored the passages in the manifesto which glorified war and proclaimed the domination of the male sex. But there is another point of difference which is less obvious and which needs to be stressed considerably more. The German writers were generally conscious at the beginning that anarchy could so easily spill over into tyranny, that the means by which freedom could be achieved might be turned with bewildering suddenness against freedom. Again it was Döblin, who, despite his general approval of their radicalism, saw that the fanaticism of the Futurists could defeat itself, replace the dominance of the museum by the dominance of the machine, and subject them to a new kind of Naturalism :

> Surely you do not think that there could be only one reality, surely you do not identify the world of your automobiles, aeroplanes and machine-guns with the world? . . . Or do you ascribe to the world of angles, colours and sound an absolute reality, which we should approach as reverently as minute secretaries?[9]

Döblin objected to specific aspects of Futurism. But his protests were also directed against a general tendency to bring everybody into their own fold.[10] Although the Expressionists of the pre-war years had willingly entered into the communities of the clubs and the journals, they were chiefly distinguished by the individuality of their literary style and technique. It is true that the war and particularly the revolutionary period after the war produced a spate of political writing and an always increasing tendency to stereotyped techniques after the fashionable models of Werfel, Kaiser, Toller and others. This was accompanied by a mass of theoretical writing which followed the appearance of Hermann Bahr's *Expressionismus* in 1916 and reached its high point in Kasimir Edschmid's treatise in 1919[11] which is, despite the disservice done to it by too frequent quotation, still one of the essential documents of Expressionism. But the Expressionist before the war felt no temptation to ally himself to any literary mode and the few desultory attempts to formulate classifications[12] point to the lack of any compelling binding relationship present at the time.

These writers did not want to be pinned down, to be labelled, to be forced into a new mould at a time when development seemed to be limitless. Their minds were reaching out constantly to grasp something which lay beyond the horizon of all those who had preceded them, they wanted simultaneously to form and yet not to be formed, to create and yet to remain forever in the enticing realm where everything is possible and not yet realized, for realization is a kind of death. "Christ became Church", said Kurt Heynicke, "and thereby failed."[13] They wanted to lose themselves in a search for God and to be God themselves, to reform the structure of the world and to destroy that structure before it began to solidify around them. The only sphere in which the attempt to reconcile the irreconcilable is even remotely possible is in art, for art offers one of the few possibilities for man to assert his independence of environment.

This is a state in which only absolutes are acceptable, in which the compromises and modifications of ordinary life are rejected. A tension arises between permanence and change which is the basis of conflict in so many Expressionist works. Where permanence has established itself in its most rigid and monolithic forms the irresistible power of change is brought into play, pictorial and verbal images indicate the *action* of massive, often unseen and incomprehensible, forces in their disruption of the static and comfortably established. Thus Ludwig Meidner rejects nature in favour of city scenes in his pictures, and his apocalyptic visions show massive buildings collapsing in upon themselves, drunken structures in the first stages of rapid dissolution. Jakob van Hoddis, in his poem *Weltende*, sees the end of the world as the formless strength of wind and sea sweeping aside the most rigid forms of civilization. The geometrical patterns of the bourgeois' pointed head fitting within his hat, roofs sealing off a fixed order of domestic living, the train neatly confirming the horizontal line of a bridge; all these are swept away, and in the middle of the catastrophe the cosmic ridicule of the little man who has caught cold. Even the vast serenity of sky and earth is resented by Alfred Lichtenstein, who longs for the storm to "tear the gentle world with iron claws . . . to rend the beautiful blue eternal sky into a thousand tatters" (*Sommerfrische*).

The shattering of the cohesiveness of the universe by this juxtaposition of extreme opposites, reflects a determined rejection of the more conventional aesthetic, the cult of beauty. The opposition had been expressed crudely but effectively by the Futurist slogan, "Death to moonlight". The old sensual moon, "with the beautiful warm thighs", is replaced by another ideal of beauty which is just as absolute, by the beauty of the electric moons which dim the radiance of ancient Luna.[14] The glorification of the technical for its own sake, the speed and rhythm of the machine, the architectonic construction of steel and concrete, occurs among Expressionist writers,[15] but it is not a dominant theme and in its extreme form barely represented among the better writers. What one does find is an exact inversion of the conventional idea of beauty contained in unusual combinations : in Georg Heym's poem, *Ophelia*, the dead girl with the nest of water rats in her hair and the long white eels slipping over her breast, or, in the short story, *Der Irre*, by the same author, the radiant universe of infinite peace and eternal rest which is the product of a bloodthirsty madman's imagination. Gottfried Benn's picture of the aster folded into the chest of a drunken beer-carter during a post-mortem is even more shocking in its conciseness, and the poem about the girl, in whose body a nest of rats is found, is entitled *Schöne Jugend*. The dissonance between poem and title, and the obvious attack on cliché which is intended, represents Benn at his most sarcastic.

From the opposition to a cult of beauty it is logical transition to a cult of ugliness for its own sake, in which are contained in equal measure emotions of abhorrence and attraction, a salutary purging by the concrete expression of disgust. Very few regions which can supply loathsomely emotive details were left unexplored. The stench of pestilence and poverty, the prisons, the brothels and the thieves' dens, the insane, the crippled and the drunkards fill the landscape of the asphalt literature. This ugliness is all man-made and man is the sufferer. The factories and the hospitals are ugly enough, but they derive their horror from the wretched mass of human beings who inhabit them and who, whether seen in the mass or individually, are degraded to the point of being dehumanized. Men appear as "mucus spat on a rail" (Ehrenstein), dissected on a mortuary slab or washed by nurses "as one washes benches" (Benn), or an aimless, mindless whirling mass jerked hither and thither in a dance conducted by evil and cruel beings of whom they are totally unaware and whose gigantic stature dwarfs them to the size of ants (Heym). It is because he is not even aware of the fact that he stands on the lowest rung in the universal scale of things, because he does not know that above him and around him there is no firm protective fabric but a vast uncomprehended and uncomprehending hostility or indifference, that man excites the scorn or the pity of these writers.

This view of the predicament of man derives rarely from cynical indifference, but rather from a sense of universal agony and personal vulnerability, in which the poet himself is involved. Heym reserves the quality of love for those beings who are, like himself, tortured and torn by inner conflicts—for men such as Kleist, Grabbe, Büchner and Hölderlin, who despair in themselves, "as I daily despair in myself".[16] It is the knowledge that these men had shared the despair of the human condition which draws Heym to them, whereas in his God this essential quality is lacking. God is without love and indifferent, he is "cold and dumb as the cloud formations which forever carry their heads turned away from earth, as though they knew some terrible secret and must bear it with them throughout all time to a dark, unknown and distant goal".[17] And it is God's remoteness from human suffering to which Albert Ehrenstein points again and again in his poetry and in his prose fragments, *Briefe an Gott*.[18] Ehrenstein can recognize God in nature, but "not, almost never in man, that illegible caricature of immortality, that transitory sketch of eternity".[19]

The deepest religious feeling is to be found in those writers who acknowledge the immensity of distance, the impossibility of communication, between themselves and God. It is the combined hopefulness and hopelessness of the search for God which Franz Kafka has made the subject of one of his best-known parables, the story of the message from the dying emperor "to you, the humble subject, the insignificant shadow cowering in the remotest distance before the imperial sun".[20] The messenger can never fight his way through the infinite multitude of obstacles, through "the centre of the world, crammed to bursting with its own refuse.—But you sit at your window when evening falls and dream it to yourself."[21] In the plays of Ernst Barlach the need for God is urgent, for there is no alternative; when, in *Der Tote Tag*, the way to God is barred, the hope of man is turned in on itself and ends in self-destruction. But it is in the poetry of Georg Trakl that one can feel most keenly the crushing weight which lies on humanity in its vital need for a God, who is at every approach inaccessible and who is, one senses, in the last resort merely emptiness. But where Heym and Ehrenstein accuse God, Barlach and Trakl feel the deficiency in themselves; in Trakl's *De Profundis*, "God's silence" is within himself, plunging his whole being into darkness and sealing him off from any hope of contact. In Trakl's world, the moments of hope and ecstasy seldom maintain themselves and give way to melancholy and self-hatred; or they appear at several removes, as in the poem,

An die Verstummten, where he addresses, in the last lines, that section of humanity in whom the future hope of redemption rests, but which is now silent and in remote darkness.

The compelling sense of ineradicable evil and a threatening universe, the fear or conviction that human existence is ultimately meaningless, above all, the creation of an intensely personal literature, in which writers such as Heym, Trakl, Benn, Barlach, and Lasker-Schüler are more concerned in the struggle to come to terms with themselves than guiding the rest of humanity—this forms one end of the Expressionist spectrum. At the other end stand the so-called Activists whose chief characteristic is a fervid revolutionary optimism. They too were aware of the filth and wretchedness of a world which is hostile to mankind, but in more finite terms and not as an unalterable state of affairs. "Those who are aware should kill themselves—or acquire a will", said Kurt Hiller, one of the leading Activist theorists, in attacking the helplessness induced by resigned recognition.[22] They believed, like so many of their contemporaries, that their own time had been given over to a deadening materialism, which had spread over the face of the earth like a disease and that a tabula rasa was necessary in all fields, whether cultural, political or religious. They shared the hatred for the Wilhelminian society which was dominated by a hierarchy of officialdom and militarism, by conventional and repressive morality in state, school and home, by a traditionalism in taste which had remained almost completely unaffected by new tendencies in the arts. They shared also the contempt for the philistinism of the middle classes—most of them were themselves of middle-class origin and the violence of their reaction was undoubtedly due in great measure to the degree of repression which they had experienced as children or were still experiencing as young men.

But the Activists also designated as philistines those who withdrew, in their estimation, into aesthetic strongholds and shut themselves off from the world. Evil was, for all practical purposes, palpable and readily comprehended, and could be overcome by perfectly rational means and by political action. Their programme was at least in part political—socialistic in the sense that it would lead to the annexation from the establishment of the outward forms of control. The greatest emphasis, however, was on the preparation for this utopia through the rehabilitation of the mind (*Geist*)—as opposed to "soul" which does not distinguish between right and wrong—which was capable of reaching out and transforming the minds of all men, changing the face of society from within. Thus the legions of depressed humanity were not condemned to the permanent status of marionettes. In the poems of Ernst Stadler, the drabness of factory workers, the anxieties of madmen are lit by the premonition of happiness. In Stadler's work is the crossing of the ways, the simultaneity of bitterness and hope; in the work of political writers such as Johannes Becher and Ludwig Rubiner, misery is used as a whip to scourge complacence and to stimulate revolt. They deliberately cut themselves off from organized society and identified themselves with its waste products, the "street filth" and the "human rubbish". "We are the scum, the offal," said Rubiner. "We are the holy mob."[23] The acknowledged subservience of art to politics, the obtrusive application of moral purpose promise banality. Add to this the habit of sustained ecstatic utterance—Becher's calls to unity, Franz Werfel's and Leonhard Frank's visions of the brotherhood and ultimate goodness of man —and the promise of banality was all too frequently fulfilled.

Yet it was rare for even Activist literature to ally itself with any specific political cause. It might be revolutionary, anti-militaristic, anti-capitalistic, but a vague socialism or uncommitted sympathy with Communism were the farthest point to which they were prepared to go. In the drama with a social mission especially, hopes were centred in an undefined leader figure, as unreally magnified as Heym's figures were reduced, who was to lead his generation out of the wilderness. Into such figures are compressed ideal attributes of humanity at large; they speak for and to all those who are awakened and ripe for awakening, are confronted not by antagonists but by antagonistic forces contained in just such representative figures as himself. The "poet", the "young man", the "son", all frequently encountered sobriquets, pass through stages or spheres, into which are concentrated vital facets of human experience; at the end comes the promise rather than the realization of the ideal, for which the hero prepares the way by what often amounts to self-inflicted martyrdom. These abstractions do not allow for normal dramatic interplay of characters or for the construction of a unified comprehensive plot (which are specifically rejected), but are contained in a series of largely independent scenes which are united by theme and metaphor, and supported by the symbolic effects of stage design and lighting. The weight of the play lies in the lyrical and rhetorical intensity of each scene, condensing the emotions and experiences of a lifetime into moments of utmost significance, which are heaped one upon the other with growing fervour until the climax is reached. In the nature of things, it can be an anti-climax, for there is a limit to the extent to which intensity can be "intensified", but there are superb examples of this genre, such as Georg Kaiser's *Gas I* (1918). In the fourth act of this play, the enlightened millionaire's son is arguing the case for humanity against the representative of the conventional materialistic world (Engineer) before a mass of assembled workers who punctuate the exactly constructed dialectic of the individual speeches with staccato cries. *Gas I* provides a genuine involvement, vastly different from Franz Werfel's *Die Versuchung* (1913), in which the poet resists Satan's offer of a noble martyrdom, decides to descend humbly into the world, expose himself to insult and misunderstanding, offer the whole world to men, who will "become rich from my poverty".[24] This kind of arrogant humility is unfortunately not limited to Werfel. It can be found, understandably enough, in writers such as Hanns Johst and Kurt Heynicke, who later became Nazis, but it is also present to a quite unpleasant degree in Fritz von Unruh and not least in Georg Kaiser himself.

Such plays normally provide no concrete solution, but point forward to a coming era of light, so that in their end is a new beginning, occasionally symbolized by effects such as ascension (Kaiser : *Die Bürger von Calais*), resurrection (Johst : *Der junge Mensch*), actual rebirth after passing through the realms of the dead (Heynicke : *Der Kreis*). In place of a solution they present a constant searching, testing and questioning, demanding an answer, but seeing the ultimate answer receding interminably into the distance. In Reinhold Sorge's drama, *Der Bettler* (1911), the central figure appears successively as the poet, the son, the brother, the youth. In each of these functions an area of experience is explored, but the process cannot be finite and, at the end of the play, the poet stands on the edge of eternity : "I see many stages yet before me in the light/And many purities which I have not yet traversed ..."[25] And the young man at the end of Ludwig Rubiner's *Die Gewaltlosen* (1919) says : "We must go on ! Our way lies through many countries."[26]

The two plays by Sorge and Rubiner illustrate one of the main differences between Expressionism and Activism as defined by Wolfgang Paulsen in his book on the subject.[27] The Activist is, according to Paulsen, the theoretician for whom poetry is not an end in itself but an aid in forming the reality which he wishes to impose on society. He is less an artist than a politician, a politician of the "mind and idea". The Expressionist, who is first and foremost the poet, will make use of everday reality, but ruthlessly subordinate it to his own vision and create his own world. Rubiner's play takes place in a revolutionary setting. The reactionaries who hold material power are overcome, their main representative is converted and, before his execution, voluntarily passes over his power to the suppressed, to the "powerless". Humanity (*will* and *mind*) has become visible in the political arena and will continue into the future. In *Der Bettler* the poet makes himself independent of a society which bars his way to self-fulfilment, he establishes sovereignty over his environment by drastic means and re-creates it in terms of his dream.

Whatever the difference in their final aims, both Activist and Expressionist were united in their realization of the need to throw off the controls which bind men to the increasingly circumscribed patterns of their existence. They objected particularly to the attempt to see people in terms of the psychological factors which create personality, for this seemed to proceed from the assumption that man was a prisoner of himself, that his behaviour resulted from an unalterable combination of physical and mental character-istics and that his whole development moved on rails. In order to impose his will on reality, in whatever form, man must be freed of all restraints, and above all he must be freed from himself.

An interesting pointer to the processes involved is contained in the prose piece by Alfred Wolfenstein, *Fragment eines Daseins* (1914). There is only one character, and there is no name or other identifying detail. The outer world, the world of normality is still there and he still makes physical contact with friends, relations and strangers, but none of these has any meaning for him or any power to affect the dominance of his own thoughts. The function of other people is purely negative and merely serves to underline his own liberty of action and invulnerability to outside stimulus—he seeks out acquaintances in the certainty that they will not be able to afford him company. He has cut himself off from his own past and his own future purpose, and his mind is free to examine, with a mixture of curiosity and fear, that unexplored universe, his own self. In Wolfenstein's story the procedure is described in extreme, mechanically contrived terms and its ultimate sterility is recognized, but it admirably maps out the territory into which so many writers ventured and points the dangers to which Expressionist character-ization was exposed. The lack of any stable centre is made very clear in one sentence of the story : "Diese Nacht . . . wollte die Bodenlosigkeit vollenden, die er als Feind eines Müssens, als zer-störerischer Freund aller Möglichkeiten, als unaufhörlich *gegen sich Treuloser* lange vorbereitet hatte . . ."[28] One may of course insert into this paradoxical, self-cancelling, infinitely elastic frame all the denials of organic development and causal relationships ("the enemy of compulsion"), the radical break with the past and the transformations of character ("constantly faithless to oneself") and the infinite possibility of new combinations and developments of personality which are opened up as soon as verisimilitude is thrown overboard ("the destructive friend of all possibilities").

In fact it is, one suspects, another case of the formula which, stretched to cover a large area of Expressionism, is so all-embracing as to be virtually meaningless. It is left to Bertolt Brecht, who so often in his early plays parodied and deflated Expressionism by the use of its own techniques, to put Wolfenstein's tour de force into perspective by somewhat drastic means. In his *Mann ist Mann*, written in 1925 eleven years after *Fragment eines Daseins*, he creates an equally artificial situation by taking the simplest of harmless fellows, a piece of putty responsive to the slightest pressure, and remoulding him by a series of farcical procedures into a bloodthirsty warrior. This is in one important respect an actual reversal of Wolfenstein's theme, since in Brecht a naturally insulated character is changed by pressure from without. Yet the basic assumption is the same. There is no such thing as psychological continuity or the permanent unity and consistency of character. Nor is Brecht's attitude only a negative one for the schematic formulation in *Mann ist Mann* points forward to his later realistic technique, in which opposite and apparently self-contradictory traits, courage and cowardice, nobility and meanness, are shown in the same character emerging under the stimulus of varying situations. Or one thinks of the close link between gluttony and intellectual curiosity in his *Galileo*, especially as interpreted with Brecht's approval by Charles Laughton.

Fragment eines Daseins appears in the anthology of Expressionist prose which the compiler, Karl Otten, has entitled *Ego und Eros*, and Otten is quoted as regarding *Fragment eines Daseins* and its companion piece, *Die künstliche Liebe*, also by Wolfenstein, as central to the theme of the anthology.[29] *Die künstliche Liebe* introduces one of the most typical manifestations of Expressionism, the combination of the spiritual and the material in the power of love and the erotic urge. Here there are just the two figures involved, man and wife. The woman's whole personality is absorbed in her one dynamic rôle which is expressed neither in her features nor her character, but in her body. This is a liberated personality in a much more positive sense than appears in *Fragment eines Daseins*, for there is no alienation of the outside world; on the contrary, material things are subordinated to her existence and integrated into her activity. She is creative and acts from instinct, without any kind of self-awareness, whilst cerebration and too great a pre-occupation with self render her husband incapable of sharing genuine experience. "Ego" and "eros" are perfectly compatible, but not on any conscious or rational level.

The husband, a man with money and without occupation, has married his wife in the hope of discovering at least at second hand the enjoyment of experience. But he is unequal to the task of participating, his relegation to the rôle of observer soon palls and he realises that she too cannot maintain her powers with a passive partner. He decides to change himself or at least to make the appearance of a change, and to translate himself during love-making into a world of art, imagining that he is reading a book printed on fine paper, conjuring up in his mind a symphony or a painting. The pretence succeeds in so far as he is able to deceive her and give her happiness, he gains the cold satisfaction of achievement, of a certain selflessness even, but not of love; not even the sensation of her love is conveyed to him. What he has gained is "talent". He cannot bridge the gap and must bear the weight of loneliness.

The two factors in this story might be considered as dominant motifs of Expressionism. Firstly: eros as the liberating, creative force appears most frequently in the guise of prostitution. Prostitutes are idealized as representing the release of love from the restraints of marriage and thus in a general sense the release of creative strength itself. Even at the most sensual level there is idealization and even at the most idealized level, as in Werfel's poem *Veni Creator Spiritus*, in which the divine spirit is called upon to break through man's imprisoning walls, there are clearly recognizable erotic overtones. However, the situation which Wolfenstein envisages in *Die künstliche Liebe* is more akin to the world of Frank Wedekind, whose formative work had begun some twenty years before—the woman in Wolfenstein's story is a rational abstraction of Wedekind's Lulu, as she appears in *Erdgeist* and *Die Büchse der Pandora* (1893–1902). In Lulu's vivid person is contained the elemental force which is in itself neither good nor bad and has creative potentialities, but will turn to destruction or even self-destruction, if contained or dominated. Her nature is as instinctive, innocent and direct as that of an animal and she lacks all trace of artifice or self-knowledge. All the men with whom she is associated attempt to possess her and to adapt her to their own stature. Only the intelligent egotist, Dr. Schön, recognizes the danger and tries to keep her at a distance, but he cannot save himself. The very strength of his intellect and will make him inferior to Lulu and Wedekind sums up their relationship as the destruction of the conscious intellect, which always overrates itself so extravagantly, by the unconscious element in man.[30] Strikingly similar situations may be found in the drama of Georg Kaiser (e.g. *Die Jüdische Witwe*), and although handled in an immense variety of forms, the themes recur constantly in Expressionist literature:

the primitive and the natural are at war with the conventional (hence the popularity of animal subjects in painting and literature), hope and creativity derive from irrational and dynamic forces, and the *dominance* of the cerebral and the artificial produces a frustration, which can be either tragic or comic in its effects. Isolated within themselves, the contrivers and the manipulators remain tragically aware, or ridiculously unaware, of the fact that the gulf between themselves and the outside world cannot be bridged.

Egotism, the other main motif of *Die künstliche Liebe,* also appears in many guises. There is a clearly marked tragic frustration and isolation in the person of the husband in Wolfenstein's story. Especially in the beginning he is shown as the type of egotist who has no inner life of his own and tries to gain his sensations by living parasitically on the vitality of others. The clearest demonstration of such a relationship is contained in the drama, *König Hahnrei* (1913), in which Georg Kaiser makes use of the story of Tristan and Isolde. The absurd old king, Marke, literally warms himself at the fire of their youth, and eventually, by the burden which his weakness imposes upon them, destroys their love for each other.[31] "In the realm of sensations I am the poorest beggar."[32] This cry of Alwa Schön in *Die Büchse der Pandora* is the despairing acknowledgement of impotence, the tragedy of the author who has been unable to write since he has surrendered himself to a more vital personality. For a predicament of this kind Wedekind clearly felt a personal sympathy, but in his play, *Die Junge Welt* (written in 1889), he bitterly attacked the literary vampirism of Naturalism. The playwright Meier, a gross caricature of Gerhart Hauptmann, obtains literary recognition by using the life story told to him in confidence by another person. Like Balzac, Meier carries a notebook in which he jots down every conversation he hears. He records the reactions of his fiancée at the moment when he is kissing her and complains bitterly of her unnaturalness and lack of spontaneity when she ceases to react at all.[33]

Even more scathing in his treatment of characters with artistic and literary pretensions was Carl Sternheim. Both Scarron in *Die Hose* (1911) and Seidenschnur in *Die Kassette* (1912) are, like the weaklings in Wedekind's and Kaiser's plays, compulsive talkers. It is the poetry of cliché which Scarron adopts, compressed poetic cliché, in which the empty inflated phrases follow on one another with stunning rapidity, so that they are immensely funny when delivered with the staccato precision employed by actors in Sternheim plays. Seidenschnur's protestations of love, delivered with the same bombast, are deflated when they become entangled with the mechanics of the camera: "Your picture, Lydia, flows into the

lens, into the chambers of my heart."[34] Both Scarron and Seidenschnur are savage denunciations of the inadequacy of the romantic type, who claim to be preoccupied with their innermost selves,
claim to be superior to bourgeois philistines, to which they, the
artistic philistines, cling nevertheless like drowning men. They are
in a way the false egotists, for they remain as empty at the end as
they were at the start, they attach themselves to the body of the
"shark", and seek not strength but only protection for themselves.

Sternheim's portrayal of the middle classes, annihilating as it is, is
not intended, as Emrich forcefully reminds us, to be regarded as
satire, it is not a "scourging" but a "recognition" of reality.[35] His
main characters, his Maskes, Krulls and Ständers, are not merely
intended to show the emptiness of a life given over to materialism
and middle class ambition. They are not there as warnings, but as
signposts in a waste country. There is about them an aliveness, a
vitality which is strangely attractive and survives dedication to a
limited aim. Sternheim is therefore not sarcastic, but perfectly
genuine when he describes them as heroes, for they have gained
their freedom by overcoming the restraints which are imposed on
them by society.[36] This is very much the idea of freedom which
activates the hero in Wedekind's Der Marquis von Keith (1900),
who sets out to free himself from middle class society by dominating it. Keith fails, but Sternheim's characters have less inner life
and more tenacity and grasp of reality than Wedekind's characters. Theobald Maske (in Die Hose) and in even more extreme
fashion his son Christian Maske (in Der Snob) subordinate society
to their own goals. Christian works quite cold-bloodedly and with
exact machine-like calculation; he is the prince of the manipulators.
In Christian and his other heroes, Sternheim has created characters
who stand out as unique in Expressionism for two reasons: they
are the only contrivers and manipulators to win their way to personal freedom and they are the only liberated personalities who
do not represent some purpose greater than themselves. They are
the pure egotists, egotists unsullied as it were by frustration on the
one hand or by the intrusion of any moral, artistic or community
ideal which transcends the individual and which Sternheim despised
heartily. Yet these characters are not individuals in the orthodox
sense. They achieve their power and urgency by the fact that the
whole horrible world which Sternheim "recognizes", the wealth
and status worshippers spread over all the rungs of the social
ladder, is concentrated into them and shaped by them, or more
accurately is shaped by the words that are spoken; for Sternheim's
characters do not live by virtue of their individual fate or by their
position in an unfolding story, but through their language.

Sternheim said of Gottfried Benn that he "destroys concepts from within, so that language totters and citizens lie flat on belly and nose";[37] like Benn, Sternheim was an uncompromising critic, not only of idealistic concepts, but also—and this is more characteristic of Expressionism in general—of the platitudes which are used to paper over unpalatable and unfamiliar realities. Conventional images are seen as masks concealing the essential attributes of a person or object, and the revolt against the lazy classification of people according to comfortable and familiar categories is a recurring theme from Wedekind's *König Nicolo* (1902) to Hans Henny Jahnn's *Die Krönung Richards III* (1920). Richard III is the perfect example of the popular image which has crystallized around a name through the main external features by which he is familiar to us : the murder of the princes and his physical ugliness. Jahnn makes his Richard bitterly conscious of the process : "Have you ever really known me? Was I not always an image to you, made up of shadows, ugliness and hellish instincts?" and adds in resigned recognition : "You have again not understood me . . . but this you should know, I am not quite identical with my counterfeit."[38] Between these personal statements Richard speculates on the application of his case to life in general, on "the whole masquerade which is called life. It would be a joke to tear off their masks . . . people who are only stomachs, and women who are like cows— one covers them, they calve, give milk—and men who are only words, completely without meaning, and gifted with all the virtues of the word, with honour, wisdom, integrity ! . . . And if one were to tear off the masks, some would appear who are shaped for eternity."[39]

This one speech in Jahnn's play sums up large reaches of Expressionist literature, in which life is seen literally as a masquerade, men and women as puppets acting according to the dictates of an imposed or self-imposed image of themselves, and hidden amongst them the few (in the case of Jahnn mostly children) who contain the promise of regeneration. But words too contribute to concealment and constitute a barrier to real understanding. Language can also act as a mask unless it is rescued from its progression towards emptiness of meaning through the abrasion of common usage. In the passage about Benn quoted above, Sternheim writes of the "intoxication caused by separation from context" ("Rausch der Zusammenhangsentfernung").[40] If language is to regain its dynamic quality it must be delivered from its organization into familiar structures and associations, from the certainty that one word automatically follows another in speech and writing and—quite concretely—from the enslavement of syntax.

Language controlled by syntax was regarded as rational language and the "language of reason presupposes a world of repose and rigidity, an easily assimilable mosaic which can be mirrored in concepts and logical connections".[41] This description appeared in Oswald Pander's essay, "Revolution der Sprache" in 1918 and is typical of many approaches which add nothing substantially new to the systematic and comprehensive statements on the language revolution contained in the Futurist "Technical Manifesto" by Marinetti which appeared in *Der Sturm* in 1912.[42] Marinetti's opposition is directed basically against normal syntax as reflecting compartmentalized thinking. He advocates the removal of all defining and connecting elements. Conjunctions, adjectives and adverbs disappear, and together with them punctuation; the verb remains in the infinitive, so that it may adapt "elastically" to the noun. The "naked" nouns themselves thus retain and enhance their own essential character, and are linked directly by association and analogy, not by any logical train of thought.

In their most extreme form these requirements are scarcely practicable, but Marinetti's influence was clearly felt among members of the *Sturm* group of writers, led by August Stramm, and by certain Activists, such as Becher and Rubiner. In his poem, *Mensch stehe auf*, Becher is concerned to make his voice heard in the most primitive fashion, by hammering repetition :

Verfluchtes Jahrhundert ! Chaotisch ! Gesanglos !
Ausgehängt du Mensch, magerster der Köder, zwischen Qual
Nebel-Wahn Blitz.
(Cursed century ! Chaotic ! Songless !
You man hung out, leanest of baits, amidst torment fog-illusion
flash.)

This is Marinetti's method adopted in almost literal fashion; there is the absence of any finite verb, the chain of single words and fragmented phrases, the row of four nouns—a single noun on either side of the double noun—juxtaposed and unpunctuated. Marinetti had wanted to avoid by his technique a too even tone, but Becher's words and images, though certainly forceful, are all on the same level of extreme emphasis and the emotions are shapeless and undirected. More truly dynamic is August Stramm's *Patrouille* :

Die Steine feinden/Fenster grinst Verrat/Äste würgen/
Berge Sträucher blättern raschlig/Gellen/Tod.

The violence here, which is genuine and not a whipped-up emotion, is contained in each word, and each of the inanimate objects—

stones, window, branches, hills, bushes—acquires a hostile attitude through the verbs with which they are associated. The tension mounts to the last word as the whole scene explodes in a final shriek of death.

The Stramm poem rests upon the suspension of time, the simultaneity of the various elements, each of which carries within itself the promise of the final word. In the following excerpt from Sternheim a similar effect is obtained where the passage of time is violently compressed as Christian Maske sums up his previous existence :

> Kämpfe ums Dasein. Die habe ich auch durchgemacht und dabei ganz anders als Myriaden Boden in mir aufgerissen; von Trieben geschnellt, flog ich durch den Brei der Bequemen, weil ich wusste, jenseits fängt erst das Leben an. Du sahst ja, wie ich ankam, Fetzen mir vom Leib riss und das flatternde Band am Hals zu fester Krawatte knüpfte. Mich allmählich zur Form erzog, der der höhere Mensch im Zusammenleben bedarf.[43] (Der Snob).

The fragments of language illustrate the fragmentary nature of Christian's existence, the violence of the verbs his headlong destructive passage through life, and the whole is given a dynamic cohesion through the fusing of the fragments into a mass activated by the principle of flight, which forces him through the "mush of comfortable people" to the life which is always a stage beyond. In the second half of the passage the fragments take palpable form in the shreds of clothing which hang about him; the tatters and the fluttering ribbon are drawn together in the firmly knotted tie. It is Christian's mistress who literally knots his ties because he cannot manage them himself,[44] who disciplines his formless existence and trains him to live the life of the "higher man".

In the Stramm poem the pressure expands outwards towards the explosion, in Sternheim's passage there is a forced contraction of exploded fragments into the confining image, providing a contrast of startling and absurd proportions. Furthermore, there is a levelling of the usual hierarchy of values; the trivial object, the tie, is given a life foreign to its own and is raised to a status far above its place in the normal scale of things, whilst the notion of the "higher man" is correspondingly deflated. It is the same process which Wolfenstein describes in Die künstliche Liebe, where the inanimate objects which provide the environment of lovemaking—bed, lamp, room—are divested of their independence and their quality of "strangeness", and are drawn into the whole magical sphere of love.[45] Here, objective reality is broken up or transformed, exterior objects are diverted from their normal functions and directed to the assumption of new roles which the hand and the eye of the artist have prepared for them.

These examples differ radically from the imaginative transformations of reality which one finds for instance in the description of a fever in Rilke's *Die Aufzeichnungen des Malte Laurids Brigge* (1910). Malte describes the way in which even the most trivial objects take a new form and life under the spur of fear : the fear that a thread of wool protruding from the edge of a blanket is as hard and sharp as a needle, that the button of his nightshirt is bigger than his head, that a bread crumb falling from his bed will break like a piece of glass and that everything will be broken for ever.[46] With Rilke the fear is given an explanatory basis, for it derives from a fever which awakens childhood memories and terrors, the typical nightmares of childhood which are familiar to everybody. Moreover, no transformation has taken place and the whole passage in the original German is couched in the subjunctive, the hypothetical product of fear.

It is a characteristic of many Expressionist writers that the transformation is presented as complete, apparently without the involvement of the observer, and there is no insertion of the process of imaginative change or of the "as if" which prepares the way for a bold comparison. "Zerlumpte Bäume strolchen in die Ferne./ Betrunkene Wiesen drehen sich im Kreise." (Ragged trees stroll into the distance./Drunken meadows turn in circles.) In these lines from Lichtenstein's poem, *In den Abend...*, the intermediate stage by which the everyday is changed into an intoxicated landscape is withdrawn and the inner vision of the poet has completely displaced objective reality. The point is made more sharply in the familiar example of Kafka's *Die Verwandlung*, in English *The Metamorphosis*. As Sokel points out,[47] there is no comparison between Gregor Samsa and an insect, no pointing to a relationship between one entity, Samsa, and the other entity, the insect. Samsa *becomes* the insect, a fact described in minute physical detail. In Barlach's *Der Tote Tag*, the instrument of observation itself becomes the metaphor; the vision of the artist is objectified and the eyes—the eyes of the blind seer Kule—are "two spiders crouching in the net of their sockets and catching the images of the world", but these images, at first full of sweetness and delight, multiply till they are "juicy with bitterness and greasy with horror; so that at last my eyes could no longer bear such bitterness and they spun a web over the entrance, crouched within, preferred to hunger and die".[48]

The withering away of the physical sense of sight is, like the withering of the rational faculties of the madman, simply another pointer to the emancipation from the order and system of the representational world; but this emancipation is a constructive act which opens the way to an infinite range of possibilities, the new grouping of sensual images and the creation of new relationships which constitute the most fruitful aspect of Expressionist style. Entities which have previously had neutral contacts or no contact at all, like Samsa and the insect, lose their original identity when brought together in a meaningful relationship, and a third or transcendental identity is established.

In addition, the normal patterns of time and space, indeed the quality of both animate and inanimate objects may undergo a radical change. In Wolfenstein's sonnet, *Städter*, the meaning may be summed up tritely enough—the loneliness of man in the crowd. But the violence of the compression created by the imagery produces a transformation of reality. The windows of houses are as close as holes in a sieve, the houses themselves are packed so tightly that the streets are as grey and swollen as strangled corpses. The townspeople suffer a double transformation of compression and petrification, they are locked together on the tram-seats like "two façades", and the reality of their new state is so completely established that the comparison, "Unsere Wände sind so dünn wie Haut" (Our walls are as thin as skin), has been exactly reversed and "skin" becomes the extended meaning of "walls". Or we are shown the relationship between man and nature, not personalization of nature in the simple sense, but a physical interpenetration, an actual linking of man and world in a composite picture of decay, such as one finds in Lichtenstein's poem, *Punkt*, and in other poems contained in the anthology introduced by Benn, *Lyrik des expressionistischen Jahrzehnts*.[49] In such relationships, the idea of the grotesque and the incongruous—grass growing from a skull, a man reduced to a hand operating a lever—no longer exists, any more than atonality exists in modern music. The shock which distortions of reality produce derives only from their unfamiliarity; the eye and the ear which has grown accustomed to these combinations will not be shocked, but stimulated.

Thus the process which is observable in the modern art forms is not merely a "destruction" of the familiar world or a "dislocation" of language; it is rather the process of using the flexibility thus made possible in an increasingly personal way—personal in the sense that images and symbols acquire an independence of external and generalized criteria and can properly be understood only in their own terms and by reference to each other.[50] Nor is this process to be regarded as either subjective or arbitrary; Trakl, for instance, is one of the most personal writers in the above sense, but he was able to say in a letter about a poem which he had re-written : "I am convinced that it (the poem) will say more and mean more to you in the universal form and manner than in the limited personal manner of the first draft."[51] Moreover, the more accomplished writers were fully aware that discipline and form were necessary. It was not, however, the discipline of outward form which was the deciding factor—though in the lyric and the drama a formal framework was not infrequent—but the artist's need to construct in a way which corresponded with his own needs. Ehren-stein said of Napoleon that "he made laws but had no law in himself".[52] The criterion of the Expressionist's work is therefore to be found, not in the application of an aesthetic or ethical system, but in terms of his own view of life, his own experience and his formulation of that experience.

NOTES

Throughout the notes "Pörtner, II" = P. Pörtner, *Literaturrevolution 1910–1925*, Dokumente. Manifeste. Programme. II. Zur Begriffsbestim-mung der Ismen. 1961.

1. R. Samuel and R. H. Thomas, *Expressionism in German Life, Liter-ature and the Theatre (1910–1924)*, 1939, p. 59.
2. e.g. W. H. Sokel, *Der literarische Expressionismus*, p. 67.
3. F. Schmalenbach, "Das Wort 'Expressionismus' ", *Neue Zürcher Zeitung*, 11.3.1961, Fernausgabe Nr. 69.
4. In 1914 even the majority of painters were against the classification into "isms". Cf. Introduction to Pörtner, II, p. 18.
5. P. Scher, "Das Zeitalter der Lyrik", *Die Aktion*, 5.7.1913.
6. F. T. Marinetti, "Technisches Manifest der Futuristischen Literatur" (*Der Sturm*, 1912), Pörtner, II, p. 52.
7. "Manifest der futuristischen Maler" (*Der Sturm*, 1912), Pörtner, II, p. 44.
8. A. Döblin, "Futuristische Worttechnik" (*Der Sturm*, 1912), Pörtner, II, p. 64.
9. Ibid., p. 64 f.
10. Ibid., p. 69.
11. K. Edschmid, *Über den Expressionismus in der Literatur und die neue Dichtung* (Tribüne der Kunst I), 1919.
12. Cf. Introduction to Pörtner, II, p 22.
13. K. Heynicke, "Der Wille zur Seele" (*Masken*, 1917–18), Pörtner, II, p. 209.
14. F. T. Marinetti, "Tod dem Mondschein!" (*Der Sturm*, 1912), Pört-ner, II, p. 77.
15. Praise of the machine is to be found especially in the verse of the "Worker Poets" such as Heinrich Lersch, Gerrit Engelke, Max

278   PERIODS IN GERMAN LITERATURE

Barthel. Cf. Samuel and Thomas, *Expressionism in German Life, Literature and the Theatre*, p. 112 f.
16. Heym's diary of 20.7.1909. G. Heym, *Dichtungen und Schriften* (ed. K. L. Schneider), Hamburg, München, Vol. 3, p. 128.
17. Heym's diary of 26.6.1910, ibid., p. 136.
18. A. Ehrenstein, *Briefe an Gott* (1922). *Gedichte und Prosa* (ed. K. Otten) Neuwied am Rhein, Berlin-Spandau, 1961, pp. 180–229.
19. Ibid., p. 228.
20. F. Kafka, *The Great Wall of China* (*Beim Bau der Chinesischen Mauer*) in "Metamorphosis and Other Stories". Penguin, 1961, p. 76.
21. Ibid., p. 77.
22. K. Hiller, *Es ist an der Zeit* ("Pan", 1912), Pörtner, II, p. 388.
23. L. Rubiner, *Der Mensch in der Mitte* (1917). Extract translated by W. Sokel in *An Anthology of German Expressionist Drama* (ed. Sokel), 1963, p. 4.
24. F. Werfel, *Die Versuchung*, Gesammelte Werke (ed. A. Klarmann), Frankfurt/Main, 1959, Vol. I, p. 40.
25. R. J. Sorge, *Der Bettler*, Werke (ed. H. G. Rötzer), Nürnberg, 1964, Vol. II, p. 92.
26. L. Rubiner, "Die Gewaltlosen", in: *Schrei und Bekenntnis*, Expressionistisches Theater (ed. K. Otten), 1959, p. 380.
27. W. Paulsen, *Expressionismus und Aktivismus. Eine typologische Untersuchung*, Bern, 1935, p. 14 f.
28. A. Wolfenstein, "Fragment eines Daseins", in: *Ego und Eros. Meistererzählungen des Expressionismus* (ed. K. Otten), 1963, p. 360.
29. Heinz Schöffler, "Karl Otten, Ego und Eros", in: *Ego und Eros*, p. 566.
30. F. Wedekind, *Vorrede zu Oaha*, Gesammelte Werke (Eds. A. Kutscher and J. Friedenthal), München, Vol. IX, p. 440.
31. G. Kaiser, *König Hahnrei*, Berlin, 1913, p. 147.
32. F. Wedekind, *Die Büchse der Pandora*, Werke, III, p. 137.
33. F. Wedekind, *Die Junge Welt*, Werke, II, p. 87.
34. C. Sternheim, *Die Kassette*, Dramen (ed. W. Emrich), Neuwied am Rhein, Berlin, 1963, Vol. I, p. 400.
35. W. Emrich, Foreword to C. Sternheim, *Dramen*, I, p. 11.
36. Sternheim writing about his own work in *Europa Almanach* of 1925. Quoted in: *Expressionismus. Literatur und Kunst 1910–1923*. Eine Ausstellung des deutschen Literaturarchivs im Schiller-Nationalmuseum. Marbach a.N. vom 8. Mai bis 31. Oktober, 1960, p. 285.
37. C. Sternheim, *Die Prosa Gottfried Benns* (Prosa, 1918). Quoted in: *Expressionismus. Literatur und Kunst 1910–1923* (see note 36), p. 197.
38. H. H. Jahnn, "Die Krönung Richards III", in: *Deutsches Theater des Expressionismus* (ed. J. Schondorff), München, n.d., p. 303.
39. Ibid., p. 303.
40. C. Sternheim, *Die Prosa Gottfried Benns* (Prosa, 1918). Quoted in: *Expressionismus. Literatur und Kunst 1910–1923* (see note 36), p. 197.
41. O. Pander, "Revolution der Sprache" (*Das Junge Deutschland*, 1918), Pörtner, II, p. 234.

42. F. T. Marinetti, "Technisches Manifest der Futuristischen Literatur" (*Der Sturm*, 1912), Pörtner, II, pp. 47–56.
43. C. Sternheim, *Der Snob* (1914), *Dramen*, I, p. 179–180. "Struggles for existence. I've been through all that, too, and the turmoil taught me a lot. Impelled by an insatiable impulse, I waded through the mush of comfortable people because I had learned that life really only begins when you are through and out the other side. But you saw how I got there, how I 'arrived', how I tore strips of living flesh from my own body and wore them, twisted into an elegant cravatte, round my own neck. Little by little I approached that form which the superior being must assume among his peers."
44. Ibid., p. 145.
45. A. Wolfenstein, "Die künstliche Liebe", in: *Ego und Eros. Meistererzählungen des Expressionismus*, p. 363.
46. R. M. Rilke, *Die Aufzeichnungen des Malte Laurids Brigge*, Wiesbaden, 1951, p. 79.
47. W. H. Sokel, *Der literarische Expressionismus*, p. 64.
48. E. Barlach, "Der Tote Tag", *Die Dramen* (ed. K. Lazarowicz), München, 1956, Vol. I, p. 23–4.
49. *Lyrik des expressionistischen Jahrzehnts. Von den Wegbereitern bis zum Dada* (ed. M. Niedermayer) with an introduction by G. Benn, Wiesbaden, 1955.
50. Cf. M. Hamburger and C. Middleton in their introduction to *Modern German Poetry 1910–1960*, An anthology with verse translations, London, 1962, p. xxvii–xxviii.
51. Letter to E. Buschbeck (date unknown), in: *Erinnerung an Georg Trakl. Zeugnisse und Briefe*, Salzburg, 1959, p. 140.
52. A. Ehrenstein, *Briefe an Gott*, Gedichte und Prosa (see Note 18), p. 207.

BIBLIOGRAPHY

A. Soergel, *Dichtung und Dichter der Zeit II*, Neue Folge: Im Banne des Expressionismus (Leipzig, 1925).
A. Soergel and C. Hohoff, *Dichtung und Dichter der Zeit*, Vom Naturalismus bis zur Gegenwart, Vol. 2 (Düsseldorf, 1961–1963).
W. Paulsen, *Expressionismus und Aktivismus: Eine typologische Untersuchung* (Bern-Leipzig, 1935).
R. Samuel and R. H. Thomas, *Expressionism in German Life, Literature and the Theatre* (1910–1924) (Cambridge, 1939).
F. Martini, "Der Expressionismus", in: *Deutsche Literatur im 20. Jahrhundert. Gestalten und Strukturen*, ed. H. Friedmann and O. Mann (Heidelberg, 1955).
H. Friedmann and O. Mann (Editors), *Expressionismus. Gestalten einer literarischen Bewegung* (Heidelberg, 1956).
R. Brinkmann, *Expressionismus. Forschungsprobleme 1952–1960* (Stuttgart, 1961).
W. H. Sokel, *The Writer in Extremis. Expressionism in Twentieth-

Century German Literature (Stanford University Press, 1959). Translated into German as: *Der literarische Expressionismus. Der Expressionismus in der deutschen Literatur des Zwanzigsten Jahrhunderts* (München, 1960).

P. Raabe and H. L. Greve, *Expressionismus, Literatur und Kunst 1910–1923*, Ausstellungskatalog, Marbach: Schiller-Nationalmuseum (München, Langen-Müller), 1960.

P. Pörtner, *Literaturrevolution 1910–1925*. Dokumente. Manifeste. Programme. Darmstadt-Neuwied-Berlin-Spandau, Luchterhand. I: Zur Aesthetik und Poetik, 1960. II: Zur Begriffsbestimmung der Ismen, 1961. III: Manifeste, Pamphlete, Utopien, 1964.

W. Muschg, *Von Trakl zu Brecht. Dichter des Expressionismus* (München, 1961).

Modern German Poetry 1910–1960. An anthology with verse translations. Edited and with an introduction by M. Hamburger and C. Middleton (London, 1962).

An Anthology of German Expressionist Drama. A prelude to the Absurd. Edited and with an introduction by W. H. Sokel (New York, 1963).

P. Raabe, *Die Zeitschriften und Sammlungen des literarischen Expressionismus 1910–1921*. Repertorien zur deutschen Literaturgeschichte I (Stuttgart, 1964).

German Literature from 1945

German Literature from 1945
RODNEY LIVINGSTONE

I

THE problem besetting all literary history is how to unite the idea of literature as the totality of imaginative writing with the idea that it is necessary to give due prominence to writers of greater importance. A completely factual catalogue has its uses and so has the one-sided account with its exclusive interest in masterpieces, but a good literary history will be both comprehensive and critical. To be both it is necessary to discover an organizing principle and the reason for the noticeable decline of the older type of history can perhaps partly be found in the difficulty of finding such principles for the more recent trends. If the current histories are any guide it would seem that German literature proceeds in a fairly orderly manner until Naturalism but there has since been such a profusion of modes and movements and such a diversity of individual talents that it is difficult (and perhaps not all that rewarding?) to search for larger, more comprehensive categories. Historians of the past could console themselves for being unable to fit Hölderlin into Classicism or Romanticism, because there were any number of prominent writers who were more pliable. But to labour, as some have done, to force Rilke, Mann, Kafka, Kraus and Musil into this or that minor group is often comic : one is reminded of the cartoon showing a gigantic Tolstoy bursting out of the Lilliputian Orthodox Church.

The method of this essay must differ from that of the other contributors to this volume, for their subjects are more firmly defined. They are dealing with concepts which have atrophied or need clarifying or otherwise revising in the light of new material. But in the postwar period the situation is too fluid; such concepts as there are, are hardly so powerful as to have gained acceptance, let alone undue prominence. Such prestige is in any case the prerogative of periods firmly in the past and categories are often found for them long after they have been concluded. There is, then, no orthodoxy to attack, no dogma with awkward exceptions, no injustice to be rectified. Quite the reverse in fact. The necessary absence of a historical perspective leaves its mark on criticism.

Most commentators accept too much uncritically, judging the period as if it were totally different from previous ones, others are too unsympathetic to contemporary writing to see its achievements and they judge it rigidly by ideas no longer relevant. Hence, premature though it may be, it is perhaps desirable, while discussing recent literature and such terms as have gained currency, to keep an eye open for concepts that might provide a synoptic view.

A glance at the relevant chapters of some of the recent histories of literature reveals the following kinds of division : by genre, i.e. poetry, prose and drama, to which some add a fourth category, the essay; by author and by generation of authors; by political divisions, i.e. the German Federal Republic, the German Democratic Republic, Switzerland, Austria; by categories, often invented for the occasion, that try to distinguish along literary or philosophical lines; and finally some give prominence to the *Gruppe 47* presumably because it is a group and because it is influential.

A writer rarely confines himself to one of these types. Frequently there is an unholy mixture of all of them. In one well-known history the page headings range from "Recent Poetry" and "Fiction in Austria and Switzerland" to "Meditation and Lament" and "At the edge of the Wasteland".[1] In another belonging to a type now fortunately dying out we find a general division into "Simplicity and Ambivalence" and within that there are chapters entitled "Unity and Symbol", "Christian Poets", and even "The Struggle against the Leviathan of Nihilism in the daily Life of Germany".[2]

Admittedly most of these categories have some relevance or other : it is as legitimate to stress the different or related political tendencies of recent literature as it is to examine developments in the various genres. But the haphazard mixture of different categories can have no pretensions to systematic exposition. Few of the current histories reveal a developed conception of the period.[3] Within the particular discussions, of course, interesting relationships are established (e.g. the link between Brecht's epic theatre and his politics has been thoroughly analysed) but there is no general study of the period which analyses such relations throughout. The only kind of unity that can be found is that rooted in the personality of the historian.

One cannot stress too heavily the unsystematic nature of existing expositions if only because it has so often been the proud boast of literary history as opposed to literary criticism that it is "scientific" and objective while the latter, above all in Germany, is still generally thought of as subjective and arbitrary. On the other hand the difficulties facing the historian in the field of contemporary literature are indeed formidable, as most writers would agree. But hard as it is to pick one's way through the uncertainties of contemporary fashions and trends, the impulse to search for a total image of the age is not to be denied. The completely sceptical critic will object that such "total images" are dangerous everywhere, and especially so in literature where it is more important to grasp the individual work in all its originality than to chase after large generalizations which resound so splendidly only because they are hollow. The sceptic's doubts are justified particularly when the excesses of literary history are borne in mind; yet they go too far. Generalizations have become indispensable now that everyone, at least to some extent, thinks historically. There are standard views of the Victorian Age, the Nazis, the Renaissance and so on. On one level these views are clichés, on other levels this need not be so. But at whatever level they operate it is right that someone should have worked them out properly and in accordance with the facts. This is not just the problem of popularizing knowledge; it is the problem of discovering the truth.

I cannot claim to offer more than notes towards a definition of the period and to consider some of the problems. Chief among them are these :

(1) What is a satisfactory historical concept and how is it arrived at?

(2) How useful are the concepts at present in fashion and what aspects of the literary situation do they ignore?

What purpose is served by a term like Romanticism? Is it merely a mnemonic for students to prevent them from mixing up their centuries and committing other historical faux pas? (To mention Zesen and Brentano in one breath, unless they are joined by the word "influence", is a much greater solecism than to bracket Hoffmann and Wordsworth who after all are both "Romantics".) Clearly such uses are trivial (though not uncommon). A more serious abuse is the use of categories for ideological purposes. Thus terms like "Enlightenment" or "Realism" in a critic like Lukács normally imply i.a. "progressive". Perhaps the following quotation can illustrate a correct use of a period-concept :

> Pope's peculiar greatness is that he can be a complete Augustan, realizing in his poetry the strength of that actual concentrated civilization immediately around him, and at the same time ... achieve a strength so closely related to Marvell's (F. R. Leavis).[4]

What Leavis means by the word "Augustan" is of course described elsewhere in his book; what is important is the way it is used and that is indicated by the clause "realizing in his poetry the strength of that actual concentrated civilization immediately around him". The term is not purely morphological, it is not confined to a neutral catalogue of a writer's characteristics and above all Leavis' method is not to try to fit Pope into a category. On the contrary, the category itself is not the final court of appeal (in addition to the Augustan virtues Pope has those of Marvell). Furthermore the notion of the Augustan is not a place of safety to which the critic, harassed by the uniqueness of the writer, can repair, but is a kind of key that, in the hands of the right critic can unlock the works.

We may still enquire, however, what kind of concepts are the most likely to yield such a key? From what aspects of literature are they most profitably to be deduced? Literature is essentially various and our attention is focused more on an author's individual distinction than on what he shares with others. Where can unity be found? Should we look for it in (external) stylistic devices such as the pervasiveness of "epic" elements in postwar drama? Should it be sought in the subject-matter, for example in the many descriptions of the war? Or perhaps in the predominance of particular genres? Thus we might point to the widely held opinion that all literary forms are currently in a state of crisis : that the novel is attempting to do away with the story (as if the story had ever been a salient feature of the German novel!), that the drama is striving to eliminate conflict and, under Brecht's influence, is becoming more "epic", that poetry is driven to increasingly desperate devices to assert its existence at all ("Most of what is thought to be poetry becomes the crassest kind of irony if I confront it for a single day with my actual life." Max Frisch). Perhaps one should consider the most prominent themes; bad conscience or the dehumanization of modern life. Perhaps the religious or political beliefs of a writer would yield a unified view although in the contemporary conflicts between rival ideologies that is unlikely. Or perhaps the age has produced a style in which all writers participate, regardless of their views.

Clearly all these factors have a part to play but how can they all be integrated into a single point of view without giving rise to the kind of confusion noted earlier on? Perhaps after all literary history is an art, not a science. However that may be it is worth stating that the search for a single all-embracing principle is likely to go unrewarded. Such principles have in any case long been the bane of literary history. As the phenomena themselves are complex their relations must be complex too, and it may be more profitable to relate a work to some others by theme and to yet others by its style. The whole matter has been well formulated by Ludwig Wittgenstein in his famous definition of a game :

> I mean board-games, card-games, ball-games, Olympic games and so on What do all these have in common?—Don't say . They *must* have something in common otherwise they wouldn't be "games", but *look* and see whether they do have anything in common. For when you look at them you will not in fact find something common to *all* of them, but you will notice similarities, relationships, and moreover a whole series of them.[5]

Wittgenstein then speaks of a "complex network of similarities" and of "multifarious relationships"; this manner of describing the definition of a game seems especially useful as it implies a more complex notion of a "system" than has been current in literary history, one therefore eminently suited to the variousness of literature. For if Wittgenstein is sceptical of finding a single quality all games have in common, his view is not nominalistic; for the "complex network of similarities" does entitle us to link all the phenomena together—by the word "games".

II

Many of the terms that have actually been applied to postwar German literature, terms like *Heimkehrerliteratur, Trümmerliteratur* (literature of the returned soldiers and of the ruins), do not aspire to describe more than a part of the field. They are self-explanatory and apply chiefly to the subjects of the works. Many writers have made contributions to works of this type : Kasack, Böll, Schnurre, Wiechert, Holthusen, etc. Moreover the terms, although they suffer from the drawback of yoking together writers who do not really belong together, have at least the advantage of cutting across the genres. A brief discussion of the best-known (although hardly the best) of these works Wolfgang Borchert's *Draußen vor der Tür*, will reveal the limitations of concepts derived from the subject-matter.

Walter Jens briefly contrasts the play with two *Heimkehrer* plays of the 'twenties :

> what an abyss separates Ernst Toller's realistic tear-jerker *Hinkemann* and Bert Brecht's cheerfully cynical *Trommeln in der Nacht* from Wolfgang Borchert's scream of horror. *Draußen vor der Tür* as the legend of our time, Beckmann as Everyman, the Colonel as the Devil, the Cabaret Owner as the Mistress of the World (Frau Welt), decked out in remnants from the arsenal of cynicism from the Year Nought.[6]

Jens' point is primarily historical and is accurate enough. Borchert's play moreover does tend in the direction he indicates though
his allegorising goes too far (the *Male* Cabaret Owner as *Frau
Welt*!). But the mere fact of the comparison with Toller and
Brecht shows that a term like *Heimkehrerliteratur* is too vague to
give a precise definition of a particular period. Heinrich Böll,
defending *Trümmerliteratur* (against critics who objected to its
realism and its lack of uplift), even claims Homer as a practitioner :

> Homer is the father of the European Epic, but Homer tells of
> the Trojan War, of the destruction of Troy and of Odysseus'
> return home—literature about war, the ruins and returned
> soldiers—there is no need for us to be ashamed of the epithets.[7]

Böll's defence and Jens' comments enable us to analyse the terms
a little more deeply. We should note first that, according to Jens,
Borchert's play is "a scream of horror" (*ein Aufschrei*). Where
Toller is realistic, Borchert gives expression to an agony more
fundamental than realism can convey; (*larmoyant* = tearful, suggests moreover that Toller's experience too is less considerable than
Borchert's : only a man of our time can know the real horrors of
existence). So we can see why Borchert has recourse to Expres-
sionist-Surrealistic devices to render his apocalyptic vision. Thus the
dream of the general playing on a xylophone made of human
bones :

> I see a man standing playing the xylophone. He's beating out a
> frantic rhythm; and he sweats the whole time, he does, because
> he's extremely fat. And the xylophone he's playing is enormous.
> And because it's so big he has to run up and down at every note.
> And he sweats the whole time because he really is very fat. But
> he doesn't sweat perspiration, that's the funny thing. He sweats
> blood, dark, steaming blood. And the blood runs down the side
> of his trousers in two broad red stripes so that from far away
> he looks like a general ... He has lost both his arms. Yes, he's
> playing with long thin artificial hands that look like the pins of
> hand-grenades ...[8]

Passages like this one make it comprehensible that several critics
should speak of postwar writing in terms of a development of
Expressionism. Heselhaus talks of a Post-Expressionism which (with
Loerke, Konrad Weiss and Weinheber) bridges the gap, and as late
as 1956 W. Höllerer speaks of a Neo-Expressionism, distinguishing
it from the original movement by the absence of :

> programmatic formulations which conflict more and more with the
> experience of the individual in the twentieth century. The

"Crash and Cry" (*Sturz und Schrei*), "Uprise and Uproar" (*Aufruhr und Empörung*) of Expressionism gave way to a more restrained manner and to the attempt to replace oratorical pathos by verse with a firmer backbone.[9]

Improbable as it may sound, there is even a lone voice claiming that "the only real chance for humanity is the New Man" (Herbert Eisenreich).

Thus *Heimkehrer-* and *Trümmerliteratur* must be seen, at least in part, against the background of a Neo-Expressionism which derives its own precise application only from within the yet wider notion of *Nullpunktliteratur* (literature of the "Year Nought"). This is probably the most widely accepted term in German literature since the war. Jens' remarks on Borchert occur under the heading of "The Situation in the Year Nought" (*Die Lage im Jahre Null*). The very fact that in this chapter I deal with German literature since the war is evidence of its influence. For what could be the *literary* justification (as distinct from the political one) for making a period division at 1945? This question obvious as it is, is never asked. The "Year Nought" is a holy concept. True, its defenders could point not only to the complete destruction of Germany, the apparent end of a tradition, the younger generation with its complete mistrust of its elders, i.e. not only to political, economic and social convulsions, but also to literary changes : the turning away from the Nazi prescription, the adoption of techniques from foreign writers like Sartre, Hemingway, Dos Passos, rather than from the German Classics, the failure of writers (who, like Wiechert and Carossa, persist in traditional paths) to keep pace with the *Zeitgeist*, as well as of those who, having been abroad until after 1945, have missed the decisive German experiences :

> Before the smoke-blackened image of this ruined occidental landscape in which man, loosed from all traditional bonds wanders staggering, all the standards of the past fade into nothing.[10]

There is some truth in this but less than is commonly thought. The seventeenth century saw comparable disasters but the Thirty Years' War brings no hiatus in Baroque literature. It may be argued that there are special reasons for this but it may also be claimed of the period under discussion that when the political dust has settled the really valuable productions of the period will not be the *Nullpunktliteratur* or the *Gruppe 47* but the last novels of Thomas Mann, Hermann Broch, Doderer, Ernst Jünger and the poems of Benn and Brecht; i.e. that continuity was provided by both the Inner and Outer Emigration.

No one claims that the above-mentioned authors are negligible but there is an unproved but pervasive assumption that at least some of them are not in touch with the real atmosphere of postwar Germany, i.e. the atmosphere of the *Nullpunkt*. We see then that there is a circular process whereby a literary fashion is created : a literature that reflects and satisfies certain spiritual needs is highly valued regardless of its true achievement. Just how difficult it is for an author to record his experience without making concessions to the needs of his public to find their own view of themselves in his works we shall see later in the case of Andersch.

The valid element in the idea of the *Nullpunkt* can be seen not only in Borchert but everywhere in the *Trümmerliteratur* where the writer seems to be fixing the past, now in ruins, with the cool sceptical gaze of a man who does not want to be fooled. The instrument of this scepticism is a kind of irony that does not seem limited to one author but is characteristic of the period :

> The "Lord", without Whose willing it no sparrow falls from the roof, nor are 10 million people gassed in concentration camps : He must be a strange sort—if He exists now at all (Arno Schmidt).

Similarly the satirical parts of *Draußen vor der Tür* carry conviction while the things that remind Jens of a medieval mystery are often nothing but pompous cliché.

What makes for cliché in Borchert is something essentially related to the idea of the *Nullpunkt* itself, according to which 1945 is a unique historical moment : never have people been faced with such an upheaval, never have they been so helpless before the cataclysms of history, before the apocalypse itself. This claim to a unique experience is implied by Jens in his contrast between Toller whose *Hinkemann* is a "realistic tear-jerker" and Borchert whose play is a "scream of horror". And uniqueness is everywhere implied, for example in Holthusen's *Tabula Rasa* (in the very title) and, politically coloured, in an essay by Hans Werner Richter :

> And so they (the *Gruppe 47*) felt they had to begin from scratch with new methods, with better assumptions and with different goals.[11]

It is sometimes hard to distinguish between the true and the false but self-dramatization is often involved—an intoxicated self-pity at the idea of wandering through a smashed landscape without even a God to hear one's screams and witness one's agony. This, I take it, is the kind of inspiration that lies behind the visionary flights (like the dream quoted above) in Borchert's play and in much of the work associated with the idea of the *Nullpunkt*. They form an embarrassing contrast with the ironical writing of which Arno Schmidt's sentence is typical.

To revert to the subject of contemporary German literature it need only be repeated that terms like *Trümmerliteratur* have their uses but are not comprehensive. At first indeed, the chief subjects are taken from the experience of the war and its aftermath, but fairly soon (and certainly by 1950) we find writers preoccupied with the problems of living in a Germany well on the way to recovery and they tend to produce a socially critical and satirical literature. In addition there is another more subjective trend, a personal, often metaphysical examination of the individual condition of man in the present age. Many writers use the word *Bestandaufnahme*—a taking stock of the situation—to describe their activities. And the word "situation" is often rendered, as in the quotation from Jens, by the word "Lage" with all its military connotations (in much the same spirit as that in which Gottfried Benn spoke of defending the *Nietzsche-Lage*, the last philosophical bastion of the spirit). It is instructive to observe the career of Alfred Andersch, for his novels faithfully reflect the changing interests of the serious reading public. His first novel, *Die Kirschen der Freiheit* (1952), is an autobiographical account of his desertion from the front towards the end of the war. In his second novel, *Sansibar oder der letzte Grund* (1956), the reporting of his own experiences has given way to a less directly personal (though not less committed) treatment of the Nazi past; he describes the response of five people to the pressure of the police-state, showing how even when threatened by very concrete dangers they can become capable of a liberating act. This then is a contribution, one of the more moving ones, to the slightly over-fashionable, but on the whole honourable process of coming to terms with the past (*Bewältigung der Vergangenheit*). In his third novel *Die Rote* (1960), Andersch tells the story of a successful career-woman who suddenly becomes disgusted by the complacent materialism of a resurgent Germany as embodied in her husband. She leaves him in Italy where they are on holiday and undergoes some implausible adventures before settling down temporarily as a factory-worker.

Andersch's subjects not only reflect the interests of a larger segment of society than is likely to sympathize with his extreme left-wing, even anarchist, opinions, they also offer something like a standard diagnosis. In *Die Kirschen der Freiheit* the discussion centres on the vexed question of the Soldier's Oath of Loyalty: was it moral to desert from the front after swearing loyalty?

Andersch's affirmative answer, platitudinous outside Germany, has a moral righteousness there, where the book provoked a storm of criticism. It could thus have an almost programmatic value in democratic circles. It would be unfair to say that this is a typical case of a German providing himself with an alibi, for Andersch had no particular need of that. But it could certainly be used as a kind of moral buttress by those who did need alibis and who were eagerly counting heads in order to swell the size of the German Resistance. In *Sansibar* too the prose is convincing enough to make us feel that Andersch has not consciously given the public what it wants, yet the moral that a liberating act was possible even under the rule of National Socialism is not offered in a way that would make his public feel remorse at missed opportunities. Quite the reverse : the book has a soothing and ennobling effect. It is all so idealistic. The Gestapo is real enough to forestall the criticism that salvation is facile, yet too intangible to provide real opposition. The carved statue of the young monk reading is meant to incite to action and does have this effect on the hero Gregor, but the emphasis seems to be more on the idea of a contemplative freedom than an activist one. Moreover the actual dangers undergone smack more of the adventures in a spy story than of a real testing of a view of freedom. Thus in the last analysis the freedom that emerges is the contemplative freedom of the German tradition of *inwardness* where a transformation of the spirit means more than the trumpets and drums of the French Revolution, although admittedly Andersch does not go so far as to imply that the greatest freedom consists in obeying the law. It is not hard to imagine which view of freedom will cause Andersch's readers the least discomfort. Lastly, *Die Rote*, his least successful novel, is written from the point of view, of someone who feels uneasy at the thought that the present material well-being is undeserved and accords ill with the attitudes of contemporary Germans. This uneasiness is un-reasoned and reminds one of the feeling that Kierkegaard's father had when, having gone out on a heath as a little boy and cursed God, he later became rich at a time when almost everyone in Denmark went bankrupt. Andersch cannot enforce his suspicious-ness which is fatalistic and superstitious rather than genuinely critical; instead he makes his heroine romantically seek alterna-tive forms of existence. His solution for her is of course hopelessly naive (he has himself admitted to being dissatisfied with it) yet his discomfort and bad conscience are, in their vagueness, even more fashionable than the diagnoses of his earlier novels.

Andersch's subjects are limited in interest to Germany and even to the Federal Republic. But as Reich-Ranicki has shown,[12] a

theme of wider interest underlies them : they are all novels about
flight, flight from the German army, flight from the Nazis, flight
from the complacent prosperity of today. And if we examine the
more common themes of contemporary writing we find they are
more closely related than their subject matter might suggest :
flight, man imprisoned, man on trial (Frisch's *Stiller*), man alienated from society because of the past (Böll's *Billiard um Halb
Zehn*), man in search of himself, in flight from himself :

Was habe ich hier verloren
in diesem land
dahin mich gebracht haben meine älteren
durch arglosigkeit?
eingeboren doch ungetrost
abwesend bin ich hier
ansässig im gemütlichen elend,
in der netten zufriedenen grube (Enzensberger, *Landessprache*).[13]

It is no accident that H. E. Holthusen should have entitled a collection of essays *Der Unbehauste Mensch* (Man the Homeless), nor
that W. Höllerer's anthology of poems should be called *Transit*.

For all the influence of foreign writers, and for all the social
criticism (i.e. for all the real changes since the war) German literature still continues to be metaphysical and even solipsistic
(although the tendency to introduce lengthy theoretical discourse
whether of a scientific or philosophical nature into the novel
seems to have lost its popularity). The sense in which I mean
"solipsistic" here is that in which, according to J. P. Stern, the
Bildungsroman is solipsistic for the latter "leads the young hero
from self-absorbtion into society, as though social life were a
problematic task rather than a natural condition, the given
thing".[14] And it is less the question of the author's attitude to
society than his manner of depicting it that is significant, the
uncertainty and lack of definition with which it is rendered. There
are no *Bildungsromane* now but the observation still holds good.
Where society is depicted at all (and there are works which, like
Martin Walser's *Überlebensgroß Herr Krott* content themselves
with vague Expressionist allegories) it is often shown as it were
from a non-social or even anti-social point of view. This is the
case with Gerd Gaiser's novel *Schlußball* which attacks the decline
of morality in Neuspuhl, a town full of Germany's "nouveaux
riches". To tell his story Gaiser uses a technique similar to
Faulkner's in *The Sound and the Fury* of letting the characters
tell their own story, but with a significant difference : the different
parts of the story accessible to the different characters in Faulkner

throw light on those characters (most obviously in the case of Benjie the simpleton whose understanding of the matter is that of the mentally retarded). In Gaiser's book the method is not adhered to strictly and the resulting loss of intensity is fatal to the novel. The reader is left with the impression of an amorphous, darkly hostile and incomprehensible society. Even more striking is the fact that Martin Walser's *Ehen in Philippsburg* should similarly fail to give a convincing portrait of society despite its being modelled, almost to the point of plagiarism on a fairly successful social satire from the turn of the century, Heinrich Mann's *Im Schlaraffenland* (1900). These failures are less interesting for their own sake than because they are evidence that the traditional predilection for "existential"[15] themes is more fundamental than the present attempts to extend the domain of the novel to include a view of society.

If the themes of contemporary literature seem to present a fairly unified picture the wide divergences in *Weltanschauung* do little to disturb this. For at the level on which literature functions, differences in ideology are less decisive than the way in which they are incorporated into the works; despite the ordinances of governments there is still no way of logically deducing the form of art from the nature of an ideology. It might be thought that there is no significant link between the literatures of East and West Germany, that the Marxism of the East especially in the bleak form prescribed in the German Democratic Republic would create a literature as far removed from that of the West as are their respective views of life. And of course the two literatures are very different. The problem of guilt so popular in the West does not exist in the East; the unrelieved naturalism, often merging with *Reportage*, so prevalent in the East, does not exist in the West. Yet quite apart from the not inconsiderable literary traffic between the zones there are internal similarities even where one might least expect them. For instance in lyric poetry. Hans Magnus Enzensberger has discussed this in an ingenious article on Edgar Allen Poe's essay *The Philosophy of Composition*. The influence of this essay in Baudelaire's translation on the whole course of modern poetry is well known. Enzensberger refers to the introduction of the analytical, intellectual element into poetry (Poe is concerned to debunk the theory of inspiration by showing in great detail just how rationally he composed *The Raven*). He sees Poe's influence in Valéry's description of the poet as a literary engineer, in Benn's demand "to keep poetry cool", and in Eliot's dedicating *The Waste Land* to "il miglior fabbro", Ezra Pound. More original than

this is the observation that the imagery of machinery used by Poe
to stress that poetry is a contrivance, is ultimately connected with
Stalin's description of the poet as the engineer of the human soul,
as well as with Mayakovsky's aesthetics :

> He (Mayakovsky) draws the logical conclusion from the Ameri-
> can's cogs and driving-belts and speaks of poetic raw materials,
> semi- and wholly manufactured goods. So close can the aesthetics
> of "poésie pure" come to the Marxist view of history according
> to which the development of the forces of production deter-
> mines all human activity and poetry along with everything
> else.[16]

It is hardly necessary to point to the theory and practice of Brecht
as further confirmation of the possibility of crossing political fron-
tiers, albeit in different disguises. It is easy to make too much of
similarities but one suspects that too little has been made of them
rather than too much and this for reasons that have little to do
with literature.

It is also true of other *Weltanschauungen* that differences of
opinion do not entail differences at the literary level. There seems
to be general agreement that if an author wishes to validate
Christian beliefs he must demonstrate to his readers that the
"positive" solutions these often involve should not obscure or mask
the reality of evil. Truthfulness is perhaps the highest value (at least
in theory) of postwar literature and as has been remarked : "As
always when the emphasis is on 'unadorned truth', the notion is at
hand that the dirtier the truth, the truer it is".[17] So the true
"representative" of Christ in Hochhuth's *Der Stellvertreter* is not
the Pope but the priest who volunteers to die in Auschwitz, for only
the man who has faced up to the inferno of modern life deserves
salvation. While this is an almost obligatory pattern for writers with
a Christian message it is not confined to them. Günter Eich in his
well-known poem *Latrine* finds solace amidst the blood and filth in
some lines of Hölderlin :[18]

> Irr mir im Ohre schallen
> Verse von Hölderlin
> In schneeiger Reinheit spiegeln
> Wolken sich im Urin.

It is the primacy of a common view of experience over the
exigencies of a *Weltanschauung* that enables an explicitly Christian
writer like Heinrich Böll to become a representative figure of the
Gruppe 47. This is the most influential "movement" in recent

times. It is not certain that it should be described as a movement as it disclaims the fixed programme (though not the common pursuit) that have characterized earlier movements, and is instead proud of having attracted many of the best writers regardless of their ideological commitment (although the political right-wing is excluded) to the meetings held once or twice a year to read and discuss new works. However, its influence is great enough to make it hard to deny its character as a movement while its refusal to state a "party line" make it no less hard to say what kind of a movement it is. Starting out as a successor of *Der Ruf* a left-wing but independently nationalist magazine that managed to offend everyone and was finally banned by the Americans for its criticisms of the occupying powers, it gradually lost its predominantly political character (despite the personal predilections of its prime mover Hans Werner Richter) while retaining the left-wing, liberal and democratic bias, and also perhaps a greater interest in the content of literature than its form. Underlying much of the writing, divergent though the various styles may be, is the kind of cautious mistrust towards experience expressed by Ilse Aichinger :

> Have we not avoided each other's glance for long enough, whispering instead of speaking, creeping instead of walking upright? Have we not evaded each other for long enough, paralysed with fear? And where are we to-day? Don't we despise everyone placed above us, every authority, every measure not taken by us, every word that we have not uttered? We are filled with mistrust—of God, of the blackmarketeer from whom we buy, of God, of atomic research, of the growing grass . . .[19]

Mistrust as a basic attitude of the *Gruppe 47* as of post-war writers in general is an important element of Böll's work too. His Roman Catholicism would bring him few friends in the group but the valuation on the "Year Nought" (and the high praise he lavishes on Borchert), the sceptical, wary, concrete manner of writing, his essentially critical and political nature and democratic-humanist(!), anti-war outlook, and even his weaknesses like the over-conscious symbolism—all these qualities make him almost the ideal author of the group. So although there must be a sense in which his commitment to his beliefs is primary it is not this sense which matters most to the critic. We may note in passing that what marks out his purely religious essays is their extremely critical tenor, above all when treating of the ambiguous role of the Church under the Nazis; like Kierkegaard's attacks they probably have a greater appeal for the atheist than for the pious.

The *Gruppe 47* does not by any means represent the whole of contemporary German literature, yet there are writers outside it to whom its spirit is not alien. Because of his different background the Swiss writer Max Frisch might be expected to be radically different in his works. But the attitudes and qualities I have mentioned are not a purely German phenomenon. Frisch shares the group's distrust of ideology, and the phrase in which he sums up the art of the cartoonist Varlin : "intelligence without theory" would describe a large part of their essential spirit too. In addition Frisch's early plays are *Trümmerliteratur (Nun singen sie wieder* and *Als der Krieg zu Ende war)*. In general the regional divisions (Swiss, Austrian, East German) are less fundamental in literature than in politics. It is no doubt meaningful to ponder on the specifically Swiss or Austrian qualities of Dürrenmatt or Doderer without falling into Nadler's heresies, but here as everywhere in recent literary history too many concessions, and above all concessions of the wrong sort, have been made to politics. While politics has a place in literary history, and glad though one is that democratic ideas are popular with the avant-garde in Germany, it becomes tiresome to see with what monotonous regularity purely literary debates degenerate into reflections on the inadequate understanding of the fundamentals of democratic theory and practice revealed by a rival novelist in his view of narrative technique.

The aspects of post-war literature considered hitherto do not yet take us to the heart of the matter. To apprehend the true spirit of the age we must examine its style. It is true that style cannot be the sole criterion much as one would like to be able to give a purely "literary" history of literature, as one can give a musical history for music. Yet if not a magical touch-stone it can define an age more closely than any other single aspect of literature.

Many themes of post-war writing are not exclusive to the period. By comparing the treatment of the same theme by different periods we can show what is specific to ours. The theme of the death of God has played a major part in German literature since the end of the last century. Nietzsche announces it in the preface to *Also sprach Zarathustra* :

When Zarathustra was alone he spake to his heart thus :
"Can it be possible ! This old saint in his forest has not yet heard that *God is dead!*"

As a consequence of God's death our image of man has to be revised, and this revision occupies Nietzsche throughout his book. We may notice that Nietzsche introduces his theme in a strange way. The rhetorical question has something of the surprise in it with which an enlightened modern man might say : is it possible that this man should not know what a tin-opener is? Yet Zarathustra refrains from enlightening the hermit :

> when Zarathustra had heard these words he bade him farewell, saying : "What could I give you! But let me depart in haste lest I take something away from you."

So although God's death is common knowledge it remains a terrible secret; to tell the hermit the truth would liberate him only to destroy him. Nietzsche's sentences derive their tremendous power from the dramas and conflicts they reflect, not merely that his opinions are dramatic but that, as here, each sentence involves him in conflicts. The book is witty, profane, prophetic and holy, destructive and inspired, all at the same time. A philosophical treatise, it contains some of the most poetic imagery in all German literature; and the images are not mere illustrations of abstract thought but the embodiment of his "existential" battles of the mind. If man is one of the earth's diseases he is also "a rope between animal and the superman—a rope above an abyss".

The death of God is also the theme of a story by W. Schnurre, *Man sollte dagegen sein*. It is a comic story with a serious undertone. A man reads in the paper that God has died, he attends the funeral which is conducted in desolate conditions by an indifferent parson and two bored gravediggers. The style is realistic e.g. in that Schnurre makes good use of the colloquial Berlin dialect; the comedy stems from the ludicrous contrast between the grandeur of the theme and the paltriness of the world in which the news is made known by a tiny ad. in a paper :

> Loved by none, hated by none, there took place today after sufferings borne with heavenly patience the death of God.

The seriousness consists precisely in the statement that the shabby world is what remains when there is no God.

> One of the gravediggers jumped into the hole and stamped the earth into place. The other blew his nose and flicked a snot from his fingers.

The writing lacks the complexity we have noted in Nietzsche; at the same time we are incomparably nearer to the world of our common experience. Needless to say, this value would not have been one in Nietzsche's eyes, but it is of great importance for contemporary German literature, which can be satisfied by this story because it is firmly planted in "ordinary" life and yet comments on problems of cosmic importance.

Nietzsche's use of language was extraordinarily creative; Schnurre seems to be attempting to indicate his universal message with as little linguistic creativity as possible. Of course we should not underestimate the achievement of post-war writers and especially those of the *Kahlschlag* period of the *Gruppe 47* in cutting through the thick jungle of corrupt usage left over from the Nazi period—the false and hypocritical "Sprachregelungen" (the Nazi version of double-think), the would-be heroic jargon, the sentimental barbarisms, the debased language of German idealism (which enabled Eichmann to say at his trial that in all his actions he had thought of himself as a disciple of Kant). This achievement is genuine; every reader will have been struck by the fact that the German language is much *cleaner* now than it used to be and that Brecht's remark that while Horace's medium was gold "we have to work with muck" is less true than it was. Yet this achievement is largely reductive. True the contemporary colloquial language became respectable; but with it seems to have come the tacit assumption that this language is the raw material of literature from which writers may select, which they may refine or embroider (even fantastically as do Günter Grass or Arno Schmidt) but which was the indispensable starting point. How far this is from the days when Karl Kraus developed his style in *opposition* to common usage and when Rilke left Germany in order to keep his language free from corrupting influences! Nowadays there is a deeper commitment to ordinariness than has ever been observable in German literature before. It is too early to say what changes this will bring with it except that it should provide fertile soil for the growth of an indigenous commercial literature.

The situation in poetry is slightly different. It has become fashionable to talk (after the cries of agony and protest of the immediate post-war years died away) of the poet as a magician and of the poem a "structure" (the term comes from Heidegger) which does not reflect reality but provides "ciphers" (the term is Benn's) with which to decode it. The world of poetry :

> is a laboratory, a lab for words inhabited by the poet. Here he models and manufactures words, opens them up, breaks them down, smashes them to pieces, in order to fill them with tensions that endure for a few decades ... In this sense everything that happens becomes for the poet ... words, roots of words, series of words, conjunctions of words; syllables are psycho-

analysed, diphthongs re-educated, consonants transplanted. To him words are real and magical, a modern totem. (Gottfried Benn).

Some commentators talk then of a "Magic Realism", but it is hard to tell what exactly is meant by "magic" unless it refers to a form of imagism in which the poem is neither mimetic nor the expression of an inner experience (i.e. it is not *Erlebnislyrik*). Clearly only magic offers a real alternative, the magic of :

> Unauflöslich bleibt die Trauer
> Die aus schwarzem Honig ist . . . (Karl Krolow)[20]

where the seemingly incompatible is fused alchemically—sorrow made of black honey. At the same time poets and their critics are as eager as the novelists to emphasize their realism; magicians? yes, but not idealists like Novalis.

Another trend in poetry stems from Brecht. In his Diary, Max Frisch praises Brecht for writing poetry which does not need to fear contact with reality. When someone entered a room where he was reading a poem aloud to some friends, he was not embarrassed, there was no painful clash between the elevated poetic mood and the banal interruption. "I was just reading a poem", he said, "it was about . . .", and he went on reading. Brecht is for Frisch a poet without incense and for poets influenced by him magic is no virtue :

> seht in den spiegel : feig
> scheuend die mühsal der wahrheit,
> dem lernen abgeneigt, das denken
> überantwortend den wölfen,
> der nasenring euer teuerster schmuck.

(H. M. Enzensberger, *Verteidigung der wölfe gegen die lämmer*)[21]

These lines are Brechtian (without being unoriginal) in their incantatory rhetoric, the slow rhythm and the strange participial clauses, their conscious prosiness : all these are "devices" rigorously subordinated to the argument, which is presented with a kind of restrained passion.

The boundaries between the two kinds of verse are less sharp than my rough division indicates. Benn and Brecht are regarded as opposite poles (largely because of the cold war)—the one a nihilist, the other a Marxist, the one a believer in "form" as an absolute, the other putting poetry in the service of "truth", the one believing that poetry should change the world, the other that it neither can nor should do so.

Die Schlechten fürchten deine Klaue
Die Guten freuen sich deiner Grazie
Derlei
Hörte ich gern
Von meinem Vers. (Brecht)

These lines are quite radically different from :

Ach vergeblich das Fahren
Spät erst erfahren Sie sich;
bleiben und stille bewahren
das still umgrenzende Ich. (Benn)[22]

But quite apart from the fact that Benn too writes satirical verse (admittedly different from Brecht's) and that at least one critic can classify a poem by Brecht along with one by Wilhelm Lehmann,[23] the task of the future historian of literature will clearly be to see that there is less a question of two divergent traditions than of a coin with two sides.

III

If one were to invent a label for the period under discussion one might do worse than to call it the Existentialist Period. There are of course many powerful objections to the term quite apart from the reluctance one feels to the introduction of another vague term at all. The chief objections seem to be as follows. Existentialism is vague enough already as a philosophical concept, why increase the confusion by officiously bringing it into literary history? Unlike the situation in France there are no writers who are known as Existentialists; the label is therefore gratuitous. To describe the age as Existentialist would include writers who claim some other allegiance possibly hostile to Existentialism, Brecht for example is a Marxist. To define Existentialism in such a way as to include Brecht would involve depriving the word of all real meaning : it would simply mean the introduction of a term doomed from the start to become a misleading cliché. There is no way of defining it so as to embrace trends hostile to Existentialism, for example one result might be to neglect the importance of traditional elements in post-war literature. The use of the term would give the impression of a greater unity than in fact exists; much contemporary writing is highly experimental and diversified.

One might try to counter these objections in this way. The vagueness of the concept is not decisive : on the contrary all the important concepts of literary history are vague in a certain sense and necessarily so. They are approximations that indicate a trend, a concern, an atmosphere, a stance, a manner. All these things are vague, yet the term Romanticism has a use even if it is difficult to say exactly what it is, who the Romantics are, what is Romantic about them. We all use the term, albeit with reluctance on occasion. The vagueness inherent in the term does not mean that we should abolish it but that we should work at it, periodically revising it and freeing it from misconceptions. True, there is in Germany no Existentialist School in literature. But the influence of Existentialism is great, how great is a matter for speculation until it has been explored. But one can mention the influence of Sartre generally and through Andersch on the *Gruppe 47*, the influence of Kierkegaard on Max Frisch, Ingeborg Bachmann's doctoral thesis on Heidegger and so on. Brecht does not seem to be the hard case one might expect. The notion of a committed literature is fundamental in Sartre and there is (or has been at different times) a Marxist wing of Existentialism. By including Brecht the term would indeed become wide, but not disastrously so : it would still be narrow enough to exclude Wiechert. The traditional elements in post-war literature might indeed be neglected but these in fact play a subordinate rôle. The Marburg debate of 1929 between Heidegger and Cassirer in which the latter defended continuity in civilization and culture with frequent reference to Goethe, while Heidegger denied the contemporary relevance of the philosophical tradition, was no doubt a warning of what the immediate future held in store for Germany, but also points forward in a rather different sense to the spirit of post-war literature.

These arguments are too speculative perhaps to be conclusive. But the elements of contemporary literature elaborated hitherto may constitute a prima facie case. The general spirit of post-war literature may be held to be Existentialist in this sense : the themes of man cast into the world and into particular concrete situations not of his own making; the insistence on this situation as a starting point for literature; the implication that the language of literature should be that of each man's individual experience; the emphasis on choosing oneself, on authenticity, on the *Nullpunkt* (in both its good and bad i.e. over-dramatized senses), on man's tragic plight which his lack of an all inclusive *Weltanschauung* turns into the grotesque. (According to Dürrenmatt only tragi-comedy is possible in our age for it shows "den verzerrten Menschen verzerrt"—distorted humanity in distortion.) In addition there is the emphasis on commitment either public or private (Benn's "Was hast du seelisch eingesetzt?" giving valid expression to the latter), the outsider heroes, the marginal situations, the austere moral involvement, the absence of a cultural heritage. Yet as the comparison between Nietzsche and Schnurre showed, if the modern German writer is a witness to the truth, this is no longer in the sense in which Kierkegaard uses the phrase; it is nowadays a more personal, more prosaic truth in which the witness is not indeed as ambiguous and devious a figure as for Kierkegaard, he is more self-effacing and the truth has become more modest. Yet this definition is perhaps sufficient as a pointer to the criteria by which post-war writers might most profitably be judged.

NOTES

1. F. Martini, *Geschichte der deutschen Literatur* (Stuttgart, 1963).
2. H. Pongs, *Im Umbruch der Zeit* (Göttingen, 1952).
3. C. Heselhaus, *Deutsche Lyrik der Moderne* (Düsseldorf, 1961), is an interesting attempt at consistency. C. Hohoff's revision of A. Soergel's *Dichtung und Dichter der Zeit* (Düsseldorf, 1961), is a failure in this respect, despite Hohoff's awareness of the need for an "Organisationsprinzip". See his essay "Wie schreibt man Literaturgeschichte?" in *Schnittpunkte* (Stuttgart, 1963).
4. *Revaluations*, Peregrine, p. 34.
5. *Philosophische Untersuchungen* Abs. 66 (Frankfurt/M, 1964). The translations here and throughout this chapter are my own.
6. *Deutsche Literatur der Gegenwart* (München, 1962), p. 31.
7. "Bekenntnis zur Trümmerliteratur" in *Erzählungen, Hörspiele, Aufsätze* (Köln/Berlin, 1961), p. 343.
8. *Draußen vor der Tür* (Hamburg, 1956), p. 25.
9. *Transit* (Frankfurt/M., 1956), Vorwort p. xvi.
10. *Der Ruf* (München, 1962), p. 12.
11. *Almanach der Gruppe 47* (Hamburg, 1962), p. 12.
12. *Deutsche Literatur in West und Ost* (München, 1963).
13. What have I lost here in this land to which my elders have brought me unsuspectingly? A native but without solace, I am both here and not here, settled in this cosy wretchedness, in this nice contented pit.
14. J. P. Stern, *Re-interpretations* (London, 1964), p. 10.
15. See J. P. Stern, op. cit., for an elaboration of the existentialist nature of nineteenth-century German prose.
16. "Die Entstehung eines Gedichtes" in *Gedichte* (Frankfurt/M., 1962), p. 62–3.
17. J. P. Stern, op. cit., p. 99.
18. Verses by Hölderlin stray resoundingly past my ear. In snowy purity the clouds are mirrored in the urine.
19. *Aufruf zum Mißtrauen*, Plan 1, Jhrg. Okt. 45, January 47, p. 588.
20. Indissoluble remains the sorrow made of black velvet.
21. Look in the mirror; cowardly evading the labour of Truth, disciplined to learn, leaving the responsibility for thought to the wolves, a nose-ring your most precious ornament.

304   PERIODS IN GERMAN LITERATURE

22. Evil people fear your claws. Good people enjoy your gracefulness. I
should like to hear such things of my verse.
Travel, alas, is in vain. You learn but late about yourself; remain and
silently preserve the silently encompassing self.
23. B. von Wiese, "Die Deutsche Lyrik der Gegenwart" in *Deutsche
Literatur in unserer Zeit* (Göttingen, 1959).

BIBLIOGRAPHY

Balluseck, Lothar von: *Dichter im Dienst*. Der sozialistische Realismus in
der deutschen Literatur (Wiesbaden, 1956).
Bienek, H.: *Werkstattgespräche mit Schriftstellern* (München, 1962).
Blöcker, G.: *Kritisches Lesebuch* (Hamburg, 1962).
Bridgwater, P., ed: *Twentieth Century German Verse* (Penguin Poets,
1963).
Heselhaus, C.: *Deutsche Lyrik der Moderne* (Düsseldorf, 1961).
Horst, K. A.: *Die deutsche Literatur der Gegenwart* (München, 1957).
Horst, K. A.: *Kritischer Führer durch die deutsche Literatur der Gegen-
wart* (München, 1962).
Jens, W.: *Statt einer Literaturgeschichte* (München, 1957, erw. 1962).
Jens, W.: *Deutsche Literatur der Gegenwart* (München, 1961).
Lennartz, F.: *Deutsche Dichter und Schriftsteller unserer Zeit* (Stuttgart,
1959) (8. erw. Aufl.).
Nonnemann, K. ed.: *Schriftsteller der Gegenwart—Deutsche Literatur*
(Olten, 1963).
Reich-Ranicki, M.: *Deutsche Literatur in West und Ost*. Prosa seit 1945
(München, 1963).
Soergel/Hohoff: *Dichtung und Dichter der Zeit*. Vom Naturalismus bis
zur Gegenwart. Bd. 2 (Düsseldorf, 1963).
Waidson, H. M.: *The Modern German Novel*. A mid-twentieth century
survey (Oxford, 1960).
Weiskopf, F. C.: *Unter fremden Himmeln—Ein Abriß der deutschen
Literatur im Exil* (Berlin, 1948).
Weiskopf, F. C.: *Literarische Streifzüge* (Berlin, 1956).

Handbuch der deutschen Gegenwartsliteratur unter Mitwirkung von
Hans Hennecke, hrsg. von Hermann Kunisch (München, 1965), contains
the following chapters as well as entries on individual authors:
Die Deutsche Gegenwartsdichtung—Kräfte und Formen, von Hermann
Kunisch.
Deutsche Literatur im Exil 1933–47, von Hildegard Brenner.
"Innere Emigration"—die innerdeutsche Literatur im Widerstand 1933–
45, von Herbert Wiesner.
Dichter und Dichtung des Nationalsozialismus, von Rolf Geissler.
Neue Strömungen in der deutschen Literatur der Nachkriegszeit, von
K. A. Horst.
Die Literarische Situation in der DDR, von Jan Peddersen.

See also the following chapters in: *Deutsche Literatur in unserer Zeit* (Göttingen, 1959).

Das literarische Leben der Gegenwart, Wolfgang Kayser.

Die deutsche Lyrik der Gegenwart, Benno von Wiese.

Die Erzählkunst des 20. Jahrhunderts und ihr geschichtlicher Sinn, Wilhelm Emrich.

Das Drama der Gegenwart, Fritz Martini.

Gegenwartsdichtung der deutschen Schweiz, Max Wehrli.

Perspektiven österreichischer Gegenwartsdichtung, Friedrich Heer.

Name and Subject Index

Title Index